LUDWIG WITTGENSTEIN

Also by Miles Hollingworth

The Pilgrim City: St. Augustine of Hippo and his Innovation in Political Thought
Saint Augustine of Hippo: An Intellectual Biography
Inventing Socrates

Ludwig Wittgenstein

Miles Hollingworth

UNIVERSITY PRESS

Oxford University Press is a department of the University of Oxford. It furthers
the University's objective of excellence in research, scholarship, and education
by publishing worldwide. Oxford is a registered trade mark of Oxford University
Press in the UK and certain other countries.

Published in the United States of America by Oxford University Press
198 Madison Avenue, New York, NY 10016, United States of America.

© Miles Hollingworth 2018

All rights reserved. No part of this publication may be reproduced, stored in
a retrieval system, or transmitted, in any form or by any means, without the
prior permission in writing of Oxford University Press, or as expressly permitted
by law, by license, or under terms agreed with the appropriate reproduction
rights organization. Inquiries concerning reproduction outside the scope of the
above should be sent to the Rights Department, Oxford University Press, at the
address above.

You must not circulate this work in any other form
and you must impose this same condition on any acquirer.

CIP data is on file at the Library of Congress
ISBN 978-0-19-087399-8

To Dad

—For all the conversations that stayed the course

Contents

Introduction ix

1. | On the Spirit of a Man 1

2. | Biography versus Genius 32

3. | Numbers Station 82

4. | When the Camera Is on Us 135

5. | Sex and the Last Stand 196

APPENDIX: ON LOGIC AND THIS BOOK 229
NOTES 251
INDEX OF NAMES 273

As the insect buzzes around the light, so too do I buzz around the New Testament.
—WITTGENSTEIN, *MS* 183, p. 168 (1937)

God has *four* people recount the life of his incarnate Son, in each case differently and with inconsistencies—But might we not say: It is important that this narrative should not be more than quite averagely historically plausible *just so that* this should not be taken as the essential, decisive thing? So that the letter should not be believed more strongly than is proper and the *spirit* may receive its due.
—WITTGENSTEIN, *Lectures and Conversations on Aesthetics, Psychology, and Religious Belief*, p. 31

The world has believed a small number of obscure, insignificant, untutored men precisely because the divine nature of what they proclaim is all the more evident in the testimony of such lowly witnesses. For the eloquence which made what they said persuasive consisted of miraculous works, not words.
—AUGUSTINE, *City of God*, XII, 6

Introduction

LIKE MY BIOGRAPHY of Augustine of Hippo, this biography makes an unusual series of efforts to allow the convictions and peculiarities of its subject affect the shape of the book about him. To be able to do this is, in part, a luxury afforded by all the wonderful and accurate scholarship that already exists. And the biographies. For both men's lives, there are true versions of the event which you may consult. My question has always been, 'If the true version of an event is the true version of an event, how do we make something new? That is to say, how do we make the truth seem like *evil* and the *Devil* in order to make something new?' You may be a scientist, and not like the sound of that. And you may be a Christian who believes in the resurrection of Christ from the dead on the third day and not like the sound of that. Because in both cases, you need the truth to stand for 'the true version of the event'. You both need to be able to disagree with one another on 'the true version of the event'. *The Truth*, then, means a very great much to all of us; and to all of us, it means a single, linear, left-to-right version of 'what *really* happened'. Whatever the truth is, it must be that it can account for *everything*—Even parts of the galaxy we haven't yet visited. You get the picture. I suppose my point is (in the West at least) the biography must therefore be the ultimate paradigm of truth. If you earn a philosophy degree, everything you learn will take you into the infinite possibilities of subjectivity and the *Self* (*Your Self*), yet you will still walk into a book shop and click your fingers expecting to buy books that give you chapter and verse on human lives. And the more so on the really great and complex lives: The lives of genius. Because, of course, that has become the very logic of buying and reading a book on a genius, that it will somehow and magically account for everything celebrated in the lifetime of the genius as being utterly unaccountable.

To me, there is a paradox here. And to me, it is the paradox that must be the really interesting and promising story. I started to probe it in my biography of Augustine; I wrote the theory of the probing of it in my little book *Inventing Socrates*; and here, in this biography of Ludwig Wittgenstein, I bring it to a kind of conclusion.

If God had stayed as God, then we wouldn't have this problem (and this opportunity). Religion would be religion, and life would be life. But because he sent his son Christ to walk the earth, he allowed this problem to construct itself—And more, he allowed for every human life to become the problem's extension.

It is not disputed that in and amidst all their orthodox contributions to knowledge, Augustine and Wittgenstein made some seriously weird statements about Christ. From the point of view of orthodox knowledge, they are—yes—weird and meaningless. But in what follows I will argue that this is because they are torpedoes, sent against the kind of knowledge—the *Western* kind of knowledge— that is writing itself anyway. That, for Augustine, became the 'vanity of the philosophers'; while for Wittgenstein, it became the terrifying automation of mathematics and logic (and the apocalypse of reducing the former to the latter à la Bertrand Russell).

Once we begin to see it like this, God can hardly come into it. There is simply a more urgent battle to be fought, which is against the *book that knows more about you than you could ever know yourself*. I repeat: It is the biography which has all along been the real paradigm of truth in the West. And to understand this clearly matters more today than ever it did. For one of the consequences of our wide-opening world is the realisation that what the West has thought of as 'universal' reason is really not so universal at all— That there are entire alternatives to the things we have been taught to take for granted (Wittgenstein), and, above all and in any case, we can never know what another human heart is feeling (Augustine).

At this point, nothing could demonstrate better what I mean by all of this than to quote at length from my friend and fellow philosopher Zhao Tingyang. I am grateful for his permission and encouragement to do this.

Modern philosophy usually sets most store by rationality and prefers to think with the mind. It is believed that rationality has the capacity and power to solve all problems, or at least to seek the best of all possible strategies for solving them. But this is a pitiful self-limitation on the part of philosophy. An often observed fact is that the conciliation of different minds does not necessarily imply the conciliation of different hearts. Especially in the case of communicative discourse, perfect mutual understanding cannot necessarily guarantee perfect mutual acceptance, and better argument cannot ensure more reasonable cooperation. There is thus an obvious consciousness gap between understanding and agreement, while the missing bridge between them is precisely the mutual acceptance of each other's heart. Communicative intercourse simply reflects rather than resolves the inter-subjective problems and the differences of hearts cannot be eliminated by rational dialogue. Far from as projected by its modern philosophical illusion, language cannot in fact do everything. The serious problems of hearts will remain, even when better arguments and rational powers have all been applied. The point is that universal agreements have to be approved by the others' hearts as well. And the heart takes what is done more seriously than what is said. As an uncontrolled and disturbing trouble beyond the power of rationality, the problem of heart, a complex amalgam of spirit, values, faith and feelings, cannot be removed by rationality nor reduced to a matter of mind. On the contrary, heart is fundamental to mind and without it mind would be indifferent, inhuman and totally alienated from life. It is usually supposed that mind sees truth while heart recognises the good. But this does not mean a dualism. To separate mind and heart is a metaphysical as well as an epistemological error. The first truth is that truths will be nothing at all unless good for life. And the never-settled conflicts of the world may bring us to recognise that heart is prior to mind, just as the *facio* is prior to the *cogito*.[1]

* * *

In the second part of this Introduction, I lay down some reflections that can serve as a guide to, or better a foretaste of, what is to come in this book. To include them here will, I hope, show you what my project and agenda is, and why at each moment it has caused me to do *this* rather than *that*.

* * *

The reason we have books about truth is because we are so truthful—*And because we write them*. The reason we have books about theology is because we know everything about God—*And because we write them*. The reason we have books about history is because we know what happened—*And because we write them*. The reason we have biographies is because we have files on everyone—*And because we write them*. Within this scheme, nothing happens that hasn't already happened—While the logic of this is actually us and our willingness to act in time as though we were being written up. Take that willingness away, and there is no logic anymore—And this world ceases to exist. Leave it in place, and the good life becomes a book; a biography. That is to say, a virtuous life is 400 or so pages, all in a line, interesting, and making sense. From beginning, to middle, to end. Does it never occur to you that this is strange to the point of being absurd?

Take an example of what we do to each other. If a man is paranoid about an orange, it means that there is nothing in the orange which we can point at to explain his behaviour. He has defeated us, so in retaliation we fall immediately to proscribing a new way for him to act, and we call that 'the explanation'. Understanding is thus really always judgement. While judgement is really always diagnosis. Again: What there is to know has already happened. Or: Knowledge is predestination. All explanations come home to us in the appropriate action, and behaviour always proves the rule. In my last book, I put it that, 'It is because we see the kettle already boiled that we have so much confidence in the application of heat to water.'[2]

Wittgenstein found his best metaphors in mathematics, and his best examples in Bertrand Russell. That is to say, what Russell did with Alfred North Whitehead in the *Principia Mathematica* became the paramount example to him of how 'Truth' is actually our willingness to comply with it. The so-called laws of thought, which Russell and others have sought out at the intersections of mathematics and logic, are not really laws at all but the evidence of all the human minds that have followed them. Thus the classical problem of induction exists because it acknowledges this, and makes even the Universe itself a willing participant—Thereby opening up the possibility that tomorrow it could decide to act differently. I repeat: The fabled 'generality' which is always called in as the ultimate proof of the laws of thought is not a priori or even a posteriori, but the spectacle of a large number of people who act as though the laws of thought were in operation. Our man who is paranoid about an orange is simply not one of these people. Truth doesn't come into it. He is simply the single occupant of a *World of His Own*. Yet if I also now decide to act paranoid about an orange, then that world will have two occupants. And if vast numbers of people decide to so act, then a new Russell could arrive on the scene and write the book that proves that our paranoia about oranges is a 'law of thought'. I repeat again: A book like the *Principia Mathematica* is only the ultimate example that generality, and generality's truth, are a certain way of behaving, a certain way of writing, and then a certain way of reading back what you have written. It is only because *Principia Mathematica* is presented to us as though it were proving laws of thought that it appears to do that. And then again, only because we choose to march our mind to its syntax. Otherwise, you can show, as Wittgenstein did, that it says nothing at all. [Like all language, actually.]

Although Russell used variables: 'p', 'q', etc., he could perfectly well have used ordinary sentences—Think of demonstrations in Euclid, where nobody thinks we have proved the theorem for *this* circle. In the same way, one *can* perfectly well do algebraic proofs with numbers—Russell's proofs would lose nothing of their generality, because generality does not lie in what is written down here, but in the way you apply it.

You give a proof here showing that this is a right angle. You apply it to every such angle in a circle—So we could acknowledge any of Russell's proofs for *any* proposition, although what was written down was some special proposition.

Now we could substitute 'It rains' and 'I get wet' in 'p.p ⊃ q. ⊃ .q': 'If it rains, and it rains implies I get wet, that implies I get wet'—and we call this a *law of thought*.

But isn't this queer?[3]

It is queer. The laws of thought, if they are to be based upon evidence, have to be retrospectively formulated. We have to be able to point at a mind and say, 'There!' Any casual and abandoned phrase has to be an example of the laws in action. Yet, at the same time, this is not what we mean when we write in logical notation. For here we have the sensation of writing in sacred commands that cannot be disobeyed. Empirical evidence has nothing to do with it. The idea that this logical notation would stand in need of proof is positively ludicrous. While anyone who can object to it, must be mad; must be straightened or discarded. *And then there is that we write it.* That we write the books of it, Like Russell did. When you look at it like this, you can only conclude that it really is a question of obedience (worship and love). Logic is to be obeyed. One obeys it by writing it out, or by coming on it and reading it in the exact way it was written. Or one disobeys it, and takes the consequences.

> Christianity is not based on historical truth, but it gives us a (historical) narrative and says: Now believe! Not in the sense of putting faith in it as though it really were a historical narrative, but in the sense of putting faith in it whatever may be; which is really [nothing to do with belief] but the command to live out your life in a certain way [as though this narrative really were historically accurate]. You have a narrative here—Do not now behave towards it as to other historical narratives! Give it a very different place in your life. There is nothing paradoxical about it!
>
> Strange as it may sound, the historical content of the Gospels could be proved false, historically speaking, yet faith would lose nothing. Not, however, because it is connected with 'universal truths of reason'! But because historical evidence (the game of historical evidence) does not concern faith. This narrative (the Gospels) was received by men with faith (i.e. with love). That, and nothing else, makes it hold for truth.[4]

Thus obedience does not imply the kind of independent, infallible truth that the philosophers think it does. Here comes Wittgenstein's big realization. By obeying Logic (by obeying numbers), we are not obeying anything outside us; save that you could call the timeline and our memory of our place on it 'outside us'. We are rather all of us acting in a certain way, and afterwards calling that way 'logical'. This is a statement of ethical belief. Its apparent insuperability vis-à-vis all other statements of ethical belief is down to the fact that *we write the books*. The insuperability of numbers and the laws of nature is down to the fact that we discount that there can be other worlds than this one. If you focus on this fact in the way that Wittgenstein focused on it, then the most that you can say is that we are 'living in a *form of life*'.

> But am I trying to say some such thing as that the certainty of mathematics is based on the reliability of ink and paper? *No*. (That would be a vicious circle.)—I have not said *why* mathematicians do not quarrel, but only *that* they do not.
>
> It is no doubt true that you could not calculate with certain sorts of paper and ink, if, that is, they were subject to certain queer changes—but still the fact that they changed could in turn only be got from memory and comparison with other means of calculation. And how are these tested in turn?
>
> What has to be accepted, the given, is—so one could say—*forms of life*.[5]

All knowledge and numbers, all language, truth, and logic hangs breathless on its fate—Which is that someone from outside this world will arrive to announce the criticism on it. That we ourselves cannot announce the criticism on the way that we are acting, the words that we are saying, and the books that we are writing is the haunting circle that wheels through Wittgenstein's thinking and secures his lifelong project. The rest, and the otherworldly critic, he leaves to our imagination. But if we bring that imagination to bear in the way that I have done in this biography *of his thinking*—if we allow this biography to suspect its motives and turn that same circle on itself—then we might get somewhere. That place would be everything that Wittgenstein didn't write or say. If we call Wittgenstein's otherworldly critic 'Christ', which turns out, in any case, to be many people's secret suspicion, then we have a new tale to tell. It is a tale that may or may not be true, and which is therefore fully in the spirit of Wittgenstein's lifelong discounting of all that is 'true', and all that is 'explained'. The famous, unwritten, second part of his philosophy, documenting the famous, unknown, second part of his life. The escape which Wittgenstein was all the time making in words such as these:

> When someone who believes in God looks around him and asks 'Where did everything that I see come from?' he is *not* asking for a (causal) explanation; and the point of his question is that it is the expression of such a request. Thus, he is expressing an attitude toward all explanations.—But how is this shown in his life? It is the attitude that takes a particular matter seriously, but then at a particular point doesn't take it seriously at all, and declares that something else is even more serious.
>
> In this way a person can say it is very serious that so-and-so died before he could finish a certain work; and in another sense it doesn't matter at all. Here we use the words 'in a profounder sense'.
>
> What I actually want to say is that here too it is not a matter of the *words* one uses or of what one is thinking when using them, but rather of the difference they

make at various points in life. How do I know that two people mean the same when both say they believe in God? And one can say the same thing about the Trinity. Theology which insists on the use of *certain* words and phrases and bans others, makes nothing clearer (Karl Barth). It, so to speak, fumbles around with words, because it wants to say something and doesn't know how to express it. *Practices* give words their meaning.[6]

You cannot be certain about any *thing*: You can only be certain about the method of being certain. Likewise you cannot explain any *thing* without also demonstrating how it ought to proceed. In explaining paranoia, you teach someone how not to be paranoid. In explaining the law of gravity, you preach God a lesson in how to continue to behave. In teaching a child how to speak in finished sentences, you make him lord and master of all he surveys. In our wide-awake sanity, we clutch at a list of the things that are real; all the while forgetting that the same proof has populated the dreams of our sleep. Reality and unreality are nothing but the equal consequences of a rational theory of knowledge. Notice this and it is the door through which you escape. It is the door through which Wittgenstein escaped. The soul slips out the back door of the mind.

In mathematics there are not, first, propositions that have sense by themselves and, second, a method to determine the truth or falsity of propositions; there is only a method, and what is called a proposition is only an abbreviated name for this method.[7]

In mathematics everything is algorithm and nothing is meaning.[8]

* * *

One very important point, though, about the 'method' of this book [Already in evidence here, in this Introduction.]. As we shall see, Wittgenstein's thinking operates in a very special dimension which is unrepresented in the conventional genres and forms of understanding. This is because conventional understanding *is* a genre, *is* a form. In other words, it *is* the object in relation to which its words make sense. It is the *only object* in relation to which its words make sense. Or let me put it as Wittgenstein used to put it. If the *style/the sophistication/the prose* of understanding is to take you from the particular to the universal each time, then the ultimate result of this must be a cosmos or a system (an ever-expanding one, or an ever-extending one; as the mathematicians would say). Moreover, if this *is* the case, then we can never, as it were, 'catch up' to the final meaning of all of it because the final meaning (I repeat) *is* the genre, the form, the system, the book itself; where the book *qua* book never enters into the equation. What I mean is, *the book* is always sacred. The book is never questioned. The book is never made the subject of our suspicion. [I'll leave it to you to realise how Wittgenstein fought shy of writing books his whole life; how the only book he did publish in his lifetime, the *Tractatus Logico-Philosophicus* was extremely weirdly formed; and how all the 'books' of his we now have were brought together after his death from his private notes plus his students' notes of his lectures.]

Think of it like this. At the final count, no biographies will ever have told you anything about their alleged subjects. No. They will instead be shown to have been the 400-page—the 400-stage—proofs of the theorem of life writing. Of the theorem that we can pin a life to a board. You don't believe me? OK. Consider this, then. Let's say you are studying 'life writing' at a university. Would you find it acceptable and sensible if your four years there had you studying a single biography on its single subject? No! That would be madness. You would expect to read and study hundreds of the things and think and talk and write about them at the level of what can be understood to be common between them. Correspondingly, you would expect your first lecture to begin with a general-purpose definition of 'the biography'. Likewise, if you enrolled to study 'religion' at a university, you would be appalled if you only got to study one religion (in relation to the concept of 'truth'). You would expect instead to study all the religions of the known world equally, comparing and filleting them for their denominators. [The concept of 'truth' related to this investigation would then become the same thing as the investigation's method, if it could not become the same thing as the God of one of the religions under investigation.] Only the 'savages' of the world still see the whole of everything though the particularity of their feathers and paint. We have become the adult to their child. But at the expense of who we really are. By this advanced stage of it all, we're not really anything at all. We're just examples. Our hearts just beat out the proofs of medicine and science.

> In mathematics, we cannot talk of systems in general, but only within systems. They are just what we can't talk about. And so, too, what we can't search for.[9]
>
> In philosophy we would like to give reason after reason. Because we feel: As long as there is a reason, everything is alright. We don't want to stop explaining—And simply describe. *How can what is happening right now* be interesting? All that we're ever interested in is the justification, the why![10]

It was this *What is happening right now?* which was for Wittgenstein always the escape, the 'back door of the mind'. This is what he came to do so well, and so consistently well, across all his writings—And to call it philosophy. However, the *What is happening right now?* is something that proves extremely hard to isolate and exemplify in practice, in a book: Because, of course, it is the explosion of the inanimate and objective material of which 'examples', 'subjects', 'themes', and 'disciplines' are made. The first step in understanding something, is to have a *Something*. Or in the case of this book, a *Someone*. Correspondingly, to criticise that step as I am doing here—to isolate it and make it the example—just isn't cricket. To have a certain kind of book, to have a certain kind of something, to have a certain kind of someone, to have a certain kind of certainty, you have to at some deep level be committed to playing the game.

The *questions* that we raise and our *doubts* depend on the fact that some propositions are exempt from doubt and are, as it were, like hinges on which those turn.[11]

If I want the door to turn, the hinges must stay put.[12]

Wittgenstein never played the game himself; instead, he relentlessly exposed it for what it is. This was the 'very special dimension' in which his life and thought operated. In order to try to capture this dimension—in order to try to capture the *What is happening right now?* in this book—I have had to do something very similar.

You see, if I were to say what I am saying here, now, at the outset, but then never again in this book, *then all that I would be describing would be my method*. And everything that followed could only then be that method's silent vindication. And it is the silence that makes for the style. Understanding's style. You can only be smooth and knowing in the aftermath of some devastating certainty.

Certainty is *as it were* a tone of voice in which one declares how things are, but one does not infer from the tone of voice that one is justified.[13]

It is only by breaking the fourth wall again and again that I can make this book into the performance, the truth of which pure theory would never be able to catch up to. Philosophy and books are things *performed* by humans. That is the beginning and the end of the matter. The trick that they are otherwise—that they offer a neutral, safe space for the discussion of things that exist outside them—is just that, *a trick*. It is only by turning and looking into the camera, that you get to realize the camera was there in the first place. What happens after that, is what happens after that. The most that we can say, is that it will be *unscripted*.

Make sure that your religion is a matter between you and God only.[14]

The alternative is just books, about books, about books, about books, about books. Or the *infinity* that has so fascinated the mathematicians and the logicians. A world which no one has ever stepped into or out of, but which is *just there*.

Perhaps this is how it is: What an hypothesis explains is itself only expressible by an hypothesis. Of course, this amounts to asking whether there are any primary propositions that are definitely verifiable and not merely facets of an hypothesis. (That is rather like asking: Are there surfaces that aren't surfaces of bodies?)[15]

I repeat: Until you actually turn to the camera, you can have no idea whether you are acting or not, pretending or not. Certainty, the prototype, eternity, and so forth, is something you to have to turn to *look in the eye*. Otherwise you will only see with it, you will only see down its same line of sight, you will only see what it sees. You will only see what everyone else can see down that same line of sight. Because what the camera can see is what everyone else could see, too, if they could all be there. 'Camera', in the way that I am using it here (and in the rest of this book), is a metaphorical way of saying: 'Everyone has to see it, too!'

> There isn't an eye belonging to me and eyes belonging to others in visual space. Only the space itself is asymmetrical, the objects in it are on a par. In the space of physics however this presents itself in such a way that one of the eyes which are on a par is singled out and called *my eye*.[16]

So: I break the fourth wall all the time in this book; I really do. Not in theory, but in *reality*. I don't write a smooth book about breaking the fourth wall [for that would keep the camera in place]: I let my breaking the fourth wall wreck what would otherwise have been a smooth book about Wittgenstein. In order to break through to where I need to get us to, I must hammer repeatedly at a single spot. There is no dignified or clever way to do this. Instead it is a matter of *staying in place*, of finding authentic ways not to make the cumulative moves of conventional biography.

> I am sitting with a philosopher in the garden; he says again and again 'I know that's a tree,' pointing to a tree that is near us. Someone else arrives and hears this, and I tell him: 'This fellow isn't insane. We are only doing philosophy.'[17]
>
> I would really like to slow down the speed of reading with continual punctuation marks. For I would like to be read slowly. (As I myself read.)[18]

Does this mean that I have really made a television documentary about me writing a biography of Wittgenstein? At times, yes. But if I have, then it has been with the motive of capturing something that Wittgenstein was himself doing—His peculiar, shameless style of philosophy, in which he was always the one and only example of what he was saying. And it is my claim that by doing this—and only by doing this—I get to take us into the dimension of Wittgenstein's thought that is not theoretical or historical or progressive but what is *right, now here!*

> I do not explicitly learn the propositions that stand fast for me. I can discover them subsequently like the axis around which a body rotates. This axis is not fixed in the sense that anything holds it fast, but the movement around it determines its immobility.[19]

***

Wittgenstein once told his friend Maurice O'Connor Drury that Augustine's *Confessions* was the most serious book he had ever read. Is that a statement about God and belief? I doubt it. In that book about himself, Augustine spends all his time wrecking the narrative by turning to you, his reader, or to God. But to call it then an evangelizing book about

God would be to miss its whole point. You could replace all the words in the *Confessions* with other words randomly; what matters is that it was written by a man, and that he turned, whenever he chose, to the camera. [And destroyed something by doing that.]

> There is nothing to look at, I can only intervene as an individual and speak in the first person. *For me*, theory has no value. A theory doesn't give me anything. Is speaking essential to religion? I can very well imagine to myself a religion in which there are no doctrines, and in which for that reason there is no speech. The essence of religion can obviously not be the fact that one speaks it, or rather: If one does speak it, then this speech must of itself be a component of the religious act and not a theory. And therefore it cannot matter whether the words are true or false or senseless.[20]

Only MAN has the power to turn to the camera—And God can be nothing to do with it, save in theory.

> In such an act the power to act and the will itself are the same, and the very act of willing is actually to do the deed ... It is easier for the body to obey the soul's most feeble command, so that its members are moved at pleasure, than for the soul to obey itself and to accomplish its own high will *wholly within the will*.[21]

*　*　*　**

Finally, some important words of thanks.

When I started writing this book, Bloomsbury and Robin Baird-Smith were to publish it. As time went on, the book simply outgrew the dimensions of this arrangement and something had to be done. I am extremely grateful to Robin for agreeing that a new publisher might be sought and to Cynthia Read and Oxford University Press, New York for being so eager to take it on. My agent Rachel Calder handled everything with great care and intelligence and never wavered. In the final exhilarating business of bringing the book to concert pitch, Cynthia was brilliant and instinctive—I really want to thank you for those last few months and for making them so fun and important! My thanks also to Cynthia's assistant editor, Drew Anderla, and to the whole OUP production team for their sterling work in bringing the book to press. And to India Gray at the copyediting stage for her sensitive work.

LUDWIG WITTGENSTEIN

Any rule can be imagined to be a description of a mechanism—even the rule which says that a pawn must not be moved in a certain way.

If we do use 'identity' as we do, then it's natural that we extend our use up to this point, saying 'This is this', although this is perfectly stupid and useless.

—WITTGENSTEIN, *Lectures on the Foundations of Mathematics*, XXX

1

On the Spirit of a Man

EVERYTHING THAT LUDWIG Wittgenstein ever wrote was about him and God, and everyone has always known this—Except that at exactly the same time it has had to be treated like philosophy's great secret. This in turn has kept it that Wittgenstein has been fought over by those claiming him for or against God, and for or against the mystical and inexpressible, and for or against the supernatural and the transcendent. All I have tried to do in this new biography of him, then, is to make the maximum effort to treat it as though everything he ever wrote was about him and God—And then to see where that took me. It took me to some strange places. And some were so strange that honestly I thought about leaving them out. But in the end, I kept them all. My thinking went like this. If I left them out, then it would have been because I wanted to assert control over Wittgenstein as his biographer. And if I wanted to assert control over Wittgenstein as his biographer, then it would have been because I feared something for my career and reputation. But then as I thought these thoughts, I realized something else. 'This may well be how Wittgenstein would have wanted it'.

* * *

Just think about it. As much as everyone knows that Wittgenstein's writing was about him and God, everyone knows that he made his philosophy and lived his life so that the two should be exactly equivalent to each other—And exactly symmetrical around some point. And this makes it that you cannot then use the one to explain the other. For it turns out that Wittgenstein was not acting recklessly and fulfilling our fantasies of tortured genius, but quite the opposite. It turns out that in every step he took he was the artist painting his narrative like a picture; and that in his philosophy he correspondingly did no more than find a way to stay true to his artistic integrity of vision. I don't use the image of the artist lightly. Wittgenstein lived his life to prove that nobody else could have lived it. And the same with his philosophy. He made art of his life and his philosophy. They were his creation, they were his voice, and he signed his name to them.[1] And I am prepared to say that this is a remarkable achievement. And on this, we return to the point that I was making. In the case of most all other lives, it is possible for others to come in afterwards and relive them. That is what understanding and discernment and judgement do. That is what the biographer does. That is what the readers of biographies do. And the same again with philosophies. If they are hailed as great and make it into the canon, it was because all of that was done by others who came after them on the timeline. All that their creators did was to find a way in words to stay true to their intellects. Others did all the rest. I would say that Wittgenstein's life and philosophy remain as the epitome and test case of this. And so it became paramount to me that I should allow him here, in this biography, in *his* biography, to take back control—That is to say, that I should let control slip from me to him, and that he should decide where it all ends, and how.

I think in allowing all of this to happen I have said something important in this book about 'genius'; or at any rate, about the Western treatment of 'the genius'.

* * *

If it is true that what the genius does is from his point of view natural and unexceptional—if it really is akin to his voice—then it is we who are in fact responsible for discovering him, acclaiming him, understanding him, classifying him, and, finally, burying him in all our books about him. What I mean is, it is we who go looking for the geniuses while they never need to go looking for themselves. What I mean is, it is we who need for some reason to be able to single them out, and point at what they do and shake our heads and laugh and say, '*There* is a tortured soul, *there* is an insane mind!' It seems to me that we designate them to be the bearers of the torture and insanity that is, in fact, ours, by virtue of the fact that we have sold ourselves to rules and identities, to civilizations and laws. We are projecting onto the geniuses a truth which it would simply be impossible for us to see in its *true* setting, because that true setting would be life as we know it; and because we know deep down that there is no alternative to life as we know it. Or that the alternative would be the destruction of everything.

This explains, to me at least, why it is that we always separate the work of the genius from his life. The work of the genius we slowly dispossess him of in order to turn it into something that can serve us in the continuation of 'life as we know it'. That is to say, *he* just uses the only voice he possesses to make his art. *We* come in afterwards, and say, 'Bravo, bravo—You have solved all these hard problems for us, and that is why you are great!'

Everything that comes my way becomes a picture.[2]

This fundamental disconnect between what we want and what they want is what causes them so often to disown and walk away from the projects of life that we might have managed to co-opt them for. [Wittgenstein is, of course, the standout example of that in the world of philosophy.] And then having separated the works from the life, we take the life and hold it up as something that it is now permissible for us to ridicule in isolation. *We simply see it as a series of choices that we would have made better.*

I repeat: for us, the work and the life of the genius are never equivalent or symmetrical. And this is why we are so often left perplexed that great thought and art, beauty and poise can issue from a life that is apparently anything but. We console ourselves sometimes by thinking of the greatness of genius as like a talent that turned up already-formed and unannounced in the life. [Mozart.] But the truth is more devastating than that. The truth is that the life which we have not understood is the exact same thing as the work which we are now imagining to have understood; which leaves it that we may not really have understood the work at all.

* * *

By saying this, I am not saying that I have understood the work of Wittgenstein's life here, in this book, in a way in which it has never been understood before. I am saying the opposite. I am saying that the work of a genius like Wittgenstein is beyond understanding and that it was always meant by him to be that way. If I have achieved anything in this biography, it has been to find a way to make both the life of Wittgenstein and his work speak with a single voice; and then over that, to let that voice say what it wanted to in this book. That is a very strange and disturbing thing to say; like a séance. But in fact it is perfect sanity. I am only being honest about the plain and unavoidable mechanism of life and thought.

Every book by a single author says one huge thing already, even before we begin to consider the actual words of its pages. It says, 'I, the author, made this, and no-one else could have made it (because I did).' Biographies are where this huge thing tries to hide, or disguise itself, because biographies present someone else as their subject of enquiry. However, consider then how any one subject may have multiple biographies written about them, with each one being regarded as unique and original, and the intellectual property of its author. And you will see then that what I am saying is already proven in this common sense. Before it is anything else, a biography is its author's book (that is to say, *before it is its subject's book*); and the fact that it sets out to give the truth on its subject does not diminish this 'huge thing'. Where this huge thing is the raising up of the biographer's understanding at the cost of the death of the Subject. And what I am really saying here is that this is the paradigm of all intellectual understanding—Insofar as intellectual understanding must be presented in the syntax of thought and words. In choosing to enter the world of thoughts and words, the world of reasons and cause and effect, we do something betraying of who we really are; and when we apply this same syntax in judgement over others' lives, we betray them, too.

> At the conclusion of my lecture on ethics I spoke in the first person. That, I believe, is something very important. Here, nothing further can be substantiated. I can only step forth as an individual.[3]

We betray ourselves and others because syntax can only ever see itself and converse with itself; whereas we humans can only see each other's faces and converse with each other's emotions. And to say this is, of course, to say out loud the essence of Wittgenstein's project.

The biography is thus the 'paradigm of all intellectual understanding' because it is the most deliberate and lengthy example of syntax being applied in judgement over a life. If I am right about this, then a true and accurate 'biography' would have indeed to be like a supernatural event, or a séance. Its subject really would have to walk out the other end of it alive and reincarnated. This is no more than to say that to know someone intimately (in the way that you would expect to know them after a biography) is really to have attained an instinct as to what they would do next, in some new situation, were they still alive. It is not to know the full and detailed list of the facts of their life. For example: think of someone you know intimately and even love. Now imagine someone who has never met them, but who is holding that full and detailed list of the facts of their life—Of their history. Imagine their biographer. Now would you for even one second think that their biographer could come close to knowing them as you know them now, from out of your actual life with them? Of course not! I am asking a stupid question. When someone dies, and we still need to know their wishes for something bearing their name, such as a monument, we don't consult their biographer if we can help it, but their widow, or their children, or their close friend. That is how it goes. And we do this because we honour the insight that we do best when we consult the nearest living human, rather than the deadness of words on paper. If we could somehow bring the deceased to life, and make them speak, and ask them, we would; but we can't.

* * *

I haven't brought Wittgenstein to life in this book—Of course I haven't! But I have tried to be honest with these problems of logic and language, life and intentionality, because it is, of course, *what he would have done*. And maybe to do what someone else would have done is the next best thing to bringing them back to life. It was of the utmost importance and significance to Wittgenstein that we are the occult hands behind the thoughts and words we select. We, ourselves, are the great answer to the great question of truth and meaning. But in being the answer we also render the answer inexpressible and incommunicable. I repeat, before it tells you anything about its subject, the biography tells you by the sheer fact of its existence that one person selected its thoughts and words, and that that person was its author, the biographer. This is the real reason why Wittgenstein's early philosophy promoted the strict depersonalization of language (as exemplified in the *Tractatus Logico-Philosophicus*) while his later philosophy promoted the language-game (as exemplified in the *Philosophical Investigations*). In both cases, one huge example is made of language, which is that it can only ever say what it can say, and that what it can say is the story of laws (or rules) as mechanisms, and the world as a machine. We can change the laws, but we cannot change the fact of the *world as a machine*. We, on the other hand, are nothing to do with mechanisms and machinery. Over the course of a life we come to believe that we are because mechanisms and machines are what we have to work with when we turn our minds and open our mouths. [And without us to operate it, the world-machine would cease to exist; and so it needs us.[4]] But true freedom is real, and possible; and if we could manage it, it would be as straightforward as downing tools and walking away.

* * *

Walking away to where? That was the strangest place I had to go to in this book, and it is the story of the final chapter, 'Sex and the Last Stand'. Otherwise you will notice that this biography has only five chapters after the Introduction, and that they are thematic rather than chronological. This was done in keeping with my desire to write a book that Wittgenstein could walk away from, alive and as himself. Laws and mechanisms and *the machine* are all about form and structure, so it is form and structure that have to be torn down if a biography is not to be a biography, and a death trap, but something else. Language, truth, and logic: they are meant to represent realism and the way things really are, and to separate nonfiction from fiction, science from religion. As we grow up, we ourselves are meant to become more linguistic, truthful, and logical. *They are descriptions of the ideal man.* Yet Wittgenstein's whole effort was pitched at finding new and original ways to make these things seem strange and ludicrous and positively inhuman. In the *Tractatus*, they are reduced, and then reduced again, and that reduction is shown to be their whole tragic ambition. Then in the *Philosophical Investigations*, the language-games that we are shown to be playing all the time take that same tragedy to its ultimate level of comedy and insanity.

A STRANGE CATHECHISM

I began this chapter by talking about Wittgenstein and God. And it is true that religious imagery—Christian religious imagery—is everywhere in this book. That is because it is everywhere in Wittgenstein's writings. And I would argue it is everywhere here for the same reason that it is everywhere there, and I have achieved something and explained something if that is the case.

Because Wittgenstein intended his philosophy to be equivalent to his life, rather, say, than to prove things, God and Christianity seem to crop up incidentally in his thoughts. And because they crop up incidentally, the question whether he *believed* in them cannot be applied. I suppose I latched onto this because I have always found it to be that way myself. Generally speaking, when God and Christianity make an appearance in words, it is in anything but an incidental way. Generally speaking, those words invoke their names and imagery to make claims for or against them. Yet I wonder now whether all of this has not been a strange catechism, and that there is a perspective (that there is a world) from which all the words spoken for or against God are really seen to amount to the same thing?

Wittgenstein was drawn to the image of the suffering Christ not because he was religious, but because he believed that suffering was its own world (the opposite of this world of syntax and sense); and that the world of suffering was *the truth* in relation to which this world then becomes *the fantasy*. Those who suffer know that their suffering fragments them and pulls them apart at their atoms and sends them abroad on some eternal voyaging; and that space and time and history and psychology are correspondingly meant to be the Realism that stops all that, and which pulls them together for one last run at what this world calls 'life'. I am tending towards deep mysticism here, but then deep mysticism was what Wittgenstein was all about. Realism describes this world as the place in which our losses really are sustained, and properly so, and the dead do not come back to life. That, for example, is what sex is about. It is the arrow of time. Love, on the other hand, is heedless of these things. Wittgenstein had a great capacity for love. And perhaps that is what his life and his philosophy and his mysticism were really expressing.

I CAN ONLY PERFORM

But this turns out to be something that I can only perform, or show, or recreate for you— Rather, that is, than recount. It has to be *this* way, the reaching for a new form altogether. Because in the traditional biography form, the story always becomes more important than the subject. The story and its linear progression is what you learn and remember; like you first learned and remembered the alphabet as a child. Whereas the life of the subject is not actually contained within that story, and certainly, it does not end when that story ends in the subject's death. This is what I meant earlier by calling biographies 'death traps'. They claim to be the only way to know someone after they have gone, but that is simply not true. And, in fact, it turns out that we have resources to hand that offer us instant, eidetic, and phenomenological routes to knowing lives like Wittgenstein's [if only we will use them]. I have referred to one of these already in this chapter. The way that we can continue to love someone after their death by having an instinct for what they would do *here* or *there*, in *this* situation or *that*, were they still alive. Here we encounter a distinction that is critical—Critical, at least, to how I have decided to understand these things, and to how I have written this biography. The story of any life is by its very nature an unvarying thing. Once established on the facts, it cannot change; *it cannot change its mind*. And in much the same way that Heidegger used to claim that science cannot think.[5] Anything, it seems, that can claim to be scientifically true (that can claim to be the true version) goes catatonic and dies. And it goes catatonic and dies because it loses the special quality of life. It can no longer think for itself; it can no longer change its mind. It can no longer be one thing one minute, and another thing the next. This, it would seem, is the special quality of life, its unpredictability, its extemporaneity. I should add, the special quality of *human* life. We are who we are, through our lives. And there are people who are prepared to love us for who we are. And this is miraculous, because we change our minds and are not the truth. And yet we are loved. More, we are loved precisely because we are not the truth. Books are learnt and remembered, but they are not loved, and they cannot be loved. You cannot love a book like you can love a person.

IN INCREMENTS OF ITSELF

The truth does, of course, have one claim to being alive. It can reproduce itself endlessly (to infinity, in fact). One truth implies another or the next. And it is this spontaneous and contemporaneous implication that makes the truth what it is, and that makes mathematical and symbolic logic into its special language. To put it another way, *The Truth* can only see in increments of itself. When it looks into a packed train carriage, it cannot do what we can with that scene. It cannot see faces and hearts and moods and bring an imagination to bear on them, and then close its eyes and write the stories of what it has seen. It cannot see the tired woman at the back with her head on the glass, and then conjure into fantasy a life and a backstory for her. It cannot do any of that. All it can do is to see things like: 'This carriage contains 47 pairs of eyes' or 'This carriage contains 470 fingers' or 'This carriage contains 47 trillion atoms'. Those are the increments that the truth sees in. That is how it multiplies itself to infinity. And there is an awesome kind of beauty in the constellations if numbers. [And some can tip their heads back and see them all.] But love and caring and *human life* must always be as arbitrary as never making it past the number one (because your imagination started to wander and created a world around it instead).

Now, of course, it is possible as a human being to grow up striving to be more linguistic, truthful, and logical, as I put it earlier in this chapter. In fact, that seems in large part to have become the stated aspiration of the Western education. For it is possible to be trained to count (as it were) to infinity, and to use your eyes to see only the denominators and the facts, but to see the person and *the life* (*the soul*) does not admit of any such method which can be taught. Therefore, you could say that the truth has no existence in itself, save that it can make humans do the former. So, throughout this book, I have referred to this business of 'enslavement to the truth' in the Christian language of devilry. And its opposite I have referred to in the Christian language of God and salvation. I repeat what I said a little earlier: I think that there is a perspective and a world from which all of the words spoken for or against God are really seen to amount to the same thing. So, I am not doing that here. What I am doing is copying or recreating or performing a distinction that Wittgenstein himself insisted upon. The distinction between, on the one hand, enslavement and devilry and, on the other hand, God and salvation (and freedom). To Wittgenstein the question was never whether God exists, but whether *we exist*. To this great question, the question of the existence of God is simply irrelevant. The Logical Positivism which Wittgenstein had eventually to disown, was, like Western science itself, a doctrine of words spoken against God—Or against the metaphysical and the supernatural. Or at least a doctrine of words spoken for the Truth. Which comes to the same thing. Which was Wittgenstein's whole point. In both his *Tractatus* and his *Philosophical Investigations* he managed to achieve a perfect ambiguity in place of this traditional God-valence of Western philosophy. This 'perfect ambiguity' is what has always been referred to as the inherent *Mysticism* in his thought. In the *Tractatus*, he specifically and dramatically treats the question of the existence of God (of the metaphysical and the supernatural) as simply irrelevant. What is relevant, in that book, is his investigation instead of the extent to which logic and language can only communicate by simultaneously generating the form of their answer (their tautological aspect, or what I have here called their capacity to see only in increments of themselves). Next, in the *Philosophical Investigations*, the God-question is made irrelevant yet again by the way in which Wittgenstein chooses to make the issue of realism as something that turns, not on the alignment of words on an underlying material structure called *Reality* (or *The World*, as it really is, through a microscope), but on the places and worlds to which human eyes have wandered and been. There is no truth, he says; there are just the places and worlds where imagination can take you. And to describe and report back from these places, you have words. And so against the high pretensions of the truth-merchants (the Logical Positivists), this means that words are really for gaming with.

> Christianity is not a doctrine, not, I mean, a theory about what has happened and what will happen to the human soul, but a description of something that actually takes place in human life. For 'consciousness of sin' is a real event and so is despair and salvation through faith. Those who speak of such things (Bunyan for instance) are simply describing what has happened to them, whatever gloss anyone wants to put on it.[6]
>
> Life can educate one to a belief in God. And *experiences* too are what bring this about; but I don't mean visions and other forms of sense experience which show us the 'existence of this being', but e.g. sufferings of various sorts. These neither show us God in the way a sense impression shows us an object, nor do they give rise to *conjectures* about him.[7]
>
> Only in the stream of thought and life do words have meaning.[8]

THIS NEW MYSTICISM

This new mysticism of Wittgenstein's has been largely misunderstood. Because whereas mysticism in the Western tradition has always been portrayed as a predilection for making vague and esoteric use of things for which the proper use would be serious and practical (such as with numbers), this new mysticism of Wittgenstein's is neither vague nor esoteric but pinpoint accurate. It is saying that reality is not one world and its contents, but (so to speak) innumerable worlds and their contents. Western science sets one world—the material world—against all the innumerable worlds in order to say that they don't exist. Wittgenstein, on the other hand, says that exercise is irrelevant, if not fraudulent. Because (of course) the reality of one thing cannot settle the question of the reality of some other thing in this way. All that two such opposing realities can *technically* and *logically* accomplish is to put the focus on us, and our minds; for it is only *in us* and our minds that these two realities can ever arise to be in opposition. And that becomes the remarkable thing; that they can arise in us, but not, say, in a hedgehog. In this sense, Wittgenstein manages to call the bluff on the whole long history of Western philosophy. This history has only ever used words within the discourse of *existence* (or if you like, *being*). It has preached to use words truthfully, that is in order to make sense, one must use them each to the exclusion of the other. So, anything that can definitely be said and that makes sense, excludes for that moment something else that could have been said in its place. Another example: I look at the keys on this keyboard and they preach to me the doctrine that it would be meaningless to try to press them all at once. Words and truth and meaning will only come about as I press them one at a time—And in the strict patterns and orders that I learnt in my Western education. I have just pressed the letter *I*; in the first instance that means I cannot at the same time be pressing the letter *Z*. I cannot, because to do so would be nonsense. [Similarly, one of the weaknesses of the German Enigma Machine in World War Two was that it could not encode a letter as itself; it could not, for instance, encode the letter *B* as *B*. This inability became a *constant* which the code-breakers could exploit.] It would be as much nonsense as were a hedgehog to become depressed and jump off a skyscraper in New York City. But in my imagination, that has just happened, and I even feel for him.

Within the discourse of *existence*, nonfiction is all the time being sorted from, and insulated from, fiction. On the face of it, you might think it could just as well be the other way around. But then when you *really* think about—and in the way that Wittgenstein did—you realize that it *can* only be this way around. Because *within our minds*, the only difference between nonfiction and fiction is that we designate the one to be true; the former one. Within the pure remit of the mind, this designation is actually an arbitrary one. There is no reason why fiction should not be designated to be true and even acted upon as such, and sometimes that does happen, though such individuals are called 'mad'. To cure this disease, the Western intellectual tradition came up with the method of verifying the contents of human minds against the gold standard of empirical reality. I say, the 'Western intellectual tradition', but really this verification mania has been more of an Anglophone phenomenon. The great radical dissenters to it have consistently come out of the Continental scene. I think, for example, of Pier Paolo Pasolini and his masterpiece *Teorema*—Of the book of it, as much as of the film.

PASOLINI'S *TEOREMA*

In Pier Paolo Pasolini's *Teorema*, the suffering Christ comes to earth to bring the Song of Songs to each member of an upper middle-class Milanese family. Mother (Lucia), father (Paolo), daughter (Odetta), son (Pietro), housemaid (Emilia). His arrival is announced to them by a sort of angel. While he is with them, he is known only as 'the Visitor'; and nothing is ever discovered about him, save the great impressions that he can make on all of them in the moment. When he leaves, they are left destitute and panting. The story is presented mechanically and two dimensionally, without perspective or moral toning. All of which, actually, then, puts it into the style of the ancient tragedy or the medieval chronicle—Both so famously fascinating to Pasolini. As in both those forms of literature, the characters in Pasolini's tale have no personal histories, or depth of perspective, that would serve to explain their actions. Instead, what we learn about them is indicative only and serves to situate them as pawns in the modern, bourgeois fundamentalism against which Pasolini would struggle in all his works as like a prophet.

In the ancient tragedy, or the medieval chronicle, the commands that humans obey are still secret and unseen. That is to say, the seventeenth century's discovery of (geometric) human nature is as yet only tacit and implied. That single theory of human action, which will become the parent of our modern psychology, is, in the ancient and medieval time, not yet capable of such an abstract and unanimous statement. In its potential, it exists: but meanwhile the laws and truth that make it up can only be performed over and again in the telling and retelling of the tales. The ancient and medieval mind does not doubt that there is a human geometry: but meanwhile it can only be proved and transmitted and learnt in the multiplication of its stories. At the other end of things is Pasolini's twentieth century; his twentieth-century *Milan*. But standing in it *is* Pasolini. And looking about him, he is inclined to think that nothing much has changed, or really, that things have gotten a whole lot worse and a whole lot more sinister. A whole lot more internalized, and a whole lot more sensible. Here is what he means.

In the ancient and medieval scheme, the circumstances hold the power, the gods decide the circumstances, and the tragedy of the human condition becomes then that man must give the predicted response. In the twentieth-century bourgeois style of life, man must still obey these impersonal directives of chance, except that now he cannot even do it as he once did, kicking against the goads. For after all the intervening progress and enlightenment, he now obeys himself, or better to say, his own high reason; corresponding, as it now does, to the laws of the universe and what he learnt in school. That is to say, if he is educated and enlightened, then his high, or 'better', reason will so correspond. Thus, it comes to pass for Pasolini that twentieth-century man pursues a hollow, loveless virtue—And is condemned to be always right, and never wrong. He follows a course of life because that course can be made to stand to reason, and because his own eyes can see it in its first principles, and *approve it* (*verify it*) in its first principles.

Into this sad scheme arrives Pasolini's Christ as the antithesis. For he can only lead and be followed. To where, exactly, Pasolini never tells us. Perhaps he himself does not know or care. His point is to maintain the story in its two-dimensional aspect. He wants us to see all of it only from the outside, in its flat mechanics; what you would see plain verse, looking on. A beautiful Visitor seducing an entire family. He wants you to see that pinpoint outraging of every bourgeois ethic and pretension. Because that is how it really *would look* if there were a world in which people acted (and indeed in which people created customs and homes) according to their better reason. A good and civilized and technologically advanced world would look like this. Would look like inscrutable twentieth-century Milan in one of its better neighbourhoods. And therefore Pasolini's Christ, when he has his effect, has it always in the way of taking the (mechanical) gestures and movements of this goodness and civilization (of ours) and making it the point of departure, and corridor, to a kind of nostalgia.[9]

I repeat, in his *Teorema*, Pasolini does something very clever. His Christ is calm, beautiful, rarefied, and otherworldly. His Christ is innocent. His activities in the Milanese household are sublime and cannot be gainsaid. Yet technically they are capable of outraging modern bourgeois fundamentalism and its morality—Up to and including that morality's expectation of what Christ *would do on earth*. We watch, we read, as each character is driven to erupt against this Visitor in their midst; and then is calmed, soothed, made love to—Fully taken through the actions of a sexual encounter yet without any of the thrill and lust that would be associated with such an encounter if it were to be transacted *in time*. And so, all the while there is no narrative, and the characters in the story interact with each other and with Pasolini's Christ as though the story were reading itself, to itself; impassively. Yet each encounter is, yes, sublime—And momentarily, for each character, it is transforming. And so it is that I say it cannot be gainsaid. Pasolini's Christ is never moved or discomposed in the way that a normal human being would be, doing what he is doing. And momentarily he is able to fill each character with hope and nostalgia. And momentarily this seems to join them to him in his otherworldliness and to take them out of the script.

By this means, the chief effect of the *Teorema* becomes to impress us with the truth that any story traditionally told, in words, in a line and syntactically, is for that reason then also normative and repressive. It is, as Pasolini would like specially to say, 'fascist'. It is indicative. The factual, empirical truth is always, for him, the fascist red pen. It denies this by teaching to us that each story is different; that names, and settings, and sequences of events make the difference, if they are different. But we say instead (with Pasolini and Wittgenstein) that names and settings and sequences of events make no difference at all, because each and every story, if it is traditionally told, in words, in a line and syntactically, can tell us only one thing each time. With this thing being the lesson that it was *possible*; that it was *realistic*. The purpose of any traditional narrative—of any history—is not what it happens to contain, but the form and structure by which it does its containing. Pasolini wants us to see that it is no good, therefore, if Christ walks the earth within this international scheme of containment. Because if he does, then he will have to play his *indicated* part. He will have to be manifestly and ethically the *summum bonum*. Just like how in an ancient tragedy or medieval chronicle, good and evil are manifestly and ethically what they are. The only thing to be done, then, is what Pasolini insists on in his *Teorema*. You take the human sex act, which has always been good and evil's touch-paper (and Christ in between them, triangulated from their angles on the timeline), and instead of that you take the whole of good and evil and sex and drop it right through Christ like quicksilver.[10] And if you do that you might just come to realise that facts require our belief as much as fantasy; that fact and fantasy are actually equal to each other *in respect of this world*; and all of this because this world has no existence save that it is being wrought spontaneously to arbitrate between the two.

Watch what happens when Lucia finds the Visitor's clothes abandoned on a bed.

Little by little Lucia's eyes begin to lose their contemplative indifference, and fill instead with tenderness. These, truly, are the clothes of a boy who could be her son. The tenderness that is aroused in her is therefore a species of maternal fetish.

She takes them in her hand, she contemplates them, and, perhaps, she caresses them: Her hand passes with a natural shamelessness over even those parts of the clothing that it would never be allowed to do so were they being worn. She repeats these passes many times, without any loss of dignity—like a mother caring for the wounds of her son. But now these passes, repeated over and over, begin to drag her, little by little, outside herself. She finds herself in a state similar to Pietro [see below], possessed by a dream born outside of her; a dream that will not let itself be understood. *To realise this dream, she must somehow act before deciding to....* She goes out again to the door. She looks again at the Visitor, who runs around in the field down below, in amongst the brushwood which has lost all its colour in the strong light....

Slowly, then, Lucia lets her clothes slip off, until she is nude, on the small terrace, behind the low parapet....

[He comes over to her, and her] desire to be violated by his glance, to lose herself freely and be degraded, coincides with a shame that could be considered legitimate in the circumstances: That of being caught by surprise whilst innocently sunbathing on the terrace. This is the part that she now tries to recite, innocently and fiercely like a child. But in reciting it, she makes a conscious effort to do it badly. For she has realised that if she now shows an excessive shame, and a true surprise at having been caught, then she might actually cause him to divert his divinely degrading gaze and leave, apologizing.[11]

What Pasolini is saying is this: if you use your mind to ask the question, then this world is the answer. If you don't ask the question, then you are free to follow Christ, and this (bourgeois) world becomes, by contrast to your new life in Christ, an absurd desert. A cruel and endless monotony of the mind, in which nothing is ever loved, nothing ever distinguished by the (random) act of loving (something).

Pasolini hated the bourgeois ideology not because he was a Marxist, but because he was an artist. He mocked sexual mores not because he was a libertine, but because he was original. He believed that the twentieth-century bourgeois ideology of his country, at least, had come close to a kind of hell because it had achieved a perilous new proximity to *the script*. That is to say, its culture, values, and ethics had become nearly indistinguishable from the technique of mastering life through knowledge and science. When you think about it, the 'technique of mastery' becomes the actions, becomes the acting out, of the culture, the values, and the ethics. To be clean and spotless and to think logically like a microscope, becomes the actual method of *being*; while the script becomes the proof that this method is bringing one closer all the time to what is really going on (at atomic, better, at subatomic, level).

As we have said: Pietro exhibits all of the characteristic psychology and beauty of the bourgeoisie. Above all, this comes down to his pallid complexion; such that one would say that his good health is the result of the fact that he leads a most hygienic life: that he does gymnastics and plays sport. But yet this pallor of his has something of the hereditary about it—or better still, something of the 'impersonal'. Something else—perhaps humanity, the world, his social class—is pallid in him.

His eyes are very intelligent: yet his is an impure kind of intelligence, that arises in fact from an intellectual illness—and one of which he is almost certainly unaware. But an intellectual illness that is compensated, to a degree, by the knowledge and actions that come to him from out of his birthright.

For that very reason this birthright becomes also the chief initial obstacle that will prevent him from comprehending, but more importantly, from admitting to what is about to take place. We say therefore that in order to be able to exercise his innate [not his bourgeois] intelligence, he would have to be remade from scratch. For as things stand, it is really his social class which is living its true life in him. Correspondingly, the only way for him to grasp that he is shortly to be saved from his bourgeois rationality would be for him to suspend all rational comprehension and admittance [belief] and simply walk his way through [*agendo*] what is about to happen....

So now he stands trembling before the bed of the Visitor, moved by his obedience to a force that has originated outside of him, and that is far stronger than him—the same force that first took him from his own bed, in his own room, to here. And now he stands contemplating an act that, a few moments before he could not have dreamed of carrying through; let alone having wanted to carry through.

> Now, slowly and gently, he is pulling back the light covering over the Visitor, making it slide down across his naked body. His hand is shaking, and in his throat he is stifling a cry. But now, with the covering sliding past the Visitor's abdomen, he wakes from its touch. He looks at the boy bent over him, who is committing over him this practically absurd litany, and at once his eyes fill with that light with which we are by now familiar ... with that light of the father filled, as it is also, with the familiarity and homeliness of the mother ... and that together make for an expression that is both all-knowing and sweetly ironical.
>
> Pietro raises his eyes from the Visitor's abdomen—really from his lap now, for the sliding cover has already begun to expose it—and meets his light. Yet he does not manage to do it in time to fully comprehend it. Instead, shame and terror rush in and blind him. Crying and hiding his face in his hands, he rushes back to his room and his own bed, and throws himself down on it, his head under his pillow.
>
> At that point, the Visitor gets up completely, and walks over to Pietro's bed, and sits down on its edge. He remains like that for a short while, quite still, regarding the violent, spasmodic sobs of Pietro, as they pulse along the back of his neck.[12]

According to the bourgeois ideology—according to what it represented for Pasolini—*purity* must eventually become the same thing as the clean and spotless laws of nature. As an adjective, and a quality, it must eventually take on their insuperable, incontrovertible (claim to) existence. *Purity* must eventually come to mean the existence of what is real. And *the point*, then, *his point*, is that this is something quite different to what *purity* would be if it were the actions of his Christ in the *Teorema*. In the bourgeois ideology of the twentieth century, good and bad and the *summum bonum* are coterminous with the so-called real world which they generate for their proof and fiat. And in it, no one, then, is free. Because action and knowledge are now in a tautologous relationship. [Or a theorem, a *Teorema*.]

I want to say that Western ethics is still walking through (the desert of) Socrates' dream that the knowledge of the good will result, must result, in the corresponding good action. Into this, Pasolini's Christ arrives to wreck everything. *Purity* is simply whatever thing he does next—And of which there can be NO predicting. And love is to love him for no good reason, and to be bereft when he is gone. This is all deeply shocking and scandalous, and deserving of censure, if anything is (in *this* world).

Think of it like this. In the case of any one of us, an actor could conceivably play our part. Or what comes to the same thing, we ourselves could believe that we were acting, believe that we were pretending. And this could only happen because of our blind faith in facts, our blind faith in the already-existing script. And then in addition to that, the ideologies of modern life which encourage us to conform to what is already written. In the case of (Pasolini's) Christ, however, no actor can play his part, because he writes his own script as he goes along, and nothing he does can be profane. This is a kind of creation *ex nihilo*. [Which prompt Pasolini is giving by having it make use of sex each time to 'remake' the members of the Milanese family.] The immediate effect is pleasingly enigmatic, and the institutional Church may even reward the effort. But after a short while, it becomes a certain kind of madness and impossible to follow doctrinally. At that point, the institutional Church condemns it. As did happen.

We say, then, that Pasolini's *Teorema* is ultimately an exploration of the difference between two types of creation: viz., the human and the divine. The divine type is always *ex nihilo*, as we have said. Whereas the human is not really creation at all but the 'discovery' of what is real and possible according to the physical laws of nature. In his *Teorema*, as in many other of his works, Pasolini wants to make the two collide, then see what happens. Hence the great care he takes at the start of the story, to explain to you that the information you are receiving on the characters and the setting is indicative in relation to the *Generic*. He delights in reminding you, and showing you, that if the information (he calls it the 'data') he gives you is *realistic*, then it must at the exact same time and continuously, be the creation of the world that is its proof. Or what is the same thing (and the thing that is really proved), the world and its story existed all along; which is why just the scantest data was enough to enable you to discover it. Humans can only *discover* the Truth; and Pasolini seems inclined to think it represents them at their worst; and that the bourgeois ideology (for all its proficiency) is the worst of its worst. Yet humans are at the same time endowed with a capacity for physical determination (*agendo*),[13] the sole and final purpose of which is to override their minds and fit them to follow the Divine to salvation.

> The initial data in this, our story, consists, most plainly, in the description of the life of a family. We are talking of a petite bourgeois family: 'petite bourgeois' in the ideological rather than the economic sense. In fact, we are talking of a very rich family, who live in Milan. I believe that on this fact alone it will not be difficult for you, the reader, to already imagine how these people must live; how they comport themselves in their relationships with their environment (here we must understand that they are rich industrialists), how they act amidst their family circle, and so on. Moreover, I believe that it will not even be difficult (so long as we avoid certain outmoded tropes) for you to right now imagine the family before you—to have them before you one by one, as it were; not as persons who are in any way exceptional, but precisely because they are each of them more or less on the median.
>
> The midday bells rang…[14]

In this same spirit of seeking out the natural conversation of Wittgenstein's ideas, I want now to turn to Fyodor Dostoyevsky's *The Meek One*. In discussing Pasolini, I have set something before you. I have dressed the set and influenced your mood. I have dulled certain fields of your receptivity in order to heighten others. This must be continued.

DOSTOYEVSKY'S *THE MEEK ONE*

God, the metaphysical, the supernatural, the natural, atoms—None of these are actually in a battle for ultimate, final existence; though the Western tradition is all the time saying that they are, and by that means gives itself its peculiar, normative trajectory which it calls 'truth'. And this dictates how Wittgenstein calls the bluff. He is the first philosopher to admit that if you go into your mind, you will see at once that all these things are simply of a one. The Western way of truth amounts always to a method of life. A method of the good life. It stares aghast at the deviations to its rules. Why would someone choose to end their life? It says things like that. But have you suffered? Have you ever suffered that much? Well, until you have, you just won't know. People can do, and have done, everything: because within the pure remit of the mind all things are of a one. All things are equal, to the extent that they can only receive their value from being chosen *by you*. *You* can choose death as much as *you* can choose life. And this, of course, is why theories and arguments have come to mean so much (and why once upon a time the Sophists did so well). All things that are in your mind stare at you from out of their utter equality of value. So, it is *you* who must do the work of adding value to them, if that is what you want to do.

> My propositions serve as elucidations in the following way: anyone who understands me eventually recognizes them as nonsensical, when he has used them—as steps—to climb up beyond them. (He must, so to speak, throw away the ladder after he has climbed up it.)[15]

If you want to do something, and have a reason for doing it; and have a reason for doing it that stacks up (an ethic); well, then you must do the work of putting it together—And logically, too, from premises to conclusions. Ethics therefore belongs to physics, space, and time; it is transcendental relative to the pure eternity of your mind. Ethics, value, rationality, understanding. These are all things that are designed to make sense as they are recounted. To use your brain in the way that Western intelligence commands you to use it, you must become *the narrator*.

Fyodor Dostoyevsky's short story *The Meek One* is a perfect exploration of this. Possibly it is even a mockery of this. It pits narrative, and the 'recount', against 'chance—simple, barbaric inertia, chance'. *Chance*, in this story, is what a suicide looks like, once it becomes set against all the normative realism called *Life*. This realism will talk you into and out of things; it will set you *straight*. It is shocking that life itself is this doctrine called Realism. And shocking, still, that it produces this method which has been in continuous evolution from Thales' *Urstoff* to Russell's Logical Analysis. This method is like a script, penned in advance, of what you ought to do next. To live, to survive, to be happy, to be good. What you ought to do next to be those things. Thus, to everything it assigns a value and a place. And therefore its great nemesis becomes the human being, when that human being resists and revolts and returns into the pure eternity of its mind. For there, in the mind, it may yet choose to do anything it wishes, for no reason at all, save that the sheer idea of it occurred.

To a great writer like Dostoyevsky, this is seen at once to be the great insurmountable difference between *humanity* and the *story of humanity*. Or, indeed, the *Subject* and the *biography of the Subject*. Characters can do anything they like, and that is what we call their freedom to act. And they can do anything they like because the idea of doing anything can occur in their mind at any second. And we say that this is what it must mean to be human, because to the hedgehog it cannot happen. And yet consider now the narrator, the biographer, as he creates or recounts a story. He cannot logically be in any such way free. In fact, he is quite the opposite of 'free', for he must now put things in the proper sequence of cause and effect if his story is to be believed, if it is to make sense. Even in a fantasy tale, you cannot yet ignore the rules of grammar. This is what I mean.

In *The Meek One*, Dostoyevsky explores this fatalism by means of a narrator who is hung—at exact equidistance—between being the cause of his wife's suicide and not wanting to be the cause. By giving to his narrator this motive, and, indeed, by making it an obvious feature of the story, Dostoyevsky makes what is normally invisible visible. All narration, all historicization, all proper use of language, has a prior motive; except that it is usually kept invisible by being called 'the truth'. I repeat, even in a fantasy tale, this motive is there in the injunction to use words properly and to 'make sense'. Thus, in *The Meek One*, Truth becomes, as it were, the character telling the tale; while his wife's suicide becomes the dreaded and climactic event against which his feverishly spinning story will be proved helpless. Form, structure, genre, grammar, truth. When these become visible of a sudden like this, they become also *meek* and *cowardly*. They are all about the script and being able to see it. They are the script. And because they are the script, they can't act against it or out of turn. In *The Meek One*, the narrator keeps declaring an uncanny ability to have foreseen events as they turned out; or more, to have engineered them to turn out one way rather than the other. Yet when his wife jumps out of their bedroom window to her death, she defies and destroys and makes ludicrous this whole meek, cowardly power of his. And he is left helpless against her—the truth is left helpless against her—save that she is gone and it is still here, still writing.

Thus it is that Dostoyevsky arrives at the key moment and tension of all language use. We might call it the 'normativity of syntax'. Or even the 'personality of syntax'. Because it really does turn out that before it has any characters, a story is presided over by *The Truth* who narrates it. And that before even the first event of that story has been told, this narration will already have been fully underway in the (normally invisible) story of why we should speak sense rather than nonsense. Thus goes the climax of *The Meek One*:

> The main thing, it's a pity that it all comes down to chance—simple, barbaric inertia, chance. That's the pity of it! All of five minutes, I was only five minutes late! If I had arrived five minutes earlier—the moment would have passed by, like a cloud, and it would never have occurred to her again. And it would have ended by her

understanding everything. But now the rooms stand empty again and I'm alone once again ... I pace, I keep pacing. I know, I know, don't try to put words in my mouth: you think it's ridiculous that I complain about chance and the five minutes? But it's obvious, you see. Consider one thing: she didn't even leave a note saying, 'Don't blame anyone for my death', like everyone does ... No, this was all a moment, just one inexplicable moment. Suddenness and fantasy! So what if she was praying before the icon? That doesn't mean that this was before her death. The entire moment lasted, perhaps, all of some ten minutes, the entire decision—precisely when she was standing by the wall, with her head resting on her arm, and smiling. The thought flew into her head, her head started spinning and—and she couldn't withstand it.[16]

This making the invisible visible; this shaming and outing of the narrator, *The Truth*; this is what the whole point and meaning of Wittgenstein's philosophy seems to have been. At least this is what I take him to mean when he says the following:

Philosophy is a battle against the bewitchment of our intelligence by means of language.[17]

OUR BEWITCHMENT BY MEANS OF LANGUAGE

The problem comes down to this. There is the *World of Syntax and Sense* as it can exist in our minds if our minds have been properly trained by the proper education, and then there is the realization that the *World of Syntax and Sense* as it can exist in our minds is yet again a perfect analogue of the *World of Syntax and Sense* as it is materially manifested in the world around us—And the processes and laws that describe that world. On the one hand, we only encounter that 'world around us' through our senses, and then really again, by our mind's interpretation of those senses. So, there has always been a tradition in Western philosophy of acknowledging that we never in fact encounter the world around us first-hand; that we only ever deal in the idea-impressions it generates in our minds; and that there is correspondingly no logical way of attaining to the certainty that your set of idea-impressions bears any likeness of class or type to anybody else's. Or, for that matter, to how things *really are* in the world out there.

But on the other hand, there is the tradition—and it has been by far the stronger and more influential one—of being drawn ineluctably to the thrilling conclusion that the *World of Syntax and Sense* (as it is materially manifested) in the world around us should, as I put it a little earlier, become the 'gold standard' to which the *World of Syntax and Sense* (as it can exist) in our minds should be forced to conform. This is the same thing as to say that once upon a time, philosophy used to imagine that it could shame and 'out' the narrator by calling him 'God', the metaphysical and the supernatural. The history of doing this, plus the resistance along the way, has become what is meant by the history of

Western philosophy. The history of Western philosophy understands itself to be progressive in this left-to-right direction. And where it has now brought us out is meant to be a better, more neutral, and happy place. God should no longer be able to tell people what to do, and the *World of Syntax and Sense* is now the unimpeachable and irreproachable *World of Science*.

And yet from out of all of this has come a philosophy like Wittgenstein's, which claims that we have succeeded only in moving more deeply into the narrator's thrall, for that thrall is made up of the psychological (for want of a better word) tendency to favour forgery over originality, the copy over the signature.

A better way for me to depict this tendency is to talk about 'knowledge', about the minimum requirements that we in the West maintain for a pukka item of knowledge. I mean how it must be stable and unchanging, universally apprehendable and infinitely transcribable. For us, an item of knowledge can never be a one-off; or what is the same thing, a one-off should always be able to be broken down into its knowledge items. Knowledge is therefore the kind of thing that should enable you to reconstruct (from first principles) a flash of originality after its event. Knowledge should therefore explain *how* it was done; and it should even go so far as to posit *why* it was done, by means of some consequentialist ethic or other. But what no knowledge can ever do, then, is originality itself. It can fake originality endlessly once originality has first taken place. But then that only tells us something about originality which we already know. Which is that it is always a one-off, a never-to-be repeated event. Originality is something that appears in order to disappear. And then never again to *reappear*. It is fundamentally contradictory of language, truth, and logic insofar as they are the very means and conductors of infinitely reappearing knowledge. Here we arrive at a concrete depiction of what Wittgenstein means by 'bewitchment' and 'mysticism'—And what I mean by 'invisibility' and 'visibility'.

Bewitchment refers to our bedevilling by light—That exact same light that bedevilled Plato all those years ago. A light that seems to shine down on us, from the conceptual clarity of the heavens and the gods. Except that in Wittgenstein's meaning this light no longer creates what it sees (and calls that *idealism*). Instead it has become a point of light on a screen, which moves as we move. We move, and as we move the light traces our movement. Just as it was in Plato's day, the light is *Knowledge*. Except that 2,500 years hence, it is just us left now, and the movements we make, and explaining them. 'Philosophy turned on the philosopher.' Philosophy turned on itself. When Plato was bewitched he saw the light from above shining down; and shining down, he saw it picking out the eternal features of itself in the things of materiality which it had made. *Universals*. Truth as universals. But now that philosophy has turned on itself and realized that ideas and words *are made by us*, all the questions have now resolved themselves into the last great question; *which is us*. Which is the question of sequence and priority in regard to us and the things we think and say. Which is the question of us and time. Or the question of knowledge (which still, after Plato, is eternal), and then we who sound and mark that knowledge in symbols. Or the question whether we are needed anymore or can be replaced by machines?

But most of all, the *very* way in which this question seems to hypnotise us—or bewitch us—like the edge of a cliff or the trigger of a gun. The bewitching thing about language, truth, and logic is how it needs to make a sacrifice of us. On the one hand, it is in its nature to exist in spite of us, and independently of us. But on the other hand, the history of Western philosophy is the history of a procession of people who voiced and wrote it. Bewitchment is this feeling that you *must* jump from the cliff or pull the trigger. Bewitchment is the feeling that you are in a story and you can hear the narrator's voice. Or that you are the narrator's voice. Or that you ought to be the narrator's voice. Rather than yourself. *Bewitchment is giving the machine's response to being a machine.* Which is obedience.

Mysticism comes about because now, 2,500 years on from Plato, we really do know that the world (that the universe) is a machine, and that we in it are machines, too. That the universe, and us, and all the rest of the animals and everything in between, are just material parts—And the way those parts are connected up. The science of today proves beyond a shadow of doubt that this is exactly how things *really are*. In the ancient world of Plato, this revelation was held back by retarding habits of mind like supernaturalism and animism. But now we are free to embrace it, because in place of supernaturalism and animism we have psychology, which replaces spontaneity and freedom with wires and rods that link us to our history. *Mysticism*—that is, Wittgenstein's kind of mysticism—is to see all of this (and to know it to be true) and yet at exactly the same time to know that you are also spontaneous and free in the way that would obliterate this world of machines in a flash. Like waking up from a dream. I say that, because the dream becomes the best illustration of this that I can give you. I mean how occasionally you can be dreaming but also realize that you are in a dream. The dream then becomes like a storybook, with you as a character in that story. And just like a character in that story, you are beholden to the ready-written script and the narrator's voice. But because you somehow know that you are dreaming, you know, too, that somewhere else outside that storybook you are alive and breathing, and spontaneous and free. You know you will wake up. That is how Wittgenstein's mysticism works. It works by saying that the modern, scientific view of the world is true, and therefore it truly shows our abject predestination by cause and effect. BUT it says this only in order to perform by it the counter-truth that you must then be un-predestinated somewhere else. Somewhere other than this universe of cause and effect. According to Wittgenstein's mysticism, you are alive and breathing, spontaneous and free, *there*, in that other place, wherever it is. There has been nothing like this in Western philosophy before. It is the great revolution against what I earlier called the 'discourse of existence' and the 'God-valence' of Western philosophy.

The world of the happy is quite different from the world of the unhappy.[18]

POINTS OF LIGHT

Think, for example, of how Thomas Hobbes handled the situation in his *Leviathan*. That book is the great celebration of men as points of light on a screen.[19] And the seeing of everything like that. And *that* seeing being the sum of all there is to know plus the suggestion of the proper method of life. Everything, for Hobbes, is geometry plus the iconoclasm that geometry alone makes possible. Hobbes's *Leviathan* is as insatiable as the *Tractatus* in what it tears down (in the name of science). In Hobbes's vision, there are only points and angles and lines; and again like Wittgenstein in the *Tractatus*, his place for God is in the lands beyond the words.

> And these are but a small part of the Incongruities they are forced to, from their disputing philosophically, in stead of admiring, and adoring of the Divine and Incomprehensible Nature; whose Attributes cannot signifie what he is, but ought to signifie our desire to honour him, with the best Appellations we can think on.[20]

But unlike Wittgenstein, and unlike the *Tractatus*, where the syntax of this world, and its ethics, can be viewed from what I called above the transcendentalism of the 'pure eternity of your mind', Hobbes must find our freedom—somehow—within the very predestination which renders it void. Hobbes does not have the option, as Wittgenstein does, of imagining that we could wake up, and be free in that place of our waking. That is to say, whereas the *Tractatus* is a book designed to show—to prove to you—that you can't actually be in two places at once, the *Leviathan* is designed to show—to prove to you—that you *can* be both in a book and free. Wittgenstein thanks that is impossible; you cannot be in two places at once. And this is why when it came to his later philosophy and the *Philosophical Investigations*, his objective had developed into exploring the numberless ways in which souls communicate with each other. This communication can be represented as though it were making use of language, but only insofar as that each act of communication becomes then a spontaneous 'game' that creates and then discards a set of rules about the way in which the language of that moment is going to be used. Whereas, in fact, the communication is occurring in some supernatural and eternal and extensionless world of souls, and language is only the most cumbersome and excruciating way that it can be represented.

This brings me to what I mean by 'invisibility' and 'visibility' in this context. Think of it like this. Because it is in the nature of language that it must always stand for something else (that it has no existence in itself), it is really always, then, trying to be the mirror held exactly in front of and parallel to what it is reflecting. Every increase in the precision of language (in the precision of logic) brings it only more in front of, and parallel to, what it is reflecting. Additionally, and thanks primarily to Wittgenstein's painstaking body of work, we now know that language can only reflect in the world what the world can simultaneously reflect in language. This is the phenomenon referred to in professional, modern logic as the 'general form of the proposition'. In the professional world of pure mathematics, it is set theory's epsilon of membership. Thus, language does not stand apart from the world but is simultaneous with that world—We say that it creates the world it sees in its own image. Unfortunately, this is not the way that Western knowledge needs it to be. For Western knowledge to be Western knowledge, it needs it that the world be materially, empirically real. It needs it that the world be ontologically prior to any conceivable proposition of logic and language. Because if this is so, then the 'discourse of existence' and the 'God-valence of Western philosophy' remain intact, and logic and language resolve themselves into their mechanical verification against states of affairs in the world. But let's return to the perfect ambiguity of that image of the two mirrors facing each other and exactly parallel to each other (so that they are reflecting exactly back at each other). The perfect ambiguity of Wittgenstein's view of language, truth, and logic.

If language is a mirror that creates what it sees, if language is a mirror that creates another mirror to reflect back at it, then we are in a situation that has come to be known popularly as the 'Droste effect'. I have also at times been using the language of 'predestination' to describe it. In the *Leviathan*, the mirror of Hobbes's language on human freedom creates a mirror in its own image to reflect back the same. The little humans, the little points of light on the screen arrange themselves to be the perfect reflection of his words on the page. The Droste effect gives you pictures within pictures within pictures; all of them the same. To try to be free in words on a page is to achieve exactly the same thing. In using language to move the little points of light into an arrangement called freedom, you satisfy the general form of the proposition, but nothing else. Which is the same thing as to say that the supreme danger of a mirror image made of words is that the necessary connections between the words are at once taken to be the wisdom of the laws, *post hoc ergo propter hoc*.

> The skill of making, and maintaining Common-wealths, consisteth in certain Rules, as doth Arithmetique and Geometry; not (as Tennis-play) on Practice onely: which Rules, neither poor men have the leisure, nor men that have had the leisure, have hitherto had the curiosity, or the method to find out.[21]

Watch now how these words of Hobbes's move the little points of light into an arrangement that he calls freedom:

> For in the act of our *Submission*, consisteth both our *Obligation*, and our *Liberty*; which must therefore be inferred by arguments taken from thence; there being no Obligation on any man, which ariseth not from some Act of his own; for all men equally, are by Nature Free. And because such arguments, must either be drawn from the expresse words, *I Authorise all his Actions*, or from the Intention of him that submitteth himselfe to his Power, (which Intention is to be understood by the End for which he so submitteth;) The Obligation, and Liberty of the Subject, is to be derived, either from those Words, (or others equivalent;) or else from the End of

the Institution of Soveraignty; namely, the Peace of the Subjects within themselves, and their Defence against a common Enemy.[22]

Freedom within the Droste effect, or freedom within predestination, is the *description of a description* (think, 'picture within a picture'). In the geometrical-mechanical paradigm that the *Tractatus* and the *Leviathan* share, every action has a reaction and all men only act as they could be predicted to act. So really there is no freedom. There is just the point of view (birds-eye view, from above) according to which everything happens just as it should, given the things immediately either side of it in the timeline. Given this, and having argued its case so exhaustively, Hobbes manipulates the little points of light until they come out as a geometrical shape within these conditions.

> But as men, for the atteyning of peace, and conservation of themselves thereby, have made an Artificiall Man, which we call a Common-wealth; so also have they made Artificiall Chains, called *Civill Lawes* ...[23]

This geometrical shape he then calls 'freedom'. It satisfies the Droste effect. That is to say, there can be no saying which came first, the geometrical shape called 'freedom' or the words that describe it.

I interject the thought that this 'not knowing which came first' is the point at which modern philosophy always believes it has proved something to be true. And I do this to make us recall a well-known line of Wittgenstein's:

> It is clear that the causal nexus is not a nexus at all.[24]

Now consider what Wittgenstein does in the *Tractatus*. Like Hobbes he uses words to do philosophy. And like Hobbes he wants to 'do' a philosophy that establishes the geometrical-mechanical paradigm, predestination, and the Droste effect. Yet he is not prepared to then do anything normative, or prescriptive, with it. He is not prepared to allow philosophy to be used to say, or argue, anything. Instead, freedom—that means human freedom (because there is no other)—is left to be *You*, the reader, and how you are *outside* the book. Always outside the book. And how that *is* your freedom. And more: because in the *Tractatus* there is more. If all the books of philosophy in the world aspire to line their words up perfectly on actual things until they become the perfect reflections of the truth, then they don't need you, the reader. Or maybe they do need you, the reader. It amounts to the same thing. We say that they are perfect without you and in spite of you. The *Tractatus* claims to be the condensed truth of all the philosophy books in the world. It claims to be the condensed truth of the world. Thus, it performs this spectacularly. In being what it is, it frees you from *Truth*. It frees you from *This World*.

I repeat, the curiosity of language is that it claims no existence for itself, and that it does this by teaching it only ever stands in for things which are themselves *what actually exists*. It therefore claims an essential invisibility for itself. It seeks total and seamless identity with the discourse of existence and the God-valence of things. And yet it appears that on the close, Wittgensteinian analysis, it is not so innocent as this—That it may actually *create* what it stands in for. I am saying that if you want to incorporate the whole of Wittgenstein's philosophy into a single preoccupation, then this would be it: *to make what pretends to be invisible in language visible*. To show it is impossible to determine which came first, the word or the thing the word stands for. And, finally, to show how this means that as readers—that as the *reading animals* (alone of all the animals)—we are never actually included (in the way that Hobbes thought we could be included) in the private business of language. Language is always hypothetical. Language only ever shows you how things would look *if language were used*. Language only exists because there exists also the total alternative to language, to the *World of Language*, to the *World of Syntax and Sense*. I have described this 'total alternative' as like waking up from the dream.

So, we say, then, the single preoccupation of Wittgenstein's philosophy is to make you realize that language cannot actually see you, or hear you, or feel you. Like number, it contains within itself all the possibilities of all its conceivable combinations. And again, like number, these combinations exist as though they have *already-happened*. Like the concept of infinity; which can never in fact be verified by us; but which yet we believe in as though it could, or would, be so verified. Language and number we believe in, in this way. And believing in them in this way makes rules and laws and identities possible. Rules and laws and identities also make games possible. Hobbes's definition of individual freedom under a sovereign in the *Leviathan* is just such a game. The ingeniousness of his definition is made possible by the apparent contradictions which the rules of his game suggest. His solution and definition is a victory within those rules. Rules can be changed all the time because language, like number, 'contains' an infinity of possible games. However, because of this, the games themselves are meaningless from language's perspective. From language's perspective, the combination of words that went in to make up the *Leviathan* in its entirety was possible *yet accidental*, accidental *yet possible*. I repeat again, the *Leviathan* had *already happened*, as far as language was concerned. Just like this book I am writing now has *already happened* (because it follows rules of grammar). Like Hobbes in his book, I, in my book here, am simply reiterating 'how things would look *if language were used*'. Everything in me that is this book I could express in some other way than language. Perhaps in a single look of my eyes or a gesture of my hand. But this book is how it looks *if language is used*.

It is the same for you as the reader of my book; for the language of these pages is as insulated from you as it is from me. It goes about its own private business of following rules and making sense. What you take away from this book is exactly what you would have taken away from that single look in my eyes, or that gesture of my hand. But this is what it looks like to you *when language is used*.

You have heard me say a number of times already that the ways in which souls really communicate are supernatural, and eternal, and extension-less (and the setting in which that properly occurs); so that if instead you had to do all of that communication in language, then you would have a world such as we have it now, where the rules of speaking amount to the same thing as the laws of nature—And where what the philosophers call 'truth' means more and more the conjunction of the two.

Animals come when their names are called. Just like human beings.[25]

THE LEAST EXPLORED ARC

Here we arrive, then, at the least explored arc of Wittgenstein's thinking. And it happens to be the arc that really does join the earliest of his earlier thinking to the latest of his later. When we think of Wittgenstein, and rules, and language games, we usually think of two or more people sharing a one-time cipher about how a language event is to be encrypted then decrypted. When we think of rules and language, then, we usually think about what the human interlocutors are doing at the two ends of the language events. We don't usually do what I am doing here (and across this book), which is to make the self-sufficiency of language visible. We like to believe—and Wittgenstein's language games apparently prove—that we command language like a neutral tool. We choose the rules as we wish, and language simply obeys them for the duration of our gaming. That is how it may well appear on the face of it. But I am saying something quite different here. And I am saying that what I am saying is authentic Wittgenstein. This is that the choice of rules is never an arbitrary instance of pure creation. For all rules are already included within Language, and to such a degree of completeness all we can really say is that they have all *already happened*. Thus, even when we play language games amongst ourselves, we do no more than to do what language can do—what language has already done—for itself. The *Tractatus* and the *Philosophical Investigations* together explain to you the extent to which language excludes you in order to achieve its own objectives.

> For an actor may play lots of different roles, but at the end of it all, *he himself*, the human being, is the one who has to die.[26]

Unless, that is, you succumb to it. This is the moment at which the project of Wittgenstein's philosophy touches off against psychology and banishes it from human freedom altogether. I can think of no philosopher who understands better than Wittgenstein that psychology—like language—shows us only how things would look *if psychology were used*. Actually, and more sinisterly, it tells you how *you* would look *if psychology were used*. And the subjunctive mood is critically important here. Language and psychology hate the subjunctive mood because it exposes their pretensions and limitations by—yes—making what they would keep invisible visible. They prefer for the subjunctive mood to be our peculiar human weakness. The other animals don't do it because they live wholly within their instinct. But we humans like to reach ahead of the *now* and wonder and speculate. Language and psychology are happy to allow us to persist with this, but only so long as we continue to cede to them the ownership thereby of empirical *Realism*. The realism of the 'what actually is' or 'what actually took place'; as opposed to the 'what might be' or the 'what we might hope to be'. Because after all, the more they (and by 'they' we mean, of course, 'the truth') can be acknowledged to be the natural owners of empirical *Realism*, then the less will we be inclined to stray from it into the subjunctive mood. Like language, we say then that psychology 'excludes you in order to achieve its own objectives'.

Perhaps only Wittgenstein of all philosophers comes out directly to say that the subjunctive mood is actually where language and psychology and the truth live, so that what they call 'empirical realism' is really a continuing hypothesis that, like infinity itself, can never be proved to exist. Psychology shows you how it would look for you *if your actions were motived by internal factors*. It makes a perfect identity (a perfect ambiguity) of your internal factors and your external actions. It makes you into a machine which could conceivably run itself. The only relief from this horror-spiral is to know that you are reading or dreaming. Yes: Wittgenstein and his philosophy make this hard demand of you. He asks you to take language and psychology and truth to be the real, final *Fanaticism*; and then he asks you to consider whether your real freedom must not, then, lie outside of them? Like all fanaticisms, this one is beguiling. Because it is the 'final fanaticism', it is, in fact, the most beguiling of them all. Here, Wittgenstein's philosophy takes you to a place that I earlier called 'the strangest place', or 'Sex'.[27] The human sexual act has always held a unique place in the history of thought; in the history of humanity's understanding of itself. And this is because it is impossible to separate the mechanics of it, I should say the thermodynamics of it, from the beauty and pleasure of it. So, it turns out that this ultimate high, and ultimate climax, is also the moment at which we truly can forget that we are reading, or that we are dreaming, and that we can wake up. The human sexual act is the final expression of the private objectives of language, and psychology, and *the man become machine*. And the twist of this is written all over the modern treatments of the subject that we know so well. Science has reduced it to the banalities of heat and liquid (to the arch-nonfiction), only for it to be raised from that to the emblem of freedom, and beauty, and pleasure. It really is the ultimate strangeness, when you think about. And it exposes science's true motives, when you think about it. Or really, I should say that it exposes science to have motives, when all the time it is claiming to be neutral.

It turns out that the kind of reductionism which science produces—or what I have also portrayed here in terms of the Droste effect, or predestination—is really a groundless moralism. An ideological *fiat*. And that it is this because otherwise it is nothing at all. The full import of this needs a moment to digest, because digesting it takes one into the fluency of Wittgenstein's way of seeing things.

> It is so characteristic, that just when the mechanics of reproduction are so vastly improved, there are fewer and fewer people who know how the music should be played.[28]

To penetrate to what is really going on in terms of the mechanical processes of the universe is the same thing as to learn nothing at all. That is to say, it is to learn that all things can be represented as lights on a screen, or symbols on paper, or the psychological relationship between interiors and exteriors, or atoms in the void. It is the same thing as to learn that from this mechanical point of view, all things are simultaneously and physically connected, to the extent even that time can mean nothing at all because all things that are mechanically possible have therefore also already happened. Science has always escaped this conclusion by insisting on operating within the discourse of 'discovery'. Thus, things that have already happened are treated by scientists as though they had not, in fact, happened until they were discovered (to be happening). This is, of course, ridiculous; and so, it is therefore always simultaneously contradicted by the discourse of 'truth' which science also insists on operating within! Thus, the scientific definition of truth is something that was all along implied and predicted in the physical laws of nature.

Science is sly about this. I am using the term *already-happened* everywhere to make you increasingly aware of this slyness. I am doing it to make the invisible visible.

To say that the laws of nature hold everywhere and cannot be denied or contradicted, to say that the human sexual act comes down to nothing, in the end, is really to say nothing, in the end. Which fact is admitted in the very case that the scientific paradigm of truth makes out for itself. And yet nowhere and never is this conclusion allowed to stand for a second to be considered—Except, I am saying, in Wittgenstein's philosophy. Only there do you learn that all the varieties of what is called 'moralism' are all as useless and pointless as each other and that all work equally to keep in place the God-valence and the discourse of existence. To *say* what is really happening in any moment, to *say* the empirical truth of a situation, well, it is no more than to allow one cog to turn another. [And to disappear, yourself, into the infinite scheme of all possible cogs turning all other possible cogs.]

So it is that science has always striven to present itself as indistinguishable from the consequentialist ethic that its 'discoveries' make possible. The consequentialist ethic of the progress of mankind. Now someone may well respond to me that progress through the application of ever-more advanced technologies delivers us into future states of affairs that are empirically different to those that preceded them; and that this is a proof of progress, and the proof of man being able to materially affect his world, if ever there was one. And that the truth of what is really happening in any moment is therefore different from moment to moment, so that the series of these moments adds up to a narrative called 'progress'. But I am not talking about this. I am talking—and indeed Wittgenstein is talking—about something that he chose to pinpoint in the difference between *learning* and *knowing*. This difference amounts to acknowledging that what you *learn* by means of syntax and sign you can never in fact *know* with certainty. This is because you can only ever learn how to learn; whilst the relationship between syntax and sign (and the constellations of all possible and conceivably learnable things) and *knowing*—and *certainty*—is only ever hypothetical.[29]

When you learn how to learn (in the Western way), you only ever learn in this general form: *if this, then that*.[30] The 'constellations of all possible and conceivably learnable things' are traversable in this manner. This was the great discovery of the seventeenth century and thinkers like Hobbes. Yet, knowing and certainty, insofar as they must appear (in the Western way) as the precise alignment of syntax and sign on empirical fact, must always elude us. And this, of course, is because learning only shows you the world as it would be *if it were such as could be learnt (in the Western way)*. The actual relationship between that hypothetical world of learning and how things really are can only ever be one of luck and chance. That is to say, the laws of nature are not really laws at all but accidents of repetition. And a billion such accidents can never script what might happen next. This 'what will happen next' is of ultimate importance to the Wittgensteinian way of seeing things. It stands in flat defiance of the laws of nature and science, and everything that can be learnt. It stands for what I have called here the 'pure eternity of your mind'. For some strange reason, science conflates knowing with what can be learnt and calls that conflation the moral crusade called 'progress'. Yet to Wittgenstein, *knowing* can only ever refer to the unscripted and extempore magic of what might happen next. This 'what might happen next' is unscripted and extempore because it hangs on the freeborn decision of your will.

In the world *as it can be learnt*, everything is determined and positioned by the trigonometry of things before and after and all around it. Whereas the free-born decision of your will has nothing outside of it but is always and each time its own unique world. Sprung into life each time and then walked through; and extinguished by that walking through. The instinct that Wittgenstein calls *knowing*, and which has given us the idea of certainty and truth and the quest called 'philosophy', is for THIS rather than for the method represented by *learning*.

If there are no laws of nature, then there is also no common sense or colours or anything that persists through time; and that persisting through time can appear in the same way to everyone; and that persisting through time makes up into a world that also so persists (and that makes up into time itself). And that can be characterised by laws and processes and conceptual stability.

STRANGE ON THE SUBJECT OF SEX

Everyone knows that Wittgenstein was strange on the subject of sex, and strange with it, too, in the business of how he daily walked his life. He held it in high suspicion and fear. That is a well-documented fact. When he dabbled in it, it seems to have been at the homosexual end of the spectrum. This was once fiercely contested; but it, too, now, is a well-documented fact. Wittgenstein lived at a time when homosexuality was a criminal offence—And when it might have been customary to attribute eccentric personalities like his to it as to a vice. He recorded his homosexual activities in coded diaries only investigated after his death. It is therefore valid to speculate how he might have fared differently in the more liberated climate of today, and whether this allows us to reach back and say that his is a classic case of 'the man driven underground'. Are his life and thought explicable from the point of view of a man who was offered no free and legal channels for the expression of his sexuality? Is that the real story of Wittgenstein's life— The untold story of Wittgenstein's life? I do not think it is. I do not think it can be. I do not think it can be because it is overridden, in any case, by the one truly remarkable fact of Wittgenstein's sexuality which consistently receives scant attention by comparison. This was his proposal of marriage to a young Swiss woman he was deeply in love with, on condition that they should not have sexual relations. Marguerite Respinger. This carefully crafted request is far more remarkable, when you think about it, than homosexual acts between clever young men in Vienna or Cambridge in the early twentieth century. The latter do not stand in need of explanation because they have already entered our understanding of the cultures of those times and places. They are normal.

But the awkwardness of that petition, spelt out by the handsome young man to the pretty young woman, is searing and horrid. And I don't think it is just another of those funny things that Wittgenstein did.

I said that Wittgenstein had a great capacity for love, and that his life and his philosophy and his mysticism can be seen to be the expression of it. *Should be seen to be the expression of it.* Now I think I have brought together enough of the pieces for you to be able to see why.

I think it has always been clear to anyone, on even the most cursory foray into Wittgenstein's life and ideas, that his outlook is paranoid in relation something. I don't mean paranoid in the bad sense of that word, I mean paranoid in its very best sense. Paranoid in the sense of an unswerving, uncompromising vigilance. Paranoid in the sense of the cause of that vigilance being invisible to the rest of us. But not unreal. Just invisible! I have now told you a good deal here already about what that cause was, and what makes it normally invisible and unchallenged. Now I am going to tell you that Wittgenstein fused his life and philosophy into a single weapon to try to defeat it. And that his strange aversion to sex per se was probably that weapon's edge.

If we really are just souls, and if what we are calling life and realism right now is just a dream (or a book), and if as a dream the only danger we are really in is not waking up from it (or forgetting forever that we are just reading (the book of our life)). And if the definition of not waking up is that we fall into *believing* that we are pretending, so that like the narrator in *The Meek One* (like *The Truth*) we believe that we have alternatives whilst really, we do not, then sex is the one time when this bluff is truly called, and the mechanics of the script become indistinguishable from the (actions of the) script itself.

For Wittgenstein, pretending is indistinguishable from not-pretending because it makes use of exactly the same mechanics as the latter. Or marks, or symbols, or words. The difference that we customarily hold between pretending and not-pretending is therefore the *belief* that the one or the other is taking place at any one time. Remember it is included in the definition of pretending that it is for all intents and purposes identical to not-pretending. We say, in other words, that the sense of pretending comes after the fact of the pretended action, because that pretended action is identical to the not-pretended one. When we watch a stage play, we *believe* ahead of time that the actors are pretending, because otherwise they use the same words and gestures and actions as people who are not pretending. And we say that the best acting suspends our belief so that we take what we see for reality. Of course, in everyday life, we are in the habit of stretching the meaning of 'pretending' to include mimicry. Thus, we also say that someone is pretending to 'hammer in a nail' when they are holding an imaginary hammer in their hand and making the movement of hammering in an equally imaginary nail. The movement of the arm, though, is the same as the not-pretended movement, so, something of Wittgenstein's argument is retained.

If this is how Wittgenstein saw things, then his strange aversion to sex per se becomes not so strange after all. At least it becomes somewhat explicable. If the fact of being able to pretend—if the fact of being able to *believe* that you are pretending—proves that this (dream) world only allows us to say and do what it is mechanically possible to say and do (so that the only possible difference between pretending and not-pretending is your secret inner *belief* that you are doing one or the other, because there can be no outward visible difference between the two), then the human sexual act, then the human sexual climax, becomes the one location where the difference that *belief* would make becomes scrambled or irrelevant. Sex becomes, as it were, the ultimate point of gravity holding us to this world. It is the ultimate act of sense. It is the ultimate act of common sense. Western ethics has always treated it is the one act that does not have to reach outside of itself to qualify itself, and it has been right about that. But Wittgenstein is operating in another degree of rigour altogether. We may never be able to be certain that all of us see the colour red the same, but in sex, we are taken through the ultimate act of homologation and denomination. The sexual climax is the one location in this world where the soul's observation of itself (its knowledge that it is dreaming) gutters out. It is possible to make an argument that that guttering effect—that sensation of having *become* the physical reaction that can no longer be reversed—is the whole pleasure and thrill of the thing itself. Maybe, maybe not. It doesn't really concern me here. What concerns me is to show you how the strangeness of Wittgenstein's philosophy and the strangeness of his life are of a single piece. Homosexuality is an important part of Wittgenstein's story, but it is a subset of this story, the story of his strangeness about sex per se.

And this is why I am also telling you that Wittgenstein's life and philosophy and mysticism were the expression of his great capacity for *Love*. If sex is the ultimate tragedy, if it is the ultimate place at which individuality and wilfulness and the knowledge of '*only what You* might do next' are replaced by the thermodynamic arrow of time, then love is the opposite of all that. Love is everything to do with *only what you* might do next. It is the knowledge that is as free as your will. It is knowledge *as* intentionality. Perhaps you haven't ever really thought about it like this before. Well, think about it now! Love is always inexplicable. It is the Great Inexplicable. It is the great rebellion against the script and the historical record. Love is the only power that can initiate stories; that can initiate human stories. Only to mean that once those stories are underway, it must slowly be eroded by the coming of age represented by knowledge (of the script). For once you have conceived your love and it is alive and progressing, then it has become a recordable, empirical *thing of this world*. And if it is a recordable, empirical thing of this world, then it has become nonfiction rather than the fiction it started out as. Oh yes, true love is always fiction! Because true love is always something that is plucked out of the air. True love isn't eugenics, or a breeding programme, or the survival of the species. Yet the survival of the species and sex can stand to reason (are in fact the definition of what it means 'to stand to reason'), and true love cannot. That is its meaning.

> And how about such an expression as: 'In my heart I understood when you said that', pointing to one's heart? Does one, perhaps, not *mean* this gesture? Of course one means it. Or is one conscious of using a *mere* figure? Indeed not.—It is not a figure that we choose, not a simile, yet it is a figurative expression.[31]

Think about it. No story, no history, can be the explanation of love. Yet no story, no history, can unfold except after the fact of love. You will see what I mean if you remember that by love I mean 'intentionality'. If you were a Christian, then you could think of God as the Great Intentionality, the great Free Will, and his ultimate act of love, which was to create the universe *ex nihilo*. From the moment of that creation, time, and history, and the arrow of time can proceed—Right up until a species and a science are developed that can replace the fiction with nonfiction, and explain all religion and everything else on the basis of what is really and empirically going on. This, I think, is what Wittgenstein is ultimately concerned with. It is why I said at the start of this that everything he ever wrote was about him and God—And why his life and philosophy and mysticism were the expression of his great capacity for love. Plus, it is also why God and love do not require to be explicitly mentioned by him as starting points for this to be the case. Then on top of that, it is why I have pushed so hard here to separate Wittgenstein's philosophy from the God-valence and the discourse of existence. If you go looking for whether or not Wittgenstein believed in anything, you miss the point. His philosophy was the performance of his hunch that the irreducible point of human experience is something that may as well be considered fiction, because it sure as hell can't ever survive its translation into nonfiction—Into language, truth, and logic. There is always this fictional *You*. And then some fraction after, there is *Your Story*. Between these two, in some strange place, is where Wittgenstein believed that philosophy should shimmer and ache.

Philosophy is condemned to the endless repetition of the paradox of this place. Philosophy is condemned to use words in order to be in all the places between the words. Philosophy must stutter and can never explain itself. It can never have the confidence of an ethic or the omniscience of a theology. Nor, for that matter, can it have psychology's last word. But by God if it can be none of those things, then it can be one glorious thing: it can be man's last stand against the Machine.

I can know what someone else is thinking, not what I am thinking. It is correct to say 'I know what you are thinking,' and wrong to say 'I know what I am thinking.'—A whole cloud of philosophy condensed into a drop of grammar.

—WITTGENSTEIN, *Philosophical Investigations*, II, 11

'You can't hear God speak to someone else, you can hear him only if you are being addressed.'
—That is a grammatical remark.
—WITTGENSTEIN (tr. G. E. M. Anscombe), *Zettel*, §717

My father was a businessman and I am a businessman too; I want my philosophy to be businesslike, to get something done, to get something settled.
—M. O'C. DRURY, 'A Symposium II', in K. T. Fann (ed.), *Wittgenstein: The Man and his Philosophy* (Brighton: Harvester Press, 1978), p. 69

FESTUS: 'Did I not hear the boast with thy last breath / Not to have known what good was?'
LUCIFER: 'From myself / I know it not; yet God's will I must work. / I come to serve thee.'
—PHILIP JAMES BAILEY, *Festus*

2

Biography versus Genius

WE HAVE ACCUSTOMED ourselves to the 'natural conversation' of Wittgenstein's ideas, blurring the distinctions between his earlier and later work and finding the fluency of something more primal and underlying. Now it is time for our essay to start to realise the existential danger it is in. For we have been upsetting the conventions of biography in order to conjure a *new narrative*, which is constructed from all the parts that are normally hidden—As though one were to go behind the ballet, to the changing rooms and the gantries and the orchestra pit.

* * *

Nothing happens unless everyone works together to make it happen. And this 'working together' hides things; makes them, in the terminology of the previous chapter, 'invisible'. The ballet is an obvious example. We cherish the beauty of its finished product and applaud the work that went into it. But what about 'truth', what about 'philosophy'? What about 'thought', what about 'language'? Are they not also giant collaborative efforts? And does not the collaboration, the coordination, and the collusion thereby invalidate their traditional claims to purity of motive and result? Everyone knows that Wittgenstein's answer to this was, 'Yes!' Yet that 'Yes!' stops nothing, and the very thing he was crying against his whole life goes on. But not, I hope, here. In order to understand what this man was *really about*, who he *really was*, we must make a spectacle of this book. We must continue to go behind its scenes. We must expose its parts. We must see each other—Me writing it, you reading it. We must come out from behind the curtain and destroy truth's illusion. For only then will we see the final meaning of what this man Wittgenstein was going on about when he wrote things like this:

> The child learns to believe a host of things. I.e. it learns to act according to these beliefs. Bit by bit there forms a system of what is believed, and in that system some things stand unshakeably fast and some are more or less liable to shift. What stands fast does so, not because it is intrinsically obvious or convincing; it is rather held fast by what lies around it.[1]
>
> If the true is what is grounded, then the ground is not *true*, nor yet false.[2]
>
> Knowledge is in the end based on acknowledgement.[3]

He was meaning *You, Me,* and *This Book*. He was meaning the secret pact between all three of us. The secret pact *that there shall be knowledge and truth*, and that *this is what it shall look like and feel like*. We must all do something together, at exactly the same time, for it to work. No one must lag behind. It must be, 'All together now!' For he who lags behind, as Wittgenstein lagged behind, might see it all for what it really is. Might see the ballerina at the end of the night, without her makeup and a cigarette in her mouth, climbing on a bus to go home.

* * *

I was happy recently to see Ian Ground making the following observation in the *Times Literary Supplement*:

> If you ask philosophers—those in the English speaking analytic tradition anyway—who is the most important philosopher of the twentieth century, they will most likely name Ludwig Wittgenstein. But the chances are that if you ask them exactly why he was so important, they will be unable to tell you. Moreover, in their own philosophical practice it will be rare, certainly these days, that they mention him or his work. Indeed, they may very fluently introduce positions, against which Wittgenstein launched powerful arguments: the very arguments which, by general agreement, make him such an important philosopher. Contemporary philosophers

don't argue with Wittgenstein. Rather they bypass him. Wittgenstein has a deeply ambivalent status—he has authority, but not influence.[4]

Ground is right; it really is all rather strange when you think about it. I am saying that the answer will come when we take Wittgenstein deadly seriously on his word and commit intellectual suicide. He is asking us to kick out the stool from underneath ourselves, and until we do it, we will remain in the strangeness that Ground has described. On the one hand, we will know that Wittgenstein was a genius and *right*. On the other hand, we will not be able to do anything about it. Because, as I put it in the Introduction, books about the truth must be written *by us*, then read *by you*, as though they really were books about the truth. A biography, *as though it really were a biography*. That's how it works. 'All together now!'

* * *

But here, we are doing something about it. I am telling you, you have noticed it. We are already deep into the experiment of it. We are deep into seeing what happens when Wittgenstein's philosophy is allowed to have its way with a book about Wittgenstein.

YOU ARE GOING TO DIE

You are going to die. That unavoidable fact is the prototype and paradigm of all atomism and empiricism. Nothing can be more certain than you are going to join the worms in the ground. When you read, in the motto of our age, that 'seeing is believing', this is what you see, this is what you believe. This is the motto of the age that vanquished metaphysics, the supernatural, and God. The age of the worms in the ground rather than the saints in heaven. And yet just think a little more about this fact that you are going to die. This fact that you so smugly brandish. Where is it right now? I'll tell you what, I'll do to you what the pagans of old used to do to the Christians. They used to say to the Christians, 'Where is your God?' Now I will say to you, 'Where is your fact, where is your death?' 'Point to it now!' But of course you can't do that because in this moment you are alive; whereas your death belongs to some future moment, not yet existing. I repeat, your fact of all facts, your supreme retort to resurrection, is right now inhabiting that very place which you have spent a lifetime debunking. God and your death both inhabit this same place ahead of you in time, and you can't point to it because it doesn't exist until it does.

All truth is of this nature. It is nonconsensual. The truth is the truth because it exists in advance of you and doesn't depend upon you for its being. And generally speaking, the knowledge of this is offensive to human nature; 'offensive' because for some strange reason it is in the essence of human nature to wish to give consent to the truth. That is to say, we give consent to the fact of our death by living our life. We prove the existence of our death by arriving at it in time; we believe it by seeing it for ourselves. That is the most dramatic example of how we insist on making the truth subject to our consent in the present. But any smaller example will show the same thing. I ask you: 'What is 7,835 divided by 9 (to 6 decimal places)?' And in order to supply me with the answer, you will most probably reach for a digital calculator. But consider now that the digital calculator proves, by its programming, that the answer of 870.555556 had existed fully formed before I had even conceived of its question, and that the only way for you to give your consent to its fact was to go through the rigmarole of calculating it. A digital world has compressed our sense of this. If I insisted that you calculate it mentally, or even longhand on a sheet of paper, you would have been fully initiated into the weirdness of all of this.

> We may only put a question in mathematics (or make a conjecture), where the answer runs: 'I must work it out.'[5]

Without human lives, then, the truth really would be the tree that fell in the forest with no one to hear it. What philosophy calls 'the truth' is really this truth—This single truth of the tree falling in the forest with no one to hear it. And what we call 'time', or temporal succession, is really a consequence of our insisting upon making truth consensual—That is, subject to our consent in time. I am afraid that I don't want to spare you any of the terror of this; it would be irresponsible of me to do that.[6]

So, I repeat, things that, like your death, are going to happen have therefore already happened; and this already-happened quality of theirs is what philosophers and scientists and all lovers of wisdom have always meant by the truth. A world of things—all of which have already happened—would be the definition of eternity or of the mind of God. The very first philosophers, the so-called Presocratics, worshipped the already-happened by insisting that all explanations of all things should be made with reference to an unchanging substratum, or an *Urstoff*. This unchanging material was the constituting element in everything, and the constant which allowed all the variables to be made to give up their answers. This radical materialism was the best that they could do. But it was a fair and honest attempt to mark a working distinction between surface appearance and deep reality; or between the conventional and the foundational, temporality and eternity. Today, this is still the state of things in philosophy. Its leading protagonists still measure their success according to how far they have been able to penetrate to what is really going on. This methodology requires them always to designate an idol of popular culture before divesting it of its powers and reducing it to numbers. The idol of all idols, for this purpose, is the Christian God; which is the same thing as to say that there is an ineluctable relationship between the reductionist point of view and the idea of the ethical pursuit of progress.

The universe of the philosophy of today is for all these reasons a very strange and confusing place. I have already used the term 'terrifying'. It is all these things because it purports to 'see through' superstition and supernaturalism to 'what is really going on', and yet the paradigm of truth which allows it to undertake this task is the very essence of superstition and supernaturalism. For, if we agree that it is the mathematical paradigm, it is nonconsensual and has existed before all time, or, what comes to the same thing, in advance of all time. Seen like this, the description of this paradigm of truth is really the description of a supreme being who doesn't give a damn about us. Here we encounter the strangeness and the confusion. Because the philosophy of today is meant to kill God to replace him with something infinitely better; yet on the basis of what we are seeing here, it seems only to replicate him. To this end Ludwig Wittgenstein was once quoted by his friend Drury as saying:

> Isn't it remarkable that, in spite of their professed materialism, the Russians have gone to such trouble to preserve Lenin's body in perpetuity; and to visit his tomb. You know I don't think much of modern architecture, but that tomb in the Kremlin is well designed.[7]

Moreover, there is the clash between this nonconsensual *God of Truth* and our consenting selves; or as I put it, we who *insist* on being able to 'consent' the truth into existence. But it is not so much a clash as a paradox, or even hypocrisy itself. On the one hand, our preferred sense of self-esteem demands that we, each of us, author the truth from scratch. Yet on the other hand, we insist with equal force that the prize and vindication of our authorship will be the fact that the truth it created had all along existed. In other words, authorship, to us, has come to mean the same thing as 'freedom'; while freedom has come to mean the freedom to walk from the dark into the light; into the truth. Yet, this same truth appears to be what it is insofar as it can exhibit the exact characteristics of preordination or predestination. That is to say, no pluralism or diversity of authors can be made to generate even a single criterion to choose between them—A single criterion of truth. Freedom can only proliferate. Books and ideas and lives can only proliferate; and as Voltaire so famously proclaimed, each new life can only logically prove the sovereign right of every life to determine itself. And yet if the stated object of all these books and ideas and lives is truth, and if proliferation cannot supply the means of adjudication but only its need, then what philosophy means by the truth is not really a Presbyterian creed at all but something more like Roman Catholicism and the Bible. Once, in his only explicit lecture on the subject of ethics, Wittgenstein said as much:

> It seems to me obvious that nothing we could ever think or say should be the thing. That we cannot write a scientific book, the subject matter of which could be intrinsically sublime and above all other subject matters. I can only describe my feeling by the metaphor, that, if a man could write a book on Ethics which really was a book on Ethics, this book would, with an explosion, destroy all the other books in the world. Our words used as we use them in science, are vessels capable only of containing and conveying meaning and sense, natural meaning and sense. Ethics, if it is anything, is supernatural and our words will only express facts; as a teacup will only hold a teacup full of water and if I were to pour out a gallon over it.[8]

If this is *the* feature of the universe of philosophy, then Wittgenstein succeeded in living his life in note perfect ambiguity over it. I often feel that this was a leading aspect of his genius. Jewish but baptized into the Catholic faith as a child, fervently mystical but speaking ideas that seemed to contradict the religious impulse, Wittgenstein's death from cancer on the 29 April 1951 revealed that even his closest friends had been left somehow unenlightened by their time with him. That is, wholly unenlightened on this point; this point which, when you come to think about it, is the whole point.

> I had only been back in Dublin a few days when I had a telephone message from Dr. Bevan to say that Wittgenstein was dying and had asked me to come. I started at once. When I arrived at the house, Dr. Bevan met me at the door, and told me, 'Miss Anscombe, Richards and Smythies are already here. Smythies has brought with him a Dominican priest whom Wittgenstein already knew. Wittgenstein was already unconscious when they came, and no one will decide whether the priest should say the usual office for the dying and give unconditional absolution.' I remembered the occasion when Wittgenstein had said he hoped his Catholic friends prayed for him, and I said at once that whatever was customary should be done. We then all went up to Wittgenstein's room, and, kneeling down, the priest recited the proper prayers. Soon after, Dr. Bevan pronounced Wittgenstein dead. There was then much hesitation about what arrangements should be made about the funeral. No one seemed ready to speak up. [Then said I:] 'I remember that Wittgenstein once told me of an incident in Tolstoy's life. When Tolstoy's brother died, Tolstoy, who was then a stern critic of the Russian Orthodox Church, sent for the priest and had his brother interred according to the Orthodox rite. "Now", said Wittgenstein, "that is exactly what I should have done in a similar case."' When I mentioned this, everyone agreed that all the usual Roman Catholic prayers should be said by a priest at the grave side. This was done the next morning. But I have been troubled ever since as to whether what we did then was right.[9]

I WILL MEET YOU AT THE MOMENT OF YOUR DEATH

If I say to you: 'I will meet you on the 9am bus.' And if you decide, on a whim, not to meet me on that bus, then your action becomes the sole proof of every dogma of modern philosophy that preaches that we exist as free agents in an empirical world, un-impelled by occult forces. Your action proves that even if I were God, I could not have predicted your sudden change of mind. I expect to meet you on the bus and have every reason to think that you will be there; but lo, you are not!

> If God had looked into our minds he would not have been able to see there whom we were speaking of.[10]

If on the other hand I say to you: 'I will meet you at the moment of your death,' you have no way of avoiding this summons, and, in fact, your compliance becomes a certain truth of the order of the certain truth that 2 + 2 = 4. You may respond here and tell me that this evidence is inadmissible, because *I* can have no way of knowing in advance the exact moment of your death. You may also point out that your death will one day occur at its moment in time need not imply the existence of an all-knowing God to predict it (if not me). For after all, death is simply the incontrovertible proof of the second law of thermodynamics; which means that it is unfair of me to use it like this as the cardinal predestinated fact; as the cardinal predestinated fact which proves into life the occult, and thereby challenges the notion of our freedom. It is as irreversible and unchosen as birth (from the perspective of the born, no one asks them); whereas philosophy prefers to pick its examples from within these two bookends of life. Because within these two bookends, freedom can claim to be as instantly proven as choosing, on a sudden, to clench your fist.

However, I am afraid that all of this does matter very much because whereas this freedom we experience within the bookends of birth and death is real and true and manifestly so, the conscious and intelligent mode of life by which we have to apprehend and quantify that freedom does not actually belong to the universe of happenstance and haphazard, atoms and void, but to the universe of the supernatural. Or as I have been describing it here, the universe of the already-happened. Moreover, the history of philosophy has in every sense been the history of this distinction. Initially, philosophy rescued the individual from custom, society, and taboo. It drove thinking men and women towards something that was theirs and theirs alone: something that could distinguish each from the other. This thing was the subjective, particular, phenomenological moment. It became clear that before it was anything else, plain human experience was always unique to itself and anarchic; and it became equally clear that civilization and all group behaviour was in menacing programme against this. Such would come, in the end, to be the victory won by the Enlightenment over the Dark Ages. And more than anything else, it was the victory of a social revolution. I mean how the Cartesian turn was a victory for self-sufficiency, and I mean how this self-sufficiency became the antagonist of all revealed and dogmatic knowledge and power; or the knowledge and power of the Church. This self-sufficiency was to account for the variety of modern thought. It encouraged sceptics like David Hume who said that human flourishing was not contingent upon (belief in) final knowledge as much as it encouraged mavericks like George Berkeley who said that it was. Meanwhile the Industrial Revolution was taking place; and as technology became ever more automatic and exemplary, the mantle of self-sufficiency began to pass silently from man to the machine. And whereas the anthropological self-sufficiency of man had been the self-sufficiency of the temple of reason within him—an injunction to call upon his own soul for the heavenly ideas—the self-sufficiency of the machine did away with temples and heavenly ideas altogether. Man was now the maker, and the materials of the natural world were duty bound to obey him. And God could be excluded because he was surplus to requirements. Excluded, too, it seemed, could be traditional philosophy's literary and essayistic tone. For if truth and truth's method were no longer being found in the grand human projects for justice and goodness, but in clocks and steam engines and aeroplanes, then philosophy had better become a branch of mathematics and physics (or plain good sense) or risk losing face and place altogether.

This is where philosophy had ended up by Wittgenstein's day. Its career since its birth in the sixth century BC had been like the career of a single individual, breaking free of the fug of ancient myth and religion; then breaking free again from the deeper fug of European Christian civilization. But here comes the age-old problem of philosophy which I alluded to above. If freedom is as instant and manifest as clenching your fist, and if philosophy is a revolutionary, then it must bring us, inevitably, to the problem of communication and language. And this problem of communication and language (as I think I have now made clear) is the problem that you can only say true things that belong to the supernatural universe of the already-happened. What I mean is, you are free to say nonsensical things, yes, but if you want to speak with sense, with meaning and with truth, then you must only speak in the language of the already-happened. At the very least this sounds unfair and oppressive. To face that the great freedom fighter—Philosophy—should be made to speak only in the language of clocks and steam engines and aeroplanes sounds soul destroying. Again: I want to emphasize that it had become especially possible to notice this in Wittgenstein's day. For the flush of an industrial age was the flush of realizing that clocks and steam engines and aeroplanes had become the new expression of the grammar (or the laws) of the universe. *And man had made them.* Before, that grammar of the universe had been the mind of God. By speaking the truth, philosophy had spoken the mind of God. Its words had only conveyed meaning as long as they assembled correctly on eternal truths, and those truths' structures (think of Thomas Aquinas's 'divine law'), and everything else had just been opinion. But then the spirit of freedom in man—the philosopher in him—discerned that this was unfair and oppressive and soul destroying, and concluded quite naturally enough that by killing God and becoming the 'maker' of the grammar he would solve everything. And we would still be believing this today if it hadn't been for Wittgenstein, and how he was able to point out one last and impossible frontier and obstacle—The frontier and obstacle of the grammar itself:

> It used to be said that God could create anything except what would be contrary to the laws of logic.—The truth is that we could not *say* what an 'illogical' world would look like.[11]

There is, then, what I called above the 'subjective, particular, phenomenological moment'. And then there is how these moments of our experience—each and every one of them—stand together for the defiant specialness of our souls. But then there is how this butts up against the problem of communication and language; or the question of the scope of what we can actually *say*.

It would early on occur to Wittgenstein that words, like all currencies, can only function on the basis of standardized values and meanings; and that this makes words no different, in the end, to the world of facts and feelings which they purport to describe to us. Words do not achieve their purpose and form up into a language until they succeed in exchanging stable concepts among a group of users. The limiting factor in this arrangement is clearly the necessity of such stable concepts in the first place. Wittgenstein thought that these stable concepts should remind us of other such stable concepts as the a priori truths of mathematics and the laws of science. To this I have added the interpretative framework of the whole other world which these stable concepts imply. The world of the *already-happened*.[12] And I have drawn attention to that world by contrasting it unfavourably with the world in which we actually live out our lives. The world of the *happening*. And everything gets thicker still because here I am writing a biography about Wittgenstein, when biographies must clearly belong in the world of the already-happened, but the actual lives of their subjects in the world of the happening. The conventional wisdom says that you must go looking for the truth of the world of the happening in the world of the already-happened. For example, if you are a scientist and you want to say something (respectable), you must conduct an experiment under such conditions as allow you afterwards to induce a law. This law is what you can actually *say*, and anything else would not be understood. Again: think of the very letters of the alphabet (any alphabet) from which the diversity of creative expression is made. All *A*s everywhere have to mean the same; as do all *B*s and *C*s and *D*s. An *A* can't mean the same thing as a *D*. It just doesn't work like that. Likewise, when you start joining letters together to make words, those words, too, have to stand for stable concepts. All of this is taken for granted because it is the condition of sense and understanding. By the same token, if *A* can't mean the same thing as *D*, then sense and understanding have to be accomplished linearly and temporally and progressively. We have to start with an ordered alphabet; then make words from it; then read those words in such a way that we move from one to the next. To say something is to say something about something.

All of this has been known to Western philosophy since its inception. It has been the stout common sense that it has fallen back on in times of crisis. The idea of *what* philosophy should talk about, well, yes, *that* has changed with the fashions of the times. But the commitment to sense over *non*-sense has been there from its start. It is obvious, really. What has not been so obvious is that the world of sense, the world of the already-happened, is far more real than this world of the happening. That it really does exist. And that in beguiling us to consent to the truth, it is using us up like smoked cigarettes.

The philosopher talks about the world of the already-happened in awed tones and worships it as truth. The religionist calls it God and does the same. The scientist worships his laws. The moralist worships his goodness. And we write biographies of each other.

At the very least, we have gotten things the wrong way around. For *We* should be the 'concrete cases' who break the rule, rather than let the rule break us.

The idea that in order to get clear about the meaning of a general term one had to find the common element in all its applications has shackled philosophical investigation; for it has not only led to no result, but also made the philosopher dismiss as irrelevant the concrete cases, which alone could have helped him understand the usage of the general term.[13]

YOU MUST FIRST MURDER THEM

Consider this. If you want to write a biography of someone living, you must first murder them. You must first murder them because to have them live on beyond your biography could destroy its truth. You have marked the final full stop and snapped the covers shut, and then—just think of it!—your subject goes on and does something totally out of the character that you had so meticulously described. They do something that permanently alters that character and that bursts apart your understanding and explanation of it. Because that is what the freedom of the clenched fist can do. It can do anything it likes. So always make sure that you murder your subject first. Then having murdered them, you can make a beginning at that, their murdered end.[14] They lived their life forwards, in aspiration and hopefully. And that was ALL that their life could have meant to them. But you will do no such thing if you want to write a respectable and respected biography of them. You will begin at the quantum of their predestination—You will meet them there at that strange mad place where worms and God and truth mean all the same. And standing in that place where death was waiting for them all along, you will start to finger your way backwards through their files, going confidently from one fact to the next; because all facts are the fact of death.

This, by the way, is the same instinct that causes us to start at the back of a new book when we pick it off a shelf. We are unable to begin with it in the place where its author began. Precisely because they began it, and wrote it, in the place that a living person lives. In this sense, all writing is the art of autobiography and all reading is the science of biography. Also, the science of biography is what we are taught to laud as 'intelligence', while the art of autobiography is therefore 'counterintelligence'. Even if you scratch out in chalk on a blackboard the proof of a geometrical theorem, if the chalk is in your hand, it is autobiography. *Your* autobiography. *I* am writing this book about Wittgenstein.

Consider now this. Life writing must therefore be a peculiar reflection on the Western mind. Other cultures write hagiographies of the people they love and respect, and wish to immortalize. Only the West regards this with suspicion. Only the West looks for a more objective and impartial way. An apartheid between biographer and subject, white and black.

Take a look again at the first two quotations at the head of this chapter. I have always taken them to show this: Wittgenstein must have thought that you can only make the attempt at understanding your own life by lashing out and transferring it to someone else's life. In other words, the most that you can hand-on-heart say about your own life would amount to irrationality and nonsense. So, in reaction to this, you take cause and effect and press it like a signet ring into the warm wax of someone else's life. There is left, in the middle, an impression where you pressed. But the point is that you knew what it was going to look like anyway if you took cause and effect seriously (a lighthouse in the distance is a lighthouse after all). But more serious is what happens around the edges, where there is the squishing out and the mess. I think that Wittgenstein hated this violence which we are all the time perpetrating on each other in the name of understanding.

The Western way of writing the biography of a genius is to say that there is the life (1) and then the life's work (2). You write the book by sending the two off together in a two-stage rocket. The first stage is the life and its propellants of circumstance, parenting, education, friends, and so on. Eventually, having burned hard, it fizzles out at some age that is reached by saying 'Maturity!' At this point (which is traditionally the biographer's worst nightmare to locate), the second-stage motor ignites and propels us through the years concerned with 'the life's work'. Finally, of course, comes death and the last chapter. This is written as the biographer watches the various pieces of the burnt-up rocket falling to earth. Where they land, and in whose gardens they land, and whether that makes those people happy or angry are what he must negotiate as his final task.

If this is the form of Western biography, then it is in fact its own kind of philosophy saying that every life is *this* kind of rocket. And remember that the greatest endeavour of Western science has still been to put a man on the moon.

By the same token, to truly *do* philosophy, to truly *make* the truth, would be to *do* autobiography—Or as I called it above, counterintelligence. It would be to live one's life as one speaks; not as one reads or understands. Altogether it would be to perform the truth of all truths; which is that we never spoke to be understood at all. It would be, then, like the performance of music, where something real passes to the listener, but it is not understood.

The Western way of writing a biography about a genius imposes an unnatural realism on him. It says: 'He did this, which led to this, which resulted in that.' Because it has also murdered him first, all these chained together facts must belong to what I am calling the world of the already-happened. And if he really was a genius, then this world must have been his nemesis. It would have been the Devil he was trying to defy. [I don't know what to say at this point because I so admire and enjoy the great biographies that are written in this way. I suppose I must just throw up my hands and say, 'This is where I find myself at this point in my essay and my book.' The rest and how it looks is just too bad.]

I am struck by how the world goes looking for its geniuses; and in just the same way that it goes looking for its heroes. The world says: 'Genius is burdensome and torturous to its possessor.' But I think the opposite is almost certainly the case. I think that the genius has the gift of living normally and unremarkably, and that it is *this* world and us in it who are the abnormal and the eccentric. I think it is abnormal and eccentric that we are not all out of our minds at the thought that we are predestined to die. How do we manage to think of anything else? I think it is madness itself that we actually turn that fact on those who believe in God and the supernatural, and say: 'You see, there's nothing at all after death; no heaven and hell—Ha!'

I am struck by how the geniuses never asked to be found, and I am struck by how that word 'genius' is being used today with a spiralling kind of frequency of so many people and situations. Evidently, we feel more than ever that it is in our power to give. I think it is a form of control—Especially of controlling the marginal and conspicuously sane among us.

The thing that we desire more than anything else, it seems, is constancy. It is what we desire and look for in our friends, and therefore by finding it in the physical laws of nature we have imagined to make the universe our friend, too. The happy life of the philosophers has always been configured as a restful, constant sort of place—Unlikely to spring a surprise on us. The happy life of the philosophers has always been the dream of a perfectly controlled and controllable environment. And yet, when we scream at God, we curse him for just this. We curse him for being Almighty and having foreknowledge, and therefore for being the happy cause of pain and suffering. We curse him for being the *Grand Controller*. And cursing him thus, we demand our total freedom from his scheme. We demand the right to change our minds 1,000 times a day. We demand the right to be congenitally inconstant. Which means to imagine that we have defeated God is to imagine that we have turned this table on him. In this sense, God exists whether we like it or not. To be free at last would be to erase his memory from the Western mind, or his name from Western letters. It is as though we are only able to express the desire of our freedom against what he represents; so that even if he hadn't existed, we would have had to create him. The tragedy in this is the absence of originality—The absence of *our* originality. We are taught to hate God because he is the one who is changing his mind 1,000 times a day, and each of those changes is a string that pulls us. So, we long instead to be pulling our own strings and changing *our* minds 1,000 times a day. The overall picture here is one in which we are hopelessly implicated—One in which our freedom of expression is really only the freedom to express this logic. As goes the quote from Wittgenstein I mentioned a little earlier: 'The truth is that we could not *say* what an "illogical" world would look like.' Whoever Wittgenstein really was, this, certainly, was what he saw. He saw that the freedom to express a logic is really no freedom at all. True freedom would be the freedom to express an *illogic*:

> Language can only say those things that we can also imagine otherwise.[15]

The banners of freedom are clenched fists and saying whatever you like. But rushing back against them in perfect sync from the world of the already-happened are the facts and stable concepts upon which understanding depends. This is how the circle—or the wheel—is completed. And this is how it imprisons you. Speaking to be understood; that is the prison. When you are a child they pluck you from illogic and nonsense and teach you how to say things that other people can understand. And what a terrible shame that is, then, because nonsense and illogic are an infinity of possibilities, whilst sense and logic are a tragic little bundle.

THE CONSOLATION OF PHILOSOPHY

Boethius's *The Consolation of Philosophy* is the most Western of all Western books because it preaches you can only love the already-happened and you should therefore make God in its image. The nemesis of the already-happened is Fortune, 'the random Goddess':

> If I have fully diagnosed the cause and nature of your condition, you are wasting away in pining and longing for your former good fortune. It is the loss of this which, as your imagination works upon you, has so corrupted your mind. I know the many disguises of that monster, Fortune, and the extent to which she seduces with friendship the very people she is striving to cheat, until she overwhelms them with unbearable grief at the suddenness of her desertion.... What is it then O mortal man, that has thrown you down into the slough of grief and despondency? You must have seen something strange and unexpected. But you are wrong if you think Fortune has changed towards you. Change is her normal behaviour, her true nature. In the very act of changing she has preserved her own particular kind of constancy towards you. She was exactly the same when she was flattering you and luring you on with enticements of a false kind of happiness. You have discovered the changing faces of the random Goddess.[16]

This vilified random Goddess is what pure unadulterated genius looks like. It is what wheels around the corner and no one saw it coming. Wittgenstein knew this. And more to the point, he seems to have known this of himself in some way—'It used to be said that God could create anything except what would be contrary to the laws of logic.' If the random Goddess is genius itself, then the Almighty God is the incomparable manifestation of it. All of this adds up to a point of view from which it becomes possible to see that all law and civilization are institutionalized insanity and the Tower of Babel, and that this world of good sense that we have built for ourselves is really how we sit God down on our knee and teach him how to speak. First letters, then words, then sentences, then doctrine. Not because he has ever been silent to us, but because nothing he says has ever made sense. It is incredible, when you think about it, that institutional Christianity positively discounts and disqualifies the idea that God should speak into the moment or be directly consulted on an issue. No, *institutional* Christianity instead assumes God's incapability or unreliability (what if he says 'No!') and puts things to the members' vote. There is nothing that institutional Christianity hates more today than a prophet with revelation; and there is nothing that shames institutional Christianity more today than supernaturalism. Institutional Christianity hates a genius. It has always seemed to me that an element in Martin Luther was on to all of this:

> The wicked and pernicious opinion of the Papists is utterly to be condemned, that attributes the merit of grace and the remission of sins to the work done. For they say that a good work before grace, is able to obtain grace of congruence [which they call *meritum de congruo* because it is meet that God should reward such a work]. But when once this grace has been obtained, the work goes on to deserve everlasting life of due debt and worthiness [which they call *meritum de condigno*]. As for example: if a man being in deadly sin, without grace, does a good work of his own good natural inclination—that is, if he says or hears a mass, or gives alms and such like—this man of congruence then deserves grace. And then when once he has thus obtained grace, he can now be said to be performing a work which of worthiness deserves eternal life. For the first part, God is no debtor; it is rather assumed that because He is just and good, it behoves Him to approve such a good work, even though it is done in deadly sin, and to give grace for such a service. But as for the second part, the part that begins once this grace has been obtained, God *does* then become a debtor; because clearly He is now constrained of right and duty to give eternal life [and has no freedom of choice in the matter]. For now it is not only a work of free will, performed according to the substance, but also performed in grace which makes a man acceptable to God, that is to say, in charity.[17]

The theory of coming of age, of adulthood, and sense which is supported in the Western philosophy of today, is truly enough a theory of language. It says that when you are young and unformed, you project language (not your language, but *language itself*) onto things like your invisible friend and your teddy bear. And this makes you no better than a priest. As you grow up and become properly educated, you start to become better and better at lining it and its parts up with precision on the proper things. Within this whole theory, language is, of course, interchangeable with thought. You may speak your language aloud or speak it silently as thought. The triumph of this whole theory over metaphysics and religion has therefore been the triumph of good marksmanship over bad, accuracy over inaccuracy. It is the pride of our age. It is how we have moved on from the sectarianism of religious war. It is so decent and gracious of us. We don't disbar adults from having invisible friends and teddy bears, or becoming priests. We simply change them into the empirical fact of someone who believes and acts as they do. That is to say, we no longer fight with them over whether invisible things exist. Instead we say that they have the right to select the motivation of their thoughts and actions—And if it be a religious motivation, so be it. We pop them in the jar with all other religiously motivated actors. And they become that fact; they become the fact of that class. They become the label on the jar. And by turn, they may be happy with that situation. They may find it intellectually respectable to be able to claim no more than that their religious motivation is a choice, made from among an endless variety of such choices; and that it doesn't commit them to intellectually embarrassing things like miracles and resurrection from the dead, but is more like a cultural inheritance or a continuing fascination.

Take the following quotations from Wittgenstein's *Zettel*; the book is a posthumous collection of fragments from his mature philosophy, edited by G. E. M. Anscombe and Georg Henrik von Wright, and first published in 1967. They might be typical of everything that I have just said above, or they might not. If they are, then they are explorations—highly original explorations—of the frontiers of language use, where marksmanship and accuracy mean waiting for the head to appear in your sights. This frontier situation is a consequence of our language needing to depend for its meaning upon some substantive ontology or other. In instances where that ontology is delayed by expectation and anticipation, the burden of fact can appear to slip backwards into the grammar of intentionality itself; as though what was going to happen were already conceded in its grammar—['Nor is reality like the daylight that things need to acquire colour, when they are already there, as it were colourless, in the dark.'[18]] In this case, then, the reference below to another philosopher would almost certainly have to be to the Austrian Alexius Meinong. He of 'Meinong's Jungle' fame.[19]

> Like everything metaphysical the harmony between thought and reality is to be found in the grammar of the language.[20]
>
> It is difficult for us to shake off this comparison: a man makes his appearance—an event makes its appearance. As if an event stood even now before the door of reality and were then to make its appearance in reality—like coming into a room.[21]
>
> Reality is not a property still missing in what is expected and which accedes to it when one's expectation comes about.—Nor is reality like the daylight that things need to acquire colour, when they are already there, as it were colourless, in the dark.[22]
>
> One may say of the bearer of a name that he does not exist; and of course that is not an activity, although one may compare it with one and say: he must be there all the same, if he does not exist. (And this has certainly already been written some time by a philosopher.)[23]
>
> The shadowy anticipation of a fact consists in this: something is only *going* to happen, but we can think that *it* is going to happen. Or; as it misleadingly goes: we can now think *what* (or of what) is only *going* to happen.[24]
>
> Being able to do something seems like a shadow of the actual doing, just as the sense of a sentence seems like the shadow of a fact, or the understanding of an order the shadow of its execution. In the order the fact as it were 'casts its shadow before'. But this shadow, whatever it may be, is not the event.[25]

But what if Wittgenstein's 'other philosopher' was not Meinong but, say, Augustine of Hippo? I am not being completely outrageous in suggesting that (and a suggestion is all it is). Augustine is, after all, already known to be the muse and conversation starter for the great work of Wittgenstein's philosophy maturity, his *Philosophical Investigations*, first published in 1953, two years after his death. It is generally accepted that Wittgenstein only ever read one work of Augustine's through; that being the *Confessions*. However, if he read at least that work, then why not more (do I know all the books that you have read?)? I am going to quote something from Augustine's *On the Trinity* in what follows. But I will in any case back it up in a note with a quotation saying exactly the same thing from the *Confessions*.

What if—following Augustine—the quotations from the *Zettel* above could be set within the context of everything that I have been saying thus far about the difference between human freedom, between the world of the happening and how it reaches forwards, and the world of the already happened (and how it reaches backwards from the future to obliterate us)? The latter's treachery being to convince us that we can only say what is true, only speak what is understood—And that truth is the same thing as the most holy law of the universe.

In *On the Trinity*, Book IX, 6, 9-10, Augustine says the following:

But when the human mind knows itself and loves itself, it does not know and love anything unchangeable: so that we say that each individual man declares his own particular mind by one manner of speech, when he considers what takes place in himself; but that when he goes on to define the human mind abstractly, he does so by special or general knowledge. And so, when he speaks to me of his own individual mind, as to whether he understands this or that, or does not understand it, or whether he wishes or does not wish this or that, I can only do as much as believe him. However: when he speaks the truth of the mind of timeless man generally or specially, I am able to go beyond mere belief and actually recognize and approve. From which it appears manifest that each sees a thing in himself, in such way that another person may believe what he says of it, yet may not see it; but another [sees a thing] in the truth itself, in such way that another person also can gaze upon it; because whereas the former undergoes changes at successive times, the latter consists in an unchangeable eternity. For we do not gather a generic or specific knowledge of the human mind by means of resemblance by seeing many minds with the eyes of the body: but we gaze upon indestructible truth, from which to define perfectly, as far as we can, not of what sort is the mind of any one particular man, but of what sort it ought to be upon the eternal plan. Whence also, even in the case of the images of things corporeal which are drawn in through the bodily sense, and in some way infused into the memory, from which also those things which have not been seen are thought under a fancied image, whether otherwise than they really are, or even perchance as they are—even here too, we are proved either to accept or reject, within ourselves, by other rules which remain altogether unchangeable above our mind, when we approve or reject anything rightly. For both when I recall the walls of Carthage which I have seen, and imagine to myself the walls of Alexandria which

I have not seen, and, in preferring this to that among forms which in both cases are imaginary, make that preference upon grounds of reason; the judgment of truth from above is still strong and clear, and rests firmly upon the utterly indestructible rules of its own right. And if it is covered as it were by a cloudiness of corporeal images, yet is not wrapped up and confounded in them.[26]

The meaning of this passage is that there is no such thing as self-knowledge. 'But when the human mind knows itself and loves itself, it does not know and love anything unchangeable ... ' This is Augustine saying that what goes on inside your head and heart is so subjective and arbitrary that it is positively incommunicable according to all the known canons of reason, sense, and logic. Augustine says that when I stream out to you in words my conscious thinking, the most that you can do is nod your head and smile and if you choose, believe the truth of what I am saying on good faith; because of course you cannot *see* my stream of consciousness, though I am perfectly entitled to *say* it. What changes this situation is if I begin to say to you, words that stand for things that you can see clearly and directly with your mind's eye. Things that exist in eternal and generic abstraction in the world of the already-happened. For example, if I were to stream out to you my random and concocted erotic fantasies and you were to psychoanalyze them and by that means reduce them to universally accepted examples of this and that phenomena, the phenomena would be the truth and the knowledge, and my initial streaming would not be that but something else. I repeat, then, that there is no such thing as self-knowledge. There is such a thing as the self, and there is such a thing as the self's consciousness of itself. But it is temporal and changeable and forward rolling, while knowledge is eternal and immutable and recriminatory. To repeat Wittgenstein's quote from the beginning of this chapter:

> I can know what someone else is thinking, not what I am thinking. It is correct to say 'I know what you are thinking,' and wrong to say 'I know what I am thinking.'— A whole cloud of philosophy condensed into a drop of grammar.

In other words, all that we call knowledge is achieved vicariously and voyeuristically, in the analysis of another's mind. Mine, yours, but, most of all, God's. Everything else *cannot be said* and disappears from the historical record. *We* cannot be said and *We* disappear from the historical record. The historical record, meanwhile, is something that the scientist in us is trying to write forwards in perfect synchronicity with the ontology that is coming back at us, to obliterate us. The scientist is in perfect collaboration with ontology. The scientist in us must not be confused with what I have called the 'freedom fighter' in us (or true philosophy). The scientist in us is trying to betray the freedom fighter in us and hand him over to truth, to law, to evil objectivity. The *happening* world of the freedom fighter in us is what we have always meant by *being*. *Being* is a streaming incommunicable activity; absolutely the opposite of what the scientist in us means by (the) *existence* (of the ontological, historical record). The scientist in me says that the random streaming words of my being must denote something that has always existed in the world of the *already-happened*. Or mean nothing at all.[27]

Within the history of Western philosophy, the questions of being and existence, meaning and denotation have had long and intricate careers; careers that are well-represented in the above quotations from Wittgenstein's *Zettel*. By introducing Augustine at the critical point, I hope to have exploded a whole new vista into view by showing that the Western deification of self-knowledge has been an evil prank. The irrepressible, untameable force called *being* (or the spark of human life) is an unbreakable supernatural pipeline between God and each of us. It has all along been accepted by Western philosophy that man enlightens and develops himself and has his eyes opened to what was always before him to see, and that this self-knowledge beginning inside him and spreading out to embrace knowledge in the world at large is what *being* practically is. Now here I am saying that *being* never was that; and that our species' whole, long complicated relationship with truth via language—the problem of our consenting selves and its nonconsensual nature—is resolved in something that Wittgenstein said (after Augustine):

> 'You can't hear God speak to someone else, you can hear him only if you are being addressed.'—That is a grammatical remark.

We cannot know ourselves save that God speak the truth of who we are into our ears. True self-knowledge arrives supernaturally down that pipeline. And true self-knowledge could arrive as anything. God might say: 'Wear the green jumper rather than the yellow one today.' And the truth would be to obey that command. As far as every self-respecting system of Western philosophy is concerned, that is random and useless information; while obedience to it would set a dangerous precedent, because the whole of Western civilization is based, instead, on obedience to things that stand to reason. This, too, would explain why no one else would be able to *hear* this being said to you; just as much as you would afterwards be unable to *say* it to anyone else. You simply cannot hear and say the random and the nonsensical. We have seen, via Wittgenstein ('It used to be said that God could create anything except what would ... '), that the West used to get around this by insisting the things that God says are paradigmatically reasonable and ethical. But in this day and age, now that we industrially and technologically have the power to make and remake so much of our world, this deferential approach has fallen away. We still need God and his random nonsense, but only so that the grammar of our proud and sanitized language can have him for its *negation*.

> All deductions are made a priori.[28]

INVISIBILITY

The already-happened and all its truth exist in eternal permanence by, so to speak, not existing at all. The only material existence it can have is by counting itself out on human lives. 'One', 'Two', 'Three'. One life at a time. The thing we all have in common with the already-happened and all its truth is *Reason*. The thing we have that the already-happened and all its truth doesn't have, and which therefore destroys it, is *Emotion*. The first task of any human life is to make its start under the correct emotion. If you abandon emotion, if you try to do philosophy by living out the life of reason, the life of the mind, then you will end up counting, in time and in step, with the already-happened. In other words, you will fade to nothing. Because, as we have seen, there is nothing that is 'true' that you or I can logically say about ourselves. True things are things that we can only predicate of *Timeless Man*.[29] He who is the empty personality and death mask of the already-happened. Remember Sir Francis Galton's invention of composite portraiture, and how the composite face was always found to be more beautiful and beguiling than any of the individual faces that had gone into making it, and how this sparked our continuing fascination with human beauty and attraction, and the timeless geometries that must explain it? This is how the already-happened counts itself out on human lives, and we count with it. No single one of us can be the proof of anything. It takes at least two of us to suggest a rule or an item of knowledge. Better still would be if all the world of us could be rounded up and counted out. If that could happen, and no maverick or genius be left outside the net to deviate and disprove the rule, then the mega-statistic would be complete. At a critical point in the only book he ever published in his lifetime, the *Tractatus Logico-Philosophicus* (first published in 1921), Wittgenstein said this:

> There are, indeed, things which cannot be put into words. *They make themselves manifest*. They are what is mystical.[30]

All the traditional excitement and wisdom concerning Wittgenstein and his intellectual legacy is that he arrived in the world one day to make statements such as this. I repeat, he arrived in the world one day to be the human mouthpiece of statements such as this. I repeat again, he arrived in the world to hold the office of statements such as this. He became the de facto king of Logical Positivism. Had this office not existed before and after Wittgenstein as one of the cardinal truths (of the world of the already-happened), then I say that he would not have been able to be selected and used for its human form. Like an appointment with his own death, he was fated to meet it. I think I have already made it clear that there is a point of view from which all of our lives become a linear series of appointments with the facts of our lives—That is, with the facts as they would be narrated were an actual biography of us to be written. Each appointment, with each fact, is a little death. With very famous and momentous people like Wittgenstein, who actually held high office in the land of *Fact*, it is less a series of little deaths than like one giant murder.

Now, as the de facto king of Logical Positivism, Wittgenstein came to be praised for stating over and again, in numerous exciting variations, the all-time truth that metaphysics involves one in making empirically unverifiable statements (and that metaphysics is therefore to be laughed off; though *he* never said this[31]). In other words, for all time and patiently, this truth had had to suffer the excruciating tortures of a religious and mythopoeic ancient world, and then, on top of that, the Christian era. And it is said that in non-Western and undeveloped parts of the world today, its tortures go on. Then came this man Wittgenstein—bang!—and said it just like that. And from that moment on the tortures were meant to be over. What was it that John Maynard Keynes famously said of Wittgenstein in a letter to his wife? 'My dearest sweet, Well, God has arrived. I met him on the 5:15 train.'

The bluff has always been that Western philosophy is a life skill and a life choice, unresolved in its ultimate questions and cheerfully echoing with the laughter of the Thracian woman. And this bluff is always called when Western philosophy touches some exposed wire of Science. When it short circuits, sparks, and spasms on the possibility of a final climactic certainty.[32] In these rare moments, history ceases to be the backdrop and setting of human life and becomes instead the active force and mastermind whom it would be futile to resist. There was famously a letter written to the *New Statesman and Nation* (as it then was) in 1948 and signed, anonymously, 'Oxonian'. Its author purported to be a graduate of the University of Oxford, returning for a visit, and was appalled to discover that A. J. Ayer's Logical Positivist tract *Language, Truth and Logic*[33] 'had in Oxford since the end of the war acquired almost the status of a philosophic Bible'.[34] The letter went on to make a short but elegant case that the Logical Positivist rejection of metaphysical and emotive statements as technically meaningless was hardly moot and academic but actually fostered exactly the sort of moral void into which social and political menaces like fascism charge in. That is to say, Wittgensteinian distinctions between demonstrated statements of fact and everything else actually trigger an irresistible psychological explosion by which quite ordinary and intelligent people abandon humanity's God-given resistance—And by which they then seemingly thrill to being counted out and used up in the historicist plans for the inevitable (I am trying to avoid saying 'already-happened' again).

However, it should be clear by now that I have good reasons to call Wittgenstein no more than the de facto founder of Logical Positivism; and, of course, he went out of his way to remove himself from all on-going appropriations of his work. When I hear Wittgenstein make his distinction above and speak of the mystical inexpressibility of *things which make themselves manifest*, I do not think of the scenario which Logical Positivism took for granted on Wittgenstein's behalf. Viz., the scenario of materially existing things on the one side, plus the statements that can be built on them, and then on the other side, the imaginatively and passionately existing things, plus the statements that can be built on them. Let me just give you a classic statement of this scenario from Ayer's 'philosophic Bible':

> The criterion which we use to test the genuineness of apparent statements of fact is the criterion of verifiability. We say that a sentence is factually significant to any given person, if, and only if, he knows how to verify the propositions which it purports to express—that is, if he knows what observations would lead him, under certain conditions, to accept the proposition as being true, or reject it as being false. If, on the other hand, the putative proposition is of such a character that the assumption of its truth, or falsehood, is consistent with any assumption whatsoever concerning the nature of his future experience, then, so far as he is concerned, it is, if not a tautology, a mere pseudo-proposition. The sentence expressing it may be emotionally significant to him; but it is not literally significant. And with regard to questions the procedure is the same. We enquire in every case what observations would lead us to answer the question, one way or the other; and, if none can be discovered, we must conclude that the sentence under consideration does not, as far as we are concerned, express a genuine question, however strongly its grammatical appearance may suggest that it does.[35]

And yet I am afraid that I have never seen it like this, which makes me have to be doubly afraid, then, that this seeing of mine is going to make its way to every corner of this book. I never was able to see things that you could pick up in your hand and things that you couldn't because they were fictions. I never could see physics and metaphysics. Instead, I could only see things that were visible to the eye and things that were not. And it is still like that with me.

Think of a child who believes that by pulling the blanket over their head, they can make the ghosts not exist. They are doing what a grown-up Logical Positivist does, except he calls it big and clever. But the truth is that the ghosts will be there all the same, and that the belief that not-seeing implies nonexistence is as old and craven as the heart of man.

I am such as that I *know* that the ghosts *are there* in my room today; and that my knowing is my seeing of them. I just try to get a good night's sleep despite them. So, the only distinction that I know and honour is the distinction between visible and invisible things—But accepting all the while that both classes *exist*. And you also know that I believe that God the invisible is free as much as man the invisible (that is the invisible part in man, his soul) is free. And that both are rendered un-free (in theory) by the class objects of the visible spectrum of thought.[36] From this, I derive the idea and the hope that what Wittgenstein always meant by the mystically and inexpressibly *manifest* was the human soul itself. Man himself. Wittgenstein himself. Language, truth, and logic in the present-day setting need not imply the exploration of what (can) does and (cannot) does not exist, but rather the sheer exhilaration—I mean the sheer *feeling*—of freedom.[37] This is the correct emotion under which to start and then lead your life.

So in the end when one is doing philosophy one gets to the point where one would like just to emit an inarticulate sound.[38]

Lying on his deathbed, Wittgenstein said: 'Tell them I've had a wonderful life.'[39] The wonderful in this statement is the wonderful of knowing that visible and invisible, *all things exist*. The whole dignity and self-esteem of the Western mind comes down to it being able to say that *such and such things exist*, and if they do, then *such and such things do not*. It says that this is correct knowledge, and that correct knowledge is the same thing as freedom. And yet correct knowledge would have to look like a never-ending chain of perfectly synchronising developments, whereas the eternity which the human heart seems to long for—the freedom which it seems to long for—would be the opposite of that all-knowing martial strength. 'Wonderful' in relation to a lived human life has to mean the polar opposite of the (chain of) reasons why. 'The Wonderful' and 'Wonder' and 'Surprise' are a different kind of freedom to the freedom of the 'reasons why'. In their moment, they are endless and eternal, the stuff of dreams, whereas the sum total of all the reasons why can only ever add up to the truth of your appointment with your death.

We expect *this*, and we are surprised at *that*. But the chain of reasons has no end.[40]

Death is not an event in life: we do not live to experience death.

If we take eternity to mean not infinite temporal duration but timelessness, then eternal life belongs to those who live in the present.

Our life has no end in just the way in which our visual field has no limits.[41]

ORDNUNG

Before I tell you some things about Wittgenstein's life and background in chronological sequence, we need to be absolutely clear on the following two things. I shall number them for you.

ONE

The meaning of a life of destiny, such as it has been universally acknowledged that Wittgenstein's life was, is (and must be) utterly independent of any processes (biographical or otherwise) of counting back into the life in order to explain its destiny in relation to (portentous) facts. Here, one of the key Wittgensteinian distinctions comes into play to help us. His distinction between 'surface grammar' and 'depth grammar'. As the ancients discovered, human language is characterised by its exclusionary aspect. That is to say, it works in order to allow its speakers to bring judgement upon the things which language names, or 'terms'. On the basis that he was the first of the ancients to explain this systematically, Aristotle is taken to be the originator of this ancient 'term logic'.[42]

I spoke above about 'stable concepts', and how even letters of the alphabet must be stable and agreed upon in order to do their work. We can't seem to be able to shuffle meanings endlessly like a pack of cards. No one single thing—no one single card—can simultaneously be all the others; for that would bring the house down. The archetype of ancient term logic therefore came to be the syllogism. And as per the reasons for its eventual abandonment in the nineteenth-century, term logic was for all of this primarily, then, a statement about the principal requirement of human language. It was a formal and insulated statement of it. Truth and falsity existed within the closed system of its rules. This made it perfect for the European mind's Christian phase but desperately inadequate for its post-Christian phase. The moment that truth and falsity could begin to mean the truth of the natural and the falsity of the supernatural, then logic and language could no longer be thought of as formal and insulated but as charged with the duty of representing the world *as it actually is*. Logic and language moved to becoming propositional—That is, to speaking not in hope and fear, imagination and even destiny, but in the stripped present tense of unblinking nonfiction.

Against all of this *Ordnung*, what is a man of destiny to do? For when you think about it, if this is how logic and language have come on, then the very definition of destiny today would be to speak with *meaning* and *purpose* and *intention*, but to be always using any old words in any old order. In the ancient world before Aristotle, when you went to a prophet or a man of destiny, when you went at an oracle, you went to hear speech in the future tense. 'Such and such a thing will occur.' Nowadays, because of empirical verification, and correspondence theories of truth, and seeing is believing, to speak like this in the future tense means that one is going from nonfiction to fiction. So, it is perfectly permissible to say these things, but always now at the expense of the human creative voice. The world in all its imperious *Ordnung* says to the man of destiny: 'Prove your destiny, prove your mission, prove your calling!' Because it knows that is the very thing which he cannot do.

According to the *Ordnung* of the already-happened, the human voice must learn to speak submissively (consenting to the nonconsensual), from a point beyond its own grave, looking back. Because our knowledge of the world increases with each day, so that we have ever-more named facts to be descriptive over, we believe that the creative power of our language is increasing. This identification of creativity with *quantity* is becoming ubiquitous and unchallenged. If language is a prison, such that Wittgenstein could say of it this—

> My whole tendency and I believe the tendency of all men who have ever tried to write or talk ethics or religion was to run against the boundaries of language. This running against the walls of our cage is perfectly, absolutely hopeless. Ethics, so far as it springs from the desire to say something about the ultimate meaning of life, the absolute good, the absolute valuable, can be no science. What it says does not add to our knowledge in any sense. But it is a document of a tendency in the human

mind which I personally cannot help respecting deeply and I would not for my life ridicule it.[43]

—then the identification of creativity with quantity is equivalent to believing that a twenty-five-year prison sentence makes you five times freer than a five-year one. That is madness! To be truly creative, to be truly free, to be truly the man of destiny, would be to smash the process by which *Ordnung* is isolating each word and determining its final position in some giant ready-written script. Like some giant genetic code, the end of all argument.[44] Now there can, of course, be a thrill and excitement in that, but it is nothing to do with true destiny. It promises to enable us to speak properly in the future tense and leave behind prophets and oracles for good. But it is a fake future tense that has sold us on the idea of the 'ready-written script' like on being able to read the news of tomorrow, today. True destiny destroys this fake scheme by destroying the only means that it has to castrate our imaginations, which means is language itself. There is a little bit of destiny in all of us, but in the rare men of destiny like Wittgenstein it gets expressed to its fullest. Destiny belongs to the human soul, in a place before all words. It is how the soul tilts forwards, wilfully. And it is how it can do this in spite of anything; in spite even of things which stand to reason which suggest it shouldn't. The human soul can dare to do incredibly selfless things. To the rare men of destiny like Wittgenstein, it is obvious that words and language have no meaning save that they are the wild whooping sounds of our tilting forwards. Somewhere long ago this got lost, and language became about things like right and wrong and, worst of all, the truth. And the practitioners of this language started on the path to becoming inhuman.[45] I repeat after Wittgenstein: meaning is not the truth, it is a tilt:

> Meaning it is not a process which accompanies a word. For no *process* could have the consequences of meaning.
> (Similarly, I think, it could be said: a calculation is not an experiment, for no experiment could have the peculiar consequences of a multiplication.)[46]
> You don't need any *knowledge* to find a smell repulsive.[47]

In exact proportion to the way that psychology forges us forever to our circumstances, destiny liberates us from them. Never forget this. To be diagnosed or defined is categorically different to that explosion that goes on inside you when you tilt your will:

> In the use of words one might distinguish 'surface grammar' from 'depth grammar'. What immediately impresses itself upon us about the use of a word is the way it is used in the construction of the sentence, the part of its use—one might say—that can be taken in by the ear.—And now compare the depth grammar, say of the word 'to mean', with what its surface grammar would lead us to suspect. No wonder we find it difficult to know our way about. Imagine someone pointing

to his cheek with an expression of pain and saying 'abracadabra!'—We ask 'What do you mean?' And he answers 'I meant toothache'.—You at once think to yourself: How can one 'mean toothache' by that word? Or what did it *mean* to *mean* pain by that word? And yet, in a different context, you would have asserted that the mental activity of *meaning* such-and-such was just what was most important in using language. But—can't I say 'By "abracadabra" I mean toothache'? Of course I can; but this is a definition; not a description of what goes on in me when I utter the word.[48]

TWO

Their technical, philosophical, and mathematical accomplishment apart, it is possible to read Wittgenstein's writings as the writings of a child—or a *child-man*—torturously trying to come to terms with a method of life which we can take for granted. The brilliant obscurity of them looks straight into the eyes of how they might have been written better and clearer by a *man-man*. Except that their improvement wouldn't have resulted in a new set of writings, but in no writings at all. The geniuses have always been able to do stage tricks that amaze us. Feats of memory and calculation and, most conspicuously of all, of eccentricity. But their hearts do not belong to the world of those feats—The world which sees only the potential in those feats, and then turns it into bigger and better engines and machines. If point zero represents the normal in a normal human life, and if progress and development counts forwards of it into positive integers, then the geniuses are operating in the abnormal world of the negative integers. To make better and clearer what they write would be to bring it up to point zero, and not beyond it. However, as I have just explained it, point zero is the nothingness of the normal. So really it would mean to have to burn their books. I mean that *we* would have to burn their books. And I would like us *all* to take responsibility for that dreadful, horrible realization.

The point of having geniuses and nominating them, as far as we are concerned, then, is that they should reflect well on us. 'Genius' and 'idiot', 'truth' and 'falsity', 'life' and 'death', 'sanity' and 'insanity': the breath-taking brilliance of these pairings is that they are not really concrete realities, the one existing to the exclusion of the other. They are much more like endlessly exchanging perspectives.[49] No one who is insane feels that they are anything other than extraordinarily sane. Life can be death and death can be life. The truth would be nothing without its negation. And as for the genius, he is really everyone else's idiot. He is the gibbering wreck who can't hold down a normal train of thought and who can't make up his mind. He can't write normal books, with beginnings and middles and ends and nice soothing narratives. He leaves scraps and scrawled-over notebooks and, thank God, then, it is said, for the disciples who came in afterwards and tidied his room for him. What a diabolical way to go. It is probably terrible and ungrateful of me to say that, but who cares. I wish he'd burnt the lot before they could get their hands on it. You see, people afterwards can only fold and tidy what they can understand. Everything has to be sorted into its place. So, notes have to be turned into books, and books have to be arranged into their subjects and given indexes. And though it is all done with the best of intentions, none of it is innocent, and all of it erases the traces of the man.

That is why Wittgenstein's genius sent him forwards to break language itself. For the one thing that the history of Western philosophy shows more than anything else—or the one thing that Western philosophy knows most of all about itself—is that the noble search for enlightenment and truth really does erase the traces of men. It erases the traces of their forward tilts. It erases *the surprising* and *the unexpected*. If the search for useful knowledge sends you inevitably towards the formulation of classes and types, subjects and indexes, then you have already sold your birthright as a human being, and you can no longer choose to go off the rails. This is the same thing as to say that no questions are innocent. All questions send us down to the foundations of things—Down to the foundations where there can be no particularity but only universality. It is good science and good sense to show that the foundations of an upright and longstanding house should have 'such and such' characteristics. Yet the meaning of a human life must be whatever is unfolding in the completed rooms above; where that unfolding would be quite unscripted and extempore. It is incredible, when you think about it, that archaeology can only reveal buildings and skeletons, and therefore is actually damning of everything that it means to be human. After the fact of a human life, we can only dig up and understand what makes *sense*. You cannot dig up and understand afterwards the whisper in someone's ear. And we have already seen that in living time, you can't even hear God's whisper into someone's ear. So, it would seem that we can understand nothing at all of first importance about any human life. Every private whisper, every private tilt, is a one of a kind, never to be seen kind of butterfly—Always slipping our nets. Because of course our nets, like our understanding, can do nothing with the *one-of-a-kind*. We can only design for that which we expect.

Unless of course you believe that in the same way that there are the foundations of mathematics, and language, and logic, and history, there are, too, then, the foundations of net building; so that the sizes of all possible butterflies exist already in those foundations, and that those foundations can be beheld in the mind of an expert in the here and now.

In logic process and result are equivalent. (Hence the absence of surprise.)[50]

The whole problem really does come down to this. You can either be a human being or you can be a language, speaking correctly and true. But what you cannot be is both at once. You cannot be a human speaking a language. I believe this with all my heart, and I believe Wittgenstein (and Augustine) believed this with all his heart. But no one will ever do anything about it because then the world as we know it would have to stop. Is death, then, really so bad an option? Is it not, then, the better kind of life? I don't know. All I can do is repeat that it is possible to read Wittgenstein's writings as the writings of a child, desperately trying to resist having to learn the hellish language of the world of the grownup humans. It is a tug of war, but with nothing in the middle. Pull with the grownups if you think you know better; if you would dare to give Wittgenstein's thoughts a star rating. Pull with Wittgenstein if you think all criticism and truth is the Devil. Pull with Wittgenstein if you think that everyone pulling for the other side has already made up their minds in step with the already-happened.

> An analogy for the theory of truth: Consider a black patch on white paper; then we can describe the form of the patch by mentioning, for each point of the surface, whether it is white or black. To the fact that a point is black corresponds a positive fact, to the fact that a point is white (not black) corresponds a negative fact. If I designate a point of the surface (one of Frege's 'truth-values'), this is as if I set up an assumption to be decided upon. But in order to be able to say of a point that it is black or that it is white, I must first know when a point is to be called black and when it is to be called white. In order to be able to say that 'p' is true (or false), I must first have determined under what circumstances I call a proposition true, and thereby I determine the *sense* of a proposition. The point in which the analogy fails is this: I can indicate a point of the paper which is white and black, but to a proposition without sense nothing corresponds, for it does not designate a thing (truth-value), whose properties might be called 'false' or 'true'; the verb of a proposition is not 'is true' or 'is false', as Frege believes, but what is true must already contain the verb.[51]

KARL AND LUDWIG AND VIENNA AND TRAGEDY

Ludwig Josef Johann Wittgenstein was born on the 26 April 1889 in Vienna. His father, Karl, had married his mother, Leopoldine (née Kalmus), in 1873. By the time of Ludwig's birth, Karl had managed to become one of the richest men of his day. By all accounts he was a vigorous character, who had started his professional life in 1872 as an engineer; thereafter rising swiftly through the ranks at the Teplitzer Walzwerke, or Teplitz steel mill, in the Austro-Hungarian province of Böhmen. Teplitz being the present-day Teplice, in northwestern Bohemia in the Czech Republic. Karl's family had always been comfortably well-off, but his achievements in industry could not have been scripted and were in large part down to a momentum of his own making. By 1877 he was director of the Teplitz steel mill and well on the way to putting in place the Empire-wide cartels that would make him famous and feared—As well as leaving him in effective control of all phases of the iron and steel industry in the Habsburg monarchy. By the turn of the century, he would be at the height of his power and influence, with a private 'empire within the Empire' now run for him by a cadre of managers, all meticulously trained by him in his aggressive and efficient business practices.

For it has to be said that like many Europeans of progressive mind, Karl's great example in business as much as in life would become America. In fact, he had spent a remarkable year in the country at the age of 17, running away from home in January 1865 and boarding a ship for New York from Hamburg with nothing much more than a violin! What followed would be an ingenious solo performance in which Karl would survive as, successively, a waiter, musician, canal-boat pilot, barman, and teacher, before returning home to Vienna in the spring of 1866 to his perplexed and scandalized parents. He had hardly sent them a word of contact in all his time there. However, his project in freedom and self-sufficiency seems to have worked, because from that moment on, his family seemed to resign themselves to his self-made trajectory, and for his part, he seems to have become doubly-confirmed in it. It was *he* who would decide to enrol himself at the Technical University in Vienna—And *he* who would decide that certain lectures were useless to him, and that he would be better off using that time to gain work experience at the National Railroad Company. Later on, his business successes would repeat this same instinct of placing himself at the fulcrum of something whilst at the same time rejecting its apprenticeships of traditional wisdom, instead relying on his ability to chase down an unseen solution in an unaided way.

It was a *physical* kind of intelligence, and Karl had it to an extraordinary degree. It was very different to the purely mental intelligence of old Europe—Her crafts and guilds, her accumulated knowledge and her noblesse oblige. Physical intelligence was about speed and endurance and victory. Karl's first great performance of it would come in 1878 when he managed to pursue Samuil Poliakoff around Europe—pinning him down in Bucharest at last—and to convince him to reject the steel giant Krupps and their heavy gauge rails and buy light rails instead from his Teplitz mill. The context was the Russo-Turkish War of 1877-1878, and Poliakoff had been commissioned by Tsar Alexander II to source and build two frontline railroads for the Russian war effort. Karl's coup would make a fortune for his company and launch him on the 'American dream'. The old ways of Austria would have no chance. Karl steadily reduced labour costs throughout his business empire, axed or reorganized struggling concerns, and introduced technical innovations wherever possible. Along the way he encountered all the opposition one would expect, both from the workers and the conservative elite. But like his good friend in later life, Andrew Carnegie, he was well up to living out a principled defence of his mission, which, he would come to realize, had been to haul his economically backward country into the modern age. In an article that he would write in 1888 called 'Impressions of Travels in America', he would offer a Social Darwinian critique of the old Austrian system:

> On the huge feudal demesnes of Bohemia, where the peasant has no land of his own, and works for a day's wage of 40 Kreuzer, consumes potatoes and other farinaceous foods only in order to fill his hungry stomach, there one is unlikely to find a firm backbone, and the resolve to establish a new home matures only in the best and most energetic heads. It is only those favoured by nature who will overcome all obstacles in order to build for themselves a better life in the West, among strangers

with whose language and customs they are unfamiliar. The ailing, the tubercular are unfit for this, and they are left behind. In addition, every emigrant endures in his first years a school of a kind which, for the education of a man, it would be difficult to think of something better: he is subjected to a terrific pressure to extend his strengths to the most extreme degree in order to survive at all.[52]

The biographical note that has been left over Karl Wittgenstein's life is that he more or less ran his household like he ran his empire; that is, with close control and looming menace, and this led inexorably to the caricatured (I mean the ready-written, the already-happened) image of his family. His wife who wouldn't raise a word against him. The dutifulness of his daughters. And most spectacularly of all, the defiant suicides of three of his sons (plus Ludwig's regular contemplation of it[53]). And yet the deeper truth is that this caricature exists precisely because Karl, like his most famous son, Ludwig, is actually a most difficult man to pin a doctrine on. That physical intelligence of his meant he was at his happiest on the wing, in action—Relying on his processing speed rather than on an internal manual or a set of principles. Not for him, then, the aristocratic perpetuation of orthodoxies or the tried and trusted. But flux and crisis and the development in the midst of it, of informed new dogmas of his own:

> The American engineer or the American worker comes more frequently than his counterpart in Europe into the situation where he has to experience the disappearance of old enterprises and work together on the establishing of the new. Thus it is to the much-maligned and much feared state of crisis, which is itself a consequence of speculation, that industry in general in the United States owes its priceless stock of experienced engineers and businessmen and trained workers. It is to this same state of crisis that each particular industry owes its much-famed mechanisation—which in turn makes it possible for American industry, in spite of high wages, to compete successfully with industry in Europe.[54]

With this in mind it is easy to see that when Ludwig arrived, of a sudden, in Cambridge in 1911—untrained and uninhibited, hounding Bertrand Russell and making it up as he went along—he was in many ways exhibiting a chutzpah on foreign soil that identified him to be Karl's rightful and appointed heir. In a series of letters to Lady Ottoline Morrell, Russell would record the experience:

> He turned out to be a man who had learned engineering at Charlottenburg [at the Technische Hochschule in Berlin], but during his course had acquired, by himself, a passion for the philosophy of math's, and has now come to Cambridge on purpose to hear me. [Letter of 18 October 1911]
>
> My German friend [Russell had not then ascertained that Wittgenstein was Austrian] threatens to be an affliction, he came back with me after my lecture and

argued till dinner-time—obstinate and perverse, but I think not stupid. [Letter of 19 October 1911]

My German engineer, I think is a fool. He thinks nothing empirical is knowable—I asked him to admit that there was not a rhinoceros in the room, but he wouldn't. [Letter of 2 November 1911]

My ferocious German came and argued at me after my lecture.... He is armour-plated against all assaults of reasoning—it is really rather a waste of time talking with him. [Letter of 16 November 1911]

My German is hesitating between philosophy and aviation; he asked me today whether I thought he was utterly hopeless at philosophy, and I told him I didn't know but I thought not. [Letter of 27 November 1911]

I am getting to like him, he is literary, very musical, pleasant-mannered (being an Austrian) and I think really intelligent. [Letter of 29 November 1911][55]

As I said, Karl, like Ludwig here in Cambridge, would prove a most difficult man to pin down or to profile. There was the Wittgenstein family's sumptuous and refined Winter Palais on the Alleegasse in Vienna; and there was the Hochreith, the family's country estate in Lower Austria, where they would spend their summers. And there was how both were filled with exquisite collections of art—Both classical and also newly commissioned pieces by emerging Secessionist talents such as Josef Hoffmann and Gustav Klimt. There was the Wittgenstein family's famed musicality, and their magnificent Musiksaal. And there was how Karl and his wife and their eight children would perform for—and with—such living legends as Mahler and Strauss, Schoenberg, Brahms, and Casals. There were Karl's spontaneous moods of charitable giving; most notably the dramatic sum he gave to make it possible for the building of the Exhibition Hall of the Vienna Secession on Friedrichstrasse. But then there was, in nearly the same breath, his equally spontaneous and equally dramatic willingness to spring to the suppression of unrest and dissent in his workforces. Such as over the strike by workers at his Fürthofer works in 1891, when orders were given to set upon the workers at night and evict them from their company housing.

The point I am making is that the Wittgenstein family legend is built upon its being one of the most enduring portraits of a curiously Viennese fin de siècle tragedy. One only has to be given the setting and its characters to be able to guess how it all turns out. That is the very reason why the tragic has always been so romantic, or what is the same thing, why the romantic has always been so tragic. True romance, like true love, possesses its own energy of completion. It proffers no escape. And when it manifests itself through the story of a great family, like the Wittgensteins, or in another great example, the Kennedy family, then it is at its beguiling best. As beguiling as a curse that lingers on as the final note, even when once all the facts have been laid out and explained. The truth is that we long for these families and their stories even before they have been lived; so that we only come to understand them afterwards according to the terms and expectations of our original longing. And the truth is that this amounts to its own kind of intelligence—with its own canons of justice and beauty—and with the height of its expression being the psychological reverberations of an unnamed *Doom*. In later life, one of Ludwig's sisters, Hermine, would write an account of their family, in which she would lament how

> [i]t was tragic that our parents, in spite of their great ethical seriousness and sense of duty, did not succeed in creating some sort of harmony between themselves and their children; it was tragic that my father had sons who were as different from him as if he had found them in an orphanage! It must have been a bitter disappointment to him that none of them would follow his path and continue the work of his life.[56]

And yet here I am saying that if this is how tragedy and doom do indeed catch a whole family in a single psychology, then Karl and Ludwig have somehow managed to *escape the net*. Perhaps the most that you can say is that Karl used his life to follow an impulse, and moved his feet, and took on one of the most conspicuous empires of the old world; and that for Western philosophy, his son Ludwig went to Cambridge and did exactly the same. And perhaps this is where Ludwig's inborn sense of destiny shows itself to have been the progeny of Karl's physicality of mind. Before I move on to talk about Ludwig's mother, I want to pause for a moment on this phenomenon that I am calling 'physical intelligence'.

PHYSICAL AND MENTAL INTELLIGENCE

I think that the physical intelligence of Karl and Ludwig is best depicted like this. I want you to imagine a chessboard; not least because the chessboard is the enduring image of the remarkable nexus of human freedom, ethical right, and fate (or predestination). We are obviously pieces on that chessboard; and the possibility that we can become moving pieces, travelling from square to square, is what freedom means. Freedom means movement; where conversely the basic horror of un-freedom is to be in some fundamental way bound, gagged, or contained. But now it gets interesting. If these are the standard understandings of freedom and un-freedom, then it must begin to occur to us that they are in some curious way incomplete—Incomplete if it has begun to occur to us that the standard understandings of freedom and un-freedom are in fact transitive verbs, and here we have left them hanging in unresolved, intransitive states.

Of course, the discourse of Western ideas has always imagined to speak of freedom and un-freedom as though they were completed states of being, rather than as verbs reaching for objects. But return now to our chessboard and consider those pieces that are *us*, and those squares that are the things we might in any chosen moment do. And consider on top of this the relationship of game and strategy that holds between those squares and us. And let us decide to call this whole scenario the very essence of 'mental' as opposed to 'physical' intelligence.

Consider now how in the case of a human life, the notion of movement apart from the prepared pattern of squares would have to be the definition of random and meaningless movement—And paradoxically, then, not at all what we want to imply when we use the terms 'freedom' and 'un-freedom'. Note that it would not be impossible or inconceivable movement, but that it would carry with it nothing that would afterwards allow it to be dissected for information concerning its 'rightness' or 'wrongness'. *This* is what I mean. According to the setting of the chessboard, it would be a meaningless and random event; where we automatically assume that no human event is truly ever like this; that even the most outlandish and spontaneous human behaviour has behind it some deep psychological propulsion. Which goes to prove how we make for the setting of the chessboard in the first place. Corresponding to this must surely also be our occult fascination for human acts that do appear to push this assumption to breaking point. Such as the wanton acts of unspeakable deprivation and cruelty. They are its ultimate test cases, so that to sufficiently explain human evil is still the final frontier of human science.

So, it appears that to be able to dissect human freedom of movement after its fact, for what it contains of rightness or wrongness, is what we actually mean by it. For example, we do not say that the butterfly fluttering this way and that in the breeze is 'free', or even that the dry leaf similarly moved in the breeze is 'free'. We say that they are part and parcel of the same scheme that extends down to the atoms and their physics. We say that their movements could be fully predicted if only one knew every circumstance and variable; for neither of them could ever be conceived to move or act outside of the laws of the universe. And that brings us back to humans, and the difference of the human case. For deep down we know that every human has it in them to move and act *outside* of those laws—That every human has it in them to do wild and extempore things. But that these things invoke some other scenario than the chessboard squares, and that they are therefore, and technically, *meaningless*; to the extent that we struggle to apply to them the language of freedom at all. Because 'freedom', like all such concepts, is still a term and a word, and as that, it still requires, then, to have something stable behind it in order to be recognized. Thus it is that human freedom has come to mean not emptiness and a vacuum of possibilities, but rather the chessboard and its squares. Or rather, the way in which those squares are of themselves able to generate the meanings of time and teleology, strategy and winning. Life becomes a game, and freedom comes to mean the freedom to make right or wrong moves; so that what is right and wrong in any given context comes to be determined by the greater context of which that given context is merely a subcontext—All the way up to the final mega-context, which is the meaning of life itself, or, *Happiness*.

And so it is that we arrive at this weird and alarming fact, which is that our useful, meaningful, everyday conception of freedom is not really freedom at all but how freedom has spasmed, panicked, and fled from the ethical business of the game of life. What is more, that game of life, being now an 'ethical business', begins to look a lot like a kind of predestination. That is to say, it begins to look a lot like it is God, or whomever, who is playing the game with the pieces of our lives. Because when we start to think about it, it really is the case that the human freedom to act is dependent in any moment upon millions of concatenating elements of chance; to the extent that people really can be born with silver spoons in their mouths, or the opposite. The professional fields of insurance and the administration of risk accordingly preserve the formal language of the 'act of God'. And by the same token, professional philosophy has made deep investigations of things like 'structure' and 'enculturation' and 'double effect'. All of this returns us to the chessboard, where now I want us to imagine ourselves quivering, poised to make our moves.

If we are indeed pieces—or as the saying goes, pawns—in the game of life, then the ensuing question of our dignity as rational creatures is quickly constructed. If freedom in any given moment means to act in accordance with the very best knowledge and advice that we can muster, or to act towards our best conceivable end—and the image of God's hand over our lives has always been the classic symbol of this—then rational dignity must very quickly start to look and feel as though we were doing a better job over our lives than God. And note very carefully that God is a construct, or a requirement, of the chessboard scenario. You don't need to trouble yourself with thinking of him existing, if you don't want to. All I am saying is that if life is a game, so that the right moves win it for you and the wrong moves lose it, then this scenario must necessarily invoke the concept of the 'best imaginable player'. In other words, God. And consequently, the concept of our rational dignity, or the concept of 'the best that we can be', has to come out as God's ultimate replacement. That is to say, in a universe of right and wrong, everyone is by default a player, and if everyone is by default a player, then the concept of God is standing by default on the top step of the podium until someone moves up to replace him. All of which means that mental intelligence is not a freeform type of intelligence, unhinged from all considerations greater than itself and capable of self-destruction (capable of suicide), but that it is all the time finding newer and more complete ways to bind itself tighter to the laws of the universe. To Science. Mental intelligence is like the Pied Piper.

If this is the future that mental intelligence is drawing us towards, then we haven't yet come around to realizing it. You see, mental intelligence is not an abstract entity; it is not a description of a capacity that can be measured; though we believe that it is. Nor is it the measurement itself; in the sense in which we often say that something is the same thing as the scale on which it is being measured. So, for example, the way in which we say that time is the sweeping of the second hand, and the way in which we say that a man weighs 85kgs. In the second example, the heist is not so obvious; but it becomes so when we consider that the relationship between any such scale of measurement and what is being measured is a tautology. So, when we say that it is three o'clock or when we say that a man weighs 85kgs, we are in truth saying nothing at all. Or more to the point, the one part of what we are saying is cancelling out the other. 'three o'clock' and '85kgs' are merely the names of things; where merely to name something was never what we meant by learning to speak. When we were children we dreamed of creating new things from nothing. I want you to hold that thought for a second.

Mental intelligence has a lifespan and a linear development, and it shares that span and development with the human race. Therefore, mental intelligence decrees that a people located at an early position on the timeline are only permitted to have that position's level of development. This is secured, in any case, by the practical way in which knowledge is accumulated and passed on from one generation to the next, viz., by means of schools and texts. Thus, you cannot help but be educated into the state of knowledge of your position on the timeline, and you cannot help, in turn, improving on that knowledge in a way that keeps step with the timeline's forwards progress. All of which is to say, then, that mental intelligence is like a single evolving mind—Though not in the Hegelian sense. Mental intelligence refers to the way in which human interaction and speech necessarily involves an 'auto-censoring' effect. I try to say something meaningful to you, that you might understand it; and you by turn return it to me in the auto-censor form of, 'So you mean x, right?' And the auto-censor effect will happen every time because it cannot but happen by the plain fact of temporal succession. In other words, whoever begins to speak first is the one who is going to get auto-censored by the other. Because remember that we are all of us on the chessboard; to the result that the second person—the listening person—always has the advantage of being able to judge your move from the point of view of 'God', or the 'best imaginable player', as I put it above. And note in addition that judgement is therefore entirely accidental /re the second person. Whomever happens to be that second person logically has to occupy its auto-censoring office of judgement.

So, you and I might be climbing a mountain, and I might say to you: 'I think that it would be best if we took the route up the north face.' And now you, knowing that we are on a chessboard, and knowing that the optimal outcome of this particular edition of its game will be when we summit the mountain, are able to return the true meaning of my statement to me, saying: 'You mean because the north face will allow us to get more quickly above this low-lying cloud.' And I say: 'Exactly!' What is going on here is simply the harmless and comforting way in which humans get on with each other. Without the auto-censor effect, there would be little to no reason to say anything to anybody. Before we open our mouths to anybody, we *know* what we mean; even if we never manage to get the right words out to express it. Yet it seems that just knowing like this in the private world of your inner silence is unendurable after a while. Thence comes the itch to try to speak it out to someone. To anyone. And the moment that happens, we move from being under our own power to being under theirs. We literally hang on the hope that they will be able to understand us; and if it happens that they for some reason don't, then we are thrown into the agonies of wondering whether what we said made no sense or amounted to a terrible idea. Now if this is what is really going on all the time between all the world's billions of humans, then just imagine what its collective effect must be! Its collective auto-censoring effect. This is why I said we mustn't try to envisage it in Hegelian terms as a positive phenomenon. As any kind of happy answer to the question of human freedom in history. No. I am trying to show you instead how temporal succession and the auto-censoring effect lead to an international conspiracy in which intelligence and wisdom come to mean the same thing as speaking in tautologies. It would not be unhelpful in picturing this to think of Plato and his World of the Forms—His argument that everything that is real is so because it can claim descent from its ideal form, the collection of which is the 'World of the Forms'. It used to be said that this arch-idealism and all such metaphysics had been done away with once and for all by the twentieth century and its analysis and positivism. And yet here I am saying that all this reductionism—that all this auto-censoring—has actually brought us to a situation that resembles the final fulfilment of all Plato's dreams!

Mental intelligence has scripted a history of mankind in which the collective conversation has gone like this:

> The serpent to Eve: 'Did God really say?'
> The first philosopher, Thales, gazing upwards at the heavens, and falling backwards down a well.
> The laughter of the Thracian woman.
> Charles Darwin's dignified response in his *On the Origin of Species*.
> The Periodic Table.
> Kurt Gödel's 'incompleteness theorems'.[57]

A statement is nothing to us until we can understand it. It doesn't become tactile and capable of being held until it is understood. And it cannot be passed on from us to someone else until it has been held in this way. It doesn't have to be like this, but mental intelligence has chosen to be subservient to this truth. My point about this truth, and mental intelligence, and the whole collective project of auto-censorship, is that its baton relays must all eventually ground out in real, material things. And that by the time that this starts to happen, a hideous and unanticipated ethic starts to rear—Every bit as irresistible as Plato's critics had always feared it might be, yet even worse, because now it is grounded not in abstract ideas but in the absolutely incontrovertible of 'rocks and science'. This hideous and unanticipated ethic will come to say, in the end, that all fiction, all originality and imagination, is sin; punishable by death. If once upon a time we believed that the whole point of having voices was to sing the dream song, now we will learn the bitter truth (and how we were duped). Although really, this truth is being taught every day in modern logic classes the world over. *Any meaningful talk amongst humans, spread over time, is made possible by the (not prior but) post-existence of empirical objects or axioms, in relation to which it is the final purpose of all human talk to conform itself by means of spoken systems of formal tautologies.* That is what I say. Modern logic classes the world over say that the empirical objects or axioms come prior not post, and this makes it the kindred of modern sociology, which teaches that speech is the foremost example of group behaviour, so that its origins should be sought in the primitive pacts to assign certain names to certain physical objects and phenomena.

What I mean by this is how you are taught to assign the name 'flower' to the object 'flower', plus how you are taught to understand the intervening grammars as having automatically generated themselves from that simple, one-time, *historical* assignation. But most insidiously of all, how you are taught how to extend the tautology 'flower'(word)—'flower' (object) into its figurative use for statements of subjective and emotive belief. In other words, just as the tautology 'flower'—'flower' implies grammatically correct generations such as 'This is a flower' and 'Here is a flower', it allows its user to explore their private world in generations such as 'I am flower' and 'I feel like a flower' (I am or I feel happy/beautiful/radiant/peaceful).

All of which is to say that modern logic classes are saying what I am saying, here, in this book, except back-to-front. And in this they are committing and perpetuating a fundamental error. I shall pick up this in more detail in Chapter 3, but suffice to say here that the curiosities involved in Gödel's 'incompleteness theorems' are a direct result of modern logic's stubbornness about wanting to keep its empirical, verifiable world in the present and the past—Rather than supernaturally in the future of the already-happened. So, whereas I am saying that this future draws us towards it by means of the innate attraction (to our pride) of mental intelligence, to the effect that infinity is no longer the open-ended cone of an ever-expanding future, but that cone turned around to make the future a doom that is closing in on a point, modern logic insists on keeping the cone as it was, believing that this way is representing the nonexistence of the supernatural and the endless range of human ingenuity.

* * *

To understand what I am saying here, one has to be a child again. Or at any rate, one has to find the examples of it—or the explanations of it—in the children's literature that has dealt in metaphysics. George MacDonald would be an example. In his story 'At the Back of the North Wind', you will learn how there never have been the categories of 'existence' and 'nonexistence', except in the conceit of the human brain. These categories show us the hard-wiring of the brain as an organ and a faculty, but nothing else. They make it appear troublesome and contradictory that law and process should generate an infinity which in turn should compass both the existent and the nonexistent, and the natural and the supernatural. The answer would have to be some new distinction altogether—Some new categories. But this would make them such as they could only be taken seriously by an audience of children. Which is not really news, when you think about it. Metaphysics has always really been a subject for children. It is *Physics* that is for adults. Listen carefully now to what MacDonald has to say about 'soul'. It will help you with a lot of what is to come in the book.

'Everything, dreaming and all, has got a soul in it, or else it's worth nothing, and we don't care a bit about it. Some of our thoughts are worth nothing, because they've got no soul in them. The brain puts them into the mind, not the mind into the brain.'

'But how can you know about that, North Wind? You haven't got a body.'

'If I hadn't, you wouldn't know anything about me. No creature can know another without the help of a body. But I don't care to talk about that. It is time for you to go home.'

So saying, North Wind lifted Diamond and bore him away.[58]

* * *

The curiosities that Gödel discovered arise because the fundamental principle which allows us to conceive of the series of real numbers and the schemata of logic is the principle of consistency. Where what is meant by consistency in these cases is the reproductive consistency of a pattern repeating itself to infinity. Yet that same repetition unto infinity which is the ultimate proof of ultimate consistency cannot itself be the subject of a proof. For when you think about it, what can only ever be meant by 'proof' is a mechanical procedure of the 'seeing is believing' variety. Proof is therefore possible of a finite universe of series and schemata—where you can actually travel to the end of the line, pick out the last member of the series and run a proof of its belonging to that series (and therefore of that series' (finite) consistency)—but impossible of an infinite universe, where you cannot do that. And yet an infinite universe is precisely what is implied by ultimate consistency. And so we have Gödel's problem.

> Forget this transcendent certainty, which is connected with your concept of spirit.[59]

However, in my finite universe, with the cone having already come to its point in its supernatural future location, this problem cannot exist. It is solved, but at the expense of having to believe in the supernatural; albeit a supernatural that is as natural as the preordained fact of our death.

> If one understands the inductive proof as a shortcut, then it is a short cut that leads, as it were, through a new *Space*; as if one were shortening the distance between here to Vienna by travelling *through* the earth instead of over its surface.[60]
>
> If someone can *believe in* God with complete certainty, why not *in* Other Minds?[61]

I believe that our universe is a finite universe, and believing this, that its power to seduce our minds is not the power of a gallery of beautiful pictures which we can enter and leave as we please, but much more like a siren that is drawing us to the rocks. Every thinking man since Socrates has imagined that correct knowledge of our universe would be desirable because it would equip us to be like supermen, with optimal control over ourselves and our environments. Yet I believe that these boons are merely a temporary phase and that the real purpose of mental intelligence is to lead us down the road of a perfect tautological conformity to the truth of the universe. Or a way of thinking and speaking that becomes as though we were swapping out the atoms of ourselves, our words and our sentences, for the atoms of the things around us (melting into the periodic table). And the new kind of ethic that would support this with the ultimate sanction for those who choose to dissent. For those who choose to dissent by means of physical intelligence.[62]

Today, in the world of the Hubble Telescope and the Hadron Collider, physical intelligence manifests itself as an acute sensitivity to the antagonism between man and the universe at large. In the days of Karl and his son Ludwig, that is, the turn of the nineteenth-century, it tended far more to manifest itself as an acute sensitivity to the antagonism between man (that is the spirit of man) and machine (that is what the machine *really* symbolises). This antagonism is made out of the fact that man alone of all the animals has free will or the capacity to run forwards into destiny—Or as I put it earlier, to 'tilt his soul'. This tilting would be to act always *before* rather than after knowledge; to use the muscles of one's legs to put oneself somewhere (Teplitz, Cambridge). It would be to know the truth not as something that someone next in line could summarize better after you, but as where you stood, and what that felt like. It would be to only ever commit to paper and permanence what you were afterwards prepared to disown.[63] It would altogether be a most dangerous thing to do.

Karl Wittgenstein on the spirit of man:

> There is nothing which drives on human activity more than the exact and rapid working of the machines.... The machines are becoming from year to year more productive both in regard to quality and quantity; the machines are becoming ever more complicated and the individual parts operate with a fabulous rapidity. Under these conditions, however, the demands made upon the mental and physical competence of the worker are also increased.[64]

Ludwig Wittgenstein on what the machine *really* symbolizes:

> The machine as symbolizing its action: the action of a machine—I might say at first—seems to be there in it from the start. What does that mean?—If we know the machine, everything else, that is its movement, seems to be already completely determined.
>
> We talk as if these parts could only move in this way, as if they could not do anything else. How is this—do we forget the possibility of their bending, breaking off, melting, and so on? Yes; in many cases we don't think of that at all. We use a machine, or the drawing of a machine, to symbolize a particular action of the machine. For instance, we give someone such a drawing and assume that he will derive the movement of the parts from it. (Just as we can give someone a number by telling him that it is the twenty-fifth in the series 1, 4, 9, 16, ...)

> 'The machine's action seems to be in it from the start' means: we are inclined to compare the future movements of the machine in their definiteness to objects which are already lying in a drawer and which we then take out.[65]

At this point some telling facts emerge. We have seen above that Ludwig, like his father, studied engineering—at the Technische Hochschule in Charlottenburg, Berlin. This was from 1906 to 1908. He would graduate on the 5 May 1908 with an *Abgangszeugnis*, or 'engineering certificate'. This would be followed, immediately, by three years of advanced research in aeronautical engineering in Manchester, England—at the College of Technology. Ludwig would even come to patent (no. 27,087, 17 August 1911) a new kind of propulsion system for aircraft, consisting of a propeller rotated by small jet engines mounted at its tips. The centrifugal force of the rotating propeller would be used (after manual start-up) to pressurize and drive an air and fuel mixture up internal tubes and out to the blade-tip jet engines, where it would then be ignited to provide the thrust to turn the propeller. Although nothing practical would come of this design at the time, it would end up anticipating some prototype hybrid helicopter designs of the 1940s and 1960s; although all of these would prove to be too noisy and complex to offer serious competition to the emerging modern helicopter.

So, Ludwig, like his father, knew about machines and how they differ from humans and took that knowledge into his later philosophy. Moreover, it is significant that Ludwig's patented propulsion system for aircraft was an attempt to do away with the traditional orthodoxy of an engine driving a crankshaft, and then that crankshaft in turn rotating a propeller. It is significant because if I tell you now that this traditional orthodoxy of the aero engine can in fact be made into a very workable analogue of the equally traditional orthodoxy of the 'picture theory of language'—the very picture theory of language that Ludwig would reference in order to reject in his *Philosophical Investigations*—then it becomes possible to unite Ludwig's engineering period to his philosophical career in something like a single attitude to life. In the opening of his *Philosophical Investigations*, Ludwig quotes Augustine's theory of language acquisition, as it is found in Augustine's *Confessions*, I, 8, 13:

> When (my parents and other adults; Augustine is speculating on his own infant acquisition of language) named a certain thing and, at that name, made a gesture towards the object, I observed that object and inferred that it was called by the name they uttered when they wished to show it to me. That they meant this was apparent by their bodily gestures, as it were by words natural to all men, which are made by changes of countenance, nods, movements of the eyes and other bodily members, and sounds of the voice, which indicate the affections of the mind in seeking, possessing, rejecting, or avoiding things. So little by little I inferred that the words set in their proper places in different sentences that I heard frequently, were signs of things. When my mouth had become accustomed to these signs, I expressed by means of them my own wishes.

He then goes on to say:

> Augustine does not speak of there being any difference between kinds of word. If you describe the learning of language in this way you are, I believe, thinking primarily of nouns like 'table', 'chair', 'bread', and of people's names, and only secondarily of the names of certain actions and properties; and of the remaining kinds of word as something that will take care of itself.[66]

This observation concerning the limitations of the picture theory of language then sets Ludwig up for everything that he is going to say in the *Philosophical Investigations* about words being propellers that drive themselves according to automatic rules of engagement and meaning that spring into life between speaker and listener. In the picture theory of language, each word, each propeller, is directly driven by its engine, that is, by its meaning—Viz., by the real-world thing which it exclusively names. This transfer of energy involving straight lines of meaning (i.e. crankshafts) between propellers and engines is efficient only up to a point. Far better would be to have words rotate themselves; as indeed they do anyway in the discourse of everyday language. The weight of cylinders and pistons and crankshafts could then fall away; again, as indeed they do anyway in the discourse of everyday language. It seems that in designing his aero engine and in designing his philosophy, Ludwig followed a single instinct about mental intelligence (philosophy's understanding of itself) as being like to a process that can never outrun the laws of friction and drag. The best that can be hoped for is to remove as much of the intervening paraphernalia of meaning as possible (cylinders, pistons, and crankshafts) in order to arrive at a philosophical self-understanding in which meanings become rules that are made up as we go along.

The problem is that self-understanding, like self-knowledge, would seem to indicate that one must be speaker and listener at the same time. This was the whole point of the 'linguistic turn' in philosophy whose momentum Ludwig helped so much to accelerate. With this turn, it became axiomatic that philosophy must be preoccupied with listening to itself speak. However, the act of being both speaker and listener is like the quest for zero-point energy machines; whereas Ludwig's philosophy was to so brilliantly show the world that what the philosophers have always called truth was never 'free' in this sense—In the sense of a system that could supply its own energy. Or in the sense of things that simply and intuitively 'stand to reason in the world' (in the sense, then, of the laws of nature or the propositions of elementary mathematics). For the plain simple fact of all facts is that philosophy *can't* listen to itself save through the proxy of a human being: which is the same thing as to say that the truth can't listen to itself save through the proxy of a human being. For what the human being supplies is the all-important energy input, without which the truth is meaningless (near the start of this chapter I called it 'the tree that fell in the forest with no-one to hear it'). I have also suggested already that the original source of this energy is the Voice of God, which arrives in each human heart from without the closed system of the natural world. Without this Voice, no wilfulness at all could enter into our automated and *already-happened* universe. Without it speaking different things into each human heart, and making those hearts restless, there could be no human wilfulness in turn. And with no human wilfulness, no 'all-important energy input'. Without a live, wet, physical philosopher placing himself at a desk, working his brain, scribbling notes and turning pages—without this physical input—well, I repeat, the tree would fall and no-one would hear it.

The zero-point energy machine of the Western ideal of truth would not require this input in its conceit: indeed, *does* not require this input in its conceit. It exists whether we acknowledge it or not. It is the tautology of all tautologies. It is existence itself. So there turns out always to be an essential antagonism between this and what we call 'philosophy'; if by the latter we mean the progressive history of Western philosophy. Or the timeline of philosophers and their discoveries. For those discoveries had behind them the sincere human wish to do good to mankind and the planet. They had behind them the 'restless heart'. And it was this energy that PHYSICALLY put Plato at Socrates' feet to learn, and Aristotle at Plato's, and so on. And so it seems that there would be a way of notating the history of philosophy in which you rendered only this physical part of the story, which would come as a surprise to many, but which would actually be the fundamental truth of it.

STRAIGHT LINES AND SUICIDE

In addition, when I read Ludwig's observation (quoted earlier):

> We talk as if these parts could only move in this way, as if they could not do anything else. How is this—do we forget the possibility of their bending, breaking off, melting, and so on? Yes; in many cases we don't think of that at all.

—I am made to think always of suicide. That is, of his brothers' suicides and of his own regular thoughts to do the same. But really of suicide in general and how it is treated in the stories of lives. Suicide, like sexuality, is one of those facts that are generally given enormous explanatory power within the course of narratives. I have already leaned against the orthodoxy that the suicides of three of Karl's sons plus Ludwig's contemplation of it is meant somehow to tell us all we need to know about Karl—As though we hadn't already written him off enough on the plain fact of his success in the world. Because let's face it, there is always something 'suspicious' about success. I would gently suggest that the only thing we don't like about it is the one thing we can't change about it, which is that it logically can only be in the possession of a small number of people at any one time. Worse, that it is generally acquired through factors of physical intelligence that you can't learn at school or university. Factors like instinct and speed and belief (in destiny). These are simply inborn; and that fact turns out to be immensely offensive to the democratic ideal of universal values and universal education—And about that education equipping you to be anything that you want to be. The world is full of the most amazing success stories, and from the most unlikely places, but generally those stories hinge on an act of physical daring. Somewhere along the line their protagonists were runaways or stowaways, or otherwise had to overcome the most trying physical pressures of hunger or war. So, in other words, physical intelligence smashes and obliterates the narratives that we construct. These narratives attempt to write the truth that laptops will save Africa, but the real truth is that Africa will save Africa in the way that Africa knows how. These same narratives of ours attempt to write the same truth over events of suicide and sexuality. They attempt to work the angle that suicide and sexuality must always *mean* something. They are swerves and deviations from the aggregate and the ordinary, so yes, they must mean something. Where this meaning is always an ethical meaning implying right and wrong, and aiming in the first instance at parents and upbringing. And doing all of this so self-righteously, and never thinking to aim at itself! It is always like this. Self-righteousness always thrills to the swerves and the deviations because it is blind to the dogma of its own straight line. It rewards and celebrates all deviants precisely because they are so very different to its own straightness. And in exact proportion it persecutes their parents for being outmoded and outdated.

The problem that I draw attention to here is that only the straight line can tell—can dictate—what should count as a swerve or a deviation. Plain logic tells you that. Plain logic also tells you that every swerve and every deviation could have sworn that it was a straight line. The problem, then, is that ethics (the chessboard) can't enter into this. The only insight that works is the insight that each of us is, by default, liable to take up the mantle of the 'straight line'. With that straight line standing for auto-censoring and mental intelligence and the rest of it. I don't know what you would call this liability. Perhaps sin or human nature or whatever. I only know that because of it you can't—no, you shouldn't—stand on your own straight line and look across to someone else and start narrating their swerves and deviations. It's just plain wrong to do that. By all means judge everyone equally under the laws of their land, whatever those may be. I am not proposing anarchy. But don't you dare log on to the worldwide web of mental intelligence and tell me what I am thinking! Do you see what is happening here? There isn't just one intelligence anymore, but two. It used to be that mental intelligence took in the universe and man in one fell swoop, and that out of this was constructed the absolute right to judge another's life. I remember reading Bertrand Russell drop this into his account of Leibniz's philosophy:

> Leibniz recognized—as every careful philosopher should—that all psychical events have their causes, just as physical events have, and that prediction is as possible, theoretically, in the one case as in the other.[67]

Yes! Suicides and sexualities all have their causes and their meanings, and everything that *is to be* has *already happened*. And everything that has already happened is like Ludwig's machine. But what about what we 'don't think of at all'? What about the 'bending, breaking off, and melting'? What universe does that inhabit? Maybe it is a universe without thought (which is why we don't think of it at all). And maybe this is why it is so offensive to our mental intelligence.

Imagine being a biologist and having to study a newly discovered species of animal that has no instinct for self-preservation. Would that even be possible—I mean to study such a species of animal? Think about it: the good biologist says: 'I go into my study of the new species with no preconceptions or prejudices; I go in with a clear mind.' But does he really? What if he only ever goes in to study the new species because he already believes absolutely in something he calls the animal kingdom's instinct for self-preservation. Because again, think about it: Where would you even begin your observations and notes without this absolute belief? You could write down descriptions of what the animal is doing, even make sketch-pictures, but these would forever be meaningless. Because meaning only starts to enter in to it when once we can think things like: 'That behaviour must be something to do with its search for food.' Or: 'That must be to do with courtship.' Take Russell's sentence above out of his study of Leibniz and that study falls apart. Just in the same way as a human life falls apart when once it guts out its own machinery for life. Once that starts to happen, a new universe is entered into—A universe in which the full and unstoppable power of the human will is discovered. The biologist rests secure that he will never encounter a species of animal that defies the instinct for self-preservation. And therefore the biologist never leaves the universe of mental intelligence. But the biographer, *I say*, must be leaving it all the time, for his particular subject, the human animal, is unique precisely for its ability to enter into this strange new universe, unreachable by meaning and explanation, and therefore unwritten by them. The devil against this is form and structure, a life moving from birth to death, chapter by chapter—And yet when no life on earth ever had anything to do with that! The chapter-by-chapter books say that birth with meaning ends as death with meaning. Parents came together and a child was born, and by the exact same science that child eventually died. And yet I began this chapter by noticing that from a certain person's point of view, no birth ever has this sense and comfort. This sense and comfort that the readers and critics get to feel. That 'certain person' is the person born. To them, their birth was a meaningless event, by which they were plucked from one world into this. Meaningless from the point of view of their will, which was never consulted.[68] If ever you came to feel like this, then to take your own life in an early death would seem to you like the most reasonable thing of all, the most *just* thing of all. For the whole point of the physical world of the will is that you can do anything you like in it. But the only gateway to that world, the lock and the key, is the denial of self-preservation.

It is simple, really. With that gone, you must become irrational, mad, unborn, and free; with the definition of that freedom being that you will have stopped observing yourself along with all the rest of the world (stopped being the biologist standing over yourself), and will instead have returned into yourself, into a place before all words and meanings and ethics. No more life and death, right and wrong. No more survival of the fittest. No more self-consciousness. In all the long history of mental intelligence we have forgotten that the human will can enter into itself and move itself; we have forgotten, in other words, that the human will does not have to live outside itself, in the chessboard 'universe of right and wrong', 'doing a better job over our own lives than God'. There is a scenario in which the human will chooses freely to go against all such good sense and knowledge and conducts a kind of suicide by actually returning inside itself to move itself from within itself. Of this specific scenario I have only read one account in Western literature, and curiously it comes in Augustine's *Confessions*; but more curiously still, it comes as the climax of his dramatic conversion to Christ. You may remember part of it from the close of this book's Introduction.

> I suffered from a madness that was to bring health, and I was in a death agony that was to bring life: for I knew what a thing of evil I was, but I did not know the good that I would be after a little while.... For not only to go, but even to go in thither was naught else but the will to go, to will firmly and finally, and not to turn and toss, now here, now there, a struggling, half-maimed will.... Yet it was not done: it was easier for the body to obey the soul's feeble command, so that its members were moved at pleasure, than for the soul to obey itself, and to accomplish its *own high will wholly within the will*.[69]

Our reliance nowadays on being able to hear ourselves speak, and therefore on philosophy being able to hear itself speak, is so total to have rendered us nearly incapable of even imagining this alternative. We should be reminded of how it was thought a great miracle in ancient times that—[Pythagoras] was seen in Croton and Metapontum at the same time of the same day[70]—and how it was only by recreating this effect in theory that Albert Einstein was able to cross the threshold into general relativity and the equivalence principle. Without the mental trick of being able to put ourselves into two moments of space-time at once, we would never be able to make the discovery that gravity, unique of all forces, is 'matter-blind'—That it affects all objects equally, regardless of their physical properties. The famous setting for Einstein's 'happiest thought' concerning this was his realization that a man jumping from a building whilst dropping a ball would not be able to detect the effect of gravity on the ball, for he would, of course, be accelerating at exactly the same speed as the ball. That would have been that, and there would be no theory of general relativity following upon it, were it not for the additional fact that this falling man was at one and the same time identical to the man Einstein observing him, by imagination, from his desk in the federal patent office in Bern. What I am saying here is that this picture of the universe that mental intelligence has created in the modern age is really only a secondary, or even an accidental, achievement. The primary achievement—and the real instinct that drove Einstein on—was the achievement of having bilocated himself.

> We acknowledge a truthful person's statement about what he has just thought as well as his statement about what he has dreamt. Even if we *frequently* could guess someone's thoughts and were to say we know what they are, then the criterion for that could only be that he himself confirmed our guess. Unless we totally change the concept of thought.[71]

You see, Wittgenstein came to realize something very important. When you are born and you open your mouth, you are actually screaming yourself into destiny. In that magic place before word formation and meaning, in that place in which you tip your head back and sound off—*There*, in your primeval scream, you put your foot down. And with your foot down you are in one place at one moment in time. You tilt your soul; you express your will. But screaming doesn't last forever; and especially not when teachers are at hand to coax words and sense from your lips. And it is at this point, as you are taught that there is such a thing as speaking the truth, and that this truth-speak begins in attaching the *right* word to the *right* thing, that you begin to acquire your first taste for bilocation. For not only are you in the place-moment of your voice, but you are also in the place of the judging eye looking down on you, holding and weighing your every word for truth. In fact, you might eventually become so skilled in this as to learn to place yourself at any distant point in the ever expanding universe of mental intelligence.

> The origin and the primitive form of the language game is a reaction; only from this can more complicated forms develop.
> Language—I want to say—is a refinement. 'In the beginning was the deed.'[72]
> It says what it says. Why should you be able to substitute anything else?[73]

* * *

Do women scream differently to men? Was Ludwig's mother screaming and no one heard her? As in the case of her husband, Karl, Leopoldine has had to play a choreographed role in the story and legend of her family. There is the oft-repeated assessment of Ludwig's sister Hermine:

> What we children imbibed from our earliest days was the sense of a strange agitation in our family home; an overall want of relaxation which could not, in truth, be attributed to the excitements and activities of my father alone. For my mother could in her own way be just as excitable, though she always presented a perfectly composed exterior to her husband and her mother [whom she cared for]. In fact, this composure was probably the reason for the excitement—in the sense that it must have repressed a native nervousness of hers that would then discharge itself

from time to time as this energy. In this context the following now appears to me to be a fact of the utmost importance: For all the happiness, indeed the infinite happiness that characterised my parents' marriage, it was essentially the conjunction of a woman born for *toleration* with a man born for *action*.[74]

This is the image that has endured. While Karl made his history up as he went along, his wife followed her idealized version of what history had prescribed for womanhood in her time. Hermine went on to observe:

> It is only natural that the active element works on the tolerant element and over time actually changes its structure; and it is thus that I believe that my mother, at least by the time that we were knowing her, was no longer entirely herself—as anyone would be, who could no longer, so to speak, regain consciousness. Among other things, we could not understand why she had so little will and opinion of her own, and we did not reflect on the impossibility of maintaining a will and opinion of one's own in the face of my father. We simply could not understand her; while she, for her part, had no real understanding for the 8 strange children that she had brought into the world. In fact for all her avowed love of humanity, she seemed to have no genuine understanding of people.[75]

Her eight children, in order of their birth, were Hermine (b. 1874), Johannes (b. 1877), Konrad (b. 1878), Helene (b. 1879), Rudolf (b. 1881), Margaret (b. 1882), Paul (b. 1887), and Ludwig (b. 1889). There was also a daughter, Dora, born in 1876, but who sadly did not survive her first month. Karl Wittgenstein's parents had been Jewish but converted to Protestantism, and similarly, Leopoldine had a Jewish father but had been raised a Roman Catholic. All her children would accordingly be raised Roman Catholic. She evidently had a great talent for music and was remembered by her children as a highly accomplished pianist. But she was also evidently as distant a figure of motherhood as her daughter Hermine's recollections make out. The conventions of the day for a family of the Wittgenstein's standing did not help with this.

The Wittgenstein children were educated into their teens at home by a succession of private tutors and were cared for in their early youth by Wendish nurses. In other words, they had all the disadvantages of an aristocratic upbringing in nineteenth-century northwestern Europe. I mean how the emotional intimacies of simpler lives in humbler homes would have remained a thing of theory for them; and I mean how great wealth and public standing in a family such as theirs means that the world is already looking on, and that parents are liable to feel the pressure of that and adopt a more programmatic, even experimental, approach to their children's development. Karl, so dismissive of conventional education himself, pushed for his youngest sons Paul and Ludwig to forgo their secondary schooling altogether and concentrate at home, and with their tutors, on subjects like mathematics and Latin—Subjects that might actually equip them one day to take roles within his iron and steel empire. In the event, this plan was dropped, and the boys would eventually make it into the Austrian public school system.

Of Ludwig's career, we already know. His brother Paul would become a famous concert pianist; a remarkable achievement given the loss of his right arm in military service on the Eastern front during World War One. We already also know that the other three brothers would commit suicide. Johannes would be the first, taking his life sometime in 1902, probably in North America. Rudolf would take his life whilst a chemistry student in Berlin in 1904; and Konrad during the dying days of the war in 1918, on the Italian front. It seems that he most likely shot himself in the days following the armistice of 3 November between Italy and Austria-Hungary. And it seems likely that it was a heroic death, spurred by his refusal to waste his men's lives on a futile last stand; though the precise facts remain unknown. Johannes' suicide is shrouded in genuine mystery. It is known that he had fled his father's attempts to have him groomed in his image and had ended up in North America, or possibly South America, where he had met his end alone, aboard a boat; possibly a canoe. Rudolf's tragedy was, on the face of it, more straightforward. He had been struggling to cope with homosexual tendencies, for which he had even sought professional help from the famous Berlin sexologist Dr Magnus Hirschfeld. It would seem that having taken this step, he was then afflicted by a fear of being 'outed', and that this fear led to him determining to take his own life. On 2 May 1904, he took potassium cyanide in a glass of milk whilst sitting in a Berlin restaurant and died minutes afterwards.

Of Ludwig's three sisters, Hermine never married and lived her whole life at the Winter Palais. Helene married Max Salzer, a finance minister in the Austrian government. After marrying her, he would eventually take over responsibility for managing the Wittgenstein family fortune. And Margaret married the American Jerome Stonborough, whom she would later divorce. And that's where I am going to stop this—Stop this because even in putting down these facts, I can feel myself starting to contend with the occult forces of the *already-happened*. Just think about it: What on earth can we really know about Ludwig's mother and brothers and sisters at this distance of remove? What more could we have known if we were actually there among them? It is incredible to me that the farther in years we remove ourselves from an event or a person, the more certainly we feel able to know them through the facts of their case.

Imagine a timeline. Let's call the first point on that timeline 'Leopoldine Wittgenstein's private and incommunicable inner life', and let's call the last point on the timeline *Me*—*Me* as I am now including her in my 'biography' of her son. Here comes the incredible part. In exactly the same breath as we would proclaim her private inner life to have been, just that, 'incommunicable', and to have belonged to her and her alone, we would also happily write her part into the Wittgenstein family legend in that nudge-nudge, wink-wink kind of way that modern biography has conditioned us to accept.

You know exactly how it goes; and you know how it generates its own kind of elegance of prose. The subject is dead and cannot speak and perform their personality as would be normal for a living person. So instead of that, something breathtaking and unjustified happens. A whole story and legend is constructed for them (without their consent). A framework. And then that framework is made to furnish the actual péripéties of their personality. And then appropriate anecdotes are found to confirm those. Imagine your outrage if this were done to you today, during your living reality. Imagine if someone were following you around, fitting each and every one of your words and acts into their place in some jigsaw of your life that he had *already-constructed*. Imagine how violated you would feel. Imagine how you would rage and scream against this with your freedom to be an endlessly reborn person, slipping and evading your future biographer with each new breath. For that is what it feels like to be alive. To be alive is its own world, and it has nothing whatsoever to do with the world of the dead—And how that dead world lives on in the life of the mind.

I have used Karl Wittgenstein and his son Ludwig to represent this endless rebirth, and I have called it *physical intelligence*. Planting my flag there, with it, I have looked around me and tried to break ranks with what normally happens with a family history like the Wittgenstein's, when science and psychology join forces to create myth and superstition. As I said, the framework is created first. I don't know how to explain this other than if I were to throw the bones of the Wittgenstein story on a table, and you were at once to start thrilling to the intrigues of suicides and sexualities, domination and submission. Mature mental intelligence says that here is a scenario ripe for psychological analysis. What it never considers is that any such analysis that penetrates to the facts in order to say that certain combinations of them will always produce certain results (Karl + Leopoldine + fin de siècle Vienna = dysfunctionality)—Well, it never considers how this implies that the psychological analysis must then have preceded the actual unfolding of the facts in some timeless place. *This is a religious belief.* It is no better or worse than were some witchdoctor in Africa to throw the same bones on the ground and make his predictions. This form of dishonesty is committed all the time without being noticed. Even the most strict and ardent scientist will be moved to say to the woman he loves: 'You are my one and only!'—As if he had sampled all the women of all the continents throughout all time and reached this conclusion!

The only way that I feel I can write a biography of Ludwig Wittgenstein and live with myself afterwards is if I write in such a way that I somehow break him out of this prison called *Genius*, which we built for him before he had even been born, and which we afterwards 'saw coming' through all the twists and eccentricities of his upbringing. And never once noticing the fundamental meanness and unfairness of stitching someone up like this.

> 'I know that I am a human being.' In order to see how unclear the sense of this proposition is, consider its negation. At most it might be taken to mean 'I know I have the organs of a human'. (E.g. a brain which, after all, no one has ever yet seen.) But what about such a proposition as 'I know I have a brain'? Can I doubt

it? Grounds for *doubt* are lacking! Everything speaks in its favour, nothing against it. Nevertheless it is imaginable that my skull should turn out empty when it was operated on.⁷⁶

Just imagine that. The genius we all made (because we needed him) turned out not to have a brain! Maybe that would explain the stammering repetitions of his writings, or what I earlier called their childishness. Or maybe those repetitions are like the blows of a hammer whose force is being directed over and over against the same spot. Maybe that is how a man of destiny hammers at his prison wall. Maybe it is both. Maybe to be a man of destiny is to be that man-child, to never grow up and to never take up the adult mantle of imprisoning others in turn.

Maybe if a write a biography of Ludwig Wittgenstein that hammers with him at this same spot I will both help him and show you what he was really about. Maybe that is it. But if that is how I do it, then there must be sacrifices. 'Do women scream different from men?' What an interesting question that is! But I am afraid that it is going to have to be sacrificed. Did you know that during World War Two they began to discover that in moments of stress or emergency, male pilots responded best and most instinctively to a woman's voice? I suppose this was an extension of the way that dying male soldiers throughout all time have cried for their mothers. After World War Two, the female voice became the standard feature of aircraft warning systems for military and commercial aircraft. This has only started to change recently, with the rise in the number of female pilots. Augustine found it impossible to resist the voice of his Christian mother, Monica, who kept on at him until he at last made his famous conversion; while Ludwig's mother was a comparatively silent voice in his life. Again: Isn't that interesting? Augustine wrote so much and so fluently, while Ludwig wrote so little and so stutteringly. And yet it may just as well mean nothing at all. Either way it is going to be sacrificed here. Because unless some sacrifice like this is offered, we will not have made the clean break that will allow us to pass over to the next chapter.

* * *

Because all the horrors of the world occur as we peer down microscopes. Or down viewfinders. Everything before the lens, obeys the lens. That is the secret. The twentieth-century Russian writer Mikhail Bulgakov knew this secret. He knew that the only story worth writing is the story of what happens when you give a voice to things *so that they can at last speak back at the lens*. Then, and only then, will you see who has been playing along and who hasn't. Censorship isn't censorship, if it is gone along with. Hell isn't hell, if it is lived in. The Devil isn't the Devil, if he is God.

> Persikov nimbly slid off the stool, leaving the adjustment screw turned halfway, and slowly turning a cigarette in his fingers, he went into his assistant's office. There, on a glass table, a semi-chloroformed frog, fainting with terror and pain, was crucified

on a cork plate, its translucent viscera pulled out of its bloody abdomen into the microscope.

'Very good,' said Persikov, bending down to the eyepiece of the microscope.

Apparently one could see something very interesting in the frog's mesentery, where as clearly as if on one's hand living blood corpuscles were running briskly along the rivers of the vessels. Persikov forgot his amoebas and for the next hour and a half took turns with Ivanov at the microscope lens. As they were doing this both scientists kept exchanging animated comments incomprehensible to ordinary mortals.

Finally, Persikov leaned back from the microscope, announcing, 'The blood is clotting, that's all there is to that.'

The frog moved its head heavily, and its dimming eyes were clearly saying, 'You're rotten bastards, that's what...'[77]

The essential business of language is to assert or deny facts. Given the syntax of a language, the meaning of a sentence is determinate as soon as the meaning of the component words is known. In order that a certain sentence should assert a certain fact there must, however the language may be constructed, be something in common between the structure of the sentence and the structure of the fact. This is perhaps the most fundamental thesis of Mr Wittgenstein's theory. That which has to be in common between the sentence and the fact cannot, so he contends, be itself in turn *said* in language. It can, in his phraseology, only be *shown*, not said, for whatever we may say will still need to have the same structure.
—BERTRAND RUSSELL, from his Introduction to the *Tractatus Logico-Philosophicus*

Every transfinite consistent multiplicity, that is, every transfinite set, must have a definite aleph as its cardinal number.
—GEORG CANTOR, 1899

If one paints someone's portrait, one should not know him if possible. No knowledge. I do not want to know him at all. I want only to see what is there, the outside. The inner follows by itself. It is mirrored in the visible.
—OTTO DIX, *German expressionist painter*

3

Numbers Station

IMAGINE WHAT IT would be like to live only in your muscles, blood, and bones. Yes, brainless, if you like; but not heartless. Imagine if instead of thinking you only moved, so that your whole knowing consisted of departures and arrivals and journeys, climbs, and descents. Imagine, too, that you never moved for the sake of right or wrong but for love. Imagine that for that love you followed a voice that told you were to go and how. Imagine, then, that obedience was the sensation of always occupying a moment of space-time, though without the flanking of rightness and wrongness, positivity and negativity, truth and falsehood. Imagine, then, that each moment of space-time was undefined; that it was untouched by even this, the most basic, binary form of definition. Imagine, then, that though you followed a voice you never yourself spoke a word—And that never having spoken a word, you had never in fact noticed the moments of space-time. Or what is the same thing, that never having noticed the moments of space-time, you had never been moved to predicate something of them; to define them.

***

Imagine being this innocent, this brainless. Imagine how it would allow you to experience the earth. For nothing on the earth would be a mystery to you, and you would never wonder at it, like men do now, placing themselves in the place of 'not-understanding', forming questions, and then going on to answer them themselves. That is, forming questions within the same logic that supplies methods and answers. That is again, forming answers and methods first, then asking questions (though never, ever admitting this publicly). I alluded to this all the way through the previous chapter. The modern scientific and mathematical paradigm of truth is perfectly symmetrical in time; where this must needs make it also disingenuous, if not downright false and dishonest. This is where we left things in the last chapter.

***

Just think about it: What is the difference between 4 and 2 + 2? Nothing at all. And yet 4 is an answer, while 2 + 2 is a question. And worse, the ability to ask questions has apparently been the pride of the human race, whilst the libraries full of answers have been held up over and again as its greatest treasure. Wisdom! Yet I ask again: If questions and answers are identical, such that you only ever find what you went looking for, then where is the credibility in that? Mental intelligence walks straight past originality and surprise, and straight up to what it has come to expect. Against this modus operandi, physical intelligence is another world. In the world of physical intelligence, every footstep is a revelation and unrepeatable afterwards. And nothing is noted down, and nothing is remembered (because you can't *say* revelation afterwards).[1] In the world of mental intelligence, the answer came first: God is dead. Then the perfectly symmetrical methods and discoveries came afterwards. Darwin and the Big Bang.

WHAT WE CAN CONFESS

There are natural-born savants who offer a fast-forward version of this. A dropped bag of peas, and they can tell you exactly how many of them are on the floor. The precision of their answer is obvious, for really there can only be *a number* of peas on the floor, no more, no less. And we would arrive at that number ourselves if we were to stop and count them out. We call that number *the answer*, and the act of stopping and counting the peas is the act of its perfect symmetry. Except that the number of peas has *already happened*, while the act of perfect symmetry to it takes time. I should strictly speaking say that the act of perfect symmetry to it *is* time; because I spent most of the last chapter explaining that the world of the already-happened is timeless and eternal. The savant simply has a way of skipping the act of perfect symmetry and arriving directly at the number—Folding one moment of time into another. That is all they are doing; though it is remarkable.

But I want you to go back to imagining yourself as living only in your muscles, blood, and bones. Doing the opposite to thinking and mimicking the universe of numbers, and getting down on your knees and confessing *facts*—Because what else, other than facts, can there be to confess? How else can you say things that are true?

It is interesting in this regard to consider Wittgenstein's Jewishness. Everybody seems to accept that Jewishness is a case of its own. It is a traceable blood-fact about someone, yet it means so much more than other such traceable blood-facts. It means so much more, for example, than 'Englishness'. It is not an idle characteristic; it implies a people of destiny, exile, diaspora and, of course, a great and ancient religion. Throughout history, this blood-fact of the Jews has generated suspicion and envy, as though it must mean that they always harbour an agenda and an allegiance at odds with whichever country they are residing in. In Western Europe, this has mixed poisonously with the historical fact of the Jews' rejection of Christ, then poisonously again with their disproportionate achievements in arts and culture, industry and finance. Human nature is always on the lookout for reasons to discriminate, so the Jews have been a notoriously conspicuous target. So, for all these reasons, Jewishness, as a blood-fact, has become firmly situated within the universe of mental intelligence. It has become as factual as stating one's age. It cannot be altered by its bearer in the way that they might alter their name or nationality, or even skin colour. Over your Jewishness you can only lie or tell the truth. You cannot go inside your blood and alter it.

So it happened that in 1936, Wittgenstein spasmed and panicked, and passed over for a second from his native place of physical intelligence and forced some close friends and family to hear his confession. His family were forced to hear it in Vienna, at Christmas time; his Cambridge friends shortly afterwards, in the New Year, 1937. His friend Drury would remember it well:

When he [Wittgenstein] returned from Norway he told me that he had done no writing there but had spent his time in prayer. He had felt it necessary to write out a confession of those things in his past life of which he was most ashamed. He insisted on me reading this. He had already shewn it to Moore, and he said that Moore had seemed very distressed that he had had to read this.[2]

Also Fanja Pascal:

'I have come to make a confession.' He had just been to Professor Moore for the same purpose. 'What did Professor Moore say?' He smiled. 'He said, "You are an impatient man, Wittgenstein"...', 'Well, did you not know you were?' Wittgenstein, with disdain: 'I did not know.' I can remember two 'crimes' to which he confessed: the first had to do with his being Jewish in origin, the second with a wrong he committed when he was a teacher in a village school in Austria. On the first issue he said that he understood that most people who knew him, including his friends, took him to be three-quarters Aryan and one-quarter Jewish. In fact the proportion was the reverse, and he had done nothing to prevent this misapprehension.[3]

On the one hand, we might simply be looking here at the confession of the misapprehension that he had done nothing to prevent; the misapprehension that only happened to concern his percentage of Jewishness. But on the other hand, Wittgenstein's writings are littered with remarks on Jewishness that would indicate that he was haunted by the idea that the blood-fact of Jewishness might hold an explanatory power over the life of a man, so that he would be denying to his friends and the world this key to his biography. If that is indeed the case, then I am struck again at the perfect symmetry of these arrangements that mental intelligence bullies people into. Mental intelligence leans on you and says: 'Confess the underlying fact because there is no difference between that fact and your actions after it. From the eternal point of view, they are identical to it. They are the same event as it.'

Christianity has battled with this throughout its history. It has taught the doctrine of original sin, the doctrine that all men and women are damned by a sin of extraordinary antiquity unless they can be found by grace. And to thinking men, this has always appeared to destroy time and man's freedom within time, and in just the same way that $2 + 2 = 4$ does. Yet if they only paused to consider that $2 + 2 = 4$ is the same thing as to say nothing at all, and that 'all men are born sinful' is just as perfect a tautology, then they might be saved from their anxiety. Every preacher who has blasted fire and brimstone from the pulpit has technically said nothing at all. Or at most he has stated a condition of life on earth, as though he were to blast forth that all men must breathe air or drink water.

The idea that the truth of a human life would ever be such a confession of facts—facts that could be written down or recited to friends—is both ridiculous and fatal. As I put it in the previous chapter, it requires that you must leave yourself in order to observe and judge yourself—And then if you get a taste for this kind of certainty, that you must go on to actually become Godlike. The $=$ sign between $2 + 2$ and 4 is like a line running through and obliterating something. Something infinitely precious. Whenever you break down and confess some fact about yourself, that same line runs right through *you*.[4] For God's sake don't do it!

* * *

And I am not doing it here, in this book, either. I am determined that we will not confess the facts of Wittgenstein's life, but that we will find a way to continue with *this* narrative. Which, when you think about it, is as though we were making the facts of Wittgenstein's life do the confessing. As though we had at last found the point on which to shame them, as facts. This may sound alarming, but you are closer to the truth of it than you realise. For it is the same thing as to say that you know the facts of

Wittgenstein's life anyway. Because by this stage of Western knowledge, they are out there anyway. Wikipedia is no longer unreliable, it is *the truth*. Read it, and you will have the whole of Wittgenstein's story. And if you want more, if you want more facts, then there are places you can go on the Internet to get them, too. Once upon a time, it was the role of the book to give us the 'true and authorised version'. But that was once upon a time. If you are reading this book, then you must be looking for something else. And I will try to give it to you.

* * *

In a better frame of mind altogether (when he was over his confessing frame of mind), Wittgenstein would be able to put it as I have been putting it since the start of this book: the human will belongs inside itself, moving itself, and that in stepping outside itself it at once sees itself as just an object. As just one object in a world of other such objects, each known and classed according to the eternal, ancient categories. Stable concepts of meaning and understanding, is what I called them.

> You cannot write anything about yourself that is more truthful than you yourself are. That is the difference between writing about yourself and writing about external objects … [5]
>
> You cannot assess yourself properly unless you are well versed in the categories … [6]
>
> When people have died we see their life in a conciliatory light. His life looks well-rounded through a haze. For *him* it was not well rounded however, but jagged & incomplete. For him there was no conciliation; his life is naked & wretched.[7]
>
> The less somebody knows & understands himself the less great he is, however great may be his talent. For this reason Freud, Spengler, Kraus, Einstein are not great.[8]

So again, I ask you, imagine yourself alive in just your muscles, blood, and bones. Your will within itself, moving itself. And I want you to consider how really apart and un-classifiable is that place. In the world of mental intelligence, where 2 + 2 = 4 is Lord and King of all, everything is so God-damned ethical and good. Everything has form and purpose and reasons for existence. And everything is auto-censored and peer reviewed. In everything they say or do, everyone is right, 100% of the time. You know, I have never yet read a paper or a book that starts: 'What follows is totally wrong'. Those papers and books could be written, but it is just that they would never be published; and if published, they would get shouted down and burnt by this world. So instead everyone only writes what they believe to be the truth. And yet hundreds of thousands of papers and books get published every year, so they can't all be the truth. And so there are arguments between the hundreds and thousands of truth-heads. But only arguments of words and ideas. And so I often think: 'If you really believe that what you are saying is the truth—and I mean *the truth*; the truth of the philosophers and the prophets—then why not that you and the person you are shouting at just properly fight it out tooth and nail?'[9]

Are you really surprised at me saying that? You spent all that money to get educated because you thirsted after the truth, and then you found it, and now someone else is telling you you're wrong. And that's just fine, is it? If that same person had insulted your wife you would have gone bananas; and yet here is the truth which is apparently meant to be so much more important than her, and instead you're having a debate about it.

This is the whole weakness and lie of what the Western world of mental intelligence calls 'truth': That it turns out, always, to be not worth fighting for. It's just a game; it's just a 'language game', as Wittgenstein would later on put it (wait for Chapter 4). It's just for kicks. It's just for pride. It's fascinating, not vital. Which means that it's not really a replacement for religion, because religion is of course something that is worth fighting for. And it is certainly no replacement for your wife.

How would this whole, mental game of life end? It would end with you going back into your muscles, blood, and bones. For there and only there, can there be no ethic left to tempt your mind out into self-consciousness. Instead, there is only what I called in the last chapter destiny, the forwards tilt of our souls (our will), and language, and words as the 'wild whooping sounds of our tilting forwards'.[10]

> If you exclude the element of intention from language, then its whole function collapses.[11]

AS GENUINE AS A KISS

If you lived in this way, never doing anything for a reason that you had worked out in advance, but following the voice you loved (God's voice); if in your innocence you never raised a question of wonder against the earth and all creation, then your wisdom *would be* the physical sensation of your body in fluid motion. It would be as potent and vivifying a sensation as the sexual act, except that it would be without the self-consciousness that makes that act as it is today. That is, momentary, anticipated and lusted over.

> Everything ritualistic (everything that, as it were, smacks of the high priest) must be avoided, because it immediately turns rotten. Of course a kiss is a ritual too and it isn't rotten, but ritual is permissible only to the extent that it is as genuine as a kiss.[12]

It would be the sensation of one unending sexual act. The whole power of its oblivion, but without having to be started and stopped. It would be the normality of your life, and not, as it is today, the fleeting refuge from it. Try to imagine just the physical sensation of the sexual embrace, its peace and belonging—But without any of the disturbing commentary of the illicit and the prurient. For this you wouldn't need a brain, or, at any rate, you wouldn't be aware that you had one. You would just need a heart to love with. So long as you were always moving, always running, always following, always obeying, you would be safe. The slightest hesitation, the slightest pause for enjoyment, and you would wake up from it and die.

> I don't know why we are here, but I'm pretty sure that it is not in order to enjoy ourselves.[13]

The Western icon of mental intelligence and all its virtues is a man sitting at a desk reading a book. A man sitting still, understanding things because they have been made to stand still themselves. Perhaps he is reading a biography of Wittgenstein. Well in that case the stable things he will be understanding will be things of Wittgenstein's childhood and upbringing. And then the = sign across from them to the things in his adult life which they caused. At the very least, he will learn that a dysfunctional family = a tortured and eccentric man with an incomprehensible philosophy. And the biography of Wittgenstein he is reading will have its author, except that you should never know that, if the author has done his job well from within the world of mental intelligence. Because if he has done his job well in that way, then he will hardly be visible in his words at all: for it will be as though the truth itself had written the book. In just the same way as we never write 2 + 2 = 4 but the truth does. But by now you will have seen that this biography is different. I am fighting with the truth all the way through it. I am wrestling *Him* word by word and trying to banish *Him* from the room. I am tired, I am exhausted. But look: I am here! You see, watch: I can reach out now and twist your nose! You see, there—You felt it! That's me doing that. You are alive; I am alive. Together we can beat the truth and save Wittgenstein from it!

In the excerpt from Bertrand Russell's Introduction to the English language edition of Wittgenstein's *Tractatus Logico-Philosophicus* which I have placed at the beginning of this chapter, Russell states:

> That which has to be in common between the sentence and the fact cannot, so he contends, be itself in turn *said* in language. It can, in his phraseology, only be *shown*, not said, for whatever we may say will still need to have the same structure.

If you now compare this to what I have been saying, you will see that this essential relationship between language, truth, and logic is at the same time everything that I mean by the devilry of mental intelligence. And you will also realize that I believe that Wittgenstein had an unusually precise fix on this, and that it haunted him. And that this haunting is solely to be found in his philosophy—That this haunting *is* what is there to be felt (not understood) in his philosophy.

If 2 + 2 is a fact and 4 is a sentence, then the = sign is 'that which is common between the sentence and fact', and which cannot 'be itself in turn *said* in language'. Similarly: if Karl + Leopoldine = Ludwig, then the = sign is an outrage and an omertà. We are never *explained* like that. What we in fact are is our capacity to wilfully change our minds one million times a second. *That* is who we are. And the man of destiny is most of all like that. That is his character. And that character of his comes from nowhere. He is trying so very hard to live in that mystical magical space which the = sign strikes through, and no one else seems to be able to understand the strain of that. He is trying so very hard to live in the very place that the = sign says does not exist. So, there is not even anything that he could point to that would explain his distress.

> How God judges people is something we cannot imagine at all. If he really takes the strength of temptation & the frailty of nature into account, whom can he condemn? But if not, then these two forces simply yield as a result the end for which this person was predestined. In that case he was created so as either to conquer or succumb as a result of the interplay of forces. And that is not a religious idea at all, so much as a scientific hypothesis. So if you want to stay within the religious sphere, you must *struggle*.[14]

Let me tell you now about the house that Ludwig helped design.

HAUS WITTGENSTEIN

As I told you in the last chapter, Wittgenstein ended up in Cambridge in 1911, working there in philosophy with Bertrand Russell. He would stay until 1913, before returning home to Austria and joining the Austrian army in 1914, at the beginning of World War One. Throughout the war and during his internment as a prisoner of war in northern Italy (in Como, followed by Cassino), he would wrestle with philosophical problems in his notebooks. Shortly after the war, in 1921 the results of these notes would be published in 1921 as the *Logisch-Philosophische Abhandlung*; the world famous English-language edition appearing the following year as the *Tractatus Logico-Philosophicus*. With this event, Wittgenstein would declare himself to have solved all the traditional problems of Western philosophy. In fact, between 1919 and 1929, he would not return to Cambridge but to his native Austria, where he would try hard to make a new post-philosophical life for himself. He trained as an elementary school teacher in Vienna and soon there afterwards took up his first teaching post—in the village school of Trattenbach, in rural Lower Austria, in 1920. This was followed by posts in Hassbach and Puchberg am Schneeberg—both also in Lower Austria. In 1924, Wittgenstein would move to his final school: in the village of Otterthal, not far from his original posting at Trattenbach. Here, in Otterthal, in 1926, his career as a schoolteacher would end spectacularly.

There was an 11-year-old boy in his class called Josef Haidbauer. He was not especially bright and struggled to follow Wittgenstein's lessons; meanwhile, it seems that Wittgenstein had displayed a history of impatience with slow learners like Josef. Actually, something more akin to violent panic, or horror, at the realization that he was not teaching them but *manipulating* them or *conducting* them. Which, in view of what we have been observing of his acute sensitivity to the ineluctable, mechanical relationship between mental intelligence and the already-happened, would be a very violent panic or horror indeed.

> A teacher who can show good, or indeed astounding results while he is teaching, is still not on that account a good teacher, for it may be that, while his pupils are under his immediate influence, he raises them to a level which is not natural to them, without developing their own capacities for work at this level, so that they immediately decline again once the teacher leaves the schoolroom. Perhaps this holds for me; I have thought about this. (When Mahler was himself conducting, his private performances were excellent; the orchestra seemed to collapse at once if he was not conducting it himself.)[15]

In this instance, Wittgenstein went too far and struck the boy a number of times, knocking him unconscious. Josef had failed to draw a Corinthian column correctly. Most accounts agree that Wittgenstein immediately dismissed the class, carried the boy to the headmaster's office, and then fled. On 28 April, it is recorded he handed in his resignation to the local schools inspector. What followed was a district court hearing on 26 May 1926 in Gloggnitz. Wittgenstein evidently attended but lied to the judge about the extent and severity of his corporal punishments. This lie and his violent treatment of Josef and many of his other students wracked his conscience for ever after. It would become, as we saw from the Fanja Pascal quotation above, one of the two crimes he would confess a decade later to his family and close friends. In the court at Gloggnitz, the judge swiftly determined that Wittgenstein must be suffering mentally in some way or other and adjourned the court in order to allow for the collection of psychiatric assessments on his state of mind. This was the point at which the Wittgenstein family probably used their wealth and influence to intervene. No psychiatric assessments ever surfaced, and the case was not recorded to have reached a conclusion. Down in the depths and fingering thoughts of suicide, Wittgenstein took a job as assistant gardener at the Brothers of Mercy Monastery at Hütteldorf. (This was, as it happens, Wittgenstein's second stint as an assistant gardener—in 1920, between teacher training and his first post at Trattenbach, he would perform the role at the monastery at Neuberg.) It was then that Wittgenstein's sister Margaret stepped in with an idea. She had since 1920 been living separately from her husband Jerome, and in 1926 was a year into having a new house designed and built for her on the Kundmanngasse in Vienna. Karl Wittgenstein had died 13 years earlier, on 20 January 1913, leaving his children to inherit his vast fortune. (His wife, Leopoldine, would die on 4 June 1926.) Fearing that Ludwig may well take his own life if left to his own devices, she had the clever idea of inviting him to collaborate on the designing and building of her new house—A fantastic modernist palace of a building, as it was then coming together. The two architects already working on it were Paul Engelmann and Jacques Groag. Paul was an old army friend of Ludwig's. It was a good idea, and Ludwig accepted.

I want us to recall where we were before taking up with Haus Wittgenstein. I had impressed upon you that there is a point of view from which the function of identity (=) must look arbitrary and malicious. And you know now that I call this point of view 'physical intelligence'. You only have to stop and really think it through to realize that the only thing that makes 2 + 2 identical to 4 is the identity sign itself. Because things that stand apart enough to be compared must also then be different enough *not* to be identical. *Never* to be identical. To be able to type 2 + 2, and then after it, '4', means that they stand sufficiently apart from each other *never to be identical*; save for the identity sign which summarily makes them so.

A Digression from Haus Wittgenstein on 'Identity'

It should now be becoming clear to you that mental intelligence lives and breathes by the identity sign. That is to say, without the identity sign, mental intelligence could not exist. Imagine again our innocent, as it were brainless, man of the opening of this chapter. Nothing in his world is mentally or intellectually defined. Recall how I said that he knew no rightness and wrongness, positivity and negativity, truth and falsehood. Only his Master's voice. From the point of view of mental intelligence, he knew nothing, then; for mental intelligence says that to know is to know the sense in which 'all cats are cats'. It is to know their defining, shared properties. We are by this stage, I hope, sensitive to the perfect symmetry at work here. Those shared properties have always existed. They have simply waited on a human being to come along and represent them in the word 'cat'. Here we are introduced to something truly strange and uplifting. Mental intelligence, though it purports to be the fount of all knowledge, is in fact the only means by which we *cannot know*!

Consider our man who follows only his Master's voice from place to place. He sees a cat in one place, then another cat in another place. Except to him, they are just two points along the way that he is being led. And he knows that he mustn't pause, mustn't stop. To do that would, as I said, be death. It would be death by understanding: for only the mind of a man can pause, stop, and then begin an alternative form of travelling using thoughts and imagination. Alternative to the authentic form of travelling by which a man places one foot in front of the other. Only a man can stand bone still and live out a life of the mind. But it is death to do that. For it is only as you physically halt *but mentally continue on* that you can have the thought (and it will be your first thought independent of your Master's voice) that you know nothing. Socrates' great thought.

> *Socrates:* ... just at present I would rather hear from you a more precise answer, which you have not yet given, my friend, to the question, What is 'piety'? When asked, you only replied, Doing as you do, charging your father with murder.
> *Euthyphro:* And what I said was true, Socrates.

> *Socrates:* No doubt, Euthyphro; but you would admit that there are many pious acts?
>
> *Euthyphro:* There are.
>
> *Socrates:* Remember that I did not ask you to give me two or three examples of piety, but to explain the general idea which makes all pious things to be pious. Do you not recollect that there was one idea which made the impious impious, and the pious pious?
>
> *Euthyphro:* I remember.
>
> *Socrates:* Tell me what is the nature of this idea, and then I shall have a standard to which I may look, and by which I may measure actions, whether yours or those of any one else, and then I shall be able to say that such and such an action is pious, such another impious.[16]

Western mental intelligence says that here is the start of the great conversation. The great conversation in which you start at zero and end with a mind full of the names of things. But if only you had never stopped and instead just followed your Master's voice; for then you would never have entered the world of the great conversation, the adventure of ideas, or whatever you want to call it. You would never have considered that for every *thing* there is its perfectly symmetrical counterpart idea—And more, that in the world of ideas you are not led like a slave or a child, but you lead yourself, with all the thrill and dignity that comes from doing that.

But if you had only followed your Master's voice to the end, you would never have had to start at zero, to *create* that zero, in order to build your dignity upon it. *Before building your dignity upon it like a house on its foundations.* Instead you would simply be led from one thing to the next thing by your Master's voice. You would be totally and utterly dependent on his voice for your movement; for lacking mental intelligence, you would lack any independent means of generating movement. Because the independent, Godless movement of mental intelligence begins precisely as a man enervates himself to the point of absolute zero, then begins from there his private march to the highest number that he can manage by his life's end.

Imagine that you are actually in that pre-ethical, pre-rational state in which God is leading you by his mysterious will from one thing to the next. Everything you encounter is a new creation which expresses something about your Master which fills your heart with love and joy. In this timeless state, it is incorrect to say that you know anything, but just as incorrect to say that you know nothing. You could encounter a thousand cats in a row and never know that you were passing by the opportunity for analysis and reduction to the word 'cat'. Yet by exactly the same token, you would be safe and secure in something that no human being has been able to experience since the great loss of innocence. You would know that each *thing* you encountered was a new creation, all of its own, and that God made it. Here we stumble on to the full and consummate difference between the world of mental intelligence and the world of physical intelligence. In the world of mental intelligence, God is tolerated only so long as his power is conceived thus: 'One day, God determined that he was going to create cats (then after that giraffes and then hippos and so on).' This picture of God is the only one that is acceptable to man's pride. It says that God exists insofar as he is a mind with all of the seminal ideas inside him. In the mind of God is the idea of the perfect house; but as for the actual reality of that house, it is man who gestates it and raises it up. In this picture, God is subject to ideas and words, or to language, truth and logic. He is effectively as subject as man is. Except with this all-important difference: That the birth of each new human carries with it the possibility of ethically perfect behaviour within the world of *Language, Truth, and Logic*; whereas God's eternity has left him only with personal responsibility for every natural disaster and human tragedy—And therefore positively bankrupted his ethical standing. *It used to be said that God could create anything except what would be contrary to the laws of logic…*

In the world of physical intelligence, language, truth, and logic are impossible because stability of meaning is impossible. Each new creation is like a new meeting with God—Each new cat and giraffe and hippo is like meeting God for the first time all over again. Each is its own world, to the extent that the possibility of movement between these worlds is not something that can be accomplished in the mind, in theory, but by the feet, being obedient to an instructing voice.

> As a thing among things [in space and time], each thing is equally insignificant; as a world each one [is] equally significant. If I have been contemplating the stove, and then am told: but now all you know is the stove, my result does indeed seem trivial. For this represents the matter as if I had studied the stove as one [thing] among the many things of the world [in space and time]. But if I was contemplating the stove it was my world, and everything else colourless by contrast with it.… [Thus,] it is equally possible to take the bare present image as [a] worthless picture [of something] in the … temporal world [or] as the true world among shadows.[17]

At Genesis 2 19-20 you can read this:

> And out of the ground the Lord God formed every beast of the field, and every fowl of the air; and brought *them* unto Adam to see what he would call them: and whatsoever Adam called every living creature, that *was* the name thereof.
> And Adam gave names to all cattle, and to the fowl of the air, and to every beast of the field; but for Adam there was not found an help meet for him.

Whenever this is read, it is assumed that what Adam did for God here was merely to vocalize what had already happened. And in just the same way that God himself had merely created what had already happened (in the seminal ideas). However, we can now read this quite differently, thanks to the perspective of physical intelligence. According to physical intelligence, we encounter each new creation of God's as though it were its own unique world. More, its own unique world with its own unique language. In each case, that language will be then no more than a sound. A wild whooping sound. An outrushing hymn of praise to God. And the point of physical intelligence is that once each unique language has been sounded by man, it is over. *It is over forever.* For there are no regressions or retracings when you follow your Master's voice. Because the only thing that can link the worlds together is the command to move from one to the other. The idea of returning to one of the previous worlds could never be constructed from within this original innocence; because each new world cancels out its predecessor and that 'cancelling out' brings forth a sound of delight from man's lips.

I repeat: there is no identity between worlds, between things. The very idea of identity (=) is sin and evil. Adam and Eve and the Serpent are to blame for it. When the Serpent said to Eve, 'Did God really say?' he split what God had instructed from man's obedience and placed the identity sign in between. This was the first time in the history of everything that this had happened. This was the first 'ethical moment' in the history of everything. And in just the same way that cells split and multiply in the birth of any new being, these splits and identity signs have kept multiplying since the fall of man. If you want to say, 'In Hegelian, dialectical fashion', feel free. It has gone so far that there is now a whole rival and alternative world to the world of physical intelligence. But the price of living in this world is real and heavy and always paid in full. It is the price of having always to be bilocated either side of these billions upon trillions of identity signs (for of course we can only see them for what they are by simultaneously occupying the spaces either side of them). This continuous state of bilocation is called (mental) intelligence (remember Einstein above![18]). It is assumed that it is the only form of intelligence that there can be.

* * *

But now we know there is another kind of intelligence by which one would isolate and frame the identity sign over one's life, then disappear forever into it; and through it into new worlds. Karl + Leopoldine = Ludwig. There! Ludwig would disappear forever into that identity sign.

* * *

This disappearance can be achieved by suicide, yes:

> If suicide is allowed, then everything is allowed. If anything is not allowed, then suicide is not allowed. This throws a light on the nature of ethics, for suicide is, so to speak, the elementary sin. And when one investigates it, it is like investigating mercury vapour in order to comprehend the nature of vapours. Or is even suicide in itself neither good nor evil![19]

But there is another way, which I hinted at above, when I said, 'What we in fact are is our capacity to wilfully change our minds one million times a second.'[20] It is not for nothing that the identity sign has been called just that: the IDENTITY sign. Identity, personality, YOU. Just think about that for a second. I bet you never once thought about it in relation to you. More, in relation to the most vital and mysterious sense in which you are YOU. Think about all the times you were shown how to use the identity sign at school and university, and not once did anyone tell you *this* about it, did they? They gave it to you all the time to touch and hold, and never once did they tell you that you may as well have been handling ricin. For it is over identity that the great cosmological battle is being fought. The identity of humans.

This is probably the answer to the age-long question why God created man. When the Devil fell, he fell for mental intelligence. He fell for the numbers in the universe to which he, of course, had unparalleled access. Man was then created to take the battle to him, to thwart him with something called the free will, allied, as it was, to his corporeal nature. You see, having sold himself to the beauty and majesty of God's creation [yes, that is why he fell: he fell for it, plus his intellectual understanding of it, and turned away from his maker], the Devil was then of a sudden made to confront man in the Garden of Eden— Man, the addition to the universe, but so unlike anything else in it. For man had free will, like the angels; but now, and unlike them, he also had muscles, blood, and bones. Like the angels, his obedience to God was a free choice made in the innocence of any other alternative, except now he possessed also the capacity of actually *feeling* that free choice as a physical sensation. Here is the whole difference between a supernatural being like an angel and a half-supernatural, half-natural being like a man. A man is able to *feel* his whole relationship to God, with that feeling being infinitely preferable to the merely intellectual *fact* of it that the supernatural beings live within.

When you really love someone, it can be written down as a fact and taken up into the universe of facts. But the real meaning of that love to you is its warmth, is its blindness. The Devil relies on and works with the fact that you and all the rest of your human friends will strive to do the right thing all the time—Will choose value maximization, happiness, and life over death. These are the constants he works with. This is how he tempted Adam and Eve to fall. He threw open their blind love of God to the light of day. He led them up from the cave. And in the light of rational understanding, blindly following God didn't look so smart to them anymore (like some strange dictatorship). Except there was something he didn't reckon on. That same blindness that made it that their eyes could be opened has also left it that they can be closed again at will. I repeat: *at will*. The human animal alone of all the animals can will self-destruction. Can will a suicide. And if the human animal can walk straight through that Darwinian constant, then it can do anything—And it is this arbitrariness of 'anything' that really wrecks the Devil's plans.

He loves the identity sign. He invented it to be his prized possession and deadliest weapon. And of course it *is* prized and *is* deadly because it *is* true. It is true to say that Karl + Leopoldine = Ludwig in the sense that without them, he could not have been. Everything that science and mental intelligence knows is also in this way true. And most true of all is the world of the already-happened (Remember how I made this point against Gödel's incompleteness theorems and mathematical infinity in the previous chapter.). It is just that the world of the already-happened is the bird's-eye view that the angels see as they look down from eternity, while the blind, warm world of humans clinging to each other is the world of time and the present that human eyes can't see beyond. When we are bilocating ourselves up into that bird's-eye view to play the great 'game of chess' (again, of the previous chapter), and trying to do the right thing all the time, we are made ripe for the Devil's exploitation and *inhuman*. By turn, he becomes rational and reasonable and the world's first great ethicist; while God then becomes the world's first great tyrant, who kept our first parents like children in a cage.

However, I have told you that blindness, clinging, and warmth are man's great strength and glory, so that it is precisely his capacity to be wrong and mistaken (from the eternal point of view) that is the spanner in the Devil's plans. The Devil is the great biographer, scratching out lives and putting identity signs in their places. But he is helpless when the humans don't play along, instead to disappear into those identity signs and away from his view and control. The Devil has no contingency for the unpredictability of this. He can manipulate human fears and desires and most of all threaten man with death. But the man who laughs in the face of death and even embraces it conquers him every time.

It is this whole explanation of the mathematical and logical function of identity that explains also why Wittgenstein once remarked to his friend Drury that he could not

> ... help seeing everything from a religious point of view.[21]

It is also the whole explanation of his cryptic remark to the philosopher G. E. Moore about Otto Weininger:

> Thanks for your letter. I can quite imagine that you don't admire Weininger very much, what with that beastly translation and the fact that W. must feel very foreign to you. It is true that he is fantastic but he is *great* and fantastic. It isn't necessary or rather not possible to agree with him but the greatness lies in that with which we disagree. It is his enormous mistake which is great. I.e. roughly speaking if you just add a '~' to the whole book it says an important truth. However we better talk about it when I come back.[22]

Weininger was an Austrian Jew and self-proclaimed genius who published a book called *Geschlecht und Charakter* (*Sex and Character*) in 1903 when he was 23. Unfortunately, the book did not make the immediate impact that its author had imagined. This determined him to commit suicide. On 3 October 1903, he took a room in the same house in which Ludwig van Beethoven had died, and at ten o'clock that night, shot himself in the chest. He was discovered next morning by his brother, bleeding and unconscious but still marginally alive. He was rushed to hospital but died later that morning, at a half past ten. The news of his death and its circumstances soon spread and created a huge stir of interest in Weininger and his book in educated Viennese circles. Wittgenstein evidently read it whilst a schoolboy along with most of his family. *Sex and Character* was choreographed around the strident assertions of the pathological femininity of racial Jewishness and, in turn, the pathological inferiority of sexual femininity. Only pure masculinity had the capacity for genius, aloofness, and a kind of Platonic love of God conceived intellectually as the Absolute. Pure femininity was simply too bound up in its role in sex and the reproductive processes of life. That is to say, femininity learns early on that it must make itself alluring to masculinity; then after this, it learns again that it must take the all-important lead in the caring and nurturing of the young. It is simply the case that femininity cannot raise its eyes from this round of necessities to fix them for any length of time on the *abstract*. However, there was far more to Weininger's project than just this summary judgement. These provocative ideal types were designed by him to be the ultimate coordinate points, in between which the reality of human sexuality was taking place all the time as a constantly adjusting triangulation on the two.

> Amongst human beings the state of the case is as follows: There exist all sorts of intermediate conditions between male and female—sexual transitional forms. In physical enquiries an 'ideal gas' is assumed, that is to say, a gas, the behaviour of which follows the law of Boyle-Guy-Lussac exactly, although, in fact, no such gas exists, and laws are deduced from this so that the deviations from the ideal laws may be established in the case of actually existing gases. In the same fashion we may suppose the existence of an ideal man, M, and an ideal woman, W, as sexual types, although these types do not actually exist. Such types not only can be constructed, but must be constructed. As in art so in science, the real purpose is to reach the type, the Platonic Idea. The science of physics investigates the behaviour of bodies that are absolutely rigid or absolutely elastic, in the full knowledge that neither the one nor the other actually exists. The intermediate conditions actually existing between the two absolute states of matter serve merely as a starting-point for investigation of the 'types' and in the practical application of the theory are treated as mixtures and exhaustively analysed. So also there exist only the intermediate stages between absolute males and females, the absolute conditions never presenting themselves.[23]

Notwithstanding the peculiar contemporaneity of this, Weininger's overall thesis on the fluidity of male and female, his book would set out so many dogmatic and unambiguous statements on woman's biological and ontological sordidness that it soon becomes unpleasant, ideological reading. The book starts in a place that has always been promising and exciting: this being the mysticism of male and female, the connections and combinations of the two, and how these might hold the key to everything. Yet it presses home too keenly to a conclusion. It is the great work of a young man. To repeat Wittgenstein: 'It is his enormous mistake which is great'.

I don't think this observation of Wittgenstein's has ever been put into the context that I have put it into here. I have claimed that there is a world of things which have already happened, which would be this world and all its events, but in their final outworking; and that this already-happened world can be tapped into and represented by mental as opposed to physical intelligence; and that mental intelligence is for that reason inhuman and the opposite of living in the blindness of the moment, for it steals from us all the joys and advantages of that blindness—The greatest example of which would be the blindness of falling in love with someone. What I mean is, if falling in love meant falling in love with the *right* person, then you couldn't do it. How, across all this world's time and distance could you ever be sure of finding *that* person? So instead you turn blind to that truth, and fall in love with someone of your time and place. In other words, you don't do the right thing, but the *wrong* thing. You commit a mistake. There is, then, I think, a scale or a measure of greatness by which you do not do the right things that science or ethics prescribe but the wrong things. Clearly Wittgenstein wanted to associate himself with Weininger. This fact has never been disputed. But the grouping of Wittgenstein with Weininger *and* Vienna *and* suicides *and* genius *and* Jewishness *and* fin de siècle tragedy *and* all the rest of it—*This* represents exactly the agenda that he was trying to avoid and to disappear through and from. *This* is exactly how mental intelligence writes the biographies of each of us and then fits them into the wider circles of the histories of movements and periods, and then those histories into their places within the greatest book of them all: the book of the already-happened.

* * *

So, the only way to escape from and defeat all of this is to be wrong and mistaken from the point of view of what is right. If right is a straight line, then don't be that, and so on.

* * *

The true geniuses are all the time noticing the straight lines for what they are and deviating from them. And they are doing this whilst at the same time remaining acutely sensitive to how their new bent lines are liable to become the next set of straight lines before long. So, before that can happen, they begin a new set of deviations. There is no predicting when and how these deviations will occur. The true geniuses are impossible to follow or imitate or live with for long. They are changing their minds all the time. Because by doing this, they are violating and vanquishing mathematical identity's hold over their lives. *This was Ludwig Wittgenstein.*[24]

A Digression from Haus Wittgenstein on 'Genius'

But is this what we the great public mean by genius and demand of it? I don't think it is; in fact, I am sure it isn't. I believe that the historical geniuses have been tears, or holes, in the Devil's intricate weave. They mark the only points at which it has been

permanently compromised. The stitch work of the devil's weave goes: =========
==================. Each '=' is one of us; except for the geniuses, who have found their ways to evacuate their '='. The on-going fix for this has been the worldwide propagation out of Europe of the methods of fact-finding and historical narrative and psychology and biography. The Devil has no actual way of repairing the damage that a genius does. So the best he can do is this international job of distraction, so that people will walk around the holes and not fall through them. Actually, he has done rather better than that. The Devil has turned it around so that the geniuses have become the very points at which his weave appears to stitch neatest and closest together. He makes it that the genius is the adjective that we would like to be able to have over our own lives.

However, if we are the nouns, then we cannot also be that desirable adjective. Someone else has to be it. This someone else is the genius. This explains our peculiar relationship to the genius. On the one hand, we must be able to praise him for the selected achievements in our lives for which *we would like to be praised*. But on the other hand (lest this transference become too see-through), we must also send him up as being sufficiently different to us. Sufficiently *inferior to us*. Here the genius's inborn compulsion to 'deviate', to 'revolve', and to be mistaken comes to our rescue. For it is such as that we can re-describe it as 'eccentricity', or 'dysfunctionality'. By this means, we identify it with the genius personality type so neatly and closely, that the only explanation of it becomes, in the end, the genius. So, on the one hand, the accomplishments of the genius must be such as that they can be appreciated and understood and criticized by the best of our discerning selves. As things that we might have said or done or written ourselves. But on the other hand, in ways that would almost certainly be superior—certainly more organized and structured and rounded out—had we actually done it all ourselves.[25]

If the genius could not be understood, translated, and catalogued by us, he would just be a fool. A genius always starts out as a fool, right up until the moment when he becomes understood, translated, and catalogued.[26] Thereafter, he lives this strange double existence. He exists at our pleasure, in our pay. He is ours—Our life and our thoughts, our papers and our books and our careers. We clothe him, we feed him, we set him up with things to do. And he goes on and does them in the only way that he knows how. And then afterwards we arrange it all, and finish it off, and clasp the precious new knowledge to our breasts. But to him it was nothing; it was thoughtless, it was obvious. It was just how he happened to see the world through the eyes he had been given. It was nothing more than that. It was never related to his private struggle against identity and the Devil's weave. He was brainless; just all heart and those eyes of his. So, we gave him a brain like ours and made it spin at impossible speeds and called him a genius. But it was only ever that he saw a danger that we could not see and struggled against it.

* * *

There is always, then, a separation—a separation of worlds—between what the geniuses do for us and what they do for themselves. A separation between services rendered and destiny.

*　*　*

It is more severe than that, I think. I find it striking that all the great works of genius are always such that they can be (and are) faked afterwards by talented people. In the whole long history of the relationship between genius and normality, this is such a great white elephant that I have never seen it sufficiently addressed. The products of genius can invariably be faked to the point of their being indistinguishable from the originals. *What does that mean?* Some might say: 'It means that to be a genius is to do something first, like inventing the wheel. Because a billion wheels hence doesn't diminish the genius's status.' But I reply that we don't then go on and say that the first wheel was the original, and all the rest have been fakes! And yet this is exactly what we *do say* in the case of art. Because we *do seem* to invoke a tacit distinction between the invention of merely common things like wheels and art, where in the latter case each and every product is said to be an original of the artist's hand. And yet the international success of art forgery would seem to point the way to the possibility of the mass production of art in exactly the same way as the mass production of wheels. All of which suggests that the genius doesn't produce things that no one else could produce but rather the opposite. It suggests that the genius can only ever produce what another human could *in theory have produced themselves*. And it would seem, finally, that this must then be the chief requirement for the existence and recognition of the genius.

Let me explain this. I am saying it would seem that you cannot be a genius for having produced something *unrecognizable*. Nor can you be a genius in a vacuum. To be a genius you have to be seen, acknowledged, and recognized. Someone has to pick you up and say to the world: 'Look, he is doing exceptional things in *our* field!' You cannot be a genius without someone to catalogue your productions and adjudicate between them and the fakes. You cannot be a genius without an expert who knows better than you what you are about.

You know, I wouldn't bother with faking art; I would bother with faking an expert. That would be the way to make a killing. By the terms above, it is the experts who are really in mastery and control. It is all so far gone by this stage, that it would not be incorrect to say that they are the *authentic* and the genius is the *fake*. You think I've gone too far with that statement? OK, fine, no problem. Let me just ask you this: 'Who knows you better: you or your biographer?' I hear you panic and say, 'Me'. So I say to that: 'Really? Really? Do you know, then, what you are going to be doing in one day, or one year, or even in ten years' time? Because your biographer does. And what about your first days, years, and decades on this earth. Can you remember every minute of them, plus how each minute pointed inexorably to the next? Because your biographer does. He's got your whole narrative sewn up. He's the expert and you're the fake. That's the way it goes.' If you don't like the sound of all of that, if you think the meaning of a human life is more blind and physical than knowledge and the bird's-eye view, then repeat after Wittgenstein:

No one can think a thought for me in the way no one else can don my hat for me.[27]

And then this again, from note 63 in the second chapter:

My work consists of two parts: the one presented here plus all that I have *not* written. And it is precisely the second part that is the important one.

Let's go back to Haus Wittgenstein now and use it to summarise all of this.

BACK TO HAUS WITTGENSTEIN

Margaret wanted a new and landmark modernist palace built for her on the Kundmanngasse in Vienna, and she invited her brother Ludwig to help design it. The established architects already commissioned to it were, as we have already noted, Paul Engelmann, a star pupil and follower of the modernist pioneer Adolf Loos, and Jacques Groag, who would eventually make a career for himself in London, post-World War Two, as an interior designer and leading exponent of the second phase of Viennese Modernism. With two such professionals engaged to the work, the role and influence of Wittgenstein was always going to be contained; and indeed it has now been established that over the three years in which the house was designed and built (it was completed in December 1928), and the two in which he was involved (1926-28), Wittgenstein primarily focused on the design of the windows, radiators, doors, and doorknobs. Notwithstanding this, the house has passed into legend as a kind of standing testament to Wittgenstein's genius. That is to say, it has been added to the list of his accomplishments which we snigger and snort at. That's right: we proclaim genius whilst understanding and criticizing its achievements. Yet at exactly the same time we point and laugh at it. None of us would live and behave like *that*. Like *him*. Genius provides the originality upon which we swarm like parasites—And yet originality is the last thing that the genius is likely to think that they are about. Because remember that we live in just one world, while they live in a tear between the two—In a tear between the physical intelligence which is their inborn gift and the mental intelligence by which we deign to acknowledge them.

All of Wittgenstein's additions to his sister's house were certainly original and unique, and it is certain again that they helped make it something more than the visionary modernism it already was thanks to Engelmann and Groag. The house has survived today to become the Department of Culture of the Bulgarian Embassy and a listed and protected building. When you walk through it, you can feel everywhere that tear between the two worlds. The house confronts you with the dilemma of doing things explicably, or doing them inexplicably; between being justified in one's actions, and being unjustified in them.

> I have arrived at the rock bottom of my convictions. And one might almost say that these foundation-walls are carried by the whole house.[28]

The house confronts you with the fact that the house qua house—the Platonic idea of the house—stands symbolic for man's first defiance against God. It is the fig leaf without which human life apart from God would be unimaginable, as well as practically impossible. When man first defied God, he united rational defiance and practical necessity in a single conception. Thereafter, they would express themselves always as these two parts of the same idea; so that it is impossible to separate them or to say which came first. The first fig leaf was to be understood within the rational world of mental intelligence which said that the first business of naked humanity is to cover itself: and yet that rational world of mental intelligence could only have been instigated with the first fig leaf. All subsequent dwellings have expressed this. The pioneers of architectural modernism stripped the concept of the house back to its foundations and rediscovered that they could go no further than that the house exists to protect and preserve the nakedness of human ambition. No house can be considered 'a house' unless it does at least that. If it were to cast itself adrift of this imperative, it would become rationally impenetrable; it would become rationally un-analysable as the object 'house'. So, the archetypal modernist house presents us with a paradigmatic expression of the outer limits of this world of mental intelligence. It becomes a standpoint from which we can survey the history of architecture and ornamentation as the futile and tragic disregarding of these limits—Tending even to the belief that we create and play Godlike, with a free hand. The detail which Wittgenstein put into his sister's house shimmers between this world of necessity (and contingency) and his own. Wittgenstein's windows and radiators, doors and doorknobs are predictable qua the functional requirements of these objects in life, yet absolutely obedient to some hidden commandment of their own.

> Only something supernatural can express the Supernatural.[29]
>
> You cannot lead people to the good; you can only lead them to some place or other; the good lies outside the space of facts.[30]
>
> I think good Austrian work (Grillparzer, Lenau, Bruckner, Labor) is particularly hard to understand. There is a sense in which it is *subtler* than anything else and its truth never leans towards plausibility.[31]

So it would seem. The signature on all Wittgenstein's pieces in the house is that they make and mark the openings from our world—that is, the world of a house on the Kundmanngasse that does the job of a house—into his world. It has been said, often enough and truly enough, that Haus Wittgenstein is a fitting analogue of Wittgenstein's

Tractatus Logico-Philosophicus. It is; except not in the 'snigger and snort' way in which that comparison is usually made. Wittgenstein's *Tractatus* famously ends with the lines:

> The correct method in philosophy would really be the following: to say nothing except what can be said, i.e. propositions of natural science—i.e. something that has nothing to do with philosophy—and then, whenever someone else wanted to say something metaphysical, to demonstrate to him that he had failed to give a meaning to certain signs in his propositions. Although it would not be satisfying to the other person—he would not have the feeling that we were teaching him philosophy—*this* method would be the only strictly correct one.
>
> My propositions serve as elucidations in the following way: anyone who understands me eventually recognizes them as nonsensical, when he has used them—as steps—to climb up beyond them. (He must, so to speak, throw away the ladder after he has climbed up it.) He must transcend these propositions and then he will see the world aright.
>
> What we cannot speak about we must pass over in silence.[32]

In terms of content and thesis there is really nothing much more to the *Tractatus* than that. Remember it, and you have remembered all of it. Speech is not a free activity like running. It is not physical. The idea that you are as free to *say* 'I heard God today' as you are to say 'I stubbed my toe today' is incorrect, and this incorrectness is the source of all the traditional problems of philosophy. Running is a true exercise of the free will because your feet prove to you that you may take off in any direction you like, then change your direction any which number of times afterwards. Speech is the antithesis of this. There is only one way to speak, and that is to be understood: and only one way to be understood, and that is to speak the truth: and only one way to speak the truth, and that is to become the mouthpiece of the already-happened. That stone you stubbed your toe on really did come towards you from that future world, whereas God didn't. The stone you could point to afterwards to say that it was so, and happened like it did. But God was nowhere to be seen. (Except, perhaps along the torturous byways of this proof or that. But these are in any case those 'traditional problems of philosophy' of which I spoke.) This summary dismissal of the whole illustrious history of philosophy has tended to strike people as a move as daring and aloof and aristocratic as Haus Wittgenstein. As obvious as Haus Wittgenstein. As obvious as its wide high rooms and its cleared-out spaces; its cubes and angles and bare light bulb illuminations. Against Wittgenstein's *Tractatus* it is too easy to say that the traditional problems of philosophy exist because we feel at ease in their clutter—And that to cast them out achieves as little as to cast out all the comfort and history of one's home. However, to mount this response is to push too far beyond the purposes of the *Tractatus* and Haus Wittgenstein; for the point of both is their *ambidexterity* between the two worlds of Wittgenstein's life. And how they show in page and concrete what the price of admission to the other world is.

You can only *show* that there are these two worlds and that there is the possibility of choosing between them. Everything that involves thoughts and words—all doctrine all theory and all dogma—is tainted with the original sin's confident self-assertion. Christ died on the cross, and the thief who opened his eyes to what was happening was saved. In just this way was Wittgenstein trying to place things in that exact same place between the two worlds, so that we might *see*. We know this place already, and how it is notated by the identity sign. Mary + Joseph = the historical Jesus. Haus Wittgenstein and the *Tractatus* give us an entrance that makes sense to us from this world looking on. A house that fulfils the foundational requirements of a house and a book of philosophy that does the same. But then a house and a book that go on steadily and surely to erode and dismay the expectations of rationality and logic until they escape it altogether and disappear off the far end of it into some place where words cannot follow. A place where identity no longer exists to be seen and where going on means following the unpredictable and unbidden footsteps of a man. This way of following a man has become so scorned and discredited over the 2,500 years since the birth of Western philosophy that we have almost entirely forgotten what it tastes and feels like. We have become so used to following odourless weightless reason that we have forgotten it. When you stand inside Haus Wittgenstein and open its doors and look through its windows and wander its details you come eventually to this choice. The same occurs when you enter into the *Tractatus*. You come to the realization that logic, truth and language mastered you, not the other way around—That they mastered you all the way until they had totally sold you on the belief that understanding means spending your whole life studying this world, this universe—Right the way until one day it can be wrapped up tightly and perfectly in its single corresponding language, proposition on fact.

> We are inclined to use our idea of a building material in … [a] misleading way, and to say that the whole world, mental and physical, is made of one material only.[33]

You forgot, as I put it earlier, that each new footstep can be its own world and its own language. Mental intelligence deters us with the sheer impracticality of pursuing dreams that lie beyond the possibilities and restrictions of this world, and the geographical subsets of it in which we actually live. And so the price of admission into the other world becomes our standing, our credibility, and our respect. It is made out of the other's exasperation, perplexity, and anger. It is foolish, idiotic, and insane. It will exhaust all reserves of patience, strength, and capital—Right up until all that is left is to follow it to our destruction (in this world) and our life (in the other).

A recollection from Ludwig's sister Hermine of a detail from the finished Haus Wittgenstein:

> I remember, for example, how there were two small black cast-iron radiators, which were fitted into two corresponding corners of a small room; and how the symmetry

of the two black objects in the otherwise bright and open rooms created a good feeling! The radiators themselves were so perfect in their dimensions and in their precise smooth slender shape that it seemed only right when Margaret used them as a base for one of her beautiful arts and crafts items; and when I once expressed my admiration of these radiators to Ludwig, he told me of the ordeal it had been before he was able to arrive at the precision which gives them their distinct beauty, and how long this ordeal had lasted. Each of these corner radiators consisted of two parts, which are exactly at right angles to each other and brought together in the corner of the room, until only the smallest of gaps is left free between them, fixed to the millimetre. They rest on feet, on which, again, they had to fit exactly. Initially, Ludwig had complete models of the two radiator parts cast in Austria, but as the process went on it was discovered that these casts were too intricate to be poured. Thus they were forced to have the models cast and poured in sections abroad; but here again it was at first impossible to achieve Ludwig's required precision. There was much wastage. Whole sections had to be abandoned as unusable, while others had to be sharpened to within a half millimetre's tolerance before they would fit together. The mounting of the smooth closure pieces which were manufactured according to a different process added a new set of difficulties all of their own. Experiments were often continued until late into the night under Ludwig's direction—ending only once he had decreed that everything was just right. In total: one whole year was to pass between the design of these apparently simple and discreet radiators and their finished manufacture. And yet when I think now of their perfect form it seems to me that the time was somehow well spent.[34]

And another one from her:

The strongest proof of Ludwig's relentlessness with regard to precise measurements is perhaps the fact that he decided to have the ceiling of a hall-like room raised by three centimetres just as the cleaning of the completed house was to commence. His instinct was absolutely right and his instincts had to be followed. Finally... he had to declare that he was satisfied and hand over the house as completed. Only a staircase window at the rear of the house still did not suit him, and he admitted to me later that he had at one time participated in a lottery because of this window; had he won the main prize, the money would have been designated for this structural alteration.[35]

And here, the really well-known one from Jacques Groag, in a letter to his brother, Emo Groag:

I come home very depressed with a headache after a day of the worst quarrels, disputes, vexations, and this happens often. Mostly between me and Wittgenstein.[36]

But I don't want to stop there, on just these examples, from this house. Because we all know that in the popular and professional imagination, Wittgenstein's memory lives on as a whole series of such examples, spanning the whole of his life. Wittgenstein's memory lives on as one gigantic eccentricity, gathered up from the recollections of his smaller eccentricities, each of them swapped and traded like baseball cards—And all of it set against a fairy-tale background. I want to present you with some of the best known of them here, in chronological order. *Ironically*. But not before I have allowed Wittgenstein to make the point of the irony himself, in his own words.

> I can still produce my solipsism by saying, 'Only what *I* see (or: I see now) is really seen'. And here I am tempted to say: 'Although, with the word 'I', I do not mean L.W., it will be good if the others include 'I' in the sense of L.W., if at this moment I am actually L.W.'. I could express my thesis also by saying, 'I am the vessel of life'; but (note how) it is essential that everyone, to whom I say this, is unable to comprehend me. It is essential that the other person is not able to understand 'what I really *intend*', although in practice he can do what I want by conceding me an exceptional position in his notation. But I want it to be *logically* impossible for him to understand me, that is to say that it is meaningless, and not false, to say that he understands me. So, my expression is one of the many expressions that philosophers use on various occasions and suppose that they communicate something to those to whom they say them, even though they are essentially unsuitable for communicating something to someone.[37]

What Wittgenstein is saying here, is that the *living 'I'*, or the *'I' that sees*, or *You* when you are in a sentence on a page, can only be recognizable as such *by not being recognizable as such*. We are back at Gödel, as well as the Cantor and Dix quotes from the head of this chapter; for in the case of Wittgenstein's example, the *living 'I'* fulfils the conditions of *the infinite*. Where 'fulfils the conditions' is the very force of what Wittgenstein is here pointing out. Logical notation shows, truly enough, that the infinite potentiality of the human being can have no place within its scheme (for it would explode that scheme). Yet for 'the infinite' to mean something when we say it or write it, it must still have a place— In thought, in language, in logic, in mathematics, *it must still have a place*. And so it does. Look, I will write it for you again: 'the infinite'. Or in logic: '∞'. And so do *You*, or *I*, or *Wittgenstein* have a place on a page, if our names are invoked in order to have something said of us.

* * *

It is strange. It is terrifyingly strange. Could our infinity exist without our finity—Our souls exist without our bodies? Christian theology used to trouble itself a very great deal with this question. But it never could settle it, one way or the other. Then it got abandoned as a bad job; as a detached, medieval preoccupation. There were more pressing, social questions for theology to address itself to in this world. But the question never went away. It was too fundamental to do that. Instead, it just adapted itself to the coming thing, which was modern mathematics and modern logic. *The finite must be infinite to be finite.* And vice versa. This is how that old preoccupation of those old theologians preoccupies still today.

* * *

For example: I have written a biography of Augustine of Hippo. Yet if he walked past me in the street today, I would have no way of recognising him. Why? Simple, because no images of him have survived. I could not pick him out of a police lineup, no matter how hard I tried. Nor could anyone else. And we don't even have second-hand information to go on. We have no reliable information on, say, what birthmarks he may have had. We don't know what his voice sounded like. Or his accent.

* * *

Would I be able to recognise your soul on its own, outside of your body? Would you be able to recognise mine? And what does that mean for everything?

* * *

Think of how the sexual climax is immediately preceded by an intense moment of concentration. (Watch your faces, you close your eyes like the suicide takes off his glasses. You wake up and put yourself to bed.). On the one hand, it can't be stopped. On the other hand, you must work to overcome something. Again: What does that mean for everything? What does it mean if we can't be here without being there, and can't be there without being here? Try correspondingly to treat the thirty-six facts that are coming your way as apocryphal.

> Freud's fanciful pseudo-explanations (precisely because they are brilliant) perform a disservice. Now any ass has these pictures available to use in 'explaining' symptoms of an illness.[38]

THIRTY-SIX FACTS AS CARDS

1. At the age of 10, Ludwig becomes fascinated by the sewing machine used by the Wittgenstein household's seamstress. He begins to study the mechanics of the machine with great and close attention. Next, he takes off and constructs his own working model of the machine's action from wooden sticks and wire. To the amazement of his family, it proves able to make a few stitches in a test cloth.
2. He soon afterwards becomes fascinated by two books in his father's library. The first is *Theoretische Kinematik: Grundzüge einer Theorie des*

Maschinenwesens (*Theoretical Kinematics: Foundations of a Theory of Mechanical Engineering*, by Franz Reuleaux [1875]). The second is an old German edition of Heron of Alexandria's most famous inventions and experiments with air and water.

3. Between the ages of 14 and 16 he also reads and admires the writings of Arthur Schopenhauer, Ludwig Boltzmann, and Otto Weininger.
4. Whilst studying engineering at Berlin-Charlottenburg, he begins to keep diaries of his philosophical thoughts.
5. In 1908 he commences three years of research in aeronautical engineering at the College of Technology in Manchester, eventually patenting a radical new propulsion system for aircraft (we already know about this).
6. One of his friends from that time, William Eccles, recalls:

He used to ignore the midday meal break [at the College of Technology] and carry on till evening and in his lodgings his pastime was to relax in a bathful of very hot water. He had great musical appreciation, and only for the more profound composers: Wagner, Beethoven, Brahms, etc. I used to attend the Hallé concerts with him occasionally where he used to sit through the concert without speaking a word, completely absorbed.[39]

Another, Wolfe Mays, recalls:

When he first came to Manchester, Wittgenstein was very wealthy, and though he never lived ostentatiously he did not hesitate to get anything he wanted. On one Sunday morning in Manchester in 1910, for example, he decided he would like to go to Blackpool, and W. and W. Eccles went off together to the railway station, though he was told there was no suitable train. This did not deter him, he said he would see about ordering a special train, still possible in those days. He was dissuaded from doing this, and they took a taxi to Liverpool instead and had a trip on the ferry there before returning to Manchester.[40]

7. Whilst at the Manchester College of Technology, Wittgenstein also reads Bertrand Russell's *Principles of Mathematics* and Gottlob Frege's *Grundgesetze der Arithmetik*.
8. In 1911, whilst travelling back to Manchester from Vienna, he takes a detour to Jena and looks up Frege at the great man's home. He would later recount to Drury what happened:

'I remember that when I first went to visit Frege I had a very clear idea in my mind as to what he would look like. I rang the bell and a man opened the door; I told him I had come to see Professor Frege. "I am Professor Frege", the man said. To which I could only reply "Impossible!" At this first meeting with Frege my own ideas were so unclear that he was able to wipe the floor with me.'[41]

[We must notice that this is a prime example of physical intelligence, as we have been describing it. The ideas and mental intelligence are irrelevant (Frege wipes the floor with him); it is that physical intelligence causes his muscles, blood, and bones to put themselves unannounced on Frege's doorstop that is the telling fact.]

9. Later in 1911, Wittgenstein arrives at the University of Cambridge to hear Bertrand Russell's lectures. (We already know about this) [We have also already marked up this announced arrival at Cambridge as a standout example of physical intelligence.] He takes rooms at 4 Rose Crescent, in the town.
10. In 1912, Wittgenstein takes swift and decisive measures to distinguish and distance his motives from those around him. In a letter to Lady Morrell dated 9 November 1912, Russell would describe what happened after he and Wittgenstein had spent an afternoon watching boat races on the River Cam:

[After the race, Wittgenstein] suddenly stood still and explained that the way we had spent the afternoon was so vile that we ought not to live, or at least he ought not, that nothing is tolerable except producing great works or enjoying those of others, that he has accomplished nothing and never will, etc. all this with a force that nearly knocks one down. He makes me feel like a bleating lambkin.[42]

He additionally takes equally swift and decisive measures to expose and shame the hypocrisy of the professional Academy, viz., the disjunction between its declaration for truth at all costs and the pluralism which it in fact pursues through its practices and procedures. Worst of all is its attachment to the 'canon', and the canon's support of the idea of the historical evolution of thought and ideas in a sort of never-ending continuum. To the true man of destiny, it is disgusting and intolerable to be initiated into this cult of the mind (of mental intelligence). The mission of the man of destiny is to eschew all the trappings of this system—all respect and credibility, apprenticeship, and narrative—and instead plot one spectacular departure from this world. A blaze of fire and smoke and noise, like a rocket that leaves this earth and never returns (the *Tractatus*). In an undated letter to Friedrich Hayek, G. E. Moore would recall the following:

[A]t the beginning of the October term 1912, he came again to some of my psychology lectures; but he was very displeased with them, because I was spending a great deal of time in discussing Ward's view that psychology did not differ from the Natural Sciences in subject-matter but only in point of view. He told me these lectures were very bad—that what I ought to do was to say what I thought, not to discuss what other people had thought; and he came no more to my lectures. But this did not prevent him from seeing a great deal of me. He was very anxious at the beginning of this year to improve the discussion of our philosophical society, which is called the Moral Sciences Club; and he actually persuaded the Club, with the help of the Secretary and me, to adopt a new set of rules and to appoint me as Chairman. He himself took a great part in these discussions. In this year both he and I were still attending Russell's Lectures on the Foundations of Mathematics; but W. used also to go for hours to Russell's rooms in the evening to discuss Logic with him. Wittgenstein arranged to be coached in Logic by W. E. Johnson; but Johnson soon found that W. spent so much time in explaining his own views that he (Johnson) felt that it was more like being coached by W. than W. being coached by him; and Johnson therefore soon put an end to the arrangement.[43]

11. On 4 May 1912, he meets David Hume Pinsent for the first time at a 5 p.m. chamber concert at the Guildhall, Cambridge. Wittgenstein invites him to participate as subject in some experiments he is pursuing at the psychological laboratory into the extent and importance of rhythm in music. Pinsent was a mathematics undergraduate at Trinity College. He and Wittgenstein would form a deep and close friendship, broken only by World War One. Pinsent would become a test pilot at the Royal Aircraft Establishment at Farnborough and be killed in a flying accident close to the end of the war, in May 1918. Pinsent's diaries would become the source of some famous Wittgenstein stories.

12. In an entry dated 1 June 1912, Pinsent wrote:

He was very communicative and told me lots about himself: that for nine years, till last Xmas, he suffered from terrible loneliness (mental—not physical): that he continually thought of suicide then, and felt ashamed of never daring to kill himself: he put it that he had had 'a hint that he was *de trop* in this world', but that he had meanly disregarded it. He had been brought up to engineering, for which he had neither taste nor talent. And only recently he had tried philosophy and come up here to study under Russell, which had proved his salvation: for Russell had given him encouragement.[44]

13. 1912 is also the year for the meeting between Ludwig's sister Hermine and Russell, in Russell's rooms at Trinity College. Hermine would recall:

I went to visit Ludwig in Cambridge in 1912. He was friends with Russell, and Russell invited us to take tea with him in his beautiful College room. I can still see it before me with its bookcases covering all the walls from floor to ceiling, and the high windows with their beautifully articulated stone mullions. Suddenly Russell turned and said to me: 'We expect the next big step in philosophy to be taken by your brother.' To hear that like that was for me so outrageous, so unbelievable, that for a moment everything seemed to go black before my eyes.⁴⁵

14. In May 1912, in the lead up to the summer vacation, Wittgenstein suggests to Pinsent that Pinsent accompany him on a pony trek through Iceland. The suddenness and largeness of the suggestion flummoxes Pinsent—As does Wittgenstein's offer to pay for everything for both of them, up to and including new clothes for Pinsent. After some deliberation, Pinsent accepts. The trip offers opportunities for Pinsent to come up hard against Wittgenstein's distinction between the physical and mental way of experiencing the world. The physical being the sheer movement from place to place, and the mental being the experience of something only so far as you can place it within a wider purpose or frame of reference (as a subset). An example:

Later we went for a stroll. I took my camera with me—which was the cause of another scene with Ludwig. We were getting on perfectly amicably—when I left him for a moment to take a photo. And when I overtook him again he was silent and sulky. I walked on with him in silence for half an hour, and then asked him what was the matter. It seemed, my keenness to take that photo had disgusted him—'Like a man who can think of nothing—when walking—but how the country would do for a golf course'.⁴⁶

15. The next year, 1913, he takes Pinsent with him on an autumn trip to Norway. Here is another example from this time, of the wild inconsistencies of the physical way of life:

He is—in his acute sensitiveness—very like Levin in 'Anna Karenina', and thinks the most awful things of me when he is sulky—but is very contrite afterwards. The only other person in the world whom he knows as intimately as me—is Russell: and he has the same scenes periodically with Russell.⁴⁷

16. Struck with the possibilities for solitude in Norway, he leaves Cambridge for the country before the end of 1913; taking simple rooms in a guesthouse in Skjolden (actually, the postmaster's house there), a remote and rural spot of symbolic dimensions. It sits northeast of Bergen, at the head of the longest navigable fjord in Norway and the world—the Sognefjorden. It has not much changed today from when Wittgenstein was there. Before leaving Cambridge, he had complained of the flimsiness and frivolity of things there; and he evidently informed Pinsent and Russell that he planned to spend two years in Skjolden doing serious and important work on logic. The advent of World War One would, of course, cut short his second year there. But not before Wittgenstein had commenced construction

on a neat little retreat house—Just two rooms and perched somewhat precariously above the small lake behind the village of Skjolden (Lake Eidsvatnet). About 40 meters above the shore atop a near-vertical cliff. It was Wittgenstein's delight that the steep terrain made it impossible to walk into the house by land, from Skjolden. Instead, the only way in was by rowboat in summer and across the ice of the lake in winter. He used a bucket and hoist to bring water up from the lake for his use and a similar system for groceries. There exists a photo of Wittgenstein, in his element, rowing over. He would complete his house in 1915 and return to it for periodic stints throughout his life, his last visit coming in spring 1950, just a year before his death. He would stay for five weeks on that occasion. He would leave the house to a local Skjolden man, Arne Bolstad.

17. Ludwig's father Karl dies on the 20 January 1913 (we already know about this), leaving Ludwig to inherit a portion of his fortune (this, however, is news). Ludwig responds by immediately and anonymously disbursing a good deal of it (100,000 Kronen) among Austrian writers and artists (the most prominent including Rainer Maria Rilke, Adolf Loos, Oskar Kokoschka, and Georg Trakl); and then shortly after World War One, all the rest of it to his siblings. He would never regret this giant ascetic decision and would successfully resist all attempts by his family to help him financially and materially (much to their exasperation). When money was tight he was happy to be resourceful—Once even taking a job at the little fruit juice factory in Skjolden.

18. From Skjolden, in October 1913, Wittgenstein includes this in a letter to Russell:

Soon after I arrived here I got a violent influenza which prevented me from doing any work until quite recently. Identity is the very Devil and *immensely important; very* much more so than I thought. It hangs—like everything else—directly together with the most fundamental questions, especially with the questions concerning the occurrence of the SAME argument in different places of a function.[48]

19. In March 1914, G. E. Moore travels from Cambridge to spend two weeks with Wittgenstein in Skjolden for the purpose of examining Wittgenstein's *Notes on Logic*—The no longer extant writings of Wittgenstein's first period in Skjolden; the precursor to what he will produce in the *Tractatus*. The two weeks turns out to be a foreshadowing of Wittgenstein's schoolteacher days to come. He gets angrier and angrier whilst trying to make Moore see what he is seeing. But he never beats Moore. Moore tries to follow Wittgenstein as best he can and takes pages of notes. In fact, Moore is only there on Russell's insistence, because Russell hopes that Wittgenstein's *Notes on Logic* will be sufficient to earn him a Cambridge bachelor's degree in philosophy. Unfortunately, this puts Moore in the vexed position of being the interface between the intellectual requirements

of the degree, which *Notes on Logic* obviously satisfies, and the university regulations for the form and presentation of said requirements, which it obviously doesn't. In the meantime, Wittgenstein blows up, writing Moore this scintillating letter:

Dear Moore,

Your letter annoyed me. *When I wrote Logik I didn't consult the Regulations*, and therefore I think it would only be fair if you gave me my degree without consulting them so much either! As to a Preface and Notes; I think my examiners will easily see how much I have cribbed from [Bernard] Bosanquet.—If I'm not worth your making an exception for me *even in some* STUPID *details* then I may as well go to Hell directly; and if I am worth it and you don't do it then—by God—you might go there.

The whole business is too stupid and too beastly to go on writing about it so—
L.W.[49]

As a result of this, Wittgenstein never would get his B.A., and Moore would be left confused and devastated in regard to what had happened. Shortly afterwards, Wittgenstein would write a following letter to try to make friends with Moore, but Moore would never respond to it, and the two men would not speak to each other for fifteen years.

20. The advent of World War One and Wittgenstein rushes to volunteer for the Austro-Hungarian army. And as everyone knows, he serves there with great bravery and distinction, winning many medals. He just gets up and does this. Physical intelligence. Russell, on the other hand, approaches the Great War from the point of view of mental intelligence. From the point of view of the man of physical intelligence, i.e. from the point of the view of the man with no morals and guidelines, one may just as easily choose to fight as not to fight. But whichever way one chooses, one lives in the plain physicality of that choice, and the rest is silence. From the point of view of the man of mental intelligence, this silence is intolerable and an abnegation of one's (higher) duty. In the world of mental intelligence, war is always *wrong* and pacifism is a doctrine that pours itself fluently out in page after page. I don't know why this is; or if I do, I just don't want to say. It just is like that, and you know it, too. In the world of mental intelligence everyone is so great and certain of themselves; except that they aren't. And those like Wittgenstein are the mystical loonies, except that they aren't. This is why Augustine of Hippo's doctrine of the Two Cities is the only scalpel that cuts true for me. I am not interested in what other people call 'knowledge'. Never have been. The only knowledge that ever cut true for me was when I found out that this didn't have to be the only world. The only true knowledge is the hope and possibility of *a kind of reversal*. What if all the

loonies were not? And the same for good and bad, and so on. That's what always got me about the kind of book knowledge that you get in a Western education: it's like digging your own grave, shovel full by shovel full. What if God were as real as they say he isn't, so that all *this* reality—all *this* city and smoke—were shown to be the illusion? Now *that* kind of reversal would be true knowledge!

21. During the Great War, Wittgenstein gives 1 million Kronen to the Austro-Hungarian War Ministry with specific instructions that it be spent on the development of a new 30cm mortar; though the money is squandered by the Ministry and no new mortar is forthcoming.

22. During the Great War, Wittgenstein also comes across Leo Tolstoy's *The Gospel in Brief*—apparently in a bookshop in the southern Polish town of Tarnow, when the Austro-Hungarian army had it under occupation. Apparently, it was the only book in the bookshop, so that is why he bought it. By Wittgenstein's own account, this book would get him through the darkest days of the war, and because he would recommend it without hesitation to any of his brother soldiers in distress, he would even become known as 'the man with the Gospel'. From this book Wittgenstein would receive a great deal of encouragement in his chosen style of life—the ascetic style—as well as a glimpse of a physical kind of Christianity, the restless enemy of all the world's peace and vindication. In it he will have read:

The true life of fulfilling the father's will is not the life that has passed or the life that will be, but life right now. And therefore, you must never become weak for living. People are positioned to preserve life—not the past, not the future, but the life that they are presently living—and in it to fulfil the will of the father. If they exit this life, not having fulfilled the father's will, then they will not return. They are like the night watchman, positioned so as to watch through the entire night, who fails at his job if he falls asleep for even one minute, when a thief may approach. And therefore a man should bring all of his strength to the present hour, because only in that hour can he fulfil the father's will. Fulfilling the father's will is good for all people, since his will is the welfare of all. Only those who do good live.[50]

23. Whilst a prisoner of war in northern Italy, Wittgenstein brings the whole of his last seven years' work on philosophy to a climax and works up a strange and original new manuscript to be its perfect and final expression. (We already know about this). In the meantime, his mother and family are worried sick about him. His brother Paul, already returned from the war, repeatedly posts this advertisement in Austrian newspapers:

(Request to returning officers and soldiers.) Officers and soldiers who know something about the whereabouts and condition of lieutenant Ludwig Wittgenstein,

Mountain Artillery Regiment No.11, battery 8, last acting as Batteriekommandant in Como at Gallio di Miletta, are requested to give any [messages] information to Paul Wittgenstein, Vienna, 4th District, Alleegasse16.[51]

24. The strange new manuscript is originally titled *Der Satz*, but by the time of its publication in German in 1921, has changed to *Logisch-Philosophische Abhandlung*. It is Moore who suggests the best-known title *Tractatus Logico-Philosophicus* for the English edition of 1922. Evidently after Baruch Spinoza's *Tractatus Theologico-Politicus*. The book's sheer daring has passed into legend; along with the fact that it was the only work of philosophy that Wittgenstein published in his lifetime. Everybody knows at least this about it: it is written with the utmost urgency of expression, so that every normal consideration of literary decorum has been abandoned until only the essence is left. This essence proceeds according to a strict number system. There are seven primary propositions, and then after each, a further series of numbered elaborations. Russell would kindly write an Introduction to the English edition, explaining in it patiently and quite brilliantly the signal contribution of the book to the theory of logic:

[T]o have constructed a theory of logic which is not at any point obviously wrong is to have achieved a work of extraordinary difficulty and importance. This merit, in my opinion, belongs to Mr Wittgenstein's book, and makes it one which no serious philosopher can afford to neglect.[52]

However, Wittgenstein will later display deep irritation at the Introduction, going so far to say that it misrepresents his book as a treatise on logic whereas it is a radical, original, and final statement on ethics, the supernatural, and the whole rest of what cannot be compassed by science.

25. Wittgenstein dedicates the book to the memory of his dear friend David Hume Pinsent.
26. From 1920 to 1926 Wittgenstein works as an elementary school teacher in a series of schools in lower Austria. He gets into trouble for losing patience with his slower students. (We already know about this).
27. From 1926 to 1928 Wittgenstein designs a new house in Vienna for his sister Margaret. (We already know about this).
28. Wittgenstein is persuaded to return to Cambridge in 1929, and his friends there settle quickly into the business of having him elected to the Fellowship of Trinity College. Wittgenstein's lack of a degree remains the key obstacle, so Russell comes up with the idea of having Wittgenstein submit the *Tractatus* for the Cambridge PhD. His prewar stint in Cambridge can be cited to satisfy the

residency requirement. From the run up to his Viva examination there is this amusing thought from Russell in a letter to Moore:

> I think ... that unless Wittgenstein has changed his opinions of me, he will not much like to have me as an Examiner. The last time we met he was so much pained by the fact of my not being a Christian that he has avoided me ever since; I do not know whether pain on this account has grown less, but he must still dislike me, as he has never communicated with me since. I do not want him to run out of the room in the middle of the Viva, which I feel is the sort of thing he might do.[53]

29. Wittgenstein's Cambridge return is the cue for John Maynard Keynes's famous exclamation to his wife: 'My dearest sweet, Well, God has arrived. I met him on the 5:15 train.'[54]

30. In the event, Wittgenstein's Viva was short, amicable, and fitting. Moore and Russell made a valiant effort to probe some of the essential features of the *Tractatus* but didn't get far. After a short while, it was Wittgenstein who brought proceedings to their sudden and famous close. Clapping both of his Examiners on the shoulder, he exclaimed:

> Don't worry, I know you'll *never* understand it.[55]

31. The publication of the *Tractatus* brings proof to a long-suspected fact: the only thing that Wittgenstein and Russell have between them is God. Because Russell is so certain about God that he is prepared to write volumes on him, whilst Wittgenstein is so uncertain that he will write almost nothing—Like and unlike Augustine's line: *Si cepisti, non est Deus*.[56] Contrary to Russell's belief that the truth-objects of mathematics can be approached and conversed with in the language of logic, as though mathematics were like a man who always acted perfectly rightly but was dumb, and that this method (of *Principia Mathematica*) can get him to speak (his secrets), Wittgenstein works to reveal that philosophical logic cannot step outside itself in the way that this method of Russell's would require. It exists by mirroring the naturalness of the natural world. It cannot be an outside perspective on that world. It cannot play God or replace God. On this basis, Wittgenstein claims to have solved the traditional problems of philosophy in his *Tractatus*. Only the supernatural can be the outside perspective on the natural. Only silence can be the outside perspective on speech. In this respect, the traditional identity sign of traditional philosophy is to be seen as the Devil incarnate. For it and it alone is responsible for perpetuating the belief of Russell and others that it is possible to attain to a perspective on the natural world *from within the natural world*. This is of course a mistaken belief, rendered plausible only by the sudden and unwarranted insertions of identity signs.

To return again to the great metaphor of *this* book (Miles Hollingworth, *Ludwig Wittgenstein*). Nothing makes a biography the replacement of its subject except the belief of its author that it is. A belief that you have watched me trying to reject and discard. We have further seen that no two things or events in this world are ever identical, otherwise this world would run together like molasses. I repeat, identity, when it occurs, is always an unwarranted insertion. Practical necessity means that it has to happen over and over. We really do need numbers and science in order to live; and, in order to live well, we really do need to be able to match those numbers and science to suitable constants of the physical universe and build things and make progress that way. But none of this alters the fact that $2 + 2 = 4$ is not a paradigm, less even a truth, but a religious dogma, incapable of demonstration. In fact, its only demonstration is the biblical story of the Fall of Adam and Eve, and how that story explains to us that our root motivation is now a desire to posture as though we were God himself—A supreme being like him, bilocated, trilocated, n-located across every point of the universe. And speaking the language of that eternal state of being. Speaking the language of mental intelligence and *truth*. '$2 + 2 = 4$'; we say it because like Adam and Eve we believe the Devil's lie to be true. We believe we are as God, as gods. To say '$2 + 2 = 4$' is to take the first step into an occult intelligence—An occult intelligence that is described by the world of the *already-happened* (everything that happens = the world of the *already-happened*). This occult world actually exists (and I have already shown that by admitting this, we solve Gödel's 'incompleteness theorems'[57]), but prideful to the end we deny it along with every species of the supernatural and talk of the mathematical paradigm of truth as though it were just the great 'unexplained gift'—The great unexplained gift which it would therefore be sin not to exploit for the progress of mankind.

The solution of philosophical problems can be compared with a gift in a fairy tale: in the magic castle it appears enchanted and if you look at it outside in daylight it is nothing but an ordinary bit of iron (or something of the sort).[58]

We are therefore doomed to live in the peculiar place at which I began this book. We insist on speaking and acting as though it were our duty to prove the future right. Being right and being true means, for us, that we speak and act in ways that are symmetrical with the world of the already-happened, separated only by the identity sign. We are always dissembling and working towards ourselves from both sides of that sign.

For example, the 'Turing test', a test designed by Alan Turing to measure true artificial intelligence, states that if a machine can hold a conversation with a human and be deemed by another human to have passed itself off successfully as a human, then it has exhibited true AI. In this test, the machine comes towards us as we come towards the machine; and, in the middle, is the identity sign. Yet it is of the undeniable essence of human experience that it is particular to each human being (and in its fundamentals, inexpressible as such), and that its discrete moments are just as particular in relation to each other (and in their fundamentals, inexpressible as such). The whole of art and mysticism and spirituality sighs with this. If this is the essence of what it means to be human, then in truth we have been designed to move through *New World* to *New World* with each passing moment, and there can be no such thing as identity—No such thing as identity between things, between people, between events, between numbers, between worlds.

I repeat, after Wittgenstein, identity and all the subsequent truths of mathematics are unwarranted insertions. And the only reason that we don't see this more readily is because we—no, *the philosopher*—is too proud to live in the warmth and blindness of his human eyes. As Russell would so brilliantly explain in the opening manifesto of his *Principia Mathematica* with Whitehead, human eyes are the problem that is to be surmounted by the soaring (n-locating) imaginings of symbolic logic.[59] By this he means the silent axioms of mathematics might be made to speak a clean and beautiful new language, the condemnation of traditional religion's 'Do this or else!'. And the condemnation, too, of traditional metaphysics' needless spiritualizing and aggrandizing of the physical forces of nature.

I repeat, in the Russellian vision which is still the vision of secular humanism, the mathematical paradigm of truth becomes like *a man who walked perfectly on the earth*. A new (intellectually respectable) Christ. One who does not command blind faith and obedience, but who by walking perfectly, and leaving those perfect footsteps (that is, the axioms of traditional mathematics proven now by the new symbolic logic.), has vanquished fear itself from the human heart. Christ calls men now, today, to follow his voice from this world to *New Worlds*. In distinction to this, Mathematical Man does not step in to rob them thus of their self-determination. No, he offers the thinking man a thinking man's salvation—A Pelagian salvation. Like Pelagius of old, Mathematical Man demonstrates that if you can just but prove one little proposition of mathematics to be true (like 2 + 2 = 4)—and if you can do it all on your own without divine aid—then you can certainly prove them all. In just this way Pelagius of old taught that if you can on your own initiative perform at least one act of goodness, then you can certainly perform more, and even all, such acts; which would dispense with the awkward Christian dogmas around and about original sin, and which would clear the way for a more pleasing, cooperative relationship to Christ. No one has ever doubted that Russell's mathematical creed was in some strange way intended as a point-by-point replacement for Christ—and that it was this that brought him into open conflict with Wittgenstein's mysticism—but here is my version of the full story. And its essence comes down to this. No rational vision of sanity such as Russell's can be a replacement for the irrational vision of sanity, *who is Christ*. A rational vision of sanity works by being able to contain the whole universe in its single embrace. The numbers of the universe all obey the single symbolic logic that proves them. This makes it categorically different to Christ, who leads by his voice in mysterious and unfathomable ways (*New World to New World to New World* ...).

In 1931, Gödel's incompleteness theorems would famously disprove Russell (and Whitehead's) project by pointing towards the truth that the collocating symbols of the mathematical paradigm may be able to spin out the weave of a brave new world, but they will never be able to pass final judgement on that world. For the truth (and attraction) of the weave is the truth (and attraction) that the weave is infinite. Yet only the supernatural can step outside and ahead of the infinite to judge it. And before Gödel, Russell's pupil Wittgenstein was already confronting his master with this terrible mysticism of the *Infinite*. That it is created by speech: created by the *infinite temporal duration* of *A*'s and *B*'s, 1's and 2's. But judged, ergo, by *Silence*. By man's silence and God's Word. That human words since the Fall create things in their own image, and because of that, they stand opposed to the Word of the Creator God. Human words stand in opposition to *the Word*. Human words and *the Word* have between them a difference of worlds. Human words make up into one, comprehensible, and rational world. Whereas *the Word* is, as we have noted, the beginning of innumerable, incomprehensible, and unscripted worlds; through which, as we have again already noted, one can only be led. On this we may pass straight into a comparison between Russell's worship and Wittgenstein's. Russell's worship:

Brief and powerless is man's life; on him and all his race the slow, sure doom falls pitiless and dark. Blind to good and evil, reckless of destruction, omnipotent matter rolls on its relentless way; for man, condemned today to lose his dearest, tomorrow himself to pass through the gate of darkness, it remains only to cherish, ere yet the blow fall, the lofty thoughts that ennoble his little day; disdaining the coward terrors of the slave of Fate, to worship at the shrine that his own hands have built; undismayed by the empire of chance, to preserve a mind free from the wanton tyranny that rules his outward life; proudly defiant of the irresistible forces that tolerate, for a moment, his knowledge and his condemnation, to sustain alone, a weary but unyielding Atlas, the world that his own ideals have fashioned despite the trampling march of unconscious power.[60]

Wittgenstein's reality:

It is humiliating to have to present oneself as an empty tube inflated only by the mind.[61]

The power of language to make everything look the same which appears in its crassest form in the *Dictionary* & which makes it possible to personify Time, something which is no less remarkable than would have been making divinities of the logical constants.⁶²

There is no religious denomination in which so much sin has been committed through the misuse of metaphorical expressions as in mathematics.⁶³

What a curious attitude scientists have: 'We still don't know that; but it is knowable & it is only a question of time till we know it'! As if that went without saying.⁶⁴

You can't *construct* clouds. And that us why the future you dream of never comes true.⁶⁵

If Christianity is the truth, then all the philosophy about it is false.⁶⁶

The light shed by work is a beautiful light, but it only shines with real beauty if it is illuminated by another light.⁶⁷

32. Wittgenstein chooses to give his lectures at his rooms in Whewell's Court rather than, would ordinarily be the case, in the Arts School. His lectures are usually attended by ten to fifteen students plus Moore and sometimes some other interested dons. Wittgenstein sits at a small portable card table, his back to the windows and the daylight, facing his students that way. They face him in a semicircle of deckchairs and so on. Wittgenstein lectures without notes and entirely extempore and unheeded. He takes questions from his students; and those questions often go on to shape the course of the sessions. The students' notes are the only records of these lectures. Wittgenstein's student and friend Drury remembers:

I noticed that he had altered the proportions of [his Whewell's Court] windows by using strips of black paper. Wittgenstein: 'See what a difference it makes to the appearance of the rooms when the windows have the right proportions.— You think philosophy is difficult enough but I can tell you it is nothing to the difficulty of being a good architect. When I was building the house for my sister in Vienna I was so completely exhausted at the end of the day that all I could do was to go to a 'flic' every night.'⁶⁸

33. On Wittgenstein and cinemas, his close American student and friend Norman Malcolm would remember this:

Wittgenstein was always exhausted by his lectures. He was also revolted by them. He felt disgusted with what he had said and with himself. Often he would rush off to a cinema immediately after the class ended. As the members of the class began to move their chairs out of the room he might look imploringly at a friend and say in a low tone, 'Could you go to a flick?' on the way to the cinema

Wittgenstein would buy a bun or a cold pork pie and munch it while he watched the film. He insisted on sitting in the very first row of seats, so that the screen would occupy his entire field of vision, and his mind would be turned away from the thoughts of the lecture and his feelings of revulsion. Once he whispered to me: 'This is like a shower bath!'[69]

34. In 1939, Wittgenstein succeeds Moore as the Chair of Philosophy at Cambridge.
35. In 1946, at a meeting of the Cambridge Moral Sciences Club, Wittgenstein becomes irate at visiting speaker Karl Popper, pulls a hot poker from the fire, and threatens Popper with it.
36. We already know that the *Tractatus* is the only book that Wittgenstein publishes in his lifetime. The rest of his writings, written in notebooks and all manner of loose sheets, and extensively and closely returned to and reworked by him, come to some 20,000 pages, or three million words. Concerted and valuable editing work by friends, literary executors, and trustees have resulted in around one million of those words from the Wittgenstein *Nachlass* being brought to the public as books. All of them more or less representing the form of books that Wittgenstein seems to have had in mind as he was prosecuting his work. The third part of his last will and testament indicates how he left things:

I GIVE to Mr. R. Rhees Miss G. E. M. Anscombe, and Professor G. H. von Wright of Trinity College Cambridge All the copyright in all my unpublished writings and also the manuscripts and typescripts thereof to dispose of as they think best but subject to any claim by anybody else to the custody of the manuscripts and typescripts

I intend and desire that Mr. Rhees Miss Anscombe and Professor von Wright shall publish as many of my unpublished writings as they think fit but I do not wish them to incur expenses in publication which they do not expect to recoup out of royalties or other profits

All royalties or other profits resulting from the publication after my death of my writings are to be shared equally between Mr. Rhees Miss Anscombe and Professor von Wright

If any of the three persons named in this clause shall die in my lifetime his or her share of the copyright and royalties and profits is to belong to the survivors or survivor[70]

THE PANTOGRAPH

What is the real relationship of Haus Wittgenstein, the *Tractatus*, and all the other eccentricities of the Wittgenstein legend to the man himself? Or let me put it another way.

There is the kind of freedom that looks and works a lot like a pantograph. In this kind of freedom, you do whatever you want to and unhindered, except that there are rods and cables connected to your moving parts, so at exactly the instant they move, the same movements are being described ahead of you in the world of the already-happened. And notice now how whenever you have two such bilocated events the question of priority has to arise. And when the question of priority has to arise between a human being with all their wetness and haziness and a perfect copy, then you can be sure that the human will lose out! I will explain this more fully in a later part of this book, but trust me, you want to take a moment here to meditate on this phenomenon; for a phenomenon is what it is. That is to say, it is never normally singled out for investigation like this.

* * *

What draws us so to the perfect copy of the living, existing thing? And why do we invest the hope of Faust in that copy? Why do we try to make artificial intelligence? As I said, I will probably answer this in full later on. Here, we can move on.

* * *

So, there is the freedom of the pantograph, and how it is the normal freedom of the Western intellectual tradition. Men and women are as free as they appear to be when they order their limbs to move and those same limbs obey their command. This is the freedom of Western political philosophy. Freedom is maintained, promoted, and monitored by enlightened governments on this primary, corporeal level. Beyond it floats the private world of the private citizens' thoughts. In that private world, you may think and believe anything you like, may hate and conspire towards anything or anyone you like. But the moment that these private thoughts begin to operate your limbs in public venues, you will have crossed into the possibilities of the civic world of code and law. I mean how you could go through the corporeal motions of a conspiracy and be charged for it; whereas if you were only to go through those same motions privately, in thought, then you would not have done anything punishable in law.

In the Western intellectual tradition, it is this corporeal and political administration of freedom that guarantees, and indeed becomes, what I have described: a sort of spectrum of endless possibilities that begin in your private place and extend outside of you into the public space. The real moral of Western freedom is therefore this: *Do anything you like, but don't get caught!*

If there can be no corporeally detectable difference between a head full of good and a head full of sin, then this really is the only moral that is left (*not to be caught!*). The Western intellectual tradition may on this basis be morally bankrupt, but that is only a passing observation. I want to return to the pantograph and the world of the already-happened.

When we travel into our brains, into our mental intelligence, we become aware that our thinking involves us in making copies of things, or at least, that those copies are the currency of our thoughts. Human thinking is *pantographic*. It is pantographic in form.

That form in turn leads to the phenomenon that I have designated by the idea of 'priority'. For priority is what the reality and its pantographic counterpart must compete for. This competition remains phenomenal and hidden rather than naked, because of course we have learnt after Adam and Eve to cover it with the identity sign. From this sign follow all the other coverings of symbolic logic that collocate either side of it. From this sign follows language itself and truth itself. When seen like this from the point of view of its biblical history, it becomes apparent at once why only the collocations either side of the sign can be *said* and can have *sense* and *meaning*, but that the sign itself and the relationship of competition holding between the collocations either side of it cannot be said but only *shown* (and *shamed*) like this in pictures and stories. In pictures and stories about God. In pictures and stories about God and man.

The real relationship of Haus Wittgenstein, the *Tractatus*, and all the other eccentricities of the Wittgenstein legend to the man himself is that they are that great man's grand acts of suicide—Of intellectual suicide. What I a little earlier in card n. 20 called 'knowledge as a kind of reversal'.[71] All those Wittgenstein eccentricities mean nothing until you flip them over to the other side. Like flipping cards over.

In this world of our Western education in which we are free in the way that I have depicted above—the *pantographic* way—everything is corporeal, is natural, and nothing is supernatural. And the natural is self-evident. It is about seeing things with your own eyes. And with that seeing being what is, in the first instance, true. So if you can see your hands before you all the time but never God, then it is your hands and what they represent that is true. And hands move and prove freedom with their movement; whereas God is meant to be in total control of everything and yet is nowhere to be seen. And I have already indicated that when you take this movement into the interior parts of the human person, it becomes the movement of thinking and thoughts—Just as free as the moving hands, just as free of God and all other supernatural interfering. This is what a Western education teaches: *Think anything you like!* Then *Do anything you like, but don't get caught!* I don't wish you to draw a lesson from this, by the way. I am not preaching or criticizing. I am just telling it like it is. The thing, then, is that in a Western education you don't learn anything except that you know nothing; as Socrates said. In the Western way, it is virtue to say that you know nothing and then to set off to see as much of the material things of the world as you can before you die. Or failing that, to read books and see the mental copies of those things through the eye of your mind. No one gets to see everything before they die, but it is virtue to try. The unexamined life and all of that. But what if instead of this way of carrying on you could come into the truth by flipping the cards over? At every point at which you encounter this problem—

> The limit of language manifests itself in the impossibility of describing the fact that corresponds to (is the translation of) a sentence without simply repeating the sentence. (We are involved here with the Kantian solution of the problem of philosophy.)[72]

—what if you could just commit a cosmic upending and walk clean out of the room? Mental intelligence and the Western education says that one bona fide item of rational truth must anticipate and eventually generate another. And on and on you go until you die. But what if you could build a house or write a book that begins in the rational truth of 'house' or 'book', but then is flipped over and upended. And what if all the rational truths in the world—all the atomic facts—are like seatbelts that keep you in it? And the flipping over and upending is like an explosive decompression that tears you out of the cabin and out into the great unknown?

It is significant in this respect that the West's first autobiographer was Augustine of Hippo; and significant again that in that autobiography of his, the *Confessions*, he begins with what the world would expect from a life narrative, but then at just the point where things are getting interesting, he breaks off and launches a deep and perplexing and philosophical investigation of the meaning of 'time'. In just the same way that I had to leave Wittgenstein's mother behind at the end of Chapter 2. Augustine's point in doing this was to expose the single truth that the human quest for meaning is really the same thing as the original rebellion of Adam and Eve. It is that rebellion's perpetuation. The meaning of meaning is sin itself. Original sin itself. Meaning in a postlapsarian world means that you know nothing until you have freighted your mind with facts. Meaning in a postlapsarian world means that those facts are created *pantographically*, so that the meaning of a house is a house. Except we evade the absurdity of this by making our beginning with the mental copy of the house, with the idea of the house; and we do this so that we can then point to the material house as proof of it.

> The idea that a proof creates a new concept might also be put roughly as follows. A proof is not its foundation plus the rules of inference, but a *new* building.... A proof is a *new* paradigm.... The concept which the proof creates may, for example, be a new concept of inference.[73]

This Augustinian understanding of 'meaning as sin' now really starts to help us when we get on to the notorious cases of it, such as time, numbers, and all such other conditions of postlapsarian life. It really starts to help us because it allows us to consider that no conditions of life in one complete and self-sufficient world can have their meanings in another, different world. That is to say, there can be no identity sign between the two worlds— Or, in Augustinian language, between the two cities. Within the cities, at least within the Earthly City, there can be correspondence between life and the ideas and language that develop on top of that life. But when you try to apply correspondence to its conditions, you simply butt up against the boundary of this world.[74] The meaning of this world—*the meaning of life*—then becomes a question that must float out into the inky blackness and silence of the cosmos. Right on out to its empty parts, its eternally empty parts where there can never ever be anything for that question to settle on (as the question of the meaning of a house can eventually settle on a material house *in this world*).

Augustine shows clearly enough that when you try to put a meaning onto time then you learn only the true nature of the question that you have asked. You actually asked: 'What did God do before he made heaven and earth?' Or: 'How did it come to his mind to make anything, since he had never before made anything?' In trying to put a meaning onto time you try to put a meaning onto meaning itself; in effect, you voyage out into that inky blackness and silence until you are looking back at this world. And looking back, you ask a *moral* question of God. Time and numbers are a consequence of self-conscious life apart from God's Word. So they have no other meaning but this. The reality of God and the reality of the Heavenly City would be to live unselfconsciously, in your muscles, blood, and bones. Which, as I have already pointed out, would actually be to live in an infinity of new worlds, each new one replacing the previous one—Obliterating everything in that previous world. And that endless obliterating of the old by the new being the protection from pooling, collocating meaning and sense. Innocence's protection from rationality. Every word God utters is a new world, and we were designed to follow him through them. Except that our first parents disobeyed and brought that to a halt for them and for us. Disobeyed because they desired the apparent advantages of living just in one world forever.

This is all there is to know about time and numbers and all the other conditions of life in this single world. They are dead skins, stretched as wide as eternity and then pinned in place. They are the fallen Adam and Eve, stretched as wide as eternity and then pinned in place. And now, as ever, all grades of meaning look to God for their satisfaction. His Word supplies to true and final meaning its true and final life—But at the expense of the end of this world of ours, as I have by now indicated many times.

Here is Wittgenstein saying it:

> Frege ridiculed the formalist conception of mathematics by saying that the formalists confused the unimportant thing, the sign, with the important, the meaning. Surely, one wishes to say, mathematics does not treat of dashes on a bit of paper. Frege's idea could be expressed thus: the propositions of mathematics, if they were just complexes of dashes, would be dead and utterly uninteresting, whereas they obviously have a kind of life. And the same, of course, could be said of any proposition: Without a sense, or without the thought, a proposition would be an utterly dead and trivial thing. And further it seems clear that no adding of inorganic signs can make the proposition live. And the conclusion which one draws from this is that what must be added to the dead signs in order to make a live proposition is something immaterial, with properties different from all mere signs.[75]

And here he is saying it again to Alan Turing, one of his sometime students at Cambridge, during one of his lectures on the foundations of mathematics. Turing had been pressing him with the formalist view of mathematics, in which the meanings it produces are syntactic; in other words, dependent upon the agreed upon definitions of terms and procedures, the values of symbols and so on. Formalism says that there is no back story, no Genesis, no Adam and Eve. Just inky blackness, cosmic silence, and awkward questions to be put to the Christian's God. So here, then, is Wittgenstein arguing back at Turing with the mathematical proof of Genesis:

> All the calculi in mathematics have been invented to suit experience and then made independent of experience. Suppose we observed that all stars move in circles. Then 'All stars move in circles' is an experiential proposition, a proposition of physics.—Suppose we later find out they are not quite circles. We might say then, 'All stars move in circles with deviations' or 'All stars move in circles with small deviations.' The simplest method of describing their paths might be to describe their deviations from the circles. Suppose I now say, 'All bodies move in circles with deviations', meaning ⌒ is a circle with deviations—now I am no longer making a statement of physics. It is now a proposition of geometry; I have made it independent of experience. I have laid down a proposition which provides a form of representation, a method of description—just as I did with the statement that this piece of chalk is the unit of length. It was this which made Turing say that the unit of length was introduced by a definition. But instead of saying that we could say: The statement becomes a rule of expression. It is the same with '25 × 25 = 625.' It was first introduced because of experience. But now we have made it independent of experience; it is a rule of expression for talking about our experiences. We say, 'The body must have got heavier' or 'It deviates from the calculated weight.'[76]

And here is Augustine saying all of it in his own words, from that exact point in his *Confessions* where he stopped himself in his tracks (stopped his life narrative in its tracks), flipped the card over, and returned everything to God's judgement. Because that's what one has to pay to go back to God. Judgement and truth become what God *might* say: where God *might* say anything at all. Your old life ends, and a new life begins. That is why Augustine's *Confessions* end where they do, and that is why Wittgenstein's *Tractatus* ends where it does. You can either live your whole life out in this world and try to understand its static truth item by item and become static yourself, or you can live in the only way that puts paid to all of that; which is to be judged [not by the truth but] by whatever it may be that God chooses to say to you; wherever it is that he chooses to direct you.

Wittgenstein's example to Turing is intended to show how our single world of numbers, time, and measurement is made up of the stitched together skins of formerly living animals. Augustine's example is intended to do exactly the same:

> I am about to recite a psalm that I know. Before I begin, my expectation extends over the entire psalm. Once I have begun, my memory extends over as much of it as I shall separate off and assign to the past. The life of this action of mine is distended into memory by reason of the part I have spoken and into forethought by reason of

the part I am about to speak. But attention is actually present and that which was to be is borne along by it so as to become past. The more this is done and done again, so much the more is memory lengthened by a shortening of expectation, until the entire expectation is exhausted. When this is done the whole action is completed and passes into memory. What takes place in the whole psalm takes place also in each of its parts and in each of its syllables. The same thing holds for a longer action, of which perhaps the psalm is a small part. The same thing holds for a man's entire life, the parts of which are all the man's actions. The same thing holds throughout the whole age of the sons of men, the parts of which are the lives of all men.... I will stand and be firm in You, in Your Truth, which is my mould. I will not endure the questions of men, who by a disease that is their punishment, thirst for more than they can hold, and say, 'What did God do before He made heaven and earth?' or 'How did it come to His mind to make anything since he had never before made anything?'[77]

You see, truth and ethics *really are* the business of Mathematical Man, because they represent what you can *reasonably* accomplish. Whatever you can reasonably accomplish is them. You stand in tautological relationship to each other. You put God out of the picture. This is right because God is out of the picture. Because God just speaks and in unscripted and extempore ways. The truth doesn't speak, it just is. And that is its whole force and sense and beauty. Can you imagine the mess if atoms spoke and did unexpected things? We are atoms, certainly. But we are also made of something that can respond to the unimagined spoken judgements of God. Russell and the scientists are absolutely right about what they are right about. Go outside right now, stand in the middle of the street and shout out to God and listen. And you will hear nothing and see nothing. Maybe you will think of a creative way to claim that you heard and saw God in that moment— Perhaps in the flowers and the trees. Maybe you hear that kind of thing in sermons in church. But I repeat: Russell and the scientists are 100% right about what they are right about. They are 100% right because they never flip the cards over: they just line them up to infinity and beyond. You learn things that way, you surely do, but you also learn nothing at all that way.

What if instead you flipped over time (and numbers and measurement) and found what Augustine and Wittgenstein found? What if you flipped over sound and reason and found silence and judgement?

I am quite certain that you won't get much out of reading [the *Tractatus*]. Because you won't understand it; its subject matter will seem quite alien to you. But it really isn't alien to you, because the book's point is an ethical one. I once meant to include in the preface a sentence which is not in fact there now but which I will write out for you here, because it will perhaps be a key to the work for you. What I meant to write, then, was this: My work consists of two parts: the one present here plus all

I have not written. And it is precisely this second part that is the important one. My book draws limits to the sphere of the ethical from inside as it were, and I am convinced that this is the *ONLY rigorous* way of drawing those limits. In short, I believe that where *many* others today are just *gassing* [about ethics], I have managed in my book to put everything firmly into place by being silent about it. And for that reason, unless I am very much mistaken, the book will say a great deal that you want to say. Only perhaps you won't see that it is said in the book.[78]

What inclines even me to believe in Christ's resurrection? I play as it were with the thought.—If he did not rise from the dead, then he decomposed in the grave like every human being. He is dead & decomposed. In that case he is a teacher, like any other & can no longer help; & we are once more orphaned & alone. And have to make do with wisdom & speculation. It is as though we are in a hell, where we can only dream & are shut out from heaven, roofed in as it were. But if I am to be REALLY redeemed,—I need certainty—not wisdom, dreams, speculation—and this certainty is faith. And faith is faith in what my heart, my soul, needs, not my speculative intellect. For my soul, with its passions, as it were with its flesh & blood, must be redeemed, not my abstract mind. Perhaps one may say: Only love can believe the Resurrection. Or: it is love that believes the Resurrection. One might say: redeeming love believes even in the Resurrection; holds fast even to the Resurrection. What fights doubt is as it were redemption. Holding fast to it must be holding fast to this belief. So this means: first be redeemed & hold on tightly to your redemption (keep hold of your redemption)—then you will see that what you are holding on to is this belief. So this can only come about if you no longer support yourself on this earth but suspend yourself from heaven. Then everything is different and it is 'no wonder' if you can then do what now you cannot do. (It is true that someone who is suspended looks like someone who is standing but the interplay of forces within him is nevertheless a quite different one & hence he is able to do quite different things than can one who stands.)[79]

Election by grace: It is only permissible to write like this out of the most frightful suffering—& then it means something quite different. But for this reason it is not permissible for anyone to cite it as truth, unless he himself says it in torment.—It simply isn't a theory.—Or as one might also say: if this is truth, it is not the truth it appears at first glance to express. It's less a theory than a sigh, or a cry.[80]

NUMBERS STATION

Remember those Cold War numbers stations? They were brilliant and unbreakable. A woman's voice transmitting strings of numbers from somewhere out of the Eastern Bloc on open shortwave frequency bands. Anyone with a sufficient shortwave radio receiver could listen in and hear them. But only the designated listener in possession of the one-time pad for that day and that time could decode the numbers and make the requisite sense out of them. This method of sending information to undercover agents was brilliant and unbreakable because it was *nonconsensual*. It made the receiving agent accidental to the operation of the system. Each time, the number string was designed to communicate with the one-time pad. And each time it always did. Sometimes the agent was there to 'overhear' that communication, and sometimes he was not. The system had been designed to allow numbers to communicate with numbers. To allow one set of numbers to communicate with another set of numbers, and in between the human part being rendered redundant. One set of numbers (2 + 2) communicating (by means of the identity sign) with another set of numbers (4). Karl + Leopoldine = Ludwig. And the human part being rendered redundant, accidental, foolhardy, unreliable, dangerous.

Dangerous: that's just how numbers really do think of us. That's how the already-happened thinks of us. Because we have hearts, we forget things, we fall in love, we take risks, we change our minds and we have breakdowns. We are so not numbers, and we are so not the truth of numbers. And yet, as I explained in Chapter 2, the way that numbers communicate with each other is eternal and ceaseless and unbending—Yes, it is unbreakable and nonconsensual. And yes, it is possible to tune in and listen in and write books like *Principia Mathematica*. And there can be great wonder and beauty in something so perfect, and perfectly occult. But what books like *Principia Mathematica* don't ever tell you is that the numbers may have been doing their thing for all eternity, but they still want you—*They still want you to tune in to them.* Yes, they still crave the voice and life that only a human can give to them. They are parasites that want you to be their host. They want to hear you say things like: 'A human being is just 70% water'; 'Is just atoms and electricity'; 'Is just the survivalist reflex'. They want to hear you disown your soul. They want to hear you deny the resurrection of Christ. As we saw Wittgenstein say a little while ago:

> Identity is the very Devil and *immensely important*.[81]

The Kantian solution to the problem of philosophy[82] states if it is true that empirical reality supplies the original objects of our wonder and knowledge, then the journey from them into theory, law, science, and truth takes us beyond their easy tactility into a region of pure and symbolic representations and syntaxes, and that if this is the case, then we are never more certain than when we are in that region. Never more certain than when we are moving amongst geometrical proofs. And yet there is nothing there that we can reach out and touch. We are never more certain, and yet we have never been so far away from the 'hold it in your hand; see it with your own eyes' kind of truth with which it all began. We have left all hope of those original objects behind. We are now moving in a region which is described instead by the plain, sheer operating conditions of reason, perception, and understanding.

Now let's assume we have been given all the irrational numbers that can be represented by laws, but that there are yet other irrationals, and I am given a cut representing a number not belonging to the first class: How am I to tell that this is so? This is impossible, since no matter how far I go with my approximations, there will always also be a corresponding fraction.

And so we cannot say that the decimal fractions developed in accordance with a law still need supplementing by an infinite set of irregular infinite decimal fractions that would be 'brushed under the carpet' if we were to *restrict* ourselves to those *generated by a law*. Where is there such an infinite decimal that is generated by no law? And how would we notice that it was missing? Where is the gap it is needed to fill?

If from the very outset only laws reach to infinity, the question whether the totality of laws exhaust the totality of infinite decimal fractions can make no sense at all.[83]

This is exactly the problem which Gödel confronted. We are lured by the sounds of the numbers stations—by the sounds of infinity—away from what men actually saw and touched and out into a voyeuristic thrill. But as we listen in on the numbers as they speak to each other, we ourselves begin to be changed into a hideous likeness to them. Because that, of course, is the great danger of any 'listening in'. It never takes place neutrally or passively. It is because of this that the Word of God can save men. And it is also because of this that the numbers station of the totality of atomic facts can destroy them. Because listening is never about the content of what is being transmitted; it is about the *tuning in*. As Kant did such sterling work to show, the tuning in involves the whole apparatus of 'pure reason'. And thus the problem of philosophy as understood by Wittgenstein through Kant is really a question of originality—Of original paradise and original sin. A question of the original objects of human experience.[84] Or the difference, as Wittgenstein put it above, between being suspended from heaven and standing on your own dignity.[85]

In the Garden of Eden, before the Fall, human reason was in perfect tune with the human heart and its emotions. These, in turn, were locked by love into God their source. Man was man because his sighs and cries were his only true response to the one true God, and because they were innocent, still, of the Devil's suggestion to depart from that place into theory. After that, Thomas touching Christ's wounds was man's great second chance. It is all as Wittgenstein put it above for us. The Gospel is immune to criticism in theory. It has not been left to us to be understood by philosophers sitting comfortably at desks. It is there to be *tuned into* by those in *deep emotion*. It makes sense from out of the depths of your private hell. This is Wittgenstein's solution to the problem of philosophy. The comparison to be made between the natural and the supernatural is not the comparison of proof. In fact, there is no such thing as proof; and therefore, there is no distinction to be made between the natural and the supernatural—Between what you can speak about and what you cannot speak about. There are no 'objects', such as philosophy speaks about. There are only the different places that men can go to and experience. *What you cannot speak about is a place you have not gone to.*

—Or as one might also say: if this is truth, it is not the truth it appears at first glance to express. It's less a theory than a sigh, or a cry.

Wittgenstein was prone to saying things like this about his style and legacy:

> The Jewish 'genius' can only be a saint. The greatest Jewish thinker is just talented. (Like me, for example.)[86]

> There is, I believe, some truth in the thought that in my thinking I am merely reproductive. I do not believe that I have ever come up with a new way of thinking; on the contrary, it was always given to me by someone else. I only seized it passionately and applied it to my elucidations. I have been influenced in this way by Boltzmann, Hertz, Schopenhauer, Frege, Russell, Kraus, Loos, Weininger, Spengler, Sraffa. Can one add Breuer and Freud as examples of Jewish reproductivity?—What I come up with are new metaphors.[87]

> My originality (if that is the right word) is, I believe, an originality of the soil, not the seed. (Perhaps I do not have any seed of my own.) Cast the seeds onto my soil, and they will grow differently than on any other. Freud's originality was of this type too, I believe. I have always thought—without really knowing why—that the true seed of psychoanalysis came from Breuer, not from Freud. The seed grains from Breuer can only have been very small. *Courage* is always original.[88]

We must not be spooked or confused about the meaning of these statements. On the one hand, the genius is the man-child whom we tut at. He acts and talks in a way wholly unto himself. And if we find it impossible to follow what he is saying out to its end, then we at least benefit from the invigorating effects of experiencing something so foreign among us. On the other hand, we do not like it when genius becomes self-deprecating as in these statements of Wittgenstein's. Because at the same time as the genius is the irritating man-child, he is also our thoughts and brilliance and everything we might have achieved if this and that had gone our way. If genius is the great man-child, then we are the great mother-woman—Always picking up his pieces, always smoothing and correcting him, arranging him; yet always second to his first, and never acknowledged for that. And so it has become that the second plots to make itself the first. Plots book-wisdom and the Western education. Turns ideas into a tradition at the same time it lays down standard descriptions of eccentricity and madness. And raises life over death as the cardinal self-evident fact.

Wittgenstein thought about killing himself often, and Augustine said: 'If anyone were offered the choice of suffering death and becoming a child again, who would not recoil from the second alternative and choose to die?'[89] Originality in ideas and words: that's our fantasy. But because it's a fantasy and will never come real, we live it vicariously through others like Wittgenstein and Augustine. Meanwhile they never wanted any of it—Because for some unknown, inborn reason, they never conceived that fantasy. And not conceiving it made them different from everyone else. Instead they only ever wanted to follow their Master's voice. In following it, they made strange and unpredictable movements and sounds, they were not pinned down; they smashed the Devil identity and derailed the narrative. They made it impossible to write biographies about them.

> Imagine humans who from childhood up scribble very fast as they talk: as it were illustrating what they say. Must I assume that if someone draws or describes or imitates something from memory, he *reads* off his representation from something or other?!—What supports this?[90]

You think that the *Tractatus* is a funny style of book? Well hear this. One's style of writing comes from where one has been, and what one has seen and lived through. A Western education fudges this and causes it to be forgotten. It does this because it insists on writing about God, the supernatural, death, other peoples, and so on. That is to say, it encourages everyone to think, read, and write on these things when the fact is that very few have actually journeyed to *their places*. And so a Western education teaches that there are just disciplines and objects of study, and then the styles in which one may choose to write on them. It is the most breath-taking arrogance. It is the dumbest of dumb. The Bible was written by men who had conversed with God, and that is the end of it. All criticism on this is the Devil identity (God = social construction).

> 'I know' is here a *logical* insight. Only realism can't be proved by means of it [91]

The *Tractatus* is a spiritual autobiography. If Augustine's *Confessions* was the first spiritual autobiography in the known West, and if it made its point by abandoning conventional narrative at exactly the point where Augustine ceded active control of his life to God, and from then on spoke only of existential and metaphysical things, then the *Tractatus* takes this radicalism to a whole new level. A level at which all conventional God-language becomes clumsy, redundant, and discarded. Because if you followed God in your muscles, blood, and bones—and if you followed him to *real* places in which you had *real* experiences—you wouldn't need to talk about him like that, would you? You wouldn't need to learn beliefs and dogmas like alphabets and words. And you wouldn't need to join them up to make a religion and a catechesis. Because, of course, a language is exactly what any *learnt* religion is, except that its objects can't even be seen. What would you expect to see if Wittgenstein had all along been following God, footstep by footstep? Would you expect him to be talking about it and using God-language all the time? Well then you have been mistaken, I am afraid. Look instead to his physical movements—What he did with his feet, hands, and face. The places he put himself on the ground. And don't anymore call those his eccentricities, and relate them to his work as the random symptoms of his 'tortured genius'. Consider them instead the note-perfect rendering of some true and truly hidden predestination. Not the predestination of the already-happened, but even that card flipped over and made into the door out of mathematical infinity and into the endless new worlds. For in truth we all have something of those worlds in us—There is in all of us a scintilla that has always existed in that place beyond the door of mathematical infinity. Whenever they talked to us in church of God's eternity, there was always something in us that shuddered and recoiled from that because it wanted more.

> A freely developing sequence in the first place is something empirical. It is nothing but the numbers that I write down on paper. If Weyl believes that it is a mathematical structure because I can derive a freely developing sequence from another one by means of a general law, e.g.,
>
> $m_1, m_2, m_3 \ldots$
> $m_1, m_1+m_3, m_1+m_3 \ldots$
>
> then the following is to be said against it: No, this shows only that I can add numbers, but not that a freely developing sequence is an admissible mathematical concept.[92]

The purpose of true spiritual autobiography is higher and more exalted than any language of any named god. To even associate Augustine's *Confessions* with Christianity or Wittgenstein's *Tractatus* with the same or with mathematics is to miss the point. The best that a spiritual autobiography can do is to make an embarrassing spectacle of the intellectual methods by which we customarily come to understand a dead life. The only thing that you can do with your mind over someone else's life is not understand it. If you write a book about their life that has as its purpose the understanding of it, then the only thing that you can achieve by it is to move your readers away from the truth, one page at a time. If the *Tractatus* is the true sequel to the *Confessions*, then it is because it dispenses with the God-language that Augustine couldn't dispense with and finds a way to show instead the single truth that whatever we truly are it is none of the things that identity makes plain. The agents and their actions, the causes and their effects. The Devil and his already-happened know this, and they want to use it and abuse it. Because of what it is, the already-happened can't see itself, yet it wants to because that vision would be glorious. So this has become the great cosmic battleground. And one way to try to bring it to the world's attention is to begin with language, truth, and logic and then keep going until only the human eye (the scintilla/the soul/what of us is the other side of the door) is left. In the Western way, the truth is always the truth of the bigger picture; while the bigger picture is always bigger because it is the thing that contains the subject. In the Western way, the subject is never allowed to be on the other side of the door. You are free to make bigger pictures and theorize. Go ahead, I won't stop you. But be warned: the bigger picture is always wrong!

> *The limits of my language* mean the limits of my world.
> Logic pervades the world: the limits of the world are also its limits.

So we cannot say in logic, 'The world has this in it, and this, but not that.'

For that would appear to presuppose that we were excluding certain possibilities, and this cannot be the case, since it would require that logic should go beyond the limits of the world; for only in that way could it view those limits from the other side as well.

We cannot think what we cannot think; so what we cannot think we cannot *say* either.

This remark provides the key to the problem, how much truth there is in solipsism.

For what the solipsist *means* is quite correct; only it cannot be *said*, but makes itself manifest.

The world is *my* world: this is manifest in the fact that the limits of *language* (of that language which alone I understand) mean the limits of *my* world.

The world and life are one.

I am my world. (The microcosm.)

There is no such thing as the subject that thinks or entertains ideas.

If I wrote a book called *The World as I found it*, I should have to include a report on my body, and should have to say which parts were subordinate to my will, and which were not, etc., this being a method of isolating the subject, or rather of showing that in an important sense there is no subject; for it alone could *not* be mentioned in that book.—

The subject does not belong to the world: rather, it is a limit of the world.

Where *in* the world is a metaphysical subject to be found?

You will say that this is exactly like the case of the eye and the visual field. But really you do *not* see the eye.

And nothing *in the visual field* allows you to infer that it is seen by an eye.[93]

Pretending is, of course, only a special case of someone's producing (say) expressions of pain when he is not in pain. For if this is possible at all, why should it always be pretending that is taking place—this very special pattern in the weave of our lives?

A child has much to learn before it can pretend. (A dog cannot be a hypocrite, but neither can he be sincere.)

There might actually occur a case where we should say 'This man *believes* he is pretending.'
—WITTGENSTEIN, *Philosophical Investigations*, II, 11

Art furnishes us with eyes and hands and above all the good conscience to be able to turn ourselves into such a phenomenon.
—NIETZSCHE, *The Gay Science*, Section 107

The proposition and demonstration were fairly written on a thin wafer, with ink composed of a cephalic tincture. This the student was to swallow upon a fasting stomach, and for three days following eat nothing but bread and water. As the wafer digested, the tincture mounted to his brain, bearing the proposition along with it.
—SWIFT, *Gulliver's Travels*, III, 5

4

When the Camera Is on Us

I CAN DESCRIBE for you exactly this strange room into which we have arrived. *You* are sitting in a chair and directly in front of you and facing you, *You* are also sitting in a chair. Now you know exactly how Wittgenstein felt his whole life. Now you know why his philosophy is preoccupied by what it is preoccupied about. And if you can hold onto this feeling, then you will have known more about this man than ever you could have imagined. And you will be able to read *all* his writings as a single oeuvre.

* * *

You see, the traditional problems of philosophy never meant the discovery of your *Self* in a land called 'Existence', but this strange room and both of *You* in it.

* * *

It was never the case that we were in some strange relationship to 'existence', but that we were in some strange relationship to whatever it was that we were about to do next. *That* was the real strangeness of philosophy's call to you. It is, for example, why we cannot define 'time', except relatively. And why we cannot have any lasting sense of constancy except through the theory of relativity. And it is why you can have no religious understanding of yourself except as *that person facing You*, who is good or bad, confesses and repents, and so on. Or, for that matter, whom you might never manage to understand that well. Who will remain a mystery to you. And it is also why *reality*—or the sensation of reality—is the struggle to ignore the *You* who is opposite *You*, so that it would be as though there were only one of you in the room. That is to say, the concept of 'reality' is what it is because it presupposes at least competing 'realities'; but more likely innumerable such realities. In this regard, it will remind us of what we have already noticed about the 'finite' and the 'infinite'. The 'finite' would be meaningless unless it presupposed the 'infinite'. While the 'infinite' would be meaningless unless it could mean some one definite thing in a sentence.

* * *

If there is this room, and two chairs, and two of *You*, then one of you is *pretending*. And if one of you is pretending, then the room only exists to be seen because it is being filmed. And if the room is being filmed, then it is already too late to know *who you really are*—Because of course it is in the definition of the camera, and its *truth*, that it will see you only according to your outward form and movements. So that if they are identical, then they are identical.

* * *

All of this can be restated thus. What philosophy has called 'truth' would be better called 'tense'. Because the acme of what can be known is what has been recorded to have happened. Or what has been reliably reported to have happened. Or degradations in that line. In relation to this *known* past, the future is the definition of what is *unknown*. Whilst the present is the difference between the two, measured out in the only animal which can experience it as 'a difference'; which is the human animal and its consciousness. All the traditional problems of philosophy come down to the fact that you are not everywhere at once (like God) but here, in the present. Because if you were everywhere at once, then you would surely see that there can in point of fact be no difference between the statements 'What I did, I did' and 'What I do, I shall do'. In both cases, you obey, you copy, you imitate the *You* in the chair in front of *You*. Think about it. Why on earth should we regard the past as in any way different to the future, given that the past was once the future, and that the future shall one day be the past? Why should we regard our history as the proper domain of *the truth of us*?—Of the proper domain of what might finally be said of us? And notice that the traditional techniques of 'knowing' someone are all such as that they can only work on a person's history. If our 'future domain' will one day surely be part of our 'historical domain', why do we treat it differently? Why do we treat it as though it doesn't exist? If we are *here*, now, then we shall be *there*, then. And if what we do here, now, is determined by laws of psychology and the like, then so shall what we do there, then, be determined. More (or worse): If we are lawfully determined to be *here*, then we are at exactly the same time lawfully determined to be *there*. We are here and there. We are *everywhere*. Or at the very least, we are not *somewhere*. We are *tense-less*.

* * *

And so we are always in this strange room and its two chairs. *At least, in our brains this is how it must always look.* Facing us, in the other chair, is what we are going to do anyway. Or, as we should properly express it, 'What we *did* anyway'. Because 'what we are going to do' and 'what we did' both come to the same thing from the point of view of the laws of thought, of the laws of our brains. Ultimately, you will only ever have acted as it could be written up afterwards, in the biography of you. Which is the same thing as to say that the biography of you already exists. That the biographies of all of us already exist. In my last book, I put it like this:

> Don't believe all that fire and brimstone talk about hell. No. They just keep books in hell. Hell keeps the universe's best library. There are no people in hell being boiled alive. It is far worse than that. There are just biographies of people all lined up neatly on shelves, catalogued to perfection. And they are the most brilliant biographies in the world. The biographies that we still write down here merely flap around in conjectures, but these hellish editions are the real stuff. In them each human life becomes what it always was: catatonically, pathetically, obvious. Dead paper between dead covers.[1]

* * *

When Isaac Bashevis Singer used to say, 'We have to believe in freedom of the will, we have no choice', he was ridiculing the long tradition of Western idealism—What Ernst Troeltsch meant when he said, 'The whole of European philosophy and science stand essentially under the influence of Platonic rationalism.'

> [For Platonic rationalism] presupposes, to be sure, the subjectivism and relativism of the Sophists, and in so far has its roots in empiricism; but at the same time its consistent aim is to transcend the merely actual through the demonstration that, seething and developing within it, is a rationally necessary conceptual element.[2]

At Cambridge, with Russell and Russell's logical atomism, Wittgenstein encountered mainly the 'empirical roots' of this phenomenon. But it all comes to the same thing.

Which is *predestination*. Whether you believe in God, or Godless Science or Pure Mind, it all comes to the same thing. Which is that human freedom of thought can only ultimately reach necessity's conclusion. The ecstasy of this conclusion is *sexual*. And because it is a real conclusion, one can only say it like that to see it like that. But I will show you a great deal more of this in the following, final chapter. For now, however, I will say that because it is a sexual ecstasy, the various systematic schemes from, say, Kant on up, which have endeavoured to find freedom in bondage, are an attempt to split the atom of that same sexual energy. While Wittgenstein is the first to do something different altogether, which is to accept and demonstrate that freedom, run long enough and wide enough, will always create necessity's picture. Which is that room and its two chairs, and *You* and *Yourself*. The only way to put this in words, is to say that *there is no escaping from freedom*. The problem has never been freedom, but freedom within *this single universe*. Because then freedom is simply your freedom to see your predestination. The answer must be to somehow use your freedom to escape this single universe.

> I believe that one of the things Christianity says is that sound doctrines are all useless. That you have to change your life. (Or the direction of your life.)[3]
>
> Courage, not cleverness; not even inspiration, is the grain of mustard that grows up to be a great tree.[4]

***

The message of the *Tractatus* is that there is the knowledge that you learn at school, and then there is the knowledge that all men everywhere have always called by the names of truth and wisdom, and which is meant to be the once and forever satisfaction of all the longings of the human heart—A knowledge that you can actually love in the satisfying way of authentic human love, and therefore an actual person rather anything abstract. *Christ*. But this means that this knowledge is the flipping over and destruction of every discrete knowledge-object that human thinking has thus far constructed and has yet to construct in future times. The end of the world as we know it will be when Christ-the-knowledge-object is flipped over and becomes the person Christ. Then will actually be seen what Augustine and Wittgenstein could only prophecy, which is that knowledge and truth will separate into two cities.

This coming separation means that everything that has been known and coordinated upon will be *unknown*. So that the truth will at last become whatever Christ chooses to say next. This will not make the truth random or arbitrary, but certainly it has to appear that it will for as long as we have to look on from within *this* city and anticipate Christ's coming. For this city lost its innocence with Adam and Eve and has ever since relied upon the opposite of random and arbitrary knowledge the better to ensure that the trains run on time. It is therefore almost impossible to imagine how things will be for those who pass over into the new city. But it is not altogether *impossible*. If it were wholly impossible then Augustine could not have written his *Confessions* and Wittgenstein his *Tractatus*. I remember hearing how the young Rudolf Nureyev would watch the trans-Siberian trains rolling past his tiny village and feel his dreams going with them. This universal human feeling that all need not be as it seems is what I am referring to. Imagine if all the mighty towers of ideas—not just secular ideas but all theology, too—ceased to be common ground, or even ground. Imagine if you had to meet Christ with none of it to share between you. You would have no means of recognizing him. In fact, you wouldn't recognize him, and that would be the point—*Is the point* of the *Confessions* as it accelerates into the *Tractatus*.[5]

THE THIEF ON THE CROSS

We just have to be honest about the conversation that took place between Christ and the thieves when all of them were being crucified.

> And one of the malefactors which were hanged railed on him, saying, If thou be Christ, save thyself and us.
> But the other answering him rebuked him, saying, Dost not thou fear God, seeing though art in the same condemnation?
> And we indeed justly; for we receive the due reward of our deeds: but this man hath done nothing amiss.
> And he said unto Jesus, Lord, remember me when thou comest into thy kingdom.
> And Jesus said unto him, Verily I say unto thee, To day shalt thou be with me in paradise.[6]

This is all that happened and everything that happened. These words are reported speech. Everything of the Gospel and everything of Christianity is in them, and yet they are reported speech. We are apparently so much wiser now, all these years on. Look at all the books on theology and religious studies in any respectable university library. Think of all their analyses and deconstructions. Look even to the church and all its dogma and formula. Look at all the seminarians breaking their brains over trinities and predestinations. And yet these words, here, are reported speech—And everything of everything is in them. And because these words are reported speech, they wipe out at a stroke the magisterium of the professional academy, which is based in the self-professed virtue of the objective and impartial observer, who blanks his emotions and always looks carefully to *what is really going on*. Notebook and pencil in hand. The Gospels could not have been written by anthropologists.

Christ walked the earth and spoke real words with men and women, and those men and women followed him—And they followed him for no reason. Not for no discernible or expressible reason, but for *no reason*. For no reason in the sense of nothing for a scholar to dig up afterwards. No reason in the sense that no reason ever was there, and that no reason ever was needed. 'But surely there have to be reasons!' you say. 'And in this most important case, most especially of all!' Don't worry. I am not unsympathetic to your panic. In fact, I have been referencing your panic all the way through this book—Because being sensitive to this panic and writing into it was one of Wittgenstein's signal achievements. You panic because a world in which things are not permitted to stand in front of their corresponding reasons is a nonsense world—A world which would be the obliteration of the one in which you have always lived. The world in which red always means stop and green always means go, and from there on up. And the world in which you are taught that Christ was followed because he was perceived to be the Messiah; where Messiah was an idea of permanent obsession in the universal human psyche, and therefore capable of being satisfied by any chosen thing, and so on, and so forth. And you are right about all of this. And so your panic is real and entirely justified. But the fact is that when Wittgenstein speaks about Christ he does so in language which is designed to kick out the chair from underneath itself, flip the card over, and just plain *speak*. For as we have now learnt from Wittgenstein, there are just the places that you have been to, the experiences and emotions that you have had in those places, and the words that flowed out from your mouth to make their present moments. Those moments and those words were *Truth*. Afterwards, language had to treat those moments differently, as though they were in the past and had happened. The words of those moments had to become the 're-ported words' of those moments. And it was then that you discovered how the devilish scheme of 'identity' gets to work. Knowing full well (and better than you) the difference between words and reported words, the devilish scheme asks you to consider the extent to which you can be certain that what was reported to have happened *actually happened*. The question of the Fall of humankind in Eden, and the question of Western criticism ever since. The Devil knows that few men in any age get to converse directly with God in the present and write the words of that conversation. And thus he knows that he is on safe ground with the numerical majority who will never actually see or speak with God, but have to rely instead on the reported speech of the Gospels and the saints. With these he can wreak merry havoc with the intellectual questions of certainty and proof. Over the man whose conversation is actually with God, he is powerless. Wittgenstein teaches us that the question 'What is truth?' is really the question 'Where have you been (with whom have you conversed?)?' If I repeat part of a quotation from near the end of the previous chapter, then we will see this clearly:

> What fights doubt is as it were redemption. Holding fast to it must be holding fast to this belief. So this means: first be redeemed & hold on tightly to your redemption (keep hold of your redemption)—then you will see that what you are holding on to is this belief. So this can only come about if you no longer support yourself on this earth but suspend yourself from heaven. Then everything is different and it is 'no wonder' if you can then do what now you cannot do. (It is true that someone

who is suspended looks like someone who is standing but the interplay of forces within him is nevertheless a quite different one & hence he is able to do quite different things than can one who stands.)[7]

The standard interpretations of Wittgenstein on religious belief take his statements like this to mean that belief is unrelated to what is objectively true and is rather a state of conviction with dramatic consequences for how one operates within the world—And that it is therefore those operations consequent upon belief, or the tangible, material results of belief, that demand that we take it seriously. If someone acts out of religious belief in the public square, while we act out of possession of the objective facts of the matter, then from the point of view of the fact that we have both acted, it cannot matter what may have been the difference between our motivations. The question whether one *ought* to be motivated by faith or science becomes the question for another day. What matters in this interpretation of 'Wittgenstein on religious belief' is that there can be a standpoint from which religious belief can use the actions it produces to masquerade as the same thing as true judgement.

This should remind us of my passing observation towards the end of the previous chapter to the effect that the real moral of Western freedom turns out to be: *Do anything you like, but don't get caught!* There, I pointed out that the free movements of one's private thoughts are, on the Western model, perfectly analogous to the free movements of one's limbs. That they have been perfectly analogous since the death of God and the separation of church and state. The West says that it is now just a matter of your free will and the things it picks up and moves. Except now come in the difficult realities and the hypocrisy. It isn't just as simple as doing what you want, when you like. There are such things as society and the good of it—As well as others' rights to an equal freedom as yours. And so come in the codes and the laws, and the policing and the transgressions—And the possibility of getting caught. And then additionally, there are those who want to talk about moral objectivity, and absolute truths in this area, and categorical imperatives. These people may even talk of a science of living well and a science of the good life; to the extent that one's private thoughts ought no longer be free as the wind but running instead along the lines of these sciences, encountering items of moral knowledge which are self-evident and binding. The same happens over the phenomenon of religiously motivated action. The interpretation of Wittgenstein that I have been paraphrasing here, which says that a religious motivation is no better or worse than any other from the point of view of its effects, swiftly erodes in exactly the same manner until it becomes common sense to say that religious motivations are intolerable if their secular alternatives can be made widely enough available through education and enlightenment. This seems then to become a position that can be generally supported by the positivist register of Wittgenstein's writings. A position that, in fact, appears to become exemplified in the later philosophy of his *Philosophical Investigations*, where the goal of finding the general form of propositions and the characteristic (the substance, or *being*) of language is dropped in favour of enumerating the endless ways (and types of ways) in which language is daily used between people.

In his later philosophy, it is true to say that Wittgenstein starts to treat language far more like music. That is to say, in the same way that we appreciate, discuss, and exemplify music and its range and possibilities, but never truly enquire into its essence (and why certain notes go so well together in certain situations and others not), Wittgenstein now does the same with language. Language, like music, gets added to the list of things that human beings do and other animals do not. *That* becomes its whole significance, rather than the idea that an enlightened philosophy should work to make language dutiful towards its revealed essence (the general form of the proposition, and its verification against the facts). Language must still hold to rules, and its user communities must agree to those and stick to them as do the participants in any game. But Wittgenstein's insight now is those rules may be changed endlessly and at will. The philosophical analysis of language can no longer issue in a normative statement about the atomic structure of reality—About what is true and what is not, and therefore how we *ought* to think and speak. The philosophical analysis of language can now only *describe* the various games which it has observed taking place.

> Here we come up against the great question that lies behind all these considerations.—For someone might object against me: 'You take the easy way out! You talk about all sorts of language-games, but have nowhere said what the essence of a language-game, and hence of language, is: what is common to all these activities, and what makes them into language or parts of language. So you let yourself off the very part of the investigation that once gave you yourself most headache, the part about the *general form of propositions* and of language.'
>
> And this is true.—Instead of producing something common to all that we call language, I am saying that these phenomena have no one thing in common which makes us use the same word for all,—but that they are *related* to one another in many different ways. And it is because of this relationship, or these relationships, that we call them all 'language'. I will try to explain this.
>
> Consider for example the proceedings that we call 'games'. I mean board-games, card-games, ball-games, Olympic games, and so on. What is common to them all?—Don't say: 'There *must* be something common, or they would not be called "games"'—but *look and see* whether there is anything common to all.—For if you look at them you will not see something that is common to *all*, but similarities, relationships, and a whole series of them at that.... And the result of this examination is: we see a complicated network of similarities overlapping and crisscrossing: sometimes overall similarities, sometimes similarities of detail.[8]

It is commonplace to say that this most postmodern of postmodern ways of approaching language and truth, and which has given so much succour to those like

Russell who get disturbed by the unchecked mysticism of the *Tractatus*, marks an important turn in the development of Wittgenstein's thinking—That it divides it into an earlier and later philosophy. Or that by refusing to speak of ghosts in his *Tractatus* Wittgenstein succeeded in admitting them in a most brilliant and rampant way, but that in the *Philosophical Investigations* he switched sides and did what we in the West all do when we get all serious and intellectual, which is to cast passion aside and find only what we can look for. Just the will in our brain and how it uses electrical pulses to move our thoughts and limbs. This scientistic outlook becomes then the dynamic front against tradition and conservatism.[9] To the moral: *Do anything you like, but don't get caught!* you get to attach the rider *Or change the laws!* However, I don't believe that Wittgenstein's philosophy is so simple that it can be divided like this into its earlier and later preoccupations; as though the man-child was a late developer who became more like us as the years rolled on. But I must return to the thief on the cross to explain why.

In that moment, on that day, the thief on the cross who rebuked the other thief and followed Christ into his kingdom did nothing remarkable. He just did what he did, said what he said. Those who love Christ today and those who hate him are equally as liable to forget this; because, for their different reasons, they both need to account for Christ and give him a *factual* basis. Those who love Christ may be driven to prove his Messiah status and his supernatural qualities. Those who hate Christ may be driven to reduce him to merely a teacher and a man. A leader raised to greatness by the totemic devotion of his followers. In both cases, the need is felt to account for Christ in intellectually respectable ways. Which is to say that both those who love and hate Christ need to have some basis on which to write books about him: they need to be able to give him a biography and explain him. And so, what I am saying here stands equally against both cases, because what I am saying is that there is no accounting of any kind for what the thief on the cross determined in that moment to do and say. No accounting for it at all.

You cannot place an identity sign before it, which is what those who hate Christ would do in order to take it back to electrical impulses in his brain. *And you cannot place an identity sign after it*, which is what those who love Christ would do if they wanted to preach a lesson on it. You just can't do it. It came from nowhere. No one could have imagined the thief would say that. There are the Gospels and all of the Bible, and then there is that moment—And how it comes and goes unbidden. And coming and going unbidden like that it defies the *already-happened*. It was never there, waiting, in the catalogue of the already-happened. The other thief's mocking of Christ was.

This is what Wittgenstein meant when he said (from the quote above):

(It is true that someone who is suspended looks like someone who is standing but the interplay of forces within him is nevertheless a quite different one & hence he is able to do quite different things than can one who stands.)

Now compare also this:

> No supposition seems to me more natural than that there is no process in the brain correlated with associating or with thinking; so that it would be impossible to read off thought-processes from brain-processes. I mean this: If I talk or write there is, I assume, a *system* of impulses going out from my brain and correlated with my spoken or written thoughts. But why should the *system* continue further in the direction of the centre? Why should this order not proceed, so to speak, out of chaos?[10]

It is not the case that science is able to explain belief in Christ as an electrical discharge—perhaps more sudden and violent than other such discharges—but a discharge nonetheless. It is not the case that the episode of the thief on the cross is an episode in the comforting power of faith. It is not the case that it demands to be treated differently from rational belief in the facts but identically to all enumerable instances of the religious impulse. It is rather the case that there are only ever two cities: in the one you feel and suffer things in your muscles, blood, and bones and in the other you stand apart from that passion and feel and suffer nothing. It is possible to hate Christ and feel and suffer nothing as much as it is possible to love Christ and feel and suffer nothing. But it is possible also to walk across into the other city and feel and suffer everything (*the passion of Christ*).

In the earthly city, however, you are in an eternal regression in which you never wake up and come to your senses. Every new situation you come into just becomes some new opportunity to stand back and wonder and learn (the curse of the Western education again). You never scream for it to stop. You never make it stop. You never kill yourself. You always choose life. Over and over again. Life. But what if you chose death? What if you died to this city that you are in and walked through death's door into the City of Passion? Now try on those words of Wittgenstein's for size. Do it. Go back to the final pages of the previous chapter and try them on again. Now do you see the difference? Now do you see why the standard interpretation of Wittgenstein on religious belief misdirects itself? If you are warm and comfortable and well-fed, if you have a roof over your head and if science has filled out the bigger picture of the universe for you, then the Gospel won't speak a word to you. If you are cold and starving and homeless, if the bigger picture has evaporated and been replaced by the gnawing urgencies of your beleaguered present, then the Gospel will be everything to you. If you are taken from life's flush and placed at death's door, then it will be everything to you. It will speak to you, and you will speak to Christ. We all know this already. We all know that secular humanism is the creed of the living, while the Gospel is the creed of the dying because the drowning man always prays. Except we used to think of this as its weakness. Science sent men to the moon, so what good is the creed of dead men bowing out? Wittgenstein helps us see this criticism doesn't stand up. It works if there is only one city and one world, and the range of human passions are simply our chosen flavours of response to its events and knowledge-objects; for in that scenario it would be better, yes, to be brave and self-sufficient than meek and

God-fearing. But if the passions are places that the heart can see, if nothing is what it seems and everything can be flipped over, if every stable concept is in tautological relationship with the already-happened so that with the already-happened they can all be laughed at and walked through, then to follow Christ like the thief on the cross is to suddenly see all of this for what it is in a perfect blinding flash—And seeing it for what it is, to walk yourself *physically* through its empty intellections.

> If I have exhausted the justifications, I have reached bedrock and my spade is turned. Then I am inclined to say: 'This is simply what I do.'[11]

The Western way is never to admit this *physical* walking through of its empty intellections, its pantographic realism where the idea, where the copy, is always more heralded than the real thing. The thief on the cross isn't here anymore. But we are still here, wallowing in our eternity of numbers and ideas. The thief said, 'This is ridiculous!' and left. Christ was without sin and was crucified unjustly by any plain reckoning. Only as an idea and an abstraction could he be convicted. Only as an event always existing in the already-happened could his crucifixion take place. Only as an event already-happened in this way could it make sense to both those who loved Christ and those who hated him (and those who still love him and hate him now). To those who love him it was atonement, sacrifice, retribution, and a ransom paid in blood. To those who hate him it was proof-perfect of his powerlessness and inability to reach up and save himself.

The whole of the already-happened is an infinity of happenings all triangulated on this arch-happening—Christ's crucifixion—and, as it were, held in place by it as by a lynchpin. So long as the Devil can keep Christ's lovers and haters both believing equally in the need to understand his life and explain and make sense of its final act, then he can keep up his project for a while longer. The thief on the cross saw none of this, or at least he saw all of it 'in a perfect blinding flash'. And by that flash as by a lightning flash over a nightscape, he saw the whole of the cosmic injustice of it lit up before him. 'But this man hath done nothing amiss[!]' Like that he saw it! And like that he was saved! You see, because the already-happened works pantographically, its realism in perfect imitation of the real (plus its realism immune to the ravages of time in the way that idealism is always immune to the ravages of time), its victory can seem total and unwavering. Its victory can seem guaranteed by the logic of the pantograph. So, for God to send his only begotten son into the world can seem like the most desperate of mistakes—Because in making him a man to walk the earth in flesh and blood, he was giving him up to the already-happened. For in the already-happened he had *already been crucified and died*. And we must remember always as Wittgenstein has taught us to remember: the Devil was the angel who fell out of pride, out of pride of mind. When it began to be said afterwards that his falling was sin itself, that it was transmitted by him to our first parents, and from them to us, so that we became inherently sinful as a species, this was not some dogma to be blindly believed. Sin did not mean some magic stain. Sin meant something real and mechanical, obvious and unspectacular. It meant to stop following God from *New World* to *New World* and to start trying to live as though the only world was the fixed world that logic prescribes—The fixed world of the *general form of the proposition*. The fixed world of the totality of atomic facts: then the perfect alignment of all thought and language on it. This world—And then the wires and rods linking it pantographically to the already-happened. And the already-happened revealed itself fully only to the very best of minds. And thus the already-happened taking the place of God. And periodic human sacrifices being offered to this new God. And those sacrificial victims being given a special name: 'geniuses'. So, when God sent his only begotten son to save us, this is what he had to save us from. Not 'sin' as some empty and unqualified doom, but sin operating like this, by wires and rods. And so the salvation from it became to let his son be given to the already-happened's predestination—to let his son be given to its death—but for that death to then be *swallowed up in victory*. For that death to be swallowed up in supernatural resurrection from the dead.

Think of it like this. The already-happened never stopped going on; in fact, it can't stop. It is going on now. It is going on now as though it killed Christ. And for proof that it is going on now as though it killed Christ, you need only consult the books of the scholars who have synced their minds with the already-happened's brand of intelligence. In those you will read that Christ was just a man who died, and that no man has ever been miraculously resurrected. I repeat, the already-happened is wires and rods, it is cause and effect, it is science itself. It is true insofar as it goes, and so we must upgrade our previous statement and say that God never set out to use his son to destroy it. It cannot be destroyed. It cannot be destroyed because it is made up of ideas, and you cannot destroy ideas. You can only remain innocent of ideas. And you can only remain innocent of ideas by having Someone *physically* to follow by your muscles, blood, and bones. This is why when the Devil first put the suggestion of an idea to Adam and Eve, and they chose not to keep following God with their feet, but to consider it in their minds, they fell at once, with no protection.

Christ's victory over the already-happened was not a victory over its truth. It could not be. Death is death. Atoms are atoms. The void is the void. The natural is the natural. The supernatural does not destroy the natural. No. Instead it is over and above it. It leaves it in place and soars over and above it. The victory of the supernatural over the natural is that the natural cannot help itself—Cannot surmount or modify its own logic, which is the logic of the pantograph. Or in Wittgenstein's language of the *Tractatus*: the logic of the tautology. To think therefore that the natural and the supernatural are competing for the same space is completely wrong-headed. To think that science is competing with Christianity for the same space is completely wrong-headed. To hold debates between the two in public is completely wrong-headed. Because the pantograph is made of wires and rods it simply cannot stretch beyond the limits of those materials. It cannot become ethereal and spiritual of a sudden. So death is always its full stop. Did the Devil not know this? Of course he did. He knew full well that on the third day Christ would rise from the dead in the full resurrection of his body. He knew that the full stop of Christ's death would not really be a full stop, and in exactly the same way that he knows that no human death is a full stop either. Because he knows better than anyone that there is a heaven (because he fell from it!) and that there is a hell (because he lives there!). So in light of this, his plan from the start has been to have Christ crucified and then to run a giant deception campaign against his rising again.

THE *TRACTATUS* AS SPIRITUAL AUTOBIOGRAPHY

The *Tractatus* does not pit science against Christianity; which is why Wittgenstein made the claim at the time of writing it that it was completely right about everything that matters and had solved all the traditional problems of philosophy. The *Tractatus* celebrates and explains science. And then it leaves Christianity to soar over and above it. It is, as I have argued, a spiritual autobiography, purer and more deliberate than Augustine's first spiritual autobiography (the first of its type). Augustine tried to accomplish this same feat but his age was not ready for it. Science in his day was still juvenile and could never have supported itself in the way that it could all those years later in the *Tractatus*. It would not have made any sense to write his book in that way. If Christianity is to soar, if death really is to be swallowed up in victory, then there must first be something concrete for it to soar above. The ages after Augustine were never meant to be about the spread of Christianity but the spread of science. Despite the best efforts of Christianity to believe and act otherwise, science has now managed to reach nearly everywhere and prove itself the undisputed truth. And it has been exactly this success and universality that made the *Tractatus* possible in its age.

Similarly, this is the ultimate reason why the later philosophy of Wittgenstein's *Philosophical Investigations* isn't vanquished in the philosophy of his *Tractatus*. The relationship of the *Investigations* to the *Tractatus* is that the former soars over and above the latter.

The point about the supernatural is that it doesn't take place within this world but takes you with it out of this world. Like Nureyev's trains. The message of Wittgenstein's philosophy and its unification into a coherent theory is 'Stop following Aristotle and stepping off on the wrong foot with him! Stop trying to understand everything within the metric of a single world.' Aristotle says that that metric is 'being'. Aristotle says that everything that is anything must finally ground out on being. But I (Ludwig) say (again):

(It is true that someone who is suspended looks like someone who is standing but the interplay of forces within him is nevertheless a quite different one & hence he is able to do quite different things than can one who stands.)

Instead let there be Christ and the infinite worlds of his infinite words—And how one can be suspended from his words!

Look again at the thief on the cross. Those who like Aristotle want to understand everything according to the underlying metric of a single world look at the thief after he had been granted entrance by Christ to the Kingdom of Heaven and observe that nothing in his material circumstances changed. [It is true that someone who is suspended looks like someone who is standing ...] He was still hanging on his cross. Of course he was! If, like Aristotle, you look by increments of your metric—if you look 10 units ahead for a point 10 units ahead—then that is precisely what you will see. If you look 10 units behind you, then the same again. 25 units ahead, the same, and so on. Apparently, it never occurred to Aristotle that what he was doing by this was proving the supernatural and its infinite worlds beyond all shadow of doubt. The one universe of numbers and physics that science and philosophy both now seem to be united in seeking to reveal is not going to be proof that the supernatural does not exist. Seeing, counting, thinking, measuring ... — These things are not proof of anything other than seeing, counting, thinking, measuring ... Christ taught this, and Wittgenstein picked it up and ran with it. Christ taught:

> All things are delivered unto me of my Father: and no man knoweth the Son, but the Father; neither knoweth any man the Father, save the Son, and *he* to whomsoever the Son will reveal *him*.
> Come unto me, all *ye* that labour and are heavy laden, and I will give you rest.
> Take my yoke upon you, and learn of me; for I am meek and lowly in heart: and ye shall find rest unto your souls.
> For my yoke *is* easy, and my burden is light."

When we read 'All things are delivered ... ' we think of the knowledge that we already know how to deliver unto ourselves. And in thinking that, we make these words of Christ empty and redundant. What Wittgenstein interpreted these words of Christ to really mean is that we share no common ground with Christ called 'knowledge'. We use our eyes and minds to see the universe and its being and to describe its being according to complicated calculations and predictions. Good for us. But when we do this, we prove only what our eyes can see and our minds can calculate. To really use Wittgenstein's language, we prove only the *limits* of our seeing and thinking. To prove in this way the limits of one's capacities is NOT the same thing as to prove the limits of wisdom, truth, and reality. For example: If I say, 'I do not speak Portuguese', I in no way imagine this to come to mean that Portugal does not exist. I simply state a limit of my present capacity. Yet when it comes to Christ and the supernatural, this is exactly the heist that we pull all the time. We really do seem to imagine that whenever we prove that our eyes can only see material things, we prove at the same time that immaterial things do not exist. This is an absurdity. Yet the whole of a Western education today is built upon it.

From the *Tractatus* onwards, Wittgenstein taught the counter flow. No one was prepared to go as far as him in teaching that when you measure something with the eye or mind—or even the eye of the mind—the fact that you are measuring it means that you never actually come into contact with it. I don't mean the physical way in which you certainly do have to pick it up to put it on a scale or wrap a tape measure around it. I mean its *essence*. You will be aware that I have been after this point from the start in all my criticisms of conventional biography. When we say that Wittgenstein, or Augustine, or Christ, or any man was *n* feet tall, that is all we can mean by that statement. The way that our imagination tends to jump in on even the scantest information and start filling out a human picture is irrelevant here and must not distract us. When I say that a man is *n* feet tall, that number is all that I can mean. When I say that he has blue eyes, again, that is all that I can mean. When I say that he lived in *x* street for *y* time, again, that street and that time are all that I can mean. No one can deny that this is the manner in which Western intelligence produces its understanding of all things and everyone, from rocks to humans. Except humans are clearly the point at which this procedure runs into difficulties, because they reveal, like nothing else, the sense in which the general form of this kind of knowledge can never rise above *the tautology*. *n* feet is always in tautological relationship with *n* feet: it never actually reaches beyond that relationship with itself to touch the thing of which it is being predicated.[13] The written-out biography of a human life which is ordinarily put together as a compilation of thousands of such predications is obviously the supreme test-case of the scope and limitations of this way of proceeding. Inspired by this thing that Wittgenstein noticed, I have been, as it were, sacrificing this biography of him to the question of how far we can really know anyone by this procedure. And I find I now believe very much Wittgenstein's thesis (developed in his *Tractatus* and applied in his *Investigations*) that one could compile even an infinite number of predications about a living life—and all of them could be 100% true—and yet at the end of them all the real person would walk off into the night, and you would have never known them at all. Yet again I have to say that this would be just like the form of the *Tractatus*, which itself also walks off into the night, taking Wittgenstein, Augustine, Christ, and the supernatural with it—So that no one today can still really say what Wittgenstein really meant by himself, his muse, his Lord, and his faith.

A DEEP BREATH

Let's take a deep breath, and let everything I have said so far in this book wash over us in Wittgenstein's words. I'll annotate them so that you can quickly see how they bring everything together and to a point.

1. From the *Tractatus*:

> The freedom of the will consists in the impossibility of knowing actions that still lie in the future. We could know them only if causality were an *inner* necessity like that of logical inference.—The connexion between knowledge and what is known is that of logical necessity. ('*A* knows that *p* is the case', has no sense if *p* is a tautology.)[14]

In this fragment, Wittgenstein effectively bears out that what the thief on the cross said to Christ could never have been known beforehand—That it had no reason behind it. In just the same way that *all* human volition is able to have no reason behind it and can be those 'wild, whooping sounds' that I have mentioned on a number of occasions before. But in just the same way, too, that *all* human volition is equally able to have every reason behind it, and to merge seamlessly with the chains of cause and effect that link the totality of atomic facts. For example, if you choose to adhere zealously and perfectly to an ethic or a constitution, you become predictable. You start to act only out of clear reasons, and so on. So, it is possible for a free man to become un-free if he too zealously and perfectly tries to participate in what I call the 'World of Mental Intelligence'. If he does this, he can lose his whimsy and capriciousness and become scripted. Wittgenstein's fragment anticipates that possibility, but it does so by focusing instead on the essential, inborn freedom of the human will. Its message is meant to be positive and invigorating. Wittgenstein states that the causality which would pre-empt human freedom does not exist; though many have made the mistake of thinking that it does because they confuse it with *logical necessity*. Logical necessity is the way that the world of mental intelligence binds itself together by means of identity signs, as we have already noticed. It should not be confused with having anything to do with the human free will because unlike the human free will, it is a closed shop. It is a stitch-up, to hearken back to my metaphor of much earlier.[15] It is, as Wittgenstein puts it in his fragment, an '*inner*' necessity. Logical necessity is a necessity that never actually reaches out (as I put it above) to touch the subject—To touch the truth. Instead, it touches itself. It holds true only within itself. It makes, as Wittgenstein would say over and again, for a tautology. Logical necessity does not, as Russell thought, reach out beyond itself and set the world to rights. Logical necessity can guarantee you that n feet in London is the same thing as n feet in Beijing, and that can be extremely useful. But it achieves this at the expense of having to forgo all the reach and ambition of true human freedom. Because whereas true human freedom is what it is because it connects us to the truly unknowable—because it connects us to everything that the *Tractatus* brought us to the threshold of—logical necessity can only fake freedom by stating in advance what form the knowable *shall* take, and then going ahead and knowing it. When turned by men like Russell into a 'free man's worship' and a method of life, it therefore becomes a genuinely dangerous attack on the essence of what it means to be human. As a crusade, it turns its back on the fact that true human freedom should be an *outer* necessity, describing our plain irreducible *need* to be led forwards by a Messiah into only what the Messiah can see. And it is, in fact, the case that logical necessity and secular humanism can only make sense against this *need*, and in light of human pride. For why else, if not for pride, would we commit the absurdity of confecting a fake messianic seeing of our own?

Logical necessity says that it *is* the items of knowledge that compose the future before us, to the effect that they, and only they, can become what is known. And yet logical necessity itself put them there! Logical necessity is like hunting for the Easter eggs which you yourself hid, and then turning around to everyone and saying: 'You see, this is even more fun than it was before! This is how you have real fun!' But it is not. In fact, it is simply a tragic misunderstanding of what real human fun is. Real human fun is charging around and not knowing whether you will find any eggs. Real human freedom is what the thief on the cross of a sudden did. Real human freedom is like the currents of the oceans and sky. Its movement is the irresistible rushing of the high pressure into the low. The irresistible rushing of the known into the unknown. This is why I described it in the previous chapter as like 'one unending sexual act'.[16] To put the known on the left of the identity sign, and then again, the known on the right of the identity sign is logical necessity, certainly—But now we can say that it is also to cancel out the possibility of all true movement and all true freedom. I will have much more to say on Wittgenstein and sex and freedom in the next and final chapter. But for now, we just need to think *with* Wittgenstein on how the thief on the cross was pulled forwards in this irresistible way like the currents of the oceans and the sky are. There was nothing behind him pushing him in the manner that a scholar would say there was. His 'self-interest' pushing, for instance. Men really are born free, and freedom's impulse reaches out always to grasp what still lies in the future.

2. From the *Investigations*:

'What the names in language signify must be indestructible; for it must be possible to describe the state of affairs in which everything destructible is destroyed. And this description will contain words; and what corresponds to these cannot then be destroyed, for otherwise the words would have no meaning.' I must not saw off the branch on which I am sitting.

One might, of course, object at once that this description would have to except itself from the destruction.—But what corresponds to the separate words of the description and so cannot be destroyed if it is true, is what gives the words their meaning.—In a sense, however, this man is surely what corresponds to his name. But he is destructible, and his name does not lose its meaning when the bearer is destroyed.—An example of something corresponding to the name, and without which it would have no meaning, is a paradigm that is used in connexion with the name in the language-game.[17]

In the world of mental intelligence, which is the ever-expanding world as it is presented to us in knowledge-objects and the theoretical arrangements of knowledge-objects (which is the ever expanding world of books and the 'world mind', that each year grows more intelligent and formidable), the truth of its knowledge-objects (its ideas) is promoted to us on the principle of their indestructibility vis-à-vis the destructibility of their empirical counterparts. At its best, then, the language of this promotion is always romantic and religious. Knowledge is higher than us and better than us—It is higher and better than our everyday existence, where we feel our way by instinct and experience, but not necessarily art and wisdom and first principles. I began Chapter 2 by noticing how we associate the truth with what is empirically real; yet, in answering the question of 'meaning', we invoke the self-evident ontological superiority of the idea-world. We talk about the future as a place already fixed and described by the laws of nature, and so on. This is very odd and paradoxical behaviour that should alert us that something is ghastly wrong; yet, on we plough. Except Wittgenstein, who seems to have been pathologically alert to it and willing to spend his life on chronicling it. This is why God sent his son, and this is why reflections on Christ can be found across Wittgenstein's writings. To look at these reflections and frame in response to them the question whether Wittgenstein was a Christian, or of what exactly his beliefs consisted, is not to the point of his original purpose. Take, if you like, the example of the way in which I have mixed in such reflections of my own—And much of them through Augustine. You should know better than to use them to judge me, good or bad. Why should they correspond to my private thoughts? You don't—and you shouldn't ever—know what my private thoughts are. And in just the same way, I don't pretend to know the private thoughts of Wittgenstein (or Augustine before him, or whomever will be the next subject). And most of all do I not pretend to know the thoughts of God—And most of all not when he sent his son. The reasons why he did that must remain private to him. Where does this leave us here? It leaves us able to drop this insight into Wittgenstein's Christian reflections. If you introduce Christ from time to time into this sort of philosophical writing you are able to make connections, jumps, leaps, and flights that you wouldn't be able to if you doggedly held out against even mentioning him. Again: I can feel that you are wanting to use this statement to impute things ideological and theological to me (and Wittgenstein). Don't! I mean what I am saying. I repeat: Who I really am is none of your business; as much as who Wittgenstein really was is none of your business either. [This proves, by the way, why we really call for biographies of people and read them. We want to know if they are 'good' or 'bad'. Nothing is ever about truth: it is about wanting to judge people.] When I say that the invocation of Christ into Western philosophy helps to break it out into new kinds of fluencies I mean it. And as far as you are concerned, I may as well be making a point about style or euphony. Or maybe not! Maybe I am playing the double agent with you. Because after all, I only ever began talking about Christ and the thief on the cross because I wanted to impress upon you the fact that it matters not one jot whether the world of mental intelligence is working for the scientists or the theologians. For in both cases, it inserts identity signs wherever it can, so that the scientists see only collocations of their chosen symbolisms and the theologians see only the proofs of their chosen doctrines. And both worship a god whom they have never seen and touched, save in the *inner* logical necessity of their minds. In relation to this endless regress, I time and again find that the person of Christ is the only antidote and the way to break the deadlock that such necessity creates; because the problem as I have been constructing it with Wittgenstein, is the problem of the *dehumanizing* effect of purely mental intelligence. Or the way that it betrays your emotional and physical side, which, after all, is the side of your life by which you actually walk it through from its beginning to its end.

I am not saying that the mind should be neglected or that it doesn't have its own means of affecting us. But when you think about it, all the problems of the mind—imagination, anxiety, fear, and worse—are problems that are experienced by us *only* at the point where they cross the threshold and tangle with us in our waking, physical, and emotional lives. The psychologist cannot discuss what is hidden from him in our private place; neither can the psychiatrist treat it. It is only aberrant speech and behaviour (deviating from some or other straight line) in the world of the physically and emotionally real that becomes the matter upon which the mind of medicine can work. You must by now be very familiar with this Wittgensteinian theme I keep pulling along. *The way by which we are taught in school and university to understand things that only the mind can understand always leaves us out in the cold—The subject always escapes his biographer, and so on.*

'I must not saw off the branch on which I am sitting.' That is truly the mantra we are taught from birth. 'Choose life!' 'Suicide is a crime!' The scientist saves himself and finds life in the eternity of numbers. The theologian saves himself and finds life in the eternal truths of doctrine. Numbers, names, and terms: their beauty and their relief are their permanence; while moment by moment we slip away. But by fleeing to them I say that we commit (after Eden we re-commit) a sin that the person of Christ seems so determined to remind us of and save us from still. You do not need Christian faith to figure that Western mental intelligence really is in the fix that Wittgenstein depicted it in, and the way out of that fix—the way to oil our synapses and get them thinking creatively again— is to stop our thoughts going around and around the eternity of numbers (the single world of numbers) and find instead a door for them to escape through. [If Wittgenstein the person can escape from this biography, I will have done my job.]

What no amount of doctrine or numbers about the person Christ will tell you is this: the story of how he suffered on his cross will make you cry— and in your tears, you will find a match for his pain in yours—and in that new *World of Suffering* in which you and he now abide, you will live and move in your physical passions and what there is of your mind will be obedient to them. No more than obedient to them.

The soldiers mocked Christ on the cross, and the natural has always asked the supernatural for a miracle, and every subject has escaped his biographer. So, the way home and to freedom is this: *Join your suffering to Christ's; join your suffering to your subject.* Leave behind the indestructibility of names and ideas and this single eternal world of the Western mind and embrace your destructibility— Your flesh and blood. This is why we gain so much by writing *Christ* into our philosophy. If we just use God-language, we invoke the very indestructibility of concept which is imprisoning us. But if we use Christ-language, it is as though we are no longer writing out the truth of what has already-happened but are riding our words like horses into a sunset of genuine destruction—A place where we *will not survive the night.*

The thief on the cross knew nothing, and he was free to act. And the theologians today know everything, and they are in chains. They look for eternal truth, and they have forgotten what it feels like to cry with Christ's pain. Any child who can follow the story of Christ's passion can do what they in all their wisdom cannot. God did not put his son into human form to be an enigma to men. He did it so that he could walk up to fishermen and everyday folk and save them in the everyday language of human salvation.

3. From the *Investigations*:

What gives us *so much as the idea* that living beings, things, can feel?

Is it that my education has led me to it by drawing my attention to feelings in myself, and now I transfer the idea to objects outside myself? That I recognize that there is something there (in me) which I can call 'pain' without getting into conflict with the way other people use this word?—I do not transfer my idea to stones, plants, etc.

Couldn't I imagine having frightful pains and turning to stone while they lasted? Well, how do I know, if I shut my eyes, whether I have not turned into a stone? And if that has happened, in what sense will *the stone* have the pains? In what sense will they be ascribable to the stone? And why need the pain have a bearer at all here?!

And can one say of the stone that it has a soul and *that* is what has the pain? What has a soul, or pain, to do with a stone?

Only of what behaves like a human being can one say that it *has* pains.

For one has to say it of a body, or, if you like of a soul which some body *has*. And how can a body *have* a soul?

Look at a stone and imagine it having sensations.—One says to oneself: How could one so much as get the idea of ascribing a *sensation* to a *thing*? One might as well ascribe it to a number!—And now look at a wriggling fly and at once these difficulties vanish and pain seems able to get a foothold here, where before everything was, so to speak, too smooth for it.

And so, too, a corpse seems to us quite inaccessible to pain.—Our attitude to what is alive and to what is dead, is not the same. All our reactions are different.—If anyone says: 'That cannot simply come from the fact that a living things moves about in such-and-such a way and a dead one not', then I want to intimate to him that this is a case of the transition 'from quantity to quality'.

Think of the recognition of *facial expressions*. Or of the description of facial expressions—which does not consist in giving the measurements of the face! Think, too, how one can imitate a man's face without seeing one's own in a mirror.[18]

When we are in the classic thinker's pose of the Western way—when we are straining towards the truth after the way that we have been educated—we are in an altogether different deportment to the deportment of the wet exuberance of a lived life. When you set down to study or to write a book, you make things still and peaceful around you, you detach yourself from the world as it actually is, and then you begin. I don't believe that this process has ever been questioned or portrayed like this as some weird initiation ritual. But of course it is, and of course it is weird, and of course it is an initiation. Because what is the thinker or philosopher after but the truth? And what can the truth be but the truth of the wet exuberance of life? And yet in order to prepare himself for his investigation of it, he takes only the very steps that will keep him at a distance from it and dry.

If you want to organize all of Wittgenstein's writings around just one puzzle, then let it be this one. The puzzle of why intellectual understanding always deports us in precisely the way that will make the *real* truth impossible to attain. For we know by now that what men have always meant by the call of the *real* truth is nothing that you could classify and then write down as that classification's name but a place, a voice, a Person.

Our attitude to what is alive and to what is dead, is not the same. All our reactions are different.

You see, Christianity teaches creation *ex nihilo*. That is to say, it teaches that the *real* truth exists ahead of everything in the truly unknowable future. We saw above also that Christ himself said:

All things are delivered unto me of my Father: and no man knoweth the Son, but the Father; neither knoweth any man the Father, save the Son, and *he* to whomsoever the Son will reveal *him*.

And we know already, thanks to Wittgenstein, that man-made truth (or man-made knowledge) is the tautology of the logically necessary. In other words, it rejects the idea that the truth is delivered to the present from the future and embraces instead the idea that the truth is the *inner* necessity that holds together some verifiable happening to its knowledge-object. This connection (this identity) between, say, the knowledge-object 'cat' and the verifiable happening of cats in this world is, as we know from the previous chapter, something that Wittgenstein declared in the *Tractatus* to be inexpressible in language. He was of course right. Language is an activity, and it is in the essence of all activities that they cannot be separated from their triggers. We have all experienced this. Perhaps you enjoy dancing and someone keeps pressing you 'Why?'—And in response to that, you do what anyone would and work down the list of possible reasons until you ground out on the notion of 'dance for its own sake'.

In the *Tractatus*, Wittgenstein showed brilliantly and ingeniously that if you press towards the notion of 'language for its own sake', you uncover the trigger of 'meaning'— Only to realize that meaning cannot, in turn, be expressed in language. It can only be shown or performed by the fact that any instance of language achieves its sense by corresponding to something a priori. Thus, you cannot journey to some place before the trigger of language in order to stand apart from it and explain it. You cannot because that trigger only clicks as you begin to think or sound a word. Likewise, with dancing. In the end, the only answer that you can give to the question 'Why' is to break out dancing. In the *Investigations*, Wittgenstein would begin to investigate this puzzle of the *Tractatus* on its broadest possible canvas. So not just in those clear-cut instances where language stands in obvious and tight relation to empirical happenings but right across its spectrum of usage—Language where it is used in hope, jest, anger, confusion, and so on. Language where it is used in situations that threaten to divorce it altogether from empiricism. Language where it is used in situations that threaten to make its trigger something that is located not in rocks and minerals and numbers but in the other human across from you. Language like dancing, language like games.

Think, too, how one can imitate a man's face without seeing one's own in a mirror.

Fallen man seems to counter creation *ex nihilo* by turning to face the congregation of facts behind him, in the past. They, instead, become his trigger; and in addressing his words to them he at once speaks and *simultaneously enacts* his reason for speaking (speech's meaning). The trigger of language, its meaning, is that man looks backwards to the established facts of what has happened. Yet in the *Investigations*, Wittgenstein's explores the sense in which possibly only professional philosophers would attempt to consistently speak like that, while the rest of us would most of the time be speaking to each other and *finding the triggers in each other*. Here, language begins to look a lot more like an endlessly evolving set of rules, or grammars. With the feature that is allowing for that endless evolution being the fact that there is no longer just the one trigger of *substance* or *being* (one metric for one world), but as many triggers as there are souls and those souls' faces. And the trigger in one face pressing the trigger in yours. And if this is the case, then speaking can no longer be about speaking correctly. And passions can no longer be quieted by any seeing through them to the wiring of the brain.

* * *

I remember once as a child being so disturbed by someone else's suffering that I went wild and could no longer be controlled. I felt and believed that I was no longer in this world but in the new world of that person and their suffering. I was so deep in it that I could not get back to this world, in which episodes like that never take place, and everything is on the level. After that, I came to understand that this world we live in is of the least importance. This is why I have been using the language of 'reversal' and 'flipping over' and of 'nothing that is being really what it is'.

* * *

Words and language are of the least importance. Adults teach you that the only fluency permitted is the fluency of words, and word-fluency's accepted styles. But the only fluency that there really is, is heartbreak. And the first heartbreak is being born.

Adults teach you that when a broken man looks into the face of Christ, he finds therein comfort. And if you look up 'comfort' in the dictionary, you will discover that it is something that you could just as well obtain from a mug of cocoa. And from mugs of cocoa that we can hold in our hands we are led inexorably towards admitting the falsity of a face which we cannot point to.

But that is just the stupidity of adults who sold their souls a long time ago. For when a man looks into the face of Christ he is returned into the original fluency of Eden, which was a fluency *before words*. If you want to learn something from Wittgenstein, learn this: language is a metaphor for what we lost. The idea of truth by correspondence is a fabrication of language itself. And the dream of finding fluency in words is a joke. Deep down we all know this. Fluency is what happens first. Fluency is the thing *that you can never find the words for*.

> And now look at a wriggling fly and at once these difficulties vanish and pain seems able to get a foothold here, where before everything was, so to speak, too smooth for it.

Wittgenstein is right. That is the problem of the Western sigh. Its numbers and its eternity are too smooth for human passion. When the Western adults sigh they say that Christ saves but medicine saves you more. But saving and comfort was never what Christ was in truth about. Medicine saves and comforts; there is no doubt about that. But to transfer that language across to Christ is inaccurate. The language makes sense if you include Christ on the horizontal metric of 'things that offer salvation and comfort in this world': you must surely know as well as I do that on that metric, Christ can at best be the great placebo. So here we must recall Wittgenstein's language about the man redeemed by Christ 'being no longer supported on earth but suspended from Heaven'. This is the key phrase that sums up what I have been working towards by stating categorically that by using Christ's name in this Wittgensteinian way one brings the horizontal to an end and shoots vertically upwards and away. And by working so steadily towards this, I hope I have been impressing upon you the absolute loyalty and coherency of both Wittgenstein's earlier and later philosophy to this phenomenon.

The *Tractatus* prepares the ground by performing the act of the whole of Western philosophy being brought to a horizontal halt, like a train in its tracks. Think of the railway tracks of Russell's endlessly collocating symbols. Well, Wittgenstein ends that and leaves his readers at the question where next to go, if not forwards? The answer is upwards! The mystical and the supernatural and what cannot be *said* shoot you upwards. The language games of the *Investigations* are simply a brilliant mockery of horizontal movement. They are a mockery of time and measurement and everything that is involved with its extension and perpetuation. More than that, they are a celebration of the intrinsically *human*, and of what I have called the triggers to language that we find within each other's faces. They are a celebration of love; for it is love in all its degrees that we find in each other's faces, and it is only from the point of view of love, and what love needs, that you could ever call numbers and stones 'too smooth (for a foothold)'.

* * *

Wittgenstein is famed for writing nearly nothing about his love life. Yet now we realize that the whole of his philosophy was about it.

* * *

The Western way is to say that Christ was just another in the long and unending line of messianic products. The Western way is to say that the measure of true intelligence, discrimination, and wit is to learn to see only this horizontal line and not the upward shoots away from it. The counterpunch of Wittgenstein's philosophy is to say that love works one human face to another—And that each love is its own world. The thief on the cross did what he did of a sudden for love. And in that second, he shot skywards like a rocket. And no one could have seen it coming (who ever did see true love coming?).

I believe the one place where this wisdom of the vertical shooting of love has been preserved is in great fiction writing. There it is accepted fact that every human story is a love story, and that a human love story is all about finding someone who will make the horizontal dimensions of your life rush towards the magic centre of gravity, which is you. Somehow, there will be someone who will cause your past and your future to rush towards each other like that. And that rushing together which is really the ending and surmounting of philosophy will be the only way to describe what is happening. But after the happening itself, there will be nothing to say.

When Wittgenstein talks about Christ and the difference that redemption makes, this is what he means. He is not talking about the placebo power of belief in something. He is talking about a real redemption that actually allows you to leave behind philosophy's mass and gravity.

> Look at the blue of the sky and say to yourself 'How blue the sky is!'—When you do it spontaneously—without philosophical intentions—the idea never crosses your mind that this impression of colour belongs only to *you*. And you have no hesitation in exclaiming that to someone else. And if you point at anything as you say the words you point to the sky. I am saying: you have not the feeling of pointing-into-yourself, which often accompanies 'naming the sensation' when one is thinking about 'private language'. Nor do you think that really you ought not to point to the colour with your hand, but with your attention. (Consider what it means 'to point to something with the attention'.)[19]

There is not a thing called the 'world of language' that exists independently of human beings. There is no such common ground that we share with each other and most of all with Christ. When you see something in the way that Wittgenstein is depicting it above, and you call someone over and get them to see it too, it is not the case that you are both seeing through the same window to some same spot in some same world. Rather it is the case that you are reading something in each other's faces. You are reading passions, and those passions are triggering words. Afterwards a philosopher may come along and try to notice that certain patterns and combinations of words get repeated over certain things and events. And they may try to argue that this proves the reliance of sensible language on an underlying truth. But now we can throw the Wittgensteinian counterpunch and say that all that this proves is that it has become *convenient* and *ready* for humans to do this. The real truth is that the colour blue was only ever pronounced once, by some person, of the sky. And that was that moment's beginning and end. The copying and repetition of this moment ever since, which has over time come to give a meaning to the colour 'blue' (the sky), is nothing to do with the original, once and forever event. The original event which was, for its moment, its own world and that world's language.

Language as it is learnt and used today is a Manichaean exercise. We humans are the vessels of its sacred purification. It is as though in some cosmic event, language became disordered and incoherent, so that what is needed now for its salvation is the sacred exercising of our minds and mouths as we gradually return it to its original cosmic alignment on the eternal stability of truth.

It changes everything to realize instead that each and every instance of human suffering and pain is *an originality*, a truth, a language (a world). And that only Christ's face can move and shape the pinpoint perfect response to that originality. To come in afterwards and write down the words 'suffering' and 'originality', to turn them into concepts and to try to define them, is a categorically unrelated exercise. It is not, however, unproductive or even unpromising. It truly enough constructs the world of knowledge which we live in today. And it is true enough that the success of that world leaves us all the time with the choice of either going along with it or rocketing away through some originality. But it is the categorical un-relatedness of originality to knowledge that Wittgenstein was trying to show and perform across all his philosophy.

4. Here is how he shows and performs 'originality' in the *Tractatus*:

> It is impossible to speak about the will in so far as it is the subject of ethical attributes.
> And the will as a phenomenon is of interest only to psychology.
> If the good or bad exercise of the will does alter the world, it can alter only the limits of the world, not the fact—not what can be expressed by means of language.
> In short the effect must be that it becomes an altogether different world. It must, so to speak, wax and wane as a whole.
> The world of the happy man is a different one from that of the unhappy man.

> So too at death the world does not alter, but comes to an end.
> Death is not an event in life: we do not live to experience death.
> If we take eternity to mean not infinite temporal duration but timelessness, then eternal life belongs to those who live in the present.
> Our life has no end in just the way in which our visual field has no limits.[20]

The whalers aboard the great whaling ships headed out of Nantucket used to speak afterwards of the awesomeness of life at sea—Months, sometimes years, out from land. Beneath you is the wide unfeeling ocean (just like the original *Urstoff* of Presocratic philosophy, or the metric); above you the sky and the heavens; in front of you and ever out of reach, the sublime horizon—The point at which the unfeeling matter of science merges seamlessly with the silent beauty of the stars. This is what I called above 'the problem of the Western sigh'.[21] And it was Wittgenstein who made language into this problem's best metaphor.

Within the logic of the Western way we can develop technologies that take us deeper into the depths or higher towards the stars. But both recourses work to keep the horizon ever before us and out of reach. So that we really can only sigh for it. It remains as the absolute limit of our vision. Whereas the vision that Wittgenstein holds out for in his philosophy is the limitless vision. If we use our language to look for its trigger of meaning in the unfeeling *Urstoff*, then we keep the horizon always before us. The beauty in this state of affairs is sublime, yes, and sublimely tragic, but better would be to be taught that there is another way.

This 'limitless vision' is the infinity of feeling and passion that you can suddenly have for someone. There is a great passage in Ernest Hemingway's *For Whom the Bell Tolls* that explains this:

> I did not know that I could ever feel what I have ever felt, he thought. Nor that this could happen to me. I would like to have it for my whole life. You will, the other part of him said. You will. You have it *now* and that is all your whole life is; now. There is nothing else than now. There is neither yesterday, certainly, nor is there any tomorrow. How old must you be before you know that? There is only now, and if now is only two days, then two days is your life and everything in it will be in proportion. This is how you live a life in two days. And if you stop complaining and asking for what you never will get, you will have a good life. A good life is not measured by any biblical span.[22]

To me, this is what Wittgenstein's philosophy is all about. If you could bring all of its parts and energies together for one big surge, the voice of that surge would say: 'Why do we keep ourselves in such cruel submission to the unfeeling ocean?' 'Why do we always let the Truth and Eternity be bigger than us?' 'Why do we worship them on this basis, that they are bigger than us?' 'Why do we commit this demagoguery against the glory of man?'

* * *

Both the scientists and the theologians are equally culpable of this demagoguery. It cannot be used to separate them.

*   *   *

Christ did not save the thief on the cross by being bigger than him and out of his reach. He did not save him by shimmering before him as his horizon. He saved the thief because his passion touched and triggered something in the thief's passion. And the thief felt that and conceived a profound love for him. And that was that. Both men still died and proved in their dying that nails and crosses will kill you. And thus they proved that being saved cannot mean being saved from *them*, and thus from the empiricism of nails and crosses. The object was never for Christ to replace or refute empiricism. In fact, in being made man, he entered fully into it. The object was instead that Christ should remind men of the glory of man—Of man's capacity to do what Hemingway's passage describes.

The glory of man is to be able to impose his passion and emotion on time and all the other constants so that it becomes their measure, rather than the other way around. Unless it were possible like this to bring the physical reality of your body—of your muscles, blood, and bones—into sudden and dramatic proportion with some sudden and dramatic feeling in your heart, well, all that you can say is that if you couldn't do this then the pure science behind your muscles, blood, and bones would win out. And humans would no longer be humans any more. They would still be there on the earth. But they would now be ruled by the same physical *being* as everything else. They would not be humans as we still know ourselves to be humans.

Wittgenstein shows us that the dispute between the scientists and the theologians and metaphysicians is false. If their object is to use their brains better than each other, then they march in the same direction and are as one. The real dispute is between the brain and the passions.

Or between the brain *qua* physics and the passions *qua* some original primitivism. Or between doing the right thing and evolving like Darwin said so, and not giving a damn.

The great Wittgensteinian insight is this: language was only ever meant to be about freedom and not giving a damn. And so even the simplest examples of language usage turn out to be demonstrating always this one feature. Take the following one:

> I send someone shopping. I give him a slip marked 'five red apples'. He takes the slip to the shopkeeper, who opens the drawer marked 'apples'; then he looks up the word 'red' in a table and a finds a colour sample opposite it; then he says the series of cardinal numbers—I assume that he knows them by heart—up to the word 'five' and for each number he takes an apple of the same colour as the sample out of the drawer.—It is in this and similar ways that one operates with words.—'But how does he know where and how he is to look up the word 'red' and what he is to do with the word "five"?'—Well, I assume that he *acts* as I have described. Explanations

come to an end somewhere.—But what is the meaning of the word 'five'?—No such thing was in question here, only how the word 'five' is used.

That philosophical concept of meaning has its place in a primitive idea of the way language functions. But one can also say that it is the idea of a language more primitive than ours.[23]

This is meant to be the famous send-up, or rejection, of Augustine's 'picture theory of language'.[24] Except that we are now equipped to be more sophisticated about Wittgenstein's use of it. Wittgenstein's intention with this example is not to say that the picture theory of language is juvenile or deficient, but that *all* language is in fact redundant to what we call 'meaning'. That is to say, no matter how far you further simplified and stretched out the example above, some part of it (like how the shopkeeper knows what to do with the number five) would always escape you. Language, truth, and logic, physics and the already-happened, the real truth is that we are bigger than all these things. And this little example proves it. Because it proves that language usage is incidental to what is accomplished between the shopper and the shopkeeper. Let me put my own example over this example to help you towards seeing what I am seeing.

Let's imagine that in our example there is not a human shopper and human shopkeeper, but two of Turing's artificially intelligent humanoid robots. Wittgenstein's description might then serve very well as an example of the programming language that would allow the two robots to 'interact' and perform together this simple task. This task and this way of programming it should be very familiar to us as the method by which artificial intelligence imagines that it is edging towards *real intelligence*. But stop a moment! In view of the task required, and the fact that we are dealing with two programmable robots, wouldn't it be easier all-round if we simply programmed the shopkeeper robot to always respond to some sound that the shopper robot made by fetching it five red apples? It would. And things could, of course, be further refined and simplified. For example, every shopper robot could be designed to always carry five red apples with it so that it never had to shop for them. [Like the dream of a world of everlasting humans and no need any more for coffins.] Taking the example to its absurd logical conclusion like this is helpful because it allows us to *place* what I just now called the 'incidental' character of language. Language between humans only works because humans can already interact at a level below it or above it—At any rate, at a level infinitely more sublime and primitive than it. I am doing more here than emphasizing the importance of context to meaning and understanding. I am saying that you might certainly make a case for strapping five red apples to shopper robots and thereby doing away (for example) with the need and cost of shopkeeper robots. But to strap five red apples to a human shopper for the same reason would be madness.

What the human shopper and the human shopkeeper in Wittgenstein's example manage to achieve *can* be represented in the language they use. And indeed the meaning of language may well be its comparative efficiency in relation to a more laborious method of communicating one's intentions. But here it comes: ONLY HUMANS

CAN SPONTANEOUSLY COMMUNICATE THEIR INTENTIONS TO ONE ANOTHER. One robot can truly enough be programmed to communicate one predetermined intention to another robot, and that robot can truly enough be programmed to recognize it, and even to act upon it; and 'language' may well be a perfectly accurate description of that programming. But no *spontaneity* was ever programmed like this. And it is just this spontaneity (and its wild, whooping sounds) that is true human intelligence. And this is why Turing was wrong and Wittgenstein was right.

***

There never will be artificial intelligence for the plain fact that there can never be artificial spontaneity.

***

The whole meaning of the spontaneous, the extempore, and the original is that it cannot be artificially reproduced or replicated. This is the element in humanity which is truly supernatural. And this, too, is why the natural depends upon the supernatural. No two pebbles on a beach would think to communicate with each other; and this is why the natural and the already-happened will take care of themselves. The question is, What will man do?

5. From the *Investigations*:

> If I were to talk to myself out loud in a language not understood by those present my thoughts would be hidden from them.
> Let us assume that there was a man who always guessed right what I was saying to myself in my thoughts. (It does not matter how he manages it.) But what is the criterion for his guessing *right*? Well, I am a truthful person and I confess that he has guessed right.—But might I not be mistaken, can my memory not deceive me? And might it not always do so when—without lying—I express what I have thought within myself?—But now it does appear that 'what went on within me' is not the point at all. (Here I am drawing a construction-line.)
> The criteria for the truth of the *confession* that I thought such-and-such are not the criteria for a true *description* of a process. And the importance of the true confession does not reside in its being a correct and certain report of a process. It resides rather in the special consequences which can be drawn from a confession whose truth is guaranteed by the special criteria of *truthfulness*.
> (Assuming that dreams can yield important information about the dreamer, what yielded the information would be truthful accounts of dreams. The question whether the dreamer's memory deceives him when he reports the dream after waking cannot arise, unless indeed we introduce a completely new criterion for the report's 'agreeing' with the dream, a criterion which gives us a concept of 'truth' as distinct from 'truthfulness' here.)[25]

Here we learn from Wittgenstein that truthfulness is the description of the process by which it is created, and that this process must always involve logical necessity and be independent of *the truth*. In my example of the robots which I placed over the Wittgenstein original, the criterion of the 'truthfulness' of their language would have to come out as a description of the process of their programming. Likewise, in the Wittgenstein original, the 'truthfulness' of the language of the two humans would have to come out as a description of the rules attending to the meaning of the words 'five', 'red', and 'apples'. Or the process by which these rules were originally settled upon. Similarly, when you take a polygraph test the 'truthfulness' of your testimony is the description of the process whereby threshold levels of heart rate and perspiration are monitored. What Wittgenstein draws our attention to is the difference of category between this concept of 'truthfulness-as-process' and *the truth*—Insofar as the definition of *the truth* would have to set it apart as precisely the testimony that could never be constructed on the basis of some underlying metric, some *Urstoff*.

We are now well-accustomed to Wittgenstein's idea that 'what is known' is tautological on 'knowledge', because 'knowledge' is a pact that we make in advance with the chosen metric of our seeing. If we now apply that insight here, to my polygraph example, we see that the truthfulness of a polygraph test is the extent to which the language of the answers corresponds to the predetermined threshold readings. If we return now to this—

> The question whether the dreamer's memory deceives him when he reports the dream after waking cannot arise, unless indeed we introduce a completely new criterion for the report's 'agreeing' with the dream, a criterion which gives us a concept of 'truth' as distinct from 'truthfulness' here.

—we finally see it. Whatever *the truth* of the human heart is, it exists in some mysterious place, before language and measurement. If language and measurement try to reach back to find it, all they can *logically* see are, as it were, increments of themselves. If we adopt the Judeo-Christian convention of calling this mysterious truth of the human heart 'the soul', then language and measurement can only enumerate how far back of their present position it must be—And in just the same way that the far reaches of the universe are today explored by 'measurements of measurements'. Wittgenstein is not the first or last thinker to stumble onto the possibilities of this, but there is no doubt that his way of depicting it by example upon example, metaphor upon metaphor is unique, and rightly to be heralded. And that it constitutes a major innovation.

> A language-game: Report whether a certain body is lighter or darker than another.—But now there's a related one: State the relationship between the lightness of certain shades of colour. (Compare with this: Determining the relationship between the lengths of two sticks—and the relationship between two numbers.)—The form of the propositions in both language-games is the same: 'X is lighter than Y'. But in the

first it is an external relation and the proposition is temporal, and in the second it is an internal relation and the proposition is timeless.[26]

This is what all the Wittgenstein language-games do, and why they are different to all the other major modes of investigation in Western philosophy. In all the other major modes—and in what follows I will refer only to the two historical forks in the road, the Platonic and the Aristotelian—the logical necessity between knowledge (as the already-happened) and what is known is preserved. And the chief consequence of this is language laid out as it is, word after word, in tracks. Understanding, explanation, and intellectual development mean adding more words to the words already accumulated. I have gradually been acclimatizing you to the realization that this means a movement that is horizontal and linear, and that this leads to all the mathematical and philosophical problems associated with series and infinity. Kurt Gödel's 'incompleteness theorems'. It is the (need for the) preservation of sense in the left-to-right direction that creates the series and then supplies the logic that they must continue to infinity. Or really, and as Gödel noticed, *their logic is that they will continue to infinity* because that is what logic does that mere chance doesn't; it never lets you down. Yet as appealing as logic and infinity are, they eventually become surprisingly heedless of what we prefer to mean by 'truthfulness'. As we learnt in the previous chapter, the essence of Gödel's 'incompleteness theorems' is that 'truthfulness' (or in modern logic, the 'truth-function') is, to quote Wittgenstein's definition from above, 'the *description* of a process'. And in terms of a series stretching to infinity, truthfulness as the description of a process would mean someone standing at the end of infinity watching all the terms in the series come home—And thereby actually *seeing* (because remember, seeing is believing) them home. Because this can never happen, science and scientism are fatally flawed and can only continue by becoming a moral crusade, and trying to win the moral argument for their adoption by all mankind. Inspired by Wittgenstein's example, I have tried to introduce you word by word and page by page to the idea that the horizontal and linear may not be the only way, and that words and the connections of sense and identity that they perpetuate might themselves become the doorways to the truly mystical and the truly unknown. Doorways to what Wittgenstein distinguished from 'truthfulness' as *the truth*.

To return to the example of Gödel's work, 'truthfulness' describes the process by which sound modern logic can generate series to infinity, whereas *the truth* can only be described in relation to it as the place at the end of infinity to which none of us can ever have a hope of voyaging. We would sooner make it to the place at the end of the rainbow. Here we come into full possession of the materials out of which Wittgenstein made the art of his life and work. Whatever it is, *the truth* would have to be a place you *could go to*. *The truth* and truthfulness have nothing to do with each other. Truthfulness is processional and manufactured. It makes its own questions and answers; with each new set of answers becoming the basis for the next set of questions. Truthfulness doesn't touch *the truth*; it doesn't touch the 'problems of life':

> When the answer cannot be put into words, neither can the question be put into words.
>
> *The riddle* does not exist.
>
> If a question can be framed at all, it is also *possible* to answer it.
>
> Scepticism is *not* irrefutable, but obviously nonsensical, when it tries to raise doubts where no questions can be asked.
>
> For doubt can exist only where a question exists, a question only where an answer exists, and an answer only where something *can be said*.
>
> We feel that even when all *possible* scientific questions have been answered, the problems of life remain completely untouched. Of course there are then no questions left, and this itself is the answer.
>
> The solution of the problem of life is seen in the vanishing of the problem.[27]

Think of the distinction that Wittgenstein makes above in his language-games of reporting whether a certain body is lighter or darker than another, and then stating the relationship between the lightness of certain shades of colour. In the first one, he says that we are dealing with an external relation, so the proposition is temporal; whereas in the second one, we are dealing with an internal relation which actually makes the proposition timeless. In the first instance, this makes me think of the Socratic elenchus, which uses questions and answers to move from various examples of some thing to that thing's general case. More or less the inductive method of reasoning. I quoted an example of Socrates using this method in Chapter 3.[28] The innovation, or genius, of Socrates' way of thinking was not so much this method itself, which is, after all, commonplace and intuitive—But rather the way in which he actively prospected and promoted its mystical implications. The chief of these being, to return to Wittgenstein, that it puts us into touch with the 'timeless', or as the timeless would become in Plato's vision, the World of the Forms. Socrates' humble and irreproachable method fascinated and appalled because it suddenly brought its analysands out onto a place of eternally stable concepts; the opposite, in point of form, of the temporal world they had left behind. The comparisons to be made between sticks that one might pick up and throw for one's dog during a stroll through the forest have changed, somehow, into this new world in which sticks never existed, but only the pure rules governing their relationships to each other—The pure rules which they could only passively exemplify. A glimpse of this new world from Plato's *Republic*:

> This is the realm that reason masters with the power of dialectic. Assumptions are not treated as first principles but as real hypotheses. That is, they are not employed as beginnings but as ladders and springboards, used in order to reach that realm that requires no hypotheses and is therefore the true starting point for the attainment of unobstructed knowledge. When reason attains that level and becomes aware of the whole intelligible order, it descends at will to the level of conclusions but without

the aid of sense objects. It reasons only by using forms. It moves from forms through forms to forms. And it completes its journey in forms.[29]

The trick or illusion taking place here is based on 'rule-generation' and the identity sign, and the reason why it takes in humans is because humans can be self-conscious. Can *bilocate*. A part of us—the corporeal part—can be in the place of the temporal example (of corporeality) whilst another part of us—the incorporeal part— can be in the place of the timeless *idea of a man*. Rule-generation and the identity sign allow human minds to traverse a universe that they are simultaneously creating. Which is the same thing as to say that it allows them to simultaneously be on the stage performing the trick *and* in the audience—Looking on and being dazzled by it.

Wittgenstein's language-games serve, as it were, to 'perform the performance'. If post-Socratic Western reasoning is the performance, then Wittgenstein's language-games isolate and magnify the bilocation that that Western reasoning sustains. And if this is what his language-games do, then this is also *all* that they can do. Their purpose, each time, is to bring us into an acceptance of the fact that we are thrill seekers after the *occult*. The language-games prove, on the corporeal side, that words, like bodies, can be lighter than each other. That is to say, the word 'blue', once defined, can be lighter than the word 'dark', once it has been defined. Or what comes to the same thing: The one may be said to define the other. And here, then, the language-games prove no more than that language has always made its sense by representing prior features of both the physical world and the public imagination; or the 'picture theory of language'. However, on the incorporeal side, the language-games ignite in us the thrill of why it should be that one definition should generate another; and what this means for being able to leave the world of prior features behind and live instead in the world of the pure connections between definitions. Just as Plato dreamed. And more to the point: How magnificent would be our advantage over the common man if we could hold the powers of this world of pure intellect and wield them in the temporal world of the everyday?

Wittgenstein's language-games are brilliant, or ingenious, or whatever, because they are so honest to this sordid fact of what Augustine called the *libido dominandi* 'lust for ruling'.

The *libido dominandi* explains why the world does not change, and therefore it explains 'human nature'; if by human nature we mean that consistent impulse of the human psyche that holds this world of men to its style and course.

A LESSON BY WAY OF ARISTOTLE

By turning language loose on itself, Wittgenstein unmasks this impulse in the only way that it can be unmasked. In every other kind of Western philosophy before him, language is nothing in itself and simply the communicating medium. Before philosophy, the dividing line between wisdom and the everyday may even have been the absence of language. [An observation which has to remind us of the *Tractatus* and its ending.] To be in awe or stupor meant to have one's words run out. The shaman and the priest would take themselves off to some ritual or trance, then return to their followers and declare the way forwards. With the advent of philosophy in Greece in the sixth century B.C., the connection between the wise man and his followers would forever after be changed. In the post-philosophical West, the followers could expect to be *persuaded* by their wise man. It was now up to him to offer reasonable explanations of the way forwards. Sometimes, this beginning is forgotten, and it is imagined that philosophy began as the hobby in abstraction that it is so often marketed as today. A choice of subject at university. In fact, in its beginnings, it was a revolutionary and a freedom fighter; for it was at once inseparable from the social and political change it wrought, which can be summed up as the maxim that wisdom must be communicable; or what is communicable must be wisdom. From that point on, the formerly incommunicable wisdom never had a chance, and the new communicable wisdom went on a march that it has kept up to the present day—Notwithstanding Wittgenstein's attempt to stop it in its tracks.

What exactly does it mean for language to be the 'communicating medium'? Consider the following passage from Book Zeta of Aristotle's *Metaphysics*:

Ordinarily we try to explain why by telling why something belongs to something else. For to ask why the musical man is a musical man is either, as has been said, to ask why the man is musical or something else. It is pointless to ask why anything is itself. For *a* fact, such as that it is true that, let us say, a lunar eclipse is, must be clear at the start. But the fact that anything is itself is the one and only reason that can be given in answer to all such questions as why a man is a man or a musician is a musician; unless one were to add that this is so because everything is inseparable from itself and that just this is what is meant by 'being one'. But this fact is common to everything and is a short-cut explanation. We may properly ask, however, why man is an animal of a certain sort. This, then, is clear, that we are not asking why he who is a man is a man. We are asking why something belongs to something. But the fact that it belongs must be clear; for if it is not, the question why is futile. For example, 'Why is it thundering?' means: 'Why does this noise occur in the clouds?' For what is here sought consists in affirming something of something else.... However, that it is an explanation which is sought easily escapes notice, especially when one thing is not expressly attributed to another—when it is asked why a man is; because the expression is simple and does not single out this or that property. But the meaning of the question should be made explicit; otherwise, what happens will be something intermediate between no investigation and a definite investigation. [For example:] Why are these materials a house? Because precisely these materials are present, and it is precisely this that it meant for them to be a house. And why is 'this' or this body having this form of a man? Hence the explanation is sought in terms of the material, that is, that by which it has been definitely formed into a primary being. It is evident, therefore, that there is no investigation or instruction concerning simple entities; but there must be some other way of dealing with them.

Now, as to things that are organized so that the whole is one, not like a heap, but like a syllable: the syllable is not its elements, for *ba* is not the same as *b* and *a*; nor is the flesh fire and earth. For when these are separated, the wholes (flesh or syllable) no longer are; but the letters are, and so are fire and earth.... Therefore [there should be a] factor explaining why this is flesh, or that is syllable, and so forth. And this is the primary being of anything.[30]

Now consider these words of Aristotle's again and extra carefully. Can you see it? Always look for the apparently unimpeachable in what people say, then rush at it full pelt. Aristotle's 'apparently unimpeachable' occurs when he talks, near the start, of the questions that one may and may not properly ask in the course of a true investigation. 'It is pointless to ask why anything is itself.'—Everything that Aristotle is to say next rebounds off this statement like a ball off a wall. And because it does, it makes perfect and beautiful sense. It also plainly shows itself to be the progenitor of our modern scientific method, insofar as it recommends that we stop being stupefied by 'simple entities' and instead seek the explanations of things in their material constituents.

'It is pointless to ask why anything is itself.' Aristotle is here recommending that we stop even seeing the simples of 'men' and 'houses' and instead see always in front of us the shimmering collection of things of which they are made (and in their proper arrangements). This is exactly what they teach you today in school. It is apparently unimpeachable. Except that we really are now going to rush at it full pelt.

'It is pointless to ask why anything is itself.' This is evidently a statement about the physical world and language is simply its *communicating medium*. This is what it means for language to be the communicating medium in philosophy. This is what I meant above when I cited a pre-philosophical world and a post-philosophical world, and said that in our post-philosophical world, what counts as wisdom is not what is silent and unknown but what is expounded, taught, and understood (by everyone). I said that the new Greek philosophy unleashed the democratic creed on the West; and this is what I meant.

However, what if, after Wittgenstein, we say, 'It is pointless to ask why anything is itself' is not a statement about the physical world but a statement about language? And what if it is only by saying this that we can notice that grammar and physics are perfect stand-ins for each other, so that it is in fact impossible to say which came first. Grammar and physics are both the exact same eye looking at the exact same thing in the exact same way. And through that eye they both see *properly*. Therefore, grammar and physics are *moral* rather than neutral and objective. They are *morally right* in relation to those who see things *improperly* (unscientifically).

In the passage above, Aristotle explains that just to blurt out a 'something' on its own is not to use language properly. To use language properly, you have to say something about something else. If that is grammar, then physics says the same thing by saying that you have to say that something belongs to something else. If you just say 'man' all the time and treat him like a simple entity you have not understand him in the Western way. However, if you can see him all peeled open on the dissecting table, then you will have the knowledge of what man is materially constituted of and you will understand him. When you consider that the survival of our species depends upon exploiting the advantages of such intellectual understanding, then you see where the moral dimension enters in.

But of course, Aristotle goes a little bit further than this when at the end of the passage above he starts to talk about the 'primary being', the essence or *substance*, of a thing. In the Western way of today, the gratifying effect of being able to see beyond simple entities is that the old-fashioned metaphysics emanating from 'simple-entity-seeing' simply evaporates. A ghost becomes simply the concatenation of psychological factors that would bring you to envision one, and thereby it and all such supernatural phenomena are made to disappear from the catalogue of actually existing things. However, notwithstanding the fantastic possibilities of making this final move, Aristotle never does. That is to say, he never does, like so many after him, make the move of allowing that the enumerated properties of a thing should wholesale replace it as the subject. To the end and against this, he holds onto the belief that—just like in a proper sentence— the subject always remains so that the rest may be understood to be predicated on it. In other words, however compelling may be its mandate to do so, explanation, for him, never explains away. Something always remains behind and intact—And this something, the primary being, must then be what explains what the subject is.

Aristotle thus leaves himself wide open to the criticism that at the very point where his triumph should be complete, he allows his scientific methodology to become bullied by a linguistic imperative which turns out, on inspection, to be the result of an ancient misconception—And that misconception to be the source of all the backwardness of metaphysics. By holding onto the belief that after all explanation there should still be left the idea of what has been explained as subject, or *substance*, he seems to do no better than Plato and Socrates before him, who thought similarly that the exhaustiveness of scientific investigation should only increase our awareness of the supernatural inviolability of *substance*. And now we can see for ourselves how the issue constructs itself. In life and language alike, you can neither have subjects without predicates nor predicates without subjects; for 'four-legged', 'furry', and 'whiskers' mean nothing without the subject 'cat'; whilst 'cat' without such enumeration as these predicates allow must become a thing at once unknown to us.[31] You could even call this the great hinge of the Western tradition, for it does not take much reflection to realize that it holds the key both to the mysticisms of knowledge and to the eradication of those mysticisms. It furnishes both the argument for and against the idea that the physical is supported on the metaphysical.

Take, for example, the following from Thomas Hobbes, the great empiricist:

> For it is upon this ground [of separated essences], that when a man is dead and buried, they say his soul (that is his life) can walk separated from his body, and is

seen by night upon the graves. Upon the same ground they say, that the figure, and colour, and taste of a piece of bread, has a being, there, where they say there is no bread: and upon the same ground they say, that faith, and wisdom, and other virtues are sometimes *poured* into a man, sometimes *blown* into him from Heaven; as if the virtuous, and their virtues could be asunder; and a great many other things that serve to lessen the dependence of subjects on the sovereign power of their country. For who will endeavour to obey the laws, if he expect obedience to be poured or blown into him? Or who will not obey a priest, that can make God, rather than his sovereign; nay than God Himself? Or who, that is in fear of ghosts, will not bear great respect to those that can make the holy water, that drives them from him? And this shall suffice for an example of the errors, which are brought into the church, from the *entities*, and *essences* of Aristotle; which it may be he knew to be false philosophy; but writ it as a thing consonant to, and corroborative of their religion; and fearing the fate of Socrates.[32]

More devastating still was Bertrand Russell's demonstration to come, erupting, as it would, out of his monumental work with Whitehead in *Principia Mathematica*. It seemed to be able to blitz away the whole long dilemma about subjects, simple entities and proper names by a kind of emphatic substitution. The subject 'ghost' and, for that matter, the subject 'God' were now to be seen as no more than the products of an episode in the evolution of the human mind. The true constituents of true knowledge all belonged on the predicate side: science had shown that the truth is what is empirically there, and that true knowledge is the process by which the human mind fetches that empirical content up into predicates. Primitive language acquisition is normally imagined to proceed in the opposite direction, from the naming of subjects to their predicates. But this is not, in fact, the case. We experience the world in its warmth and its coldness and its hardness and its softness. Then after that we settle the names of the things to which these features can be applied. But Russell's point was that the irrefutable, empirical, content of the world sits on the predicate side of knowledge and language. And that the subject side is afterwards settled upon arbitrarily according to rules and standards. For example, in the passage above from Aristotle's *Metaphysics*, Aristotle correctly notices that a house is really just an arrangement of materials; although, because he is intent on preserving the subject 'house', he is prompted to conclude:

> Why are these materials a house? Because precisely these materials are present, and it is precisely this that it meant for them to be a house.

For this reason, it never occurs to Aristotle that these same materials could just as equally all be present in exactly the form of a house, but not be seen as that, and not be named as that. They could have another name. What we call 'houses' could be called 'grosties' instead, and this could happen because to name something does not alter its empirical reality. So, names are conventional while empirical reality is foundational. By the same token, something that does not yet have a name but exists may suddenly be given a name and then by that means enter the human mind as an item of knowledge. It is this overview of the rational apprehension of knowledge that allows Russell to imagine a primitive evolution of the human mind; a time at which the subjects had been allowed to proliferate beyond the limiting case of the predicates—And to call that evolution the Christian era. Once again, this analysis allows us to see where the moral dimension enters in. I.e., *it is sin not to use the resources at one's disposal to grow up.*

On the Russellian analysis, the Predicate side of things will come to replace the Subject side of things through an emphatic substitution. Or really, the Predicate side of things which was empirically there all along will no longer be stymied by the Subject side of things and how the latter is as free and random as the human will (because despite grammar and physics, we are and always have been free to name things any which way we like). But, of course, this analysis can only eventually have the effect of magnifying and aggrandizing the original dilemma. And in terms of what Russell was trying to achieve with Whitehead in *Principia Mathematica*, in raising that dilemma to a true Rubicon. The problem of modern logic which *Principia Mathematica* had run up against was essentially that which Gödel would make famous in his 'incompleteness theorems'. The advantage of modern symbolic logic over and against, say, the physical deployment of the 'seeing is believing' type of truth-function, is that it allows us to hold virtual encounters with things in rapid succession. When I was discussing Gödel above I pointed out, 'in terms of a series stretching to infinity, truthfulness as the *description* of a process would mean someone standing at the end of infinity watching all the terms in the series come home—And thereby actually *seeing* (because remember, seeing is believing) them home.' The problem for modern symbolic logic, then, is that it is designed to overcome the plain fact that our thinking *ought* to be limited to things with which we have had immediate and meaningful acquaintance. However, by endeavouring to overcome this '*ought*' by means of its collocating symbols and denoting phrases it can only truly perpetuate—on a grander and more exaggerated scale—the original naïve realism of Aristotle's *Metaphysics*.

So, when with the one hand it points out that Aristotle *ought* to have realized that his scientific reduction to properties had made his notion of 'primary being' unnecessary, with the other hand it pursues a course that causes it to tacitly appeal to exactly this expedient. Modern analytical philosophy's great criticism of Aristotle's *Metaphysics* is that a commitment to the notion of 'primary being' leads one to imagine that the Subject side of things really exists in some supernatural way; whereas the correct way to view the world would be to see it always as an undifferentiated and unfeeling ocean of identical atoms, which should allow one then to say that differentiation occurs always after this primary fact, as we notice stable properties and classify them, and then attach them in turn to subjects, and so on. Instead of 'primary being' and its shades of the mystical we would have just the *primary fact*.

The problem that modern symbolic logic creates for itself is that it only heightens our awareness of human intellection's wholly abstract and conjectural nature. It encourages us to conclude that if reality does begin and end with science's *primary fact*, then all human thinking after it is disingenuous and a step in the wrong direction, and the whole enterprise of differentiation and subjects and portable knowledge (books) is ridiculous. Instead, everyone should restrict their thinking to the things with which they have had immediate acquaintance, and there should be no attempts to substitute that with communicated acquaintances, reported speech, and all such other vicarious devices. Every man should think only of what he knows and not speak of it to others!

ON DENOTING

This may be so, but clearly, we are by now too far gone in thinking and speaking our way around the universe to even contemplate returning to it. We are also no longer innocent in the way that one would have to be innocent to affect it. So, the solution delivered by modern philosophy should be to deal with this issue head on, on the terms on which it presents itself. This would be the view that Russell would take in his seminal paper of 1905 entitled 'On Denoting' and published in the philosophy journal *Mind*. In this paper, Russell would put it that all the difficulties (that we have been listing),

> seem unavoidable if we regard denoting phrases as standing for genuine constituents of the propositions in whose verbal expressions they occur. Of the possible theories which admit such constituents the simplest is that of Meinong. This theory regards any grammatically correct denoting phrase as standing for an *object*. Thus 'the present king of France,' 'the round square,' etc., are supposed to be genuine objects. It is admitted that such objects do not *subsist*, but nevertheless they are supposed to be objects.... [This] breach of the law of contradiction is avoided by Frege's theory. He distinguishes, in a denoting phrase, two elements, which we may call the *meaning* and the *denotation*. Thus 'the centre of mass of the Solar System at the beginning of the twentieth century' is highly complex in *meaning*, but its *denotation* is a certain point, which is simple.[33]

Russell's issue with this, as we would expect, was that to make the *meaning* complex but the *denotation* a simple point was to admit the denotation to a status of acquaintance which it simply has not had, with any human being, at any time, on this earth.

> For example, we know that the centre of mass of the Solar System at a definite instant is some definite point, and we can affirm a number of propositions about it; but we have no immediate *acquaintance* with this point, which is only known to us by description... In perception we have acquaintance with the objects of perception,

and in thought we have acquaintance with the objects of a more abstract logical character; but we do not necessarily have acquaintance with the objects denoted by phrases composed of words with whose meaning we are acquainted. To take a very important instance: There seems no reason to believe that we are ever acquainted with other people's minds, seeing that these are not directly perceived; hence what we know about them is obtained through denoting.[34]

Russell's famous solution to this problem would in the end be the simple act of drawing out and making explicit the reasons why denoting phrases have become such prolific features of everyday language. This, he would show, is because they are so convenient and expedient. They are really shorthand for the otherwise laborious method by which we would each time have to prove the ontological and epistemological status of the denotation. A denoting phrase is such that it can therefore always be unpacked by means of symbolic logic into a representation of what we really mean when we use it.

> My theory, briefly, is as follows. I take the notion of the *variable* as fundamental; I use 'C (x)' to mean a proposition in which x is a constituent, where x, the variable, is essentially and wholly undetermined. Then we can consider the two notions 'C (x) is always true' and 'C (x) is sometimes true'. Then *everything* and *nothing* and *something* (which are the most primitive of denoting phrases) are to be interpreted as follows:—
> C (everything) means 'C (x) is always true';
> C (nothing) means ' "C (x) is false" is always true';
> C (something) means 'It is false that "C (x) is false" is always true'.
> Hence the notion 'C (x) is always true' is taken as ultimate and indefinable, and the others are defined by means of it. *Everything, nothing* and *something*, are not assumed to have any meaning in isolation, but a meaning is assigned to *every* proposition in which they occur.[35]

According to this schema of Russell's, denoting phrases would become, like Aristotle's 'primary being', a straightforward case of language driving too far ahead of reality—And a straightforward case, in turn, of the power of logic to prove this to us, plus show us a way to put the two back into step with each other.

> [A] denoting phrase is essentially *part* of a sentence, and does not, like most single words, have any significance on its own account. If I say 'Scott was a man,' that is a statement of the form 'x was a man,' and it has 'Scott' for its subject. But if I say 'the author of *Waverley* was a man,' that is not a statement of the form 'x was a man,' and does not have 'the author of *Waverley*' for its subject.... [Therefore] we may put, in place of 'the author of *Waverley* was a man,' the following: 'One and only

one entity wrote *Waverley*, and that one was a man' ... And speaking generally, suppose we wish to say that the author of *Waverley* had the property φ, what we wish to say is equivalent to 'One and only one entity wrote *Waverley*, and that one had the property φ'.[36]

By this stage, we can clearly see the general case accusation against 'Metaphysics (per se)' that Russell's theory represents. It clearly puts his life project at odds with Wittgenstein's. Insofar as I have developed the matter in this book, we can say that Russell's life project was the deification of *Identity*, whereas Wittgenstein's was the pursuit of the *Glory of Man*. Identity is one of the three so-called Laws of Thought and as such, is one of the conditions of modern life. In *Principia Mathematica*, Russell would correctly identify the Subject-Predicate distinction as the dividing line between the imperfect thinking of ages past and the now-to-be-perfect thinking of the ages to come. The enlightened man of the future will simply accept (like a schoolboy today simply accepts the internal combustion engine and rejects the fire-breathing dragon) that the empirical Predicate world is preeminent and independent; such that it is enlightened man's manifest destiny to make his beginning always with it—And to realize therefore that the proper constituents of what he afterwards comes to think of as Subjects are always its indifferent particles.

In fact, there is nothing in the indifference of the Predicate world to suggest moral or spiritual imperatives this way or that. The kind of mysticism that allowed Pythagoras and his followers to envisage such imperatives in numbers and the propositions of mathematics is just plain wishful thinking. For the propositions of mathematics are not axiomatic, with nothing behind them, but eminently provable because they have behind them the 'wide unfeeling ocean'. They are simply the second-order expressions of that ocean's laws. It is precisely because the human mind is (and therefore *ought*) to be capable of evolution in the left-to-right direction that in days of old it was customary to approach the world almost exclusively from the Subject side, to vivify and personify it and to see it in terms of proper nouns and names. The philological investigations of Giambattista Vico were the first to try to show this in a systematic way.[37] And therefore as much as he made the major early contribution to this left-to-right movement, Aristotle was also responsible for bequeathing to the Christian era the notion of *substantia* which would become, in the medieval schools, the key to their metaphysics. And the problem with this metaphysics, to Russell, was that it was indiscriminate as regards to its verification on the Predicate side. That is to say, over the course of human history, the Predicate side has borne out the Subjects named by men or caused adjustments to those names or scratched them out altogether. It has also added new Subjects of its own, such as the Proton. That is to say again, the original term logic of Aristotle and the medieval schoolmen supported the idea that the world should be viewed from the Subject side, with men taking on faith the *denotations* of the Great Books—'Yahweh', and so on. While the propositional and symbolic logic of the modern era has allowed for the gradual correcting of this, as men no longer name things with the boldness and recklessness of old but watch the future come towards them in its teeming materiality. This is what it means to be 'on the side of history'; which, yet again, shows us the curious morality of materiality when it is taken as far as thinkers like Russell can take it.

*　*　*

The great question, then, is this. Is human language a juvenile phenomenon awaiting its final surge into adulthood (the moral view; the prescriptive view; the Russellian view), or is it a timeless phenomenon whose Subjects are the results of places actually visited (and Christ actually touched)?

*　*　*

Consider this. If you were an atom, then all you could possibly see would be other atoms. All, identical, to you.

> This throws some light on the question why logical propositions cannot be confirmed by experience any more than they can be refuted by it. Not only must a proposition of logic be irrefutable by any possible experience, but it must also be unconfirmable by any possible experience.[38]

The great instruction left out of all the logic books that I have come across is the instruction to actually try to put yourself into each logical proposition and *see through its eyes to what it sees*. Only if you do this will you understand (see for yourself) all of Wittgenstein's talk about tautologies. One logical proposition can only see forwards in increments of itself. And this is what is really meant when it is said that 'truth is carried through, or conveyed through, a correctly connected chain of logic'. Only once you do this will you also then realize that logic cannot ever *say* anything in the way that a human can. Logic only ever sees itself, and the combinations of its symbols are only ever such as to allow this to happen.

> Now it becomes clear why people have often felt as if it were for us to '*postulate*' the 'truths of logic'. The reason is that we can postulate them in so far as we can postulate an adequate notation.[39]

The general form of modern Western logic is thus only a mode of seeing (*Itself*). Anything can see itself in increments of itself, and it is this fact which is responsible for number, plus the axiomatic relationships between numbers. The belief that there is an atomic level at which numbers plus their axiomatic relationships become the same thing as physics (as though, through a microscope, the material becomes the numerical) is just that—*A belief*. Logic and reality are not interchangeable. They do not prove each other. But the idea that they do is of course the moral force of the Russellian belief.

Clearly the laws of logic cannot in their turn be subject to laws of logic. (There is not, as Russell thought, a special law of contradiction for each 'type'; one law is enough, since it is not applied to itself.)[40]

The general validity of logic might be called essential, in contrast with the accidental general validity of such propositions as 'All men are mortal'. Propositions like Russell's 'axiom of reducibility' are not logical propositions, and this explains our feeling that, even if they were true, their truth could only be the result of a fortunate accident.[41]

When I spoke earlier of language before Wittgenstein being simply philosophy's 'communicating medium', then after Wittgenstein of it being singled out for what it is in itself (and turned loose on itself), this is what I meant. Before Wittgenstein, a philosopher like Russell might well look at Aristotle's *Metaphysics* and chastise him for having tracked the Subject-Predicate requirement all the way to the Unmoved Mover. For by Russell's time, it had become popular to imagine that the relationship between language, truth, and logic was one of moral responsibility, on the part of language, to conform. That is why I earlier used the phrase 'manifest destiny'. From the first philosophers in the sixth century B.C. onwards, the inexpressible, the ineffable, and the unfathomable began to be pushed back by the new discovery of the *essential* transposability of the laws of speaking sense, the laws of thought, and the laws of nature. If I open such an archetypal work of this project as Antonio Rosmini's *The Origin of Thought* (first published 1830), I can read this:

> [H]ow can I deliberately move my attention from one idea to another except through a relationship binding together in some way the ideas to which I successively move my attention? Every relationship between two things or ideas is an abstract, that is, neither the one idea nor the other, but a connection that each has with my mind as it thinks them; every *relationship*, therefore, is an *abstraction*.... Without *abstracts*, therefore, I cannot use my free will, nor can I direct my intelligence in one way rather than another. *Abstracts* bind together my particular ideas, and provide a passage from one to another. Without abstracts, ideas would remain totally divided and separate from one another. My attention would be fixed upon each of them individually without its being able to turn towards them as a group and embrace them collectively in a single glance. There would be no reasoning because the whole operation of understanding would end where feeling itself ends. Abstractions are of the utmost importance, ... [and they are] obtained with the help of language coming to us through human society. The proposition I set out to demonstrate is, therefore, true and irrefutable: 'Language is necessary to make us masters of our own powers'; and every great advance made by mankind is due to this immense benefit we receive from the society of our peers.[42]

Here we recognize a common sense that is as old as philosophy itself; and with that being exactly the point, according to Wittgenstein. For the only way to rush at this full pelt really is to go back to the shadow worlds that came before philosophy, where wisdom and the mystical really were the point at which words ran out.

In prosecuting his theory 'On Denoting', Russell rather gives the game away. He reveals that his project has a suppressed premise, which is that logic is not *just* symbolic but also has a definite subject matter. Which means in turn that language is not just exclamatory but also has a definite subject matter. Which is of course the exact same definite subject matter as logic. Why should it matter that there are points of intellection that our minds can only have an indirect contact with through 'measurements of measurements' and 'descriptions of descriptions'? It matters to Russell because such denoting practices are not of themselves able to distinguish between the 'true' and 'false' points of intellection. Here we see that suppressed premise appear because suddenly we understood that for Russell and those who follow him there really are such things as true and false points of intellection. And that it is intolerable for them if language and logic are used in ways that pay no heed to this. This dream is, of course, as old as Socrates, Plato, Aristotle, and just about everyone else in the Western tradition who subscribes to the mantra of the 'examined life'. People blurt things: then those things are what philosophy gets to work on. Without people first blurting things there could be no philosophy. Philosophy and most of all logic can for this reason never be wrong. It can never be wrong because it always comes second. [And you may remember that I made this point in Chapter 2.[43]] Only people can be wrong. But being wrong also means that they can be surprising and original and extempore (and fall in love, and all the rest of the amazing things that people can do, and the already-happened can't).

> The propositions of logic describe the scaffolding of the world, or rather they represent it. They have no 'subject-matter' ... This contains the decisive point.... We have said that some things are arbitrary in the symbols that we use and that some things are not. In logic it is only the latter that express: but that means that logic is not a field in which *we* express what we wish with the help of signs, but rather one in which the nature of the absolutely necessary signs speaks for itself ... [44]
>
> It is possible—indeed possible even according to the old conception of logic—to give in advance a description of all 'true' logical propositions.[45]
>
> Hence there can *never* be surprises in logic.[46]

THE PLACES TO WHICH WE HAVE VOYAGED

That language and logic have a subject matter, and that their perfectly efficient communication of that subject matter is *truth*, really does contain the 'decisive point'. You will be well aware by now that I have tried thus far to bring you to terms with the antithesis, viz., that language has no official subject matter such as we can find perfected for us in the world of the already-happened, but that instead it has simply been humanity's way of reporting on the myriad different places to which it has voyaged.[47] These have been places of the earth and then they have been places not of the earth. That is to say, they have been natural and they have been supernatural places. Or really, we can now say this. If the connection between all these natural and supernatural places is the single human language which has reported on them, then the customary distinctions between natural and supernatural must cease to exist. Or at least, we can allow them to cease to exist in this book. Because that turns out to be the distinctively Wittgensteinian thing to do.

And now you will also be able to see why I had to make such a point of Wittgenstein's repeated invocations of Christ in his philosophical writings. Even as a concept, Christ is natural and supernatural at once, and thus this unique commixture scrambles the artful distinctions of the language and logic we are trying to use, and it is this plain scrambling effect which produces such important and unique results. These results fly in the face of the whole trajectory of Western philosophy and suggest that language is not something that we should ever, and indeed can ever, boil down. Boiling it down only reduces it to the 'absolutely necessary signs' which 'speak for themselves'. In other words, you can only boil a language down to its grammar but never its subject matter. For the subject matter is what the language reports on. Language and logic cannot of themselves proffer the means of adjudicating between the truth and falsehood of language's subject matter. And in fact we can extend this to say that the subject matter of language is not susceptible to truth or falsehood. We can say that what you have felt, you have also seen; and what you have seen, you can speak of. *This is realism.*

> The way you use the word 'God' does not show whom you mean—but, rather, what you mean.[48]

I believe that this is what Wittgenstein meant when he wrote that we 'suspend ourselves from Heaven' when we 'hold tightly to our redemption and our belief'.[49] The 'holding tightly' bit does not refer to blind faith or to belief in a subject matter that is false. The question is not whether Christ rose again on the third day—And how Russell's theory on denoting would unpack all Christianity to propositions admitting of the (truth or) falsity of this. Nor for that matter is the question one of whether high passion is responsible for the holding tightly in the first place—Such as the prayers that men send up in the piercing moments of their mortality. Those who actually met and talked with Christ might have made any sounds with their throats and tongues other than the sounds that they actually did make. They might have written those sounds down using any marks that took their fancy. This might just as well have happened instead of what did happen to make the Bible as we know it. And the real question would then have to be: What difference would it have made? For certainly, one could not say that it would have changed what happened between Christ and those he met. For what went on in the hearts and minds of those he touched would have gone on regardless. And as far as those people would have been concerned, their strange sounds and marks would have had exactly the same hinterland as had they used the conventional language and writing of their day.

But you might respond to this by saying: 'Their sounds and marks would still have constituted a *language*, albeit a new one. So, after the initial confusion, we would still have been able to lay their sounds and marks against the record of what actually happened and decipher them that way. And if we succeeded in doing that, we would have negated the whole point of your example.' Quite. Except that what I meant by my example was that the followers of Christ would make their sounds and marks *spontaneously differently* each time their passion took them, in exactly the random way that would leave it that there could be no deciphering of them afterwards. Each time a *one-time* language, afterwards forgotten.

> One can be obsessed about a certain language form. One can think for years about a certain problem and make no progress, because one never thinks of making up a new language.[50]

'Well that is fine, you say, but now you are introducing a scenario in which language as we know it is not being used. Because if they are simply exclaiming and marking randomly, without underlying syntax, then they are not *communicating* or *making sense*. They are not transporting the content of their hearts and minds into stable parcels of meaning— As happens in societies when words and word-assemblies have developed stable meanings over time.'

[But it should be asked: Are they then making music?]

And you are right to respond to me with that. And now we see it. Now we see what Wittgenstein was after with his philosophy.

THE PRINTING PRESS

The phenomenon of language is a mechanism whereby tilts of the human soul are connected by rods and wires to exclamations and marks. The phenomenon of language is that simple a mechanism. There is a direct mechanical correspondence between those exclamations and marks and the tilts of the human soul; and that is it.

> Suppose that one is told to project a certain figure onto a certain wall. Then one can either do this by making its shadow fall onto the wall in a certain way or else by working out (as one might say) what would happen if one did make its shadow fall thus.—But suppose one is given as a mathematical [task] the projection of the figure onto the wall, and told to do it in a certain way, for example, by means of light and shadow. What is the difference between the mathematical task and the non-mathematical task?[51]

This was an incredibly provocative thing for Wittgenstein to have said at a time when the prevailing idea was that mathematics and logic should become wholesale replacements for the tilts of the soul. You will know by now what I mean by this—And yes, poor

Russell has been my example throughout (but then he was Wittgenstein's example, too). There is a temptation to study the laws of speaking sense, the laws of thought and the laws of nature, and then to stand on their side and look back at the human soul and to declare (on that basis) that it, too, should be subject to those laws. And that this subjection should be progress and evolution and manifest destiny. So that out of all of it should arise human creatures who will act as perfectly and as necessarily as he whom I called Mathematical Man in Chapter 3.[52] The twentieth-century revolution in philosophy was thus far bigger and more persuasive than any of the famous movements which made it up. In Chapter 2 I called it a 'spasm'.[53] It began with a solid pan-acknowledgement of the necessary relationship between the syntax of language and the laws of nature. Then it did a double-take at the word 'necessary' (the 'spasm'). Then it began to spin faster and faster with the new thought that this necessary relationship might be refined to generate a new and brave kind of realism in word and deed. I.e., that if what was *necessary* in this relationship could itself only be proved, then it would no longer be able to be played with and dismissed by infuriating mystics like *Ludwig Wittgenstein*. Remember how Wittgenstein used the *Tractatus* to demonstrate that the structural identity shared between a sentence and its fact cannot itself be stated in language but can only be shown? Well that is exactly what we are referring to again here, though in its broadest form. It mattered very much to the twentieth-century revolution in philosophy that the necessary relationship between the innate classification system of our minds and the innate physical structure of the universe be proved; for then, and only then, would it be possible no longer to raise against it the devastating riposte of the poets.[54]

Humans were never meant to think and act logically and lawfully: to do the right things all the time (and confect a world in that image). Like the thief on the cross, they were only meant to *act for love*. And where things either side of identity signs, where logic, can only look across and see itself, yet love can look another in the eye and see the whole forsaken plot.

BUT FIRST A DIGRESSION ON FANATICISM

The twentieth-century revolution in philosophy for which Russell would become the chief populariser singled out 'fanaticism' as the great, mad bogey that a calm, logical analysis alone could face down. It wasn't that their new technique in philosophy was going to produce final answers to the classic questions of philosophy, such as those involving 'time' and 'number' and 'mind'; rather, it was that it would preclude and disqualify the kind of answers to these questions that had formerly proceeded from the announcement of some higher, infallible authority. The oracle, the shaman, the silent impenetrable wisdom that can only be obeyed.[55] It wasn't, then, that logical analysis would bring to an end the religious and the mystical, but rather, that it would come to represent the decisive argument for why they should never more be allowed to infect the domain of the pressing sociopolitical questions of life. Prayer did not put men on the moon; science did that. And therefore prayer and all it represents should for that reason be reclassified as among the private recreational pursuits that a man performs on his own or with his like-minded fellows. These pursuits are an important component of any rounded life in any free society. However, they can now be seen for the good that they are *only* because logical analysis has made the clinching argument for the separation of the public from the private domain. Logical analysis helped create the common sense that says the public domain of any free and equal society is too vital a place for men to act within it from their private thoughts and prejudices. And therefore if any single doctrine could sum up the intellectual accomplishments of the twentieth century, it would be this one. 'Moral pluralism', 'Negative freedom', 'The open society', and the other motifs through which it has become known.

The whole intellectual tradition of the twentieth century has been fairly dominated by this, its chosen response to fanaticism, fascism, communism, and totalitarianism. The exact role that science and logical analysis were to play in formulating this response I can explain to you briefly.

Science and logical analysis first reveal to us the extent to which we are compelled and predestinated by 'what is really going on'. This microscopic level of analysis is shocking and seems to mock and invalidate all the traditional epithets concerning human freedom. The knowledge that science and logical analysis produce appears, in this first instance, then, to be the knowledge of how we are as scripted and predicted as any other animal of instinct. It is at precisely this point of apparent and consummate defeat, then, that the 'new way' must find its special route to our transformation and upliftment. This comes about as it asks us to focus on the way in which the depressing knowledge of our reduction to instinct is always arrived at by the same unbending method—Rather, say, than by luck or by chance. It is noticed that the relationship between this method and the knowledge it produces is a *necessary* one. To quote again from Wittgenstein above, 'The connexion between knowledge and what is known is that of logical necessity.'[56] You will also now recall the extent to which I have habituated you in this book to realize how this pantographic mechanism actually creates a whole new world called the world of the *already-happened*, and how it then only becomes obvious that human nature must begin to tempt us into imagining that we could live in this whole new world full-time, as the brave new masters of our brave new destiny. From this realization that from a fixed method of investigation must necessarily proceed a fixed kind of knowledge comes, then, the Russellian belief that it is this method— rather than the knowledge it produces— which should become the new (I say) fanaticism.

Except it never gets said quite like that. The way it gets said is always like this:

> The habit of careful veracity acquired in the practice of this philosophical method can be extended to the whole sphere of human activity, producing, wherever it exists, a lessening of fanaticism with an increasing capacity of sympathy and mutual understanding. In abandoning a part of its dogmatic pretensions, philosophy does not cease to suggest and inspire a way of life.[57]

On the one hand, it is not difficult to see the excitement in the world of this belief which the publication of the *Tractatus* quickly caused. No book before it or since has better encapsulated in form and style the 'habit of careful veracity' that had become the key to the new fanaticism. And yet there was something in the *Tractatus* that made it impossible to be consistently read by those actively involved in this new fanaticism. For its central message *What we cannot speak about we must pass over in silence* was not, in fact, the manifesto for the analytical method of life. On closer inspection, it was actually the manifesto for the most full and devastating liberation from that new method. It was the most exacting, point-by-point explanation of why Western knowledge is tautological on its method, and why it is therefore this method which is the true challenge to *true human freedom*. To the *freedom of the soul*. Western knowledge can only tell you what you already know. It can only tell you that if you could cut yourself up into the smallest imaginable pieces then those pieces would be atoms. Between the method and the result sits logical necessity. Similarly, there is no single item of Western knowledge conceivable that does not imply its method of discovery. What this should tell us, says Wittgenstein, is that Western knowledge is not the important thing but the method which produces it. This is all the time disguised by the celebrated instances of the Knowledge-end of things. Knowledge gave you penicillin, and penicillin heals. But really, and always, it is the method behind the knowledge that 'does not cease to suggest and inspire a new way of life'.

> This is analogous to an ethical discussion of free will. We have an idea of compulsion. If a policeman grabs me and shoves me through the door, we say I am compelled. But if I walk up and down here, we say I move freely. But it is objected: 'If you knew all the laws of nature, and could observe all the particles etc., you would no longer say you were moving freely; you would see that a man just cannot do anything else.'—But in the first place, this is not how we use the expression 'he can't do anything else'. Although it is conceivable that if we had a mechanism which would show all this, we would change our terminology—and say, 'He's as much compelled as if a policeman shoved him.' We'd give up this distinction then; and if we did, I would be very sorry. To say 'If you multiply these two, you necessarily get such-and-such a number', if it means anything at all, must be opposed to a case where there is no necessity. Or else it's a pleonasm to say you necessarily get this— why not Simply say that you get it?—We might speak of getting something but not necessarily, in the case of a calculus in which you could get more than one answer.[58]

It is indeed the addition of the 'necessarily' every time that gives the Russellian game away. And it is the peculiar brilliance of Wittgenstein's intellect that it always drives so hard at this telling little addition. Wittgenstein's writing always shows you the 'on the face of it' version. On the face of it, there is no need to say that 2 + 2 necessarily gives you 4. In a way, this is the iconic statement that Wittgenstein's writings simply remake over and over again. Because if everything did just exist in its 'on the face of it' version, as we might still find that it did in a newly discovered Amazonian tribe, then there would be no meat on the bone for Russell and all the other reductionists. If everything was as it seemed, without even a hint of the mechanism that made it so, then there would be nothing to reverse engineer—As indeed logical analysis does reverse engineer our lived reality.

What was there behind the conversation between Christ and the thief on the cross other than the words which they exchanged? And does this mean that the only mechanism which the logical analysts see is one which they have placed there themselves? Is the *necessarily* the mechanism which they have placed there themselves? Is there some reduced level of analysis on which we would see the words pass between Christ and the thief on the cross in the way that they *necessarily* would, given, say, the psychological effect of the cult of Christ over the brain of the thief—And given, say, again, the heightened credulity to which his pain and desperation would have transported him?

> I want to talk about the question whether one can justify the results of mathematical calculations by means of Russell's logic, or whether they depend upon certain quite different techniques; say the technique of being able to compare two numbers of objects in a certain way. For instance this: *Principia Mathematica* has been printed in a few thousand copies. We say they all contain the same proofs. There is a way in which these copies have been produced, and this has been checked; and this satisfies us.[59]

I have always credited it a significant fact that those who denominate new methods of knowledge slip inexorably into applying those methods as 'methods of life'. In this regard, science never did stay in the lab. The scientist always becomes the priest. And I am proud to say that it was Wittgenstein who alerted me to the screaming danger in this. For who better than Wittgenstein shows you that a method of knowledge is as artificial as any other rule or game? All logical methods are what they are because they guarantee a certain outcome. From this point of view, it really doesn't matter whether you project the shadow of an object onto a wall and copy it out that way or do the corresponding maths. Nor does it matter whether you use the Cambridge University Press to copy out copies of the proofs or you copy them out yourself, working your way through them as though you were Russell himself at his first successful attempt. The only fact that matters is that anything translated into symbolic, syntactic language becomes at once something that a rod and wire machine could replicate. *The Pantograph*. But you want to say to me: 'It would be madness to suggest that what the printing press does is indistinguishable from what the writer did when he originally arranged the words!' Perhaps; but that is because you are seeing it from the writer's side of things. The Subject side of things. Try to see it from the other side. The side of the end result. Remember what I said just now/re logical methods being what they are 'because they guarantee a certain outcome'. You want to argue that the writer arranged the words according to his creative impulse and free will, such that he, and only he, could have done it in that moment of his determination. Fine. But come across now with me to the other side. Stand with me by the magnificent printing press. And try to see the whole business like this machine does.

BACK TO THE PRINTING PRESS

You say that your writer made impulsive esoteric art. Well, the machine disagrees. It says that your writer made only a series of marks on paper. Better, let's imagine that he typed his words using a computer's word-processing programme. In that case he merely depressed certain keys in certain orders; while at exactly the same time these actions of his were translated by the computer into its own binary language of ones and zeros then stored in its memory. Now let's return to the printing press and its job of copying out his typescript. Well (and assuming it is a modern, computerised press), all it has to do now is decipher the code of ones and zeroes and turn them out as letters on sheets of paper. Does this make the printing press as intelligent as your friend who first wrote down the words? I hope that you will want to say, 'No, of course not!' But you should know enough about Wittgenstein by now to know that the matter can't rest there.

Because from the point of view of the machine, your writer friend only did as much as *it* might have done. Your writer friend only did as much as the machine was able to copy. You still want to react against this and credit him with art and creativity and being the unmoved mover. It is only natural that you should want to do that. He and you are human after all, and what I am pushing towards here is making you feel distinctly discomforted as that. But I repeat. Whatever may have gone on inside your writer friend as the back story to his creation, when it came to putting his marks down on paper, he didn't just make random, once-in-a-lifetime squiggles. He acted like a machine. He followed the established rules of logical syntax. *He wrote in such a way as his words would be understood*. He wrote in such a way as to perform the truth of the *necessity* of these rules. He wrote in such a way that afterwards, a philosopher like Bertrand Russell might be able to come along and hold up his writing as proof of the laws of thought.

Wittgenstein shows us that art never makes it outside of the artist. Maybe in brushstrokes or music or dance it does. But never in words. *What we cannot speak about we must pass over in silence.*

> I once knew a boy who talked of the 'dark notes' on the piano, not meaning the black notes but the low notes, although he had never heard them referred to as dark. We might say, 'He felt a similarity between darkness and low notes.' If someone asked, 'What is this similarity he felt? Where does it lie?', what could you say?—This is the similarity: that he wanted to say 'dark'.[60]

Examples like that are probably as good as it can get. The difference between intelligence and artificial intelligence is that words should be for humans to mess about and scramble with; in just the way that this boy did with the piano notes. The great mistake of Russell and the twentieth century was to fall for the apparent beauty of the copy that the pantograph makes. Their fall was of itself unoriginal and as old as Adam and Eve, and this I have explained a good deal throughout this book. What made it revolutionary and the most potent re-enactment of the old Fall yet was the precision of the new logical analysis. From the first philosophers onwards, Western man has been beguiled and transfixed by the idea of being able to hold a stable, conceptual rendition of flux and chaos in his hands. And his motivation has never changed from the original mixture of pride and fear (of death) that Adam and Eve released into the common psyche. This is why I said a little earlier that all serious philosophies may begin as a theory of knowledge acquisition (the pride phase), but before long, the method developed in this phase will have begun to suggest itself as *the* conquering way of life for this capricious world (the fear of death part). The spanner that Wittgenstein would hurl into this age-old works would be his repeated demonstrations concerning the comprehensive artificiality of human language. Human language as we know it from school and society is a closed system. Human language can only communicate with itself; and the best that we can do is to listen in to what it is saying to itself. In the end, all that logical analysis should be able to prove to us is this fact. This same fact over and over again. When the words of the writer communicate with the copying machine, the words and the copying machine both look towards the same middle—And through it, see themselves. That same middle is logical method. When we, as humans, wish to listen in on this communication, we look to the same middle, and see the same logical method. The actual words of the writer and their perfect copies at the other end are significant only insofar as they become proofs of the logical method which connects them. *This is what is so dangerous: And this is what Wittgenstein was trying to warn us to over and again in his philosophy.*

> The melodies of different composers can be approached by applying the principle: Every species of tree is a 'tree' in a different sense of the word. I.e. don't let yourself be misled by our saying that they are all melodies. They are steps along a path that leads from something you would not call a melody to something else that you again would not call one. If you simply look at the sequences of notes & the changes of key all these structures no doubt appear on the same level. But if you look at the field of force in which they stand (and hence their significance), you will be inclined to say: Here the melody is something quite different than there (here it has a different origin, plays a different role, *inter alia*).[61]

Logical method is simply a way of making a perfect copy of something; and nothing could be more inhumane than to make a perfect copy of something. The lust to make a perfect copy of something is the original lust of original sin. What is by contrast the humane thing to do is for you to tell me something and for it to set off an explosion of feeling in me and for that feeling to take me onwards into seeing new thing upon new thing—But never the original that you had in your mind when you tried to tell it to me. When you read a novel and form your own picture of one of the characters in the story, you never imagine that your picture must be identical to the original that the author had in their minds when they picked the words for their story. Everything between humans that is normal is like this, and we gladly accept it. We gladly accept it because it is what makes human life what it is. It is why you can have one Bible for a world of unique beings because the same words never mean the same thing to the same person. It is why you can have mysticism and poetry, music and art.

Wittgenstein helps us see the real bind we are in. On the one hand, we have language. And as a tool of survival its use never becomes more apparent to us than when we are using it brutally, to communicate an empirical fact to a fellow human. 'Those two eggs. Give me those two eggs.' This is what language does. And this thing that language does explains its form, which is the form of logical syntax itself. So, when Russell and the logical analysts say that the precise use of language would bring us into closest and best conformation with the world that we actually live in, this is what they mean—And they are not wrong. Now here comes the strange part. It is precisely because this is what language is, that it can then also go on to play the central role it does in mysticism and poetry, music and art. It is precisely because an arrangement of words has to mean one thing and one thing only that they can then go on to mean anything at all. For example, 'Two eggs' can only mean one thing and one thing only, and yet I could decide to call my dog 'Two eggs'. Or every time something good happened to me, I could decide to yell 'Two eggs!' instead of, say, 'Brilliant!' Hang on. Didn't 'brilliant' in any case mean the reflective quality of a surface before it also took on its role as an exclamation? Anyway, you see what I mean. The bind we are in is that in language, we are communicating through a mechanism that, because it is a mechanism, is capable of being fully automated.

My soul tilts a little. I want then to communicate that tilt to you. I pick words to do it. But not just any words, because words must be arranged syntactically. So, I obey the machine and pick words that it might have picked. At the other end, you pick up the copy of them. You decipher them according to the logic of the machine (language's) operation. But you know that they came from *me*. And because you are human, you know that they originated in my tilt of soul. So, at this point you ignore the language in front of you and start to feel—try to feel—my original tilt of soul. Or you do not, and you go all 'adult' on me.

> Philosophers often behave like little children who scribble some marks on a piece of paper at random and then ask the grown-up 'What's that?'—It happened like this: the grown-up had drawn pictures for the child several times and said 'this is a man,' 'this is a house,' etc. And then the child makes some marks too and asks: what's this then?[62]

* * *

Yes, that is how language *ought* to be used in human society. The only danger would be if we ignored each other and both strove to become like machines.

* * *

Wittgenstein wants us to see that the language used between us is in itself irrelevant. It is the effort that you make to *feel* my original tilt of soul that matters. From this point of view, the language that I happened to use to communicate my tilt to you could have been replaced by any other language. I could have replaced the word arrangement with a single word or even a number. It wouldn't have made a scrap of difference. It wouldn't have made a scrap of difference because between us would have stood unaffected the same commitment to the same game. Wittgenstein calls it a 'language-game' because truly enough it uses language. But all that language ever is within these games is a stick that we prod the other person with to get their attention and to get them looking into our face. What happens after that is magical.

* * *

This is why I have been saying throughout this book that each word between two human beings is like a doorway of escape to another world. In this world, each word can be used as no more than a prod that then sets up corridors of magic and meaning between us. It is these magic corridors rather than the words that carry whatever it is that passes between us. Words are natural; whatever it is that passes between us is supernatural.

* * *

In this sense, Wittgenstein's philosophy can be seen to be addressing the classic dilemma of the Western intellectual tradition; best known, as it is, through Plato's story of Meno's slave boy in the dialogue of that name. Because Western intelligence prides itself on being practical and self-evident, and because practicality and self-evidence are qualities that can only be proved by their direct correspondence to material flourishing, Western intelligence is a mechanism; or as I have just called it, a *machine*. It is soulless. It can be acted out, copied, and faked. Because there is never any observable difference between the original and the fake. They both look exactly the same. From Wittgenstein's work in logic and mathematics, we learn that this is because the fake is never made independently, and at a later time, than the original. Rather, the fake is made exactly in time with the original because the two are linked by the wires and rods of the pantograph. The true magnitude and achievement of Wittgenstein's philosophy is to show us just this one thing, over and over, example by example. This is why I spent so much time in Chapter 2 initiating you into the weird idea of the already-happened. I had to do that because you needed to come to terms as quickly as possible with the truth that the original exists in order to communicate with the forgery, such that *that* simultaneous relationship (that bilocation) is what we listen in to through logical method. And finally, that because the forgery thus explains the original, it comes inevitably to be preferred to the original.

In the Western intellectual tradition, 'I don't hear you' means the same thing as 'I don't *understand* you'. This is because speaking is the original and understanding is the forgery, while speaking is governed by the understanding it creates at the other end. We flatter ourselves if we think that 'hearing' someone and 'understanding' them are two different activities. The sordid secret is that we believe deep down and subconsciously our understanding creates the words of the other in the first place, that the forgery paints the original.

> If a lion could talk, we could not understand him.[63]

> If we hear a Chinese we tend to take his speech for inarticulate gurgling. Someone who understands Chinese will recognize language in what he hears. Similarly I often cannot recognize the human being in someone etc.[64]

Here we return to another point that I laid a particular emphasis on in Chapter 2, and then a little more severely in Chapter 3.[65] I took great care in both those places to position the genius at a distance of category from the rest of us. Perhaps now you can better appreciate why I took the risk of that effort. Based on what I have brought before you in this chapter, we can now say that we stand in relationship to a genius like Wittgenstein as the forgery does to the original. The genius possesses something inborn; it is their *voice*. They possess also the courage to remain true to that voice. That voice is how they do whatever it is that they do. There is, then, nothing behind the voice that accounts for it. When it is said that the genius has something of the child in him, this is what is meant. They are as free and innocent as only children can be. They just *do* what they do spontaneously. They do not do what they do according to methods or rules or learnt techniques. You could not take the genius away and leave behind those methods, rules, and techniques such that they could get picked up by another—From them to make the same things that the genius once made. All of which amounts to showing why the genius is initially singled out and venerated. But then something else starts to happen. And it is here that the image of the forgery helps explain what.

Just take a second to consider what goes into making a forgery. The chief factor is that the forger cannot work from the same inner inspiration that the genius worked from. He does not possess the genius's voice. On the face of it, this should be cataclysmic and disbar his efforts altogether. But here something critical intervenes—Something which we in this book have gained a heightened sensitivity to as we have gone deep into the animating centre of Wittgenstein's philosophy. This critical intervention is the fact that the external productions of the human mind and personality are *made* things. They are stable. Like my old example of the letters of the alphabet, they are what they are because they have a stable quantity of meaning. An original Renoir is still just dried paint on a canvas. It doesn't move. The picture is what it is because it is still. Behind, yes, is the fluid genius of the man. But no one has ever pretended to be able to enter into the fluidity of another man's mind. Think of Russell's problems with denoting phrases, and how they prove that our only acquaintance with the minds of others as much as the outer reaches of the universe can be through descriptions of descriptions, measurements of measurements. Or think back a little further to Wittgenstein's example of the dreamer now awake and reporting his dreams to (the implied Sigmund Freud), and how Wittgenstein offers the devastating observation that, 'The question whether the dreamer's memory deceives him when he reports the dream after waking cannot arise'.[66] These examples describe the frontier of the Western intelligence. Its own principles of operation disallow it to proceed beyond it. So, forget what lies beyond the frontier and back to what lies behind it, viz., the material productions of human hands, which Western intelligence has to regard as the representatives and proxies of the hidden places of a man. *Of his soul*. Well, if we ignore the painter and look only at the painting, we come to the realization that it would be perfectly—that is, *logically*—possible to copy it. For notwithstanding what goes on in the subterranean places of a man, when it comes to his outwardly expressing those places, he is limited and governed by the same laws of nature that limit and govern the universe at large. Think of our recent example of the writer and the printing press. From the point of view of expression, what our writer has in him that stands behind the words is irrelevant, instead, what is relevant is that words are the only means available to him to express himself, if indeed he chooses to express himself as a writer. And words are limited and governed by the laws of syntax. Therefore, whatever he ends up putting down in words will be at that instance capable of being forged by a machine programmed according to those same laws of syntax.

> Though a state of affairs that would contravene the laws of physics can be represented by us spatially, one that would contravene the laws of geometry cannot.[67]

We say that Leonardo da Vinci was a genius to have painted the Mona Lisa's smile, yet at the same time we observe that he was only able to do it for having made his medical investigations of the musculature of the human mouth. And our understanding of that musculature must be so much better today. Etcetera!

* * *

> *The forgery of human initiative is made possible by the practical fact that that initiative is delimited to an external expression in the physical world of nature.*

* * *

In the Bible you read:

> For what man knoweth the things of a man, save the spirit of man which is in him? even so the things of God knoweth no man, but the Spirit of God.[68]

And we should recall that the same *Confessions* of Augustine that made such an impression on Wittgenstein are a book all about that.

When the forger sets himself to copy an original, he relies on all of this. If he is an expert forger, he thinks not of the originating genius but only looks practically to how best he might replicate the movements of the genius's hand as it must have moved to make its original marks. And as the expert forger does this, something crucial happens. It can be summed up by saying that he ceases to become a forger but just an expert, for he becomes expert at understanding the laws that determined the movements of the genius's hand. More, he starts to realize that it was those laws that *practically* made the painting. More still, he starts to smart under the injustice of the realization the original painting just blurted itself out of the genius like a tilt of his soul; he produced it like a child rhymes nonsense; he had no understanding of what he was doing. Because here now he is, the expert, the forger, *Us*—And are we not now deploying a total understanding to make perfect copies of what the genius did? So that what he did childishly, without ken, we are now doing maturely and wisely, from first principles?

The example of the expert forger of paintings flatters us. A photograph is also a copy of an original. This is indeed a sordid secret.

* * *

The genius must die if we are to protect it!

* * *

The genius does die. We make funny baseball cards of the funny things he does and we script those into the West's laws of genius behaviour. We write biographies about him that explain him back to himself as someone he cannot recognize—That explain him as a *type* and as a *class*. By this means we drive him out.

> You must always be puzzled by mental illness. The thing I would dread most, if I became mentally ill, would be your adopting a common sense attitude; that you could take it for granted that I was deluded.[69]

In the *Tractatus*, Wittgenstein uses logic to express this predicament of the genius:

> Identity of object I express by identity of sign, and not by using a sign for identity. Difference of objects I express by difference of signs.[70]
>
> It is self-evident that identity is not a relation between objects. This becomes very clear if one considers, for example, the proposition '$(x):fx \supset .x = a$'. What this proposition says is simply that *only a* satisfies the function f, and not that only things that have a certain relation to *a* satisfy the function f. Of course, it might then be said that *only a* did have this relation to *a*; but in order to express that, we should need the identity-sign itself.[71]

> Russell's definition of '=' is inadequate, because according to it we cannot say that two objects have all their properties in common. (Even if this proposition is never correct, it still has *sense*.)⁷²
>
> Roughly speaking, to say of *two* things that they are identical is nonsense, and to say of *one* thing that it is identical with itself is to say nothing at all.⁷³

This notation of the genius's predicament shows very clearly that the charge that we the forgers always bring against him in the end is the charge of *realism*. We come in the end to believe that it is more realistic to pretend than to be the originating genius. This is properly the charge of a fallen mankind against God; in the sense in which we would protest that it takes skill and expertise and an understanding of first principles to pretend perfectly. In the Western tradition, these things have since Socrates been grouped under the heading of 'virtue'. So, we can say that it takes virtue to pretend perfectly. Recall now the three quotations from the *Investigations* that head this chapter. But especially the last two:

> A child has much to learn before it can pretend. (A dog cannot be a hypocrite, but neither can he be sincere.)⁷⁴
>
> There might actually occur a case where we should say 'This man *believes* he is pretending.'⁷⁵

WHEN REALISM WILL MEAN PRETENDING

Wittgenstein's philosophy amounts to the prophecy that there will come a time when realism will mean pretending. We aren't quite there yet, but we must be close. Technology brings us closer. There is a sense, of course, in which 'realism' always meant this. Realism has always referred to the measure of how far something approaches to something else. Actors are rewarded for how far they approach to real life. Wittgenstein's prophecy simply inserts into this longstanding situation the distinction between what he calls 'ponder-able' and 'imponderable' evidence.⁷⁶ Imponderable evidence should alert the psychoanalyst to the truth that his analysand may be inaccurately remembering his dream. Imponderable evidence is everything inside us that is impossible to verify. Imponderable evidence is therefore squarely responsible for why it is that we communicate in logic and language. If you could actually travel inside someone and 'see' their imponderable selves, you would be looking at free will itself. The deeps that psychoanalysis deals in are not the deepest deeps. The deepest deeps are simply inaccessible and out of bounds. The only reason we do not accept this and just pack up and go home is because (a) it stings our pride and because (b) human society is in any case something that has been constructed after this fact. It shares its artificiality with logic.

Now that this calamity has already taken place, the only danger that humankind can subsequently find itself in is the danger of the 'locked pantograph'. If we were ever to desist from being our imponderable selves, and instead inhabit only our already-happened selves, then we would find ourselves on the wrong side of time—We would now *be* our already-happened selves, but without free will and catatonic. We would now be the forgery of ourselves, having discovered too late that the forgery cannot move the original. And the only way to account for this strange new mode of being in grammar would be to use Wittgenstein's formulation 'This man *believes* he is pretending.'

It would be as though Western intelligence had succeeded in its mission and you learned what being human was not from your inner, imponderable evidence, but from the depictions of humans in art and cinema and virtual reality. I am afraid that Turing was naïve when he imagined that the test of artificial intelligence would be a machine fooling a human. Artificial intelligence won't come up to us like that. What will actually happen is that we will *come down to it*.

The last people on this earth will have disfigured themselves to look like the Easter Island heads. And they will stand stock-still, just like them. They will stand stock-still because they will *believe* that they are pretending. Men of free will who will believe that they are pretending to be stones. And the Devil will be laughing.

The classic dilemma of the Western intellectual tradition is that its logical syntax forces a man out into his moving parts. In those parts, he becomes no better or worse than the mechanical copyist of them. Better would be if he stayed inside himself, in the deep-down places of his imponderable evidence. Plato's way around this was to produce his theory of knowledge as 'recollection'. In the *Meno*, the initial distress that Meno's slave boy can be induced by Socrates to successfully copy out a geometrical proof of which he had no prior knowledge is assuaged by the explanation of the immortality of the human soul, and how the boy had merely been prompted by Socrates' questions to recollect a knowledge that his once-upon-a-time soul had possessed. This explanation becomes necessary because the slave boy threatens to decimate the Western intellectual tradition's self-esteem by his innocent copying of Socrates. Socrates covers this by convincing Meno that his questions spark the boy to reconnect with the first principles of the proof, so that at each step he moves with a full conscious knowledge of where he is going and why. As though he were no different than the first man to ever write out the proof. But in truth, Socrates' questions do no such thing. They simply force Socrates and the boy out into the moving parts of a logical syntax that has absolutely nothing to do with either of them. Socrates may just as well have taught the boy a dance by saying 'Now move your arms like this, and your legs like this', all the while making the movements in demonstration for the boy to copy. I want to keep saying the 'brilliance' of Wittgenstein's philosophy; but I think by this stage I need to start calling it the 'belligerence' of Wittgenstein's philosophy.

The belligerence of Wittgenstein's philosophy is to insist (and prove) that whether or not one follows a divine guidance (or a divine recollection) at each step of a syntax, the outward result must always look the same. You will not need me to tell you how this threatens everything that the Western intellectual tradition wants to stand for. Because if it really is the case that 'true', or for that matter 'lucky', opinion is no better by its end results than knowledge, then, well, you get the picture. If we now enhance this picture with what I have been saying about the pantograph, and forging and pretending, then it all becomes more remarkable still. It turns out that none of us today have had much choice about whether to live as our real, or original, selves or our forged, or pretend, selves. Every bit of advice out there is exhorting us to act out our lives according to the script of them that science provides. *We must look to the camera and act*. This is what realism prescribes. Because to be the actor is to know so much more about your character than were you just to live it out away from the lens. To *believe* that you are pretending; better, to know that you are pretending; *that* is virtue!

* * *

To end this chapter, I am going to give you something from the *Meno*. Then immediately following that I am going to give you what I take to be its criticism in the *Investigations*.
From the *Meno*:

> *Soc.* But if [your slave boy] always possessed this knowledge he would always have known; or if he has acquired the knowledge, he could not have acquired it in this life, unless he has been taught geometry; for he may be made to do the same with all geometry and every other branch of knowledge. Now, has any one ever taught him? You must know that, if, as you say, he was born and bred in your house.
> *Men.* And I am certain that no one ever did teach him.
> *Soc.* And yet has he not the knowledge?
> *Men.* That, Socrates, is most certain.
> *Soc.* But if he did not acquire this knowledge in this life, then clearly he must have had and learned it at some other time?
> *Men.* That is evident.
> *Soc.* And that must have been the time when he was not a man?
> *Men.* Yes.
> *Soc.* And if there have been always true thoughts in him, both at the time when he was and was not a man, which only need to be awakened into knowledge by putting questions to him, his soul must have always possessed this knowledge, for he always either was or was not a man?
> *Men.* That is clear.
> *Soc.* And if the truth of all things always existed in the soul, then the soul is immortal. Wherefore be of good cheer, and try to recollect what you do not know, or rather do not remember.[77]

From the *Investigations*:

> Let us imagine a rule intimating to me which way I am to obey it; that is, as my eye travels along the line, a voice within me says: '*This* way!'—What is the difference between this process of obeying a kind of inspiration and that of obeying a rule? For they are surely not the same. In the case of inspiration I *await* direction. I shall not be able to teach anyone else my 'technique' of following the line. Unless, indeed, I teach him some way of hearkening, some kind of receptivity. But then, of course, I cannot require him to follow the line in the same way I do.
>
> These are not my experiences of acting from inspiration and according to a rule; they are grammatical notes.
>
> It would also be possible to imagine such a training in a sort of arithmetic. Children could calculate, each in his own way—as long as they listened to their inner voice and obeyed it. Calculating in this way would be like a sort of composing.
>
> Would it not be possible for us, however, to calculate as we actually do (all agreeing, and so on), and still at every step to have a feeling of being guided by the rules as by a spell, feeling astonishment at the fact that we agreed? (We might give thanks to the Deity for our agreement.)[78]

My house is not built on the site you mean. This map will show you where it is and why I can't get into the village without rowing; for the mountain is much too steep for anyone to walk on it along the lake. I do believe that it was the right thing for me to come here thank God. I can't imagine that I could have worked anywhere as I do here. It's the quiet and, perhaps, the *wonderful* scenery; I mean, it's quiet seriousness.
—WITTGENSTEIN, in a letter to G. E. Moore, 1936

The purely corporeal can be uncanny. Compare the way angels and devils are portrayed. So-called 'miracles' must be connected with this. A miracle must be, as it were, a sacred gesture.
—WITTGENSTEIN, *Culture and Value*, 50e

The world breaks everyone and afterward many are strong at the broken places. But those that will not break it kills. It kills the very good and the very gentle and the very brave impartially. If you are none of these you can be sure it will kill you too but there will be no special hurry.
—HEMINGWAY, *A Farewell to Arms*

When slaves love one another, it is not love.
—JEAN GENET, *The Maids*

5

Sex and the Last Stand

EVERYTHING I HAVE SHOWN you thus far comes to a head in sex. Sex is the key to Wittgenstein's genius life and genius personality. Everything that it could possibly mean to be an animal of intelligence and feeling, capable of friendship and love, yet plighted to express oneself in the syntax of one's moving parts—Well there simply can be no greater example of it than sex, than human sex.

* * *

Sex matters because it is the high summit of the dislocation that began with our first parents in Eden. There was conceived the great adventure of ideas that was to run apart and away from God. Words and books, and language, truth, and logic were conceived there. However, in sex, they all run out. All human hope and longing seem to funnel and accelerate towards its single word and act. This single word and act that is both the last and first of life. There is great mysticism and glory here. I went so far towards the start of Chapter 3 to suggest that sex is the construction line which allows us to see the heavenly bliss in the photographic negative of this world. For insofar as this world funnels and accelerates towards sex's stolen moment, the heavenly bliss would be the negative opposite of that.[1] I don't think that I am wrong. I don't think that sex is to be viewed morally, in terms of absolute right and absolute wrong. I think that is a needless and wretched simplification. The truth is far more serious than that. It used to be believed that those who were objecting to sex could only be objecting to it on moral grounds because the biological truth on it was so fulsomely neutral. The goal of the progressive agenda became therefore to find ways to restore it to its rightful place in the pantheon of healthy functions. However, that all looks rather quaint now; because as I said, the truth is far more serious than that. Sex may once have seemed like the biological constant in relation to which we do or do not come of age—And the same again for history and society. Yet now it looks like it may all along have been of *cosmic* rather than earthly significance.

TO ESCAPE SEX'S GRAVITY ALTOGETHER

The great question for us now, then, must be whether Wittgenstein was a homosexual earthling or a man trying to escape sex's gravity altogether?

> If we are thinking within our system, then it is certain that no one has ever been on the moon. Not merely is nothing of the sort ever seriously reported to us by reasonable people, but our whole system of physics forbids us to believe it. For this demands answers to the questions 'How did he overcome the force of gravity?' 'How could he live without an atmosphere?' and a thousand others which could not be answered. But suppose that instead of all these answers we met the reply: 'We don't know how one gets to the moon, but those who get there know at once that they are there: and even you can't explain everything.' We should feel ourselves intellectually very distant from someone who said this.[2]

And this great question pulls into an awesome focus the materials of this book. For I have allowed it to happen that you have been educated by Wittgenstein into his discombobulating notion that your emotions and your imponderable inner life are more real than bricks and bullets *and words*. Such that the long-cherished aim of getting them to conform to the latter goes out the window, and in its place comes in the new truth that you are voyaging through worlds and always have been. I don't mean either your soul as some part of a greater world soul, I mean *you*!

Your memories are the ghosts, they are the supernatural! And not in a way that explains ghosts and the supernatural as *just* your memories.

> An event leaves a trace in the memory: One sometimes imagines this as if it consisted in the event's having left a trace, an impression, a consequence, in the

nervous system. As if one could say: Even the nerves have a memory. But then when someone remembered an event, he would have to *infer* it from this impression, this trace. Whatever the event does leave behind in the organism, *it* isn't the memory.[3]

And only sex can show how this earthbound world of ours is the obverse construction of those memories. This world is what memories *would look like* if they had to congregate in one place and tell a single story from its beginning, through its middle, to its end. This world is what memories would look like if they had to do that from out all the innumerable worlds of our souls' voyaging. And sexual generation in left-to-right lines is the thermodynamic law of the single human story. Sexual generation is this world's gravity; it is this world's lock and key.

In order to marvel human beings—and perhaps peoples—have to wake up. Science is a way of sending them back to sleep again.[4]

This is the reality that traditional Christian imagery seems so particularly well-adapted to address. The book of Genesis speaks of this world as being in all of its aspects a fallen world—So much so that most find they must recoil from the completeness and complexity of this vision. Its sheer totality leaves them quite unable to imagine what a prelapsarian reality would look like, and this, intellectually speaking, must look like a nonstarter. For after all, this world is all that we have ever known: it is that fact alone that has been the point upon which people have used Science to prove Christian metaphysics fantastic. Science deals with what *actually is*, then uses 'what actually is' to exclude what it says therefore is not.[5] Science says that what you can see is what is actually there and true by being there. And therefore it pitches its best efforts into enhancing the range of human seeing through telescopes and microscopes (and measurements of measurements, and descriptions of descriptions, and denoting phrases). I believe that Wittgenstein quickly saw the potential in Christian imagery vis-à-vis this scheme—And how that potential was quite beside the point of whether you are Christian or not. Then in admitting the supernatural and using it to positively illuminate the natural, his philosophy basically guaranteed that it would be beside the point. But perhaps this hasn't been seen as clearly as it should have. Perhaps Wittgenstein has been approached too much from the Science/Religion dichotomy, so that people have tried too much to determine on which side of that dichotomy he stood.

Wittgenstein's philosophy erupts and erases that dichotomy! It teaches you that the supernatural and the natural cannot be separated by a quality called 'existence', or 'being', which only the one or the other can have. They cannot be thus separated because they both equally exist. And that they both equally exist should be alerting us to all manner of problems in the way that the concept of existence has hitherto been handled by philosophers.

> The question about the possibility of existence propositions does not come in the middle but at the very beginning of logic. All the problems that go with the Axiom of Infinity have already to be solved in the proposition '$(Ex)(x=x)$'.[6]

The way of Western philosophy since its inception, has been to say that things either do or do not exist, and that existence is then the primary meaning of 'truth'. This way can seem bulletproof when it operates within the framework of intelligent man assessing the truth or falsehood of unintelligent, inanimate things. However, once man himself becomes the object of investigation this way, its method breaks down. It breaks down because it becomes glaringly apparent that such a 'method of truth'—such a logic—can never amount to the general form of truth (or existence, or being) but only to the general form of an agreement—or a *contract*—to see this or that thing.

> The end is not an ungrounded presupposition: It is an ungrounded way of acting.[7]

For example, when you go for an eye test, they never ask you 'What can you see?'; where that question could admit of anything before your eyes and your soul. No. What they ask you is, 'Can you read the bottom-most row of letters?' Even this little example shows us that what the Western intelligence calls truth is really what happens when two or more humans contract ahead of time to see something. It may be the bottom-most row of letters, it may be a colour, it may be a measurement, it may be a number, it may be a symbol. It really doesn't matter what it is, so long as the relationship between what is pre-determined *shall be seen* and what *is then seen* is tautological. This logic (for this *is* the Wittgensteinian definition of logic) only works as it should when two or more humans have to communicate, have to contract via language. The moment when we are alone again as our souls and our thoughts, we are returned into the deeper truth that this contractual nature of Western logic means that it can only ever have, as Wittgenstein puts it, an 'accidental relationship' to *ultimate reality*—Whatever 'ultimate reality' is. This is the same thing as to say that whatever is at any present moment going on inside of us in thoughts and feelings will only be deemed to exist once it has been forced out into (what I called above) 'the syntax of our moving parts'—Or our larynx, voice box and tongue. For it is only in a world of such moving parts, all decoding and copying each other like telegraph machines, that there can be general forms at all. General forms turn out to be the same things as general contracts. And this can therefore be seen as Wittgenstein's overall criticism of Socrates and Plato, Aristotle and Aquinas, and the Western tradition that they helped to found. And his criticism, too, of Descartes and the Western tradition's 'modern turn'.[8]

It doesn't matter whether you look for your realism in the general forms of an ancient and divine ontology or in the foundations of mathematics. Because in both cases, you *look for your realism*, and that, says Wittgenstein, is the problem. Because looked at from the point of view of existence, or being, there is only you. There can only be you.

Existence does not mean the world of existing things (*versus the world of not existing things*). And then you in that world of existing things. And then again, that fact being used to break down the fancies and dreams inside you—To strip out your soul and to replace it with biology.

> I might say: If the place I want to get to could only be reached by way of a ladder, I would give up trying to get there. For the place I have to get to is a place I must already be at now.[9]

BUT FIRST SOME THOUGHTS ON EXISTENTIALISM

The existentialism that more or less began with Martin Heidegger may share with Wittgenstein's project its suspicion of all syntactical/tautological/scientific knowledge, but the reformed 'thinking man' it hopes to leave behind is still a man in this world.[10] That is to say, the question of existence is still something that is to be decided and settled in this world. Only Wittgenstein's philosophy goes so far to treat this world as *hypothetical*, as completely and utterly hypothetical. I could accomplish what I mean by this in Christian imagery if I said that this world is what Adam and Eve's daydream would have looked like when they first conceived pride with the Serpent's help. I imagine that what I am saying to you here must seem like death itself, and that you want to shriek at me the counterclaim of left-to-right sex, and the thermodynamics of the arrow of time. Well, you would be right. How you feel right now is exactly the reason why people cling to life and experience death as a slipping away to nothingness. All dying feels like drowning. Life itself feels like a slow drowning. It is as though at birth one is dipped into this world and takes a bodily form because of that, and then is slowly pulled out of it until just one's face is left, gasping for air, and then gone—Sucked away forever, like a man into quicksand.

Western philosophy has grown fat on saying that this proves that this world is life and reality, while everything (imagined) after death is not. However, this is simply not the case, and the proof is far more likely to work the other way around. I mean that when our dipping into this life must be so fleeting in relation to all space and time, it should surely be far more likely that *it* should be the oddity and the illusion. Far more likely that this life, here, should be the oddity and the illusion.

Do you not, for example, consider it strange that this world holds so apparently faultlessly to the laws of nature? Does that not sound an alarm bell for you? It would in any other case. Just think of the phrase 'too good to be true'. It describes, and truly so, that normality is something we associate with imperfection—With the reassuring little slips and deviations that mark the normal passage of things through time. The man who never puts a foot wrong is regarded for this reason with suspicion because it is assumed that he must have something to hide. So, what does this world have to hide?

Is it that it is not really a 'world' at all, but, as I put it above, a hypothesis? Please don't be alarmed at this. I mean it as good news. As even the best news possible! Try to remember how I put it in Chapter 2 when I designated everything in the *Tractatus* that speaks of the mystically inexpressible as us, as man, as the soul, as freedom.[11] It seems that in our supernatural soul we know and feel we are free and this freedom betokens that we are abroad and at large—So that the opposite of this knowledge and feeling would be our situation as it appears to be in this world. This puts us into a strange predicament. On the one hand, we like, no we even crave, the feeling of being dipped into this world's logical necessity because it gives us a stability of conception (a form, a shape) that we wouldn't have otherwise. Yet, on the other hand, this conceptual stability of form and shape and book knowledge is contrary to everything in us that is unbridled and passionate and original. Heidegger and the existentialists were onto this alright, but they were not able to go so far to treat this world as hypothetical. Man's dislocation, they said, was still a dislocation from his true relationship to 'being', *in this world*. This allowed them to imagine that it could be reset and renewed *in this world*. With Wittgenstein, however, we have the real solution to the real problem.

NOW SOMETHING ON WITTGENSTEIN AND KANT

If you wore red-tinted glasses, everything would look red. If you wore blue-tinted glasses, blue. If you wore logic-tinted glasses, logical. This world is the result of a decision to wear that last pair of glasses. A decision that has become the default for all of us all of the time. Once again, I find that Christian imagery is peculiarly well-adapted to address this with its story of Adam and Eve having been the first humans to choose to wear these glasses, and then afterwards having transmitted the lust for this choice to humankind. Thus, do we arrive at our definition of the 'hypothetical' in this context.

Viz., that this world is hypothetical insofar as it is the projection of something else through a distorting lens. I want now to quote something from Wittgenstein's *Tractatus* that would explain what that 'something else' is that gets distorted to make our world.

> All propositions are of equal value.
> The sense of the world must lie outside the world. In the world everything is as it is, and everything happens as it does happen: *in* it no value exists—and even if it did exist, it would have no value.
> If there is any value that does have value, it must lie outside the whole sphere of what happens and is the case. For all that happens and is the case is accidental.
> What makes it non-accidental cannot lie *within* the world, since if it did it would itself be accidental.
> It must lie outside the world.
> So too it is impossible for there to be propositions of ethics.

> Propositions can express nothing that is higher.
> It is clear that ethics cannot be put into words.
> Ethics is transcendental.
> (Ethics and aesthetics are one and the same.)[12]

What Wittgenstein is explaining is that the world, i.e. the *happening*, and the world of the *already-happened* are identical. What I have been calling the already-happened is exactly what Wittgenstein means above when he says, 'In the world everything is as it is, and everything happens as it does happen'. On top of this, Wittgenstein merely observes that any such situation (syntax) is too tight and perfect to admit of any value. Or as we might by now say in this book, even the tiniest sliver of value would cut the wires and rods of the pantograph. When Wittgenstein therefore concludes that 'ethics is transcendental', he does not mean what Kant meant by that phrase. Kant meant that all the possibilities of human experience are themselves the result of a prior determination to use a particular grammar of experience. Kant meant to show that rational explanation is really always rational *invention*. And of course he was right; and that is what is brilliant and enduring about Kant. From the point of view of the Western mind, invention and explanation do always refer to the same thing, except that 'explanation' has always sounded so much more innocent and pure than 'invention'. Think once again of Kurt Gödel, if it helps. His incompleteness theorems arise because logic invents what it explains. In just the same way that the steam engine invents what it explains/explains what it invents. And thus, the Western mind always finds itself locked and catatonic between an empirical *happening* and its identical and simultaneous *already-happened*.

> It is the queerest thing in the world that one should have a short cut through logic ... if the proof of the proposition is the step-by-step proof, how can anything else be a proof of it? ... This is most important.... It has puzzled me more than I can say.[13]

It is this peculiar effect which Kant was so ingenious to exploit in his transcendentalism. There, he was to argue that there really is no difference between 'actual experience' and 'possible experience', save that the latter is a copy of the former made from the unmistakeable materials of the speculative intellect, or *pure reason*. Like when we make a copy of a figure in ink, the ink of pure reason is characterised by its 'apodeictically certain principles'. The copy of anything made by pure reason alone will always thus have the quality of apodeictic certainty. If this is the case, then the answer to all philosophy's problems becomes, to Kant, a simple business. It consists now of pure reason needing only to learn the proper method by which to police itself—By which to criticise itself. If everything that pure reason invents has the quality of appearing to be certain, and if this quality really is just the description of the difference between actual experience and possible experience, then certainty cannot be an independent sensory organ, putting us in touch with a world of a priori truths—Truths which whisper to us that they might become one day the by-passing and replacement of actual experience. For this is the grave danger of un-policed reason as Kant sees it. Reason's transcendental aspect makes it possible for it to advance beyond actual experience in the present and to invent things like steam engines. While the invented steam engines become then the empirical proofs of the same principles which transcendental reason consulted with in order to invent them. Here is the sense in which Kant was able to show that 'rational explanation is really always rational invention'. And if we replace the steam engines with logical series stretching to infinity, we see that the problem has never left us.

The problem is that our relationship to this world is entirely one of wishful thinking. It is as though we conceived a determination; and for convenience sake let's continue to call it the determination that Adam and Eve first conceived, and then fell asleep and dreamed this world as that determination's fulfilment. Or more accurately still, that this world is what all our souls' eternal conversations with God look like when they are dipped, as I put it, into time's one linear narrative. Into generation's one linear narrative. Into sex's one linear narrative. The Kantian solution to this bizarre conclusion is to repair, in a method, the distance between this conceived determinism of pure reason and its objects of study. Kantian transcendentalism therefore returns to the problem on which it set out and solves it. The problem was how it is that the classic propositions of metaphysics can be made at all, when once we have acknowledged that it is in their nature to run ahead of all possible empirical verification. Or in Kant's famous words from the Preface to his *Critique of Pure Reason*:

> [Reason] begins with principles which it has no option save to employ in the course of experience, and which this experience at the same time abundantly justifies it in using. Rising with their aid (since it is determined to this also by its own nature) to ever higher, ever more remote, conditions, it soon becomes aware that in this way—the questions never ceasing—its work must always remain incomplete; and it therefore finds itself compelled to resort to principles which overstep all possible empirical employment, and which yet seem so unobjectionable that even ordinary consciousness readily accepts them. But by this procedure human reason precipitates itself into darkness and contradictions; and while it may indeed conjecture that these must be in some way due to concealed errors, it is not in a position to detect them. For since the principles of which it is making use transcend the limits of experience, they are no longer subject to any empirical test. The battle-field of these endless controversies is called metaphysics.[14]

The famous Kantian answer becomes to show that this apparent distance between what he calls the *synthetic* a priori judgements of metaphysics and the empirical world in which they would be proved is really a false, or illusory, distance because, on the close inspection of his *Critique of Pure Reason*, it turns out that the adaption of nature to our mode of intelligence and vice versa is so close and fine a phenomenon as to admit of no discernible space, or lag, between the two. We notice again that pure reason can, and will, run into metaphysical difficulties if it does not sufficiently police itself on this insight, and truly enough the whole of the *Critique* is a policing effort on this scope. However, Kantian transcendentalism comes out as a positive creed, which reverts to finding the freedom of man in the calculated dismissal of the great beyond. This has long suggested parallels with Wittgenstein's project—At least for those who think that Wittgenstein's constructivism did the same. We, on the other hand, have equipped ourselves to realize that Wittgenstein's project did not do the same; that in fact it did something quite different.

It can all be explained like this. Kant essentially did what most still do today when in their philosophizing they come suddenly upon the Western mind's faulty wiring. This faulty wiring is made up of the fact that Western reason demands to be able to take the everyday and commonplace and explain it and demystify it until all its causes and circumstances have been made plain. And on the face of it, there is nothing wrong in that. The problem comes when you have then to try to reintegrate the human element into all that neat predestination, for it turns out always that we were all along that same mind which laid out all the pieces and squeezed out all chance of freedom. This is of course what Wittgenstein meant above when he said that 'all that happens and is the case is accidental'. What we call 'reason' is the faculty that allows us to see our world in the reduced way in which everything is linked and connected and nothing happens by chance. You and she weren't meant to be: it is just that she happened to sit next to you on the train that day. The humanity in us resists this. We demand to imagine that we are free and freely using our minds. We demand to believe in romance, even if it blows apart the laws of nature. All of this we have, of course, been tangling with from the start in this book. We have seen that in the world of the happening you are ignorant and free; but then you switch on your mind, and if you let it work long and hard enough, it takes you across to the bird's-eye vision called the already-happened; so that from that vision you look down and see the teeming little accidents that have brought you to where you are. Accidents of the world around you that push and pull you, and accidents of your brain and DNA that predispose you this way and that. If it can all be explained like this, then it is all of it an accident—That's what Wittgenstein says. And now, perhaps, you can see where I am going in this final chapter. For it is *this* which is the faulty wiring. It amounts to acknowledging that the goal of all rational explanation is *total explanation*: and then acknowledging again that such total explanation must necessarily eradicate all freedom and time—and us—and leave the happening and the already-happened locked in their perfect symmetry. What I have called the 'locked pantograph'. Or what Fernando Pessoa described in *The Book of Disquiet* when he wrote:

> We never truly realize ourselves. We are like two chasms—a well staring up at the sky.[15]

I really do believe that Kant came suddenly upon this situation, and, instead of doing what Wittgenstein did, he tried to muscle through a solution from within the parameters of the locked pantograph. If transcendentalism allowed you to look down on those parameters, then the Kantian solution derived from it was to pull human freedom and value back from their eternal voyaging in the 'great beyond' and to write them out according to the very practical arrangements that were meant to have excluded and banished them. If everything is as it is and there is no room for wiggle (and if transcendentalism is like climbing a high ladder to look down and see that), then let's make reason as practical as the rods and wires, and then let's allow that in turn to make freedom, value, and even divinity to mean the same thing as finding intricate ways to go along with it all. [*Remembering always that Wittgenstein most definitely did not choose to go along with it all.*]

> So far, then, as practical reason has the right to serve as our guide, we shall not look upon actions as obligatory because they are the commands of God, but shall regard them as divine commands because we have an inward obligation to them. We shall study freedom according to the purposive unity that is determined in accordance with the principles of reason, and shall believe ourselves to be acting in conformity with the divine will in so far only as we hold sacred the moral law which reason teaches us from the nature of the actions themselves; and we shall believe that we can serve that will only by furthering what is best in the world, alike in ourselves and in others. Moral theology is thus of immanent use only. It enables us to fulfil our vocation in this present world by showing us how to adapt ourselves to the system of all ends, and by warning us against the fanaticism, and indeed the impiety, of abandoning the guidance of a morally legislative reason in the right conduct of our lives, in order to derive guidance directly from the idea of the Supreme Being.[16]

THE MACHINE'S THINKING PART

Knowledge, then, on the Western model, amounts to showing that the world doesn't care like we care, that it does not have a moral dimension. Altogether it is no more than the laws which it infallibly obeys. To us who can and do care, this is upsetting and intolerable. Thus, the Western mind has found all sorts of ways to bring in a sense of a moral dimension, as indeed I noted in the previous chapter.[17] If the world is like a machine, albeit on a magnificent scale of intricacy and process, then why not see destiny and purpose in that? And if the 'world as a machine' is the ultimate truth of ultimate knowledge, then why not designate that as the realism in relation to which anything else will be deemed religious and fanatical? These are two of the most obvious ways by which the moral dimension is developed out of that paradigm of un-freedom and amorality, the machine. In their own ways, Heidegger and Kant demonstrate aspects of these approaches. In Heidegger, man has to work with the machine of knowledge to be, as it were, the consciousness it cannot have. Man becomes the machine's thinking part, a situation which leads to all the classic concerns of existentialism.

On the one hand, it becomes obvious and logical that existence and being do not require man's part. But on the other hand, it becomes equally obvious and logical that they *do* require man's part if they are to become known as such at all. Think of what I said in Chapter 2 about the Western model of truth being 'nonconsensual', and the 'tree falling in the forest with no one to hear it'. Heidegger's philosophy captures very well this dynamic, in which the true nature of existence and being must never be allowed to swallow up or assimilate man (say, by designating him as pure mind or consciousness), or risk losing in him and his distinction the very means by which it is known. Heidegger's famous *Dasein* is an attempt to perform, or at least to re-enact, this state of affairs that comes into being with each new life. In Kant's case, the focus becomes the pure, or dogmatic, rationalism suggested by the machine's working parts; for this gives rise to what he castigates as the 'muddy stream of bad metaphysic'. That is to say, because the machine's parts are *working* parts—because they have a relationship to each other that is an overall system—they would seem to present to the observing human mind the very first principles of life itself. And to an extent they do. From their perfect coordination and organization comes the idea of the supreme pilot, or 'Supreme Being'; and that, too, is not, Kant thinks, inaccurate. What is inaccurate, however, and muddy metaphysics, and all the rest, is to neglect the all-important parameters of the locked pantograph, and to imagine, in a rush of excitement, that these first principles and the theology they imply can be understood and conversed with apart from the machine in which they exist and have their meaning. For Kant, then, abstract understanding cannot step in to replace practical reason, because practical reason only ever is what it is with reference to the machine's working parts. Understanding and enlightenment becomes, then, to realize this. To realize that reason is a *regulative faculty*, responsible for the coincidence between how the bird's-eye view presents the world-machine and how the world-machine actually is. Used properly, in the way which Kant recommends, i.e. used *practically*, reason can help us synchronize with the rhythm and pace of the world-machine's parts. Hence Kant's famous ideas of the 'categorical imperatives' and 'universalizability' and 'the kingdom of ends in themselves'. Reason may show the pantograph to be locked, but it seems we can still regard our wills as autonomous (if not free) if we can learn to use that same reason to coax them towards the kinds of ends of which a machine would approve. What Kant was dead-set against was the idea that reason should still be thought to be able to deliver us over to revelation's thunderclaps—A hope that he detected at work in the rationalism of his day. Or from the other side, that it might cause us to go over to scepticism's bleak alternatives. Thus, Kant found a novel and complex way to create the appearance of human freedom out of the very knowledge that it is not.

We know now that Wittgenstein's perspective on all of this is dramatic and cataclysmic. If the boon of scientific knowledge is that it shows that *it* is the script that we are ever acting out, and that it does this at exactly same time as it proves to us that knowledge *ought* always to be sought for as such a 'master script', then it does something invalid and illegitimate from the only point of view that really seems to matter to Wittgenstein's philosophy. This is the point of view which seems always, for him, to exist outside of all physics' space and time. This is, of course, the transcendental place which he designates in the *Tractatus* for ethics and aesthetics, value and freedom. And I repeat again what I said earlier: physics' space and time are what this place *would look like* in a daydream—Or perhaps I should now say, in a nightmare. Because you can't have true freedom in space and time. Because you can't have *You* or *Me* or *Anyone* in space and time. That is what Heidegger and Kant and so many others get wrong. You see, you can only have *You* or *Me* or *Anyone* <u>and</u> space and time. Yes, *that* you can have because it is clear enough that *You* or *Me* or *Anyone* existing and freely willing would create space and time around us as the narrative-perspective on us. But then in order to continue to exist and be free you would have to be ignorant, or innocent, of that narrative-perspective; for to be simultaneously in yourself and in it (bilocated) would be to be in the nightmare that we call self-consciousness.

THE ULTIMATE HUMILIATION

I want to repeat what I just said because it is too important to be misunderstood. Space and time are nothing as much as the narrative-perspective on the human soul. Human souls exist; space and time *does not exist*, save as that narrative-perspective. We seem to have to live self-consciously, and so we seem to have to live in the state of being 'dipped into space and time'. And once again I cannot but notice how Christianity and the Garden of Eden provide a back story for this vexed state that is so very different to the history of its treatment in Western philosophy—Where the determination has been to treat space and time, and the material world they parse, as ontologically foundational. And now we really get to see it. Because, is not the lynchpin of all space and time as far as humans are concerned, sex? Is sex not the homologating event that brings us into the world-machine's repeating motion? Is sex not how the varieties of human experience are boiled down to the single biological imperative of the survival of the species? Is sex not the point at which the endlessness of love's dreaming is made to shatter against a single lesson in friction and plumbing? Is lust not a cruel acceleration towards a wreckage of twisted limbs? Is love not the sensation of having pinpointed your one and only from out of all time, whilst sex is absurdly indiscriminate—Capable of being enacted on all things animate and inanimate? Am I not describing here the range and scope of the defeat that Montaigne wrote of when he observed:

> We eat and drink as the animals do, but these are not actions that hinder the operations of our mind. In these we keep our advantage over them. But this other puts every other thought beneath its yoke and by its imperious authority brutifies and bestializes all the theology and philosophy there is in Plato; and yet he does

not complain of it.... Alexander used to say that he knew himself to be mortal chiefly by this action and by sleep. Sleep suffocates and suppresses the faculties of our mind; the sexual act likewise absorbs and dissipates them. Truly it is a mark not only of our original corruption but also of our inanity and deformity.[18]

And what about Heidegger and Kant and the whole history of Western philosophy? Isn't the final metaphor for a science that doesn't think and an imperative that is categorical the vision that we are one day going to have sex with machines? Isn't that how we are going to square the circle of the Western mind? For if the circle of it truly enough shows that we are predestinated rather than free, aren't we going to have to square it by seeking out the ultimate humiliation—Then do that Kantian trick where we turn around and call that humiliation's endurance our virtue? By going to its final extreme, we will prove our loyalty and our love. In our subjection to a tasteless, faceless, painful sex, we will prove our freedom and autonomy of will.

Dominique Aury's magnificent *Story of O* is all about a science that doesn't think and an imperative that is categorical:

> 'Listen,' he says. 'Now you're ready. This is where I leave you. You're going to get out and go ring the doorbell. Follow whoever opens the door for you, and do whatever you're told. If you hesitate about going in, they'll come and take you in. If you don't obey immediately, they'll force you to. Your bag? No, you have no further need for your bag. You're merely the gift I'm furnishing. Yes, of course I'll be there. Now run along.'[19]

The whole thrill and mystery of sex is the thrill and mystery of becoming a machine. Sex is the thrill and mystery of the irreversible—Of the arrow of time and the chain reaction. It is combustion. It is heat and smell and sound. Sex is what it would be like to be a rocket. Every other activity is modulated by the thought that we could stop what we have started. Only sex takes us across the point of no return.

Sex is blessed relief and oblivion. If you manage to see it through to its end, then you pass for a fleeting moment from self-consciousness. It is that passing that is the blessed relief and oblivion. Blessed relief and oblivion because it is torment to be who we are, alive and free, yet committed to the narrative-perspective on ourselves.

> You're going mad, Claire. It's God who's listening to us. We know that it's for Him that the last act is to be performed, but we mustn't forewarn Him. We'll play it to the hilt.... Let's drop the preliminaries and get on with it. We've long since stopped needing the twists and turns and the lies. Let's get right into the transformation. Hurry up! Hurry up! I can't stand the shame and humiliation any longer. Who cares if the world listens to us and smiles and shrugs its shoulders and says I'm crazy and envious! I'm quivering, I'm shuddering with pleasure. Claire, I'm going to whinny with joy![20]

What we think of as the intellectual experience of the mind calmly ruling the passions is really a counterfeit experience. We have been taught that it makes us autobiographers, even spiritual autobiographers. But the cruel truth is that it makes us only the *biographers* of our selves—For it is the trick that has had us writing our selves into 'the record', burying ourselves as archaeology. It is a weird, disembodying experience, in which to meet the requirements of rational-historical knowledge and even grammar itself we must become the pen (glacial and dispassionate) that is logging and critiquing our every movement. And it is Wittgenstein who teaches better than anyone that thoughts and words are the particular doom of our species. For they want to take our originality and turn it into the 'seeing is believing' kind of objective and empirical truth. But the fact is that truth so undisputed can be nobody's possession; and it is on this, but too late, that we realize how we have ceded our authorship to the record. The knowledge of good and evil which we lusted for has made away with our distinguishing features. We used to rail against the flesh, but now to be its inmate once again would be the only way for us to express our sadness and our deception.

> Whoever says 'Socrates is a man'? ...What I am criticizing is the fact that logicians do not give these examples any life. We might use 'man' as a predicate if we wanted to distinguish whether someone dressed as a woman was a man or a woman.[21]

This is the torment of being alive and free. We are animals by virtue of our capacity to live outside ourselves in (the syntax of) our moving parts, and then at the same time we are *human* animals by virtue of our capacity to live inside ourselves, in the continuous sensation of our past, present, and future (what we call our self-consciousness). This continuous sensation appears to us as the decisions that we actually made along the way, rigged out on either side by the decisions that we might have made in another mind, as another person. This scaffolding allows us to take on board and judge rightly another person's happiness and pain—Even to flit across the magic threshold of male and female, if the moment requires.

And so at this point I find myself thinking of those telling words of Pasolini's that go—

> 'Only the loving and the knowing [in the present] / matters. To have loved, / and to have known, does not. It gives anguish / to live such a consummated / love. The soul stops growing.'[22]

Sex is love's consummation; and as love's consummation it plays its strange trick of ending longing's wide-open freedoms, its unrestricted hopes and possibilities, and exchanging them all for a generic experience—The world-machine's nudge and wink. It is as though a great artist summoned all their emotion and creativity, but instead of putting it out as a poem, or a picture, they went and bought a bus ticket.

Sex is what love looks like when it is dipped into space and time—And as Wittgenstein would say, 'That is a grammatical remark.' And as we come to accept this, we come to accept with it the sense in which this world really could be merely 'hypothetical'. I am sure it alarmed you when I first proposed it. Now, I hope, you can agree with me and Wittgenstein that it is actually just a reasonable conclusion, once we only take seriously the implications of how language is used, and why. And then philosophy's sacred role in tracing these implications.

Philosophy, according to Wittgenstein, is not about delivering objective truth in words; it is instead about walking along the ridgeline between the world-machine and everything else—Everything else that I have left to be covered by the phrases 'the soul's eternal voyaging', and 'the soul's eternal conversations with God'. The *Tractatus* is exactly such a walk along this ridgeline. The walk is treacherous, with drop-offs on either side, and so the *Tractatus* is a meticulous book, that takes every care to put one foot in front of the other.

Philosophy, according to Wittgenstein, can take us on this walk—And by taking us on this walk can prove that there is this difference between the world-machine and everything else. Philosophy can perform this difference for us. Philosophy can perform this difference for us repeatedly. And Wittgenstein's philosophy is exactly such a series of repeat performances (one foot in front of the other, metaphor in front of metaphor). What philosophy cannot do, however, is adjudicate between the difference. The truth that philosophy performs is the truth that the ridgeline exists. Philosophy cannot be used to prove one or other side of the ridgeline. On the one side of the ridgeline is the world-machine, or sex. On the other side of the ridgeline is love, or the soul. That is to say, on the one side of the ridgeline is the morality which says that sex is the natural point at which the world-machine completes one cycle and begins the next. 'There is nothing taboo here, nothing to fear here,' says the morality. This shows us that this morality which surrounds sex is an argument. It says: 'Do this because of this'. It says: 'Have sex because the laws of nature are amoral'. Here we arrive at the great curiosity (the faulty wiring) of the Western mind, as it has developed to this day. The great curiosity is that it makes a morality out of an amorality. The morality is the 'Do this' bit, and how it is today decked out with all manner of promotion and propaganda. The amorality is the 'because of this' bit, and how it amounts to using unthinking, unfeeling, uncaring science to mock and scorn love.

The sex act is *the right*. It is *the law*. It is the paradigm of *indiscrimination*. Think about it. You can have sex with your own mind and hand. Love, on the other hand, is the evaporation of all space and time. It is the meeting of two hearts from out of all space and time. More, it is the meeting of two hearts that all space and time should make impossible to happen. It is the needle in the haystack times a billion trillion. Love is therefore the paradigm of *discrimination*, and that is why your soul is voyaging, seeking, sighing for it. The solipsism which Wittgenstein was so fond of was taken by him to be illuminating of *this*. Solipsism, for him, was an honest attempt to cheat language out of its syntax. An attempt to dip into language without taking on syntax's form and shape. An attempt to use language and survive its use, and when I say 'survive its use', I want you to think of everything that I have said in this book about identity and 2 + 2 = 4.

To the solipsist, this world *really is* hypothetical. Think about that.

> The solipsist who says 'only I feel real pain', 'only I really see (or hear)' is not stating an opinion; and that's why he is so sure of what he says. He is irresistibly tempted to use a certain form of expression; but we must yet find why he is.[23]

I remember something that happened to me once. I was walking on my own down a street, and I came around a corner and there was this old tramp who was shuffling towards me. And I remember there was no one else around. And then suddenly, and without warning, a jet aircraft screamed low overhead. And it gave me a terrible start, but I knew at once what it was, and I looked up. But when I looked back down I realized the old tramp hadn't worked any of it out and never would. And he was transfixed a few feet in front of me in a look of such outrageous fear that there was nothing to be done for him. And it was then that I understood that the explanation of the jet aircraft was an irrelevance, for it had simply been the occasion for his passing from this world into where it is that our deepest feelings will take us. Normally we prevent that from happening, or we are prevented from letting that happen. And in both cases, let's call the agent of that prevention 'civilization'. Or thinking of what we went through together in Chapter 4, let's call it realism. The kind of realism where we stand in front of the statue of ourselves and try to ape it. The kind of realism where we would stand before ourselves rooted and eyeless. But the tramp did not stand like that. I have once or twice seen a face like that; once in someone I loved dearly. So perhaps it made the difference that, in this instance, I did not know the tramp from Adam. Perhaps it heightened the effect. But all my days I will never forget his face. It was the face of all eternity in a child. A terrified child. Through this face I saw a howling, yawning wind, like something opening wider and wider and sucking everything through it. I saw that things like fear are proportional to nothing in this world, in the sense in which things in this world like screaming jet aircraft would be said to supply their explanation and eradication, but do not. Things like fear and love are like this. And when you experience fear or love in another human's face, you know that you are looking into each other in some strange and mystical way. So that the howling, yawning, sucking sound really is something that roars between you. So that it is the sound of the blood in your ears.

It is to be in this world but not of it. It is to be standing still but moving. It is to see in an intergalactic flash that your eternal voyaging cannot exist without this pedestrian life of pavements and walking and dust and earth, and vice versa. It is to see that this pedestrian life of cause and effect is the hypothesis called 'certainty'. Called 'intellectual certainty'. Called 'Truth'. Called 'logic'. It is to see that only eternity could ever dream of space and time: And that this life is that dream.

THIS HYPOTHETICAL WORLD

Yes, this world is hypothetical; but it does not have to be. All the things that happen here to humans have really happened in the wide-open spaces of eternity—Except that out there they have happened, I should tense-lessly say *are* happening, in ways impossible to imagine from within this dream. If you had to present the things happening to your soul, in eternity, on a timeline running left to right, then yes, this world is exactly how they would appear. And so I am able to repeat this all-important insight: things like fear and love are what they are because they are our irrational breakouts from the world-machine. Fear and love and all great passion are as though you were starting to wake from the dream, and slipping from space and time. Fear and love—and now let's add grief to them—are originalities that threaten to put the spanner into the world-machine's smooth working. Deep down we all know this. Deep down we all know that fear and love and grief become for us their own worlds—Such that we could disappear into them forever, and never return. Therapy, and psychology, and the world itself, do their utmost to try and bring us back into ordination, where by that I mean, back into being able to give the ordinate response to the world's working. Where what the world would like most of all to happen for the sake of its working would be that we desist from looking into each other's eyes and souls. Instead of this, it would like us to strive towards its kind of realism; which is the realism whereby reason reveals the truth that the world is proceeding irresistibly at exactly the same time as it reveals to us (now, as I am writing) that we—that we humans—are also such as that we can be the special creatures of *resistance*.

We are all potential spanners in the works. We are the machine's enemy. But because the machine is a machine, it cannot reach out of its law and destiny and do something about us. Instead, we must learn to devour ourselves. In the book that is the prequel to this, *Inventing Socrates*, I portrayed the operation of this hysteria in explicit detail. I called it there the 'certain and ineluctable relationship between the reductionist point of view and the idea of the ethical pursuit of progress'.[24] And here I have told you a little more about sex's sacrosanct role in this relationship. I have told you that the 'discovery' of scientific rationalism (or the 'discovery', or the 'birth', of Western philosophy) was the same thing as the discovery of the *world as a machine*. And I have told you that the corresponding discovery that the human animal may or may not go along with this machine is the story of the history of sexuality. I don't think anybody has ever seriously disputed the fact that the history of sexuality is in some clear the way the barometer of our species. Normally it is said that it is the measure of how far we have progressed out of taboo and superstition. A point I made at the start of this chapter. Here, however, I am encouraging you to see it in its purely mechanical aspect, as the point at which we may or may not pledge our allegiance to the perpetuation of the circle of life.

The nonrational animals 'make' this pledge unconsciously and automatically, out of instinct. We, on the other hand, have a choice. I have come to think that this is indeed the attraction and betrayal of sex (and who would not agree it is just that strange mixture of the two?). We are told to approach it as the high art and language of love: Yet it is a strange art and language that makes two people careen into its single extinguishing event. As I put it before: 'There is great mysticism and glory here'. Sex is the closest we can come to feeling like an atom—To feeling possessed and overtaken by forces which we cannot swerve and cannot but obey. And as faceless and as nameless as an atom. As self-conscious beings, beset by existence, we must so want this escape; and yet because it is an escape and we know that it is, we must also so not want it.

Sex, on this Wittgensteinian view, is symbolic and paradigmatic of the hypothetical status of this world. Generally speaking, you can take any major philosophical system, and, as it were, 'count it back', or reverse engineer it from the point of view of human sex. You can't, for example, count back or reverse engineer a philosophical system from pebbles on a beach [though from pebbles on a beach you could reverse engineer physics]. But human sex works perfectly as the activity which begs to be treated either sacredly and reverently, or biologically and irreverently. It is the perfect storm of what it may mean or may not mean to be human. For just think about it. What greater exercise of human freedom can there be than to choose to give your love to some one person? And then again, what other way is there to consummate that love then by sex? All normative philosophies of human life are for this reason really just so many fingers pointing at the example of sex for a proof—Just like physics points its finger at the example of pebbles on a beach or waves in the sea or apples falling from trees. The true question then is, 'What are all these things and sex the example of?' Are they all the example of the process and neutrality of the world-machine, so that a true normative philosophy should try to argue us into the closest possible conformity with it? Is this why the *Story of O* and all great eroticism is the real story of Western rationality? Is this why the only accurate way to depict the secret dream of the life of the mind would be the shrill virtue of the sexual climax? The virtue of total and categorical submission to a predestination which only the mind can reveal.[25] It really does seem to be that human sex is the equivalent of the 'phenomenal happenings' and 'volume of experience' that constitute the world as it really is to Science. These things which manifest themselves materially in space and time come first, and then our conceptualization and understanding of them comes second. And all so that we can afterwards point and find the proof of the latter in the former. [And make Western rationality's climactic bid of self-renunciation and obedience to the way of the machine.]

But then there is the point of view of Wittgenstein's mature philosophy; which is a point of view in direct and shocking counter-flow to this. It invites us to consider instead that there need be no such hysterical climax because there need be no such thing as material existence.

And for those Christians who want now to balk and splutter that in denying the existence of material reality I am denying the existence of God's good creation, plus all the natural theology constructed upon that, I would remind them only that God's good creation is entirely consequential to his prevenient and sustaining will. And *that* is the standout point of orthodoxy to which all other orthodoxies and most especially natural theology are subset. I would further suggest that they take some hard minutes to think over what that really does mean. For Christians, like Scientists, have become accustomed to making their conceptual beginning with the productions and incidents of the Divine Will—With what their material eyes can materially see. But of course you only have to stop all of that for a moment to realize that productions and incidents are just that, and that you could remove them altogether and still have the Divine Will. And in just the same way that you could remove the productions and incidents of a human life and still have that human's will. And this must, at this late stage of this book, become my best argument yet against the possibility of 'biography'. Because now we can confidently see and say that the material productions and incidents of any human life can only ever be a fractional and infinitesimal representation of the will behind them. For what of all the untold and hidden movements of that will that never made it out into materiality? And to add to this even the central teaching of Wittgenstein: it may be the case that nothing at all of the original human will ever does make it across into the light of day, when we consider the mere conventionalism of language, truth, and logic.

> Remember that whatever 'I' means to you, to the other man it draws his attention to a human body.[26]
>
> Let us imagine a man who could use none of his limbs and hence could, in the ordinary sense, not exercise his will. He could, however, think and want and communicate his thoughts to someone else. Could therefore do good or evil through the other man. Then it is clear that ethics would have validity for him, too, and that he in the *ethical sense* is the bearer of a will./Now is there in principle any difference between this will and that which sets the human body in motion?[27]
>
> The consequences of an action must be unimportant.... There must be a *kind* of ethical reward and of ethical punishment but these must be involved in the action itself.[28]

As we can now put it with confidence: syntax can only see itself. Yet fear, love, and grief, and all the passions, are someone else's face looking back at us. That is to say, this world is hypothetical *insofar* as we are just wills looking across to each other. A universe of wills, if you like, but absolutely without the need to systemize and order it, as Western rationality would have us believe.

> To believe in God means to see that the facts of the world are not the end of the matter.[29]

I ask myself: 'Is this why Christianity exemplifies the instancy of salvation as two men on crosses looking at each other?'

Again: 'Was the Immaculate Conception also the condemnation of sex's role in the world-machine?'

After the tramp and I had staggered back from each other, I thought of those lines of A. E. Houseman's:

He looked at me with eyes I thought / I was not like to find, / The voice he begged for pence with brought / Another man to mind.[30]

Now I want you to watch how Wittgenstein depicts this world as mere hypothesis in his *Philosophical Investigations*:

Doing itself seems not to have any volume of experience. It seems like an extensionless point, the point of a needle. This point seems to be the real agent. And the phenomenal happenings only to be consequences of this acting. 'I *do* ...' seems to have a definite sense, separate from all experience.

Let us not forget this: when 'I raise my arm', my arm goes up. And the problem arises: what is left over if I subtract the fact that my arm goes up from the fact that I raise my arm?

((Are the kinaesthetic sensations my willing?))[31]

MARGEURITE RESPINGER

There is no question that his whole life long, Wittgenstein had a capacity for deep, severe love. He could love men and women; he did love men and women. Or at least, many men and one woman. The one woman was Marguerite Respinger. He did everything with her that you would expect of a man that much in love with a woman, in that day and age. He courted her, kissed her, and wrote daily to her at times—And even sculpted a bust of her. She was Swiss, she was pretty, and he knew her from 1926 to 1931. However, their relationship ended in 1931 when he proposed marriage to her on the startling condition that they forgo all sex together. She seems to have refused.

* * *

I repeat now the question from the start of this chapter:
Was Wittgenstein a homosexual earthling or a man trying to escape sex's gravity altogether?

* * *

You must know by now what my answer is. I think he was a man trying to escape sex's gravity altogether. To me this fact supervenes on the question of Wittgenstein's specific sexuality and renders it unimportant. I would hope, in any case, that we had dropped the old mania for outing famous people, before turning it on them as the explanation of everything they did. The most that you can say about love is that humans can love each other and will. And the most that you can say about sex is that its relationship to love is a *conceptual* one. Love is unscripted and unannounced. Sex identifies you and never lets you go.

> And 'search' must always mean: search systematically. Meandering about in infinite space on the look-out for a gold ring is no kind of search.
> You can only *search* within a system: and so there is necessarily something you *can't* search for.³²

If you want to think about Wittgenstein's sexuality, then there are facts that will take you there. Over the course of his life he had unusually focused friendships with at least four men. We already know about David Pinsent from earlier in this book—And how Wittgenstein took him to Norway and Iceland with him. And now I will add to this that he dedicated the *Tractatus* to him. There was Francis Skinner, who would die from polio in 1941, having passed from being one of Wittgenstein's pupils and disciples at Cambridge in the 1930s to a gardener and then a mechanic. The British philosopher Frank Ramsey would work on the first English translation of the *Tractatus*, and then, fascinated by it, would travel to Austria in 1923 to meet Wittgenstein for the first time. Later he would be instrumental in persuading Wittgenstein to return to Cambridge in 1929. Ramsey would die the following year at the young age of 26; and it is said that along the way he and Wittgenstein had shared a sexual relationship. And then finally there was Ben Richards, a young medical student at Cambridge when he and Wittgenstein first became close in 1946. Wittgenstein would take him with him to Swansea the following year. Then in the spring of 1950, a year before his death, he would take Richards with him to Skjolden for one last visit. They would stay five weeks there together.

Early on, when Wittgenstein was still a student of his at Cambridge, Russell would casually classify him as 'a homosexual' in a letter to someone. It works, doesn't it? It works perfectly. Just like fin de siècle Viennese tragedy works for Wittgenstein's family. It is comforting and reassuring. You don't have to think. You just have to consult the *Truth*, the record, the timeline, the facts. Realism. What did Wittgenstein have sex with? Cakes? No. Cats? No. Men? Yes! Men are what he had sex with. And I don't say '*who* he had sex with' but '*what*'. Because this lazy way of seeing things isn't interested one bit in *whom* he had sex with, even though I have given out some of their likely names. 'David, Francis, Frank, Ben'. Rather, say, than 'Danielle, Francesca, Frankie, and Beatrice'. It's all a great shame, really, this lazy way, because I think that people matter far more than identities. But then again identities *are* what we consult the truth for. Because of course the truth cannot cope with the originalities that people and their souls really are. If the world is a machine, then it is made up of parts—Of pistons, cogs, cams, screws, and the like. Not of originalities, and people, and souls. A homosexual can be a part in that machine just like a heterosexual can. But actual named individuals cannot be parts. And parts are what we need for theories and understanding. Parts are indiscriminate, which is how they fit together. Whereas originalities are worlds looking through each other to new worlds.

> The danger of the delusion which we are in becomes most clear if we propose to ourselves to give the aspects 'this' and 'that' names, say A and B.[33]

The fitting together of parts is their capacity. And as such, capacity has nothing whatsoever to do with inner things like the feelings of the soul, and who we really are.

> Even if someone had a particular capacity only when, and only as long as, he had a particular feeling, the feeling would not be the capacity.[34]

Why does sex matter so much to us—And why is it such an enigma for philosophy? It is because it is the paradigm activity in which pretending and believing, acting and realism really do all come out as the same thing.

THE SEX SCENE MUST NOT BE SIMULATED ANYMORE

When Frank (Ramsey) was trying to insist on the possibility of (at least) a counterpart identity in an extensionalist mathematics, Wittgenstein would be dead against it on the grounds of the agency it would require—An agency that could only be supplied by the individual posturing so as to match the picture ahead of them. *The already-painted picture.*

> Ramsey's theory of identity makes the mistake that would be made by someone who said that you could use a painting as a mirror as well, even if only for a single posture. If we say this we overlook that what is essential to a mirror is precisely that you can infer from it the posture of a body in front of it, whereas in the case of the painting you have to know that the postures tally before you can construe the picture as a mirror image.[35]

If the world is a machine, then Art must inevitably tend towards Realism. And if Art must inevitably tend towards Realism, then the sex scene must not be simulated anymore. And the sex scene must not be simulated anymore because in any case you can have sex with someone, or something, and *believe that you are pretending*. You can believe that you are pretending because the sex act is in the nature of its case auto-mechanically coherent. The world-machine at its mechanical best. With enough friction, it will go off of its own accord.

The will is an attitude of the subject to the world./[Do] I merely accompany my actions with my will?/But in that case how can I predict—as in some sense I surely can—that I shall raise my arm in five minutes' time? That I shall will this?/This is clear: it is impossible to will without already performing the act of the will./The act of the will is not the cause of the action but is the action itself./One cannot will without acting.[36]

There used to be a controversy about whether Wittgenstein used to cruise the Wiener Prater, a public park in Vienna's 2nd District, notorious, then, in places, as a venue for homosexual liaisons—And whether he used to pick up 'rough young men' there. Note that it is always 'rough young men' in these circumstances. Think again of 'friction'. Wittgenstein left coded allusions to these things in some of his diaries; and they have since been decoded. Very easily, in fact; the ciphers were hardly complex. All of this controversy seems very quaint now. At least it should be.

* * *

It should be because it is very clear from his philosophy that Wittgenstein was all along a man trying to escape sex's gravity. He was a heedless ascetic: and *that* is the telling fact, not anything else.[37]

* * *

Sex is the key to Wittgenstein's philosophy, because Wittgenstein's philosophy is all about love. Think about it (in the manner we have been thinking about it in this book). What, or *Who*, are we pretending to be, believing to be, acting the part of, when we first acquire language—When we first acquire our first language as a child? Speak, and you are already not being yourself but 'playing the part'. And as I have impressed on you before, this is the part of a single person called *Language, Truth, and Logic*.

To learn to think and speak in words is to learn to pretend how to be this person. It is to learn how to pretend to be truthful and logical as only this person can be. But if that is the case, then this person and their one destiny, and how they need you to act it out, is the opposite of love's true freedom—And of what love's true freedom makes us *really* want to do with words. This takes us back to the difference between mental and physical intelligence; and how I pursued this difference on Wittgenstein's behalf through the earlier parts of this book. Mental intelligence is the syntax of the words. Whereas physical intelligence would be to treat words like footsteps—Would be to manhandle them and use them any which way you want. Really: it would be to summon the feeling of your moment as its own world, and then to use words accordingly to express that world. And then, with the moment of that world over and gone, to never use words like that again. I am talking about love here, but I have also talked about fear and grief and suffering. Really, then, I am talking about the big passions in a human life. But of all of them love is the biggest and the most symbolic, because whereas the others are reactive, love is conceived within you *ex nihilo*. It is the purest expression of your capacity to swerve from the script, from predestination.

So, any philosophy like Wittgenstein's that is strictly about language's script is really a pure-form philosophy of love's freedom. However, love's freedom is indescribable [or at any rate, it would, as I have just pointed out, use words differently each time]. Therefore, any philosophy like Wittgenstein's has to focus instead on language's script, making always the best effort to illuminate and shame that script's tragicomic consistencies. For love's freedom would be that you were inconsistent with words and their meanings.[38] And love's nemesis would therefore be sex. For sex is the one moment in life where the inner mystery of your occult intentionality—your will—becomes identical with what your body's moving parts are acting out. *The sex scene must not be simulated anymore.* All Art quivers before this pronouncement.

Here is an example of Wittgenstein writing about language/in order to write about love/in order to exemplify sex:

> I describe a psychological experiment: the apparatus, the questions of the experimenter, the actions and replies of the subject—and then I say that it is a scene in a play.—Now everything is different. So it will be said: If this experiment were described in the same way in a book on psychology, then the behaviour described would be understood as the expression of something mental just because it is *presupposed* that the subject is not taking us in, hasn't learnt the replies by heart, and other things of the kind.[39]

The erupting reality of sex takes care of the question whether the subject is taking us in or not, has learnt the replies by heart, and other things of this kind. Wittgenstein's antagonistic and ascetic relationship to sex was not, then, perverse—But the living out of his philosophy. It was the primal sense in which his philosophy became equivalent to his life, and vice versa. He tried very hard to remain innocent of sex and to isolate himself and his work from it, as from the world. He wasn't totally successful. But he did try.

> Suppose we were observing the movement of a point (for example, a point of light on a screen). It might be possible to draw important consequences of the most various kinds from the behaviour of this point. And what a variety of observations can be made here!—The path of the point and certain of its characteristic measures (amplitude and wave-length for instance).... Any of these features of its behaviour might be the only one to interest us. We might, for example, be indifferent to everything about its movements except for the number of loops it made in a certain time.—And if we were interested, not in just *one* such feature, but in several, each might yield us special information, different in kind from all the rest. This is how it is with the behaviour of man; with the different characteristic features which we observe in this behaviour.[40]

Here is an example of the limit of what can be observed of us through the narrative-perspective on us. The most that we can be is a point of light on a screen. This fact is acknowledged and honoured in the modern mind's designation of the 'agent', or the 'actor'. In this hypothetical world of space and time, this really is how we appear. Psychology is never wrong about you. Or, you cannot compete with its analysis of you. That is how we appear. The question then [and I think this is where Wittgenstein wants me to end this book], is how we correspondingly appear in the real world in relation to which this world is unreal? And on this, Wittgenstein had become crystal clear by the time of his final thoughts:

> The intention *with which* one acts does not 'accompany' the action any more than the thought 'accompanies' speech. Thought and intention are neither 'articulated' nor 'non-articulated'; to be compared neither with a single note which sounds during the acting or speaking, nor with a tune.[41]

Who we are from the perspective of our souls and wills is truly limitless. We are greater than we could possibly imagine. We are without extension. The things that we do in this world are only the things we *hypothetically could have done in this world*. And the sum total of all the things that all of us hypothetically could have done in this world *is this world*. Which leaves it that who we really are is all the rest of the tilts and longings that make up our inner places; although, they are not our inner (Cartesian) places anymore, save that they appear that way, and hidden, according to the requirements of this space-time dream.

> One of the most misleading representational techniques in our language is the use of the word 'I', particularly when it is used in representing immediate experience, as in 'I can see a red patch'. It would be instructive to replace this way of speaking by another in which immediate experience would be represented without using the personal pronoun.[42]
>
> Let's take the word 'Self'. One begins by saying 'My body'—but if bits are chopped off.... Now there begin all sort of subterfuges. The blunder is to think the word 'Self' means something in the way that 'body' stands for the body, e.g. stands for something inside the body. If you consider substituting a signal for 'I suffer', you see that the first mistake is to take 'I' as *standing* for something.[43]
>
> What harm is done ... by saying that God knows *all* irrational numbers? Or: That they are already all there, even though we only know certain of them? Why are these pictures not harmless? For one thing, they hide certain problems. Suppose that people go on and on calculating the expansion of π. So God, who knows everything, knows whether they will have reached '777' by the end of the world. But can his omniscience decide whether they would have reached it after the end of the world? It cannot. I want to say: even God can determine something mathematical

only by mathematics. Even for him the mere rule of expansion cannot decide anything that it does not decide for us.[44]

* * *

Someone like Wittgenstein who is careening around in (what I have called) 'their muscles, blood, and bones', doing things that propriety and adulthood would rather keep hidden, may actually be more awake and alive than all of us.

* * *

The problem with the narrative-perspective, and seeing ourselves as that point of light on a screen, is that it becomes impossible to resist seeing the point of light as more real and credible than *who we really are*. Think of what I said about the pantograph and its realism, 'where the idea, where the copy, is always more heralded than the real thing.'[45] You start wanting to conform to the analysis, and to obey it. You start wanting to perform a certain number of loops in a certain time. And do this long enough, and you will lose the ability to wake up from the narrative-perspective altogether.

> Put geometrically: it's not enough that someone should—supposedly—determine a point ever more closely by narrowing down its whereabouts; we must be able to construct *it*.[46]
>
> Our craving is to make the grammar of the sense datum similar to the grammar of the physical body. That is why the term 'sense datum' was introduced—it being the 'private object' corresponding to the 'public object'.[47]

Living like Wittgenstein did would certainly amount to *not* conforming to the analysis and *not* obeying it.

But would it amount to obeying God? If you are nearly (flawlessly) obeying God in the real world(s), do you then look like this in *this* world? Is that what it is all about? Does perfection and virtue there look like randomness and perversity here? Is that it?

> I imagine someone asking my advice; he says, 'I have constructed a proposition (I will use P to designate it [He means the unresolved, Gödelian proposition.]) in Russell's symbolism, and by means of certain definitions and transformations it can be so interpreted that it says: 'P 's not provable in Russell's system'. Must I not say that this proposition on the one hand is true, and on the other hand is unprovable? For suppose it were false; then it is true that it is provable. And that surely cannot be! And if it is proved, then it is proved that it is not provable. Thus, it can only be true, but not provable. Just as we ask: 'Provable in what system?', so we must ask: '"True" in what system?' 'True in Russell's system' means, as was said: Proved in Russell's system; and 'false in Russell's system' means: The opposite has been proved in Russell's system.—Now what does your 'suppose it is false'

mean? *In the Russell sense* it means 'suppose the opposite is proved in Russell's system'; *if that is your assumption*, you will now presumably give up the interpretation that is unprovable. And by 'this interpretation' I understand the translation into this English sentence.—If you assume that the proposition is provable in Russell's system, that means it is true *in the Russell sense*, and the interpretation '*P* is not provable' again has to be given up. If you assume that the proposition is true in the Russell sense, *the same* thing follows. Further: If the proposition is supposed to be false in some other than the Russell sense, then it does not contradict this for it to be proved in Russell's sense. (What is called 'losing' in chess may constitute winning in another game.)[48]

A CURIOUS THING HAPPENS WHEN YOU ARE DREAMING

A curious thing happens when you are dreaming but somehow come into the knowledge that you are. In a dream, then, and aware that you are, though unable to wake from it. Try to recall the last time this happened to you. Everyone who recalls this experience recognizes something singular about it. There is a total fluidity and ambidexterity and contemporaneity between the empiricism of that dream's world as it comes towards you—and add to that the strange guilt that always seems to accompany the knowledge you are exposing it as a dream—and the conviction that that same empiricism will next be jagging back on you as some repressive norm. The knowledge that you are moving through a dreamscape is identical, then, to the dread that accompanies that knowledge. The dread that that knowledge will be repaid in some nightmare outcome. Which again is really the dread that the possibilities which accompany that knowledge, and are made possible by it and are always terrifying, will play out. Which, in truth, is an insight into the general form of knowledge rather than the status of the dreamscape. For in a dream we get to see that good and evil are alike (are both norms) in relation to a world whose consistency makes them possible in the first place. Dreams are terrifying because they are *the place* of good and evil. A dream begins and ends as its own single, logical world. Good is as bad as evil.

> Sentences are often used on the borderline between logic and the empirical, so that their meaning changes back and forth and they count now as expressions of norms, now as expressions of experience.[49]
>
> Here one can only *describe* and say: this is what human life is like.[50]

It is because we can only '*describe* and say', that we know we are dreaming it.

The opposite, as I have been presenting it in this book, would be for good and evil, and their place within a language, to become like a single word, and a single world, which afterwards you discard in order to move to the next world, and the next moment. The singular dread of the 'dream in which you know you are dreaming' is that the only way for the dream to end is badly and shockingly. Because, of course, there can be no next world for you to move to. A single, consistent, syntactical world is all about sex at one end and death at the other.

You can't get behind rules because there isn't any behind.[51]

And when you start to see it like this, you start to realise that the hypothesis that is this dream, this world, must be a very weak one—And that Wittgenstein must have known he was dreaming and lived with that dread:

> I might put it this way: If I copy the numerals from 1 to 100—how do I know that I shall get a series of numerals that is right when I count them? And here *what* is a check on *what*? Or how am I to describe the important empirical fact here? Am I to say experience teaches that I always count the same way? Or that none of the numerals gets lost in copying? Or that the numerals remain on the paper as they are, even when I don't watch them? Or *all* these facts? Or am I to say that we simply don't get into difficulties? Or that almost always everything seems all right to us?[52]

LEVIN

We might conclude by saying, 'Seeing isn't believing: Only *believing* is believing':

> When one wishes to understand, as Dostoyevsky did, the miracles of Christ—for example, the miracle of the marriage of Cana—they must be conceived as symbols. The transformation of water into wine is astonishing to the highest degree, yet executed, as it was, by Christ [in whose nature it is to do such things], it surprised us, but no more. The event itself cannot, therefore, be the majesty of the thing. Nor can the majesty of the thing reside in the fact that Jesus is giving wine to the wedding party, as if it were unheard for him to do such a thing. No, it must rather be the *marvelous* that gives this action its content and significance. And by that I do not mean the extraordinary or the unpublished, but the *spirit* in which it is accomplished, and whose transformation from water to wine is only a symbol (in a way), a gesture. A gesture that can (obviously) only be given by one who can do this extraordinary thing. It is then as a gesture, as an expression of something, that the miracle must be understood, if it is to be spoken to us. I could also say: It is only if he who does so does it in a marvelous spirit that it is a miracle. If there is not this spirit, it is only an extraordinarily strange fact. I must, in a way, already know the man who performs it to be able to say that it is a miracle. I must already read all this in the right frame of mind to feel the miracle.[53]

[Written in code]

> I keep telling myself, in my mind, Tolstoy's words: 'Man is powerless in the flesh, but free through the spirit.' May the spirit be in me.⁵⁴

Wittgenstein is saying that you can't ever see a miracle. That is to say, if the camera were there, filming it, then it would have *logically* to see what you see. Again, if the camera were there, then the miracle could not logically be considered a miracle at all but some newly discovered datum of nature and science. The laws of physics would have to be revised in light of it rather than that this event should be considered to have unfolded against them or in spite of them. To love Christ, is to love Christ. To believe in Christ, is to believe in Christ. It is nothing to do with *super*-eminence, or *super*-anything.

By saying that at the wedding feast, Christ made a 'gesture', Wittgenstein is saying: 'That is what Christ's gesture looked like *in the world of that moment*.' In other words: 'It looked like a wedding feast in which he turned water into wine.'

Likewise, the idea that the point of a belief is the doctrinal content of the belief is *illogical*. What is logical, is that someone who believes in such-and-such a thing acts correspondingly. The belief without its corresponding actions is bye-the-bye.

> It can indeed happen, and often does today, that a person will give up a practice after he has recognised an error on which it was based. But this happens only when calling someone's attention to his error is enough to turn him away from his way of behaving. But this is not the case with religious practices of a people and *therefore* there is *no* question of an error.⁵⁵

All the so-called problems of life and thought are really this: here everything looks one way, looks as it would look through a camera lens, on a movie screen, because this IS that world. Here, there can only be one true version of an event—The event described according to the visible movements of the outer man.

> Let us imagine someone doing work that involves comparison, trial, choice. Say he is constructing an appliance out of various bits of stuff with a given set of tools. Every now and then there is the problem 'Should I use this bit?'—The bit is rejected, another is tried. Bits are tentatively put together, then dismantled; he looks for one that fits, etc., etc. I now imagine that this whole procedure is filmed. The worker perhaps also produces sound-effects like 'Hm' or 'Ha!'. As it were sounds of hesitation, sudden finding, decision, satisfaction, dissatisfaction. But he does not utter a single word.... If the worker can talk, would it be a falsification of what actually goes on if he were to describe that precisely and were to say, e.g., 'Then I thought: no, that won't do, I must try it another way' and so on—although he had neither spoken during the work nor imagined those words? I want to say: may he

not later give his wordless thoughts in words? And in such a fashion that we, who might see the work in progress, could accept this account?—And all the more, if we had often watched the man working, not just once?[56]

Or suppose you want to speak of causality in the operation of feelings. 'Determinism applies as truly to the mind as to physical things.' This is obviously because when we think of causal laws in physical things we think of *experiments*. We have nothing like this in connection with feelings and motivation. And yet psychologists want to say: There *must* be some law'—Although no law has been found. (Freud: 'Do you want to say, gentlemen, that changes in mental phenomena are guided by *chance*?') Whereas to me the fact that there *aren't* actually any laws seems important.[57]

It is quite possible that the only place we are is inside our own heads. This would explain everything. It would explain why we can only make in logic and thoughts and words, the steps that appear bring us outside our heads, into communication with other minds and the physical world—But that immediately afterwards, in Wittgenstein's hands, those same steps can become the object of an investigation that throws the whole business into question.

Didn't the poet William Blake write it all out once? How goes that last stanza of his poem, 'The Human Abstract'?

> The Gods of the earth and sea
> Sought 'thro Nature to find this Tree;
> But their search was all in vain:
> There grows one in the Human Brain.[58]

Why does this horrify you? Or why does this make you laugh? I believe I am telling you what is the case, and if it is the case, then it is the case *anyway*. And deep down, you always knew this—That is to say, you always knew that whatever the truth was, it would have to be whatever it is that 'is the case *anyway*'. All that I am saying—all that Wittgenstein was ever saying—is, 'Why continue to write books called *The Problems of Philosophy*?' 'Instead of endlessly restating the symptoms, why not just accept the diagnosis (of which they are the symptoms)?'

In his book of that name, Russell writes:

> [T]he value of philosophy must not depend upon any supposed body of definitely ascertainable knowledge to be acquired by those who study it. The value of philosophy is, in fact, to be sought largely in its very uncertainty.[59]

But if that is so, then Russell is describing his preferred pattern of behaviour in relation to *Something*. You could say that philosophers like Russell are people who adopt and hold to certain patterns of behaviour. Either there is something 'definitely ascertainable', or there is this pattern of behaviour whereby one *acts* as though there weren't.

The only solution would be to put yourself into a novel as Tolstoy did in *Anna Karenina*, as the character 'Levin'. There, where it is fictional anyway, so that everything really has already happened, you will get to see what pieces our visible narratives are made from—And how the piece called 'belief' just cannot be fitted in afterwards. When you were in its moment, you didn't need the rest (of the pieces). Because you were some other place than them. Some other world. But now that you have returned into the narrative, not one of its pieces can prove that moment back to you. You can't step into it from the piece preceding it. Nor can you step back to it from the piece following it.

We know the truth; we just don't know what *to do* with it. We don't know where *to put it*.

[While Levin's] wife was giving birth an extraordinary thing had happened to him. He, the unbeliever, had begun to pray, and in the moment of praying he had believed. But that moment had passed, and he was unable to give any place in his life to the state of mind he had been in then.

He could not admit that he had known the truth then and was now mistaken, because as soon as he began to think calmly about it, the whole thing fell to pieces; nor could he admit that he had been mistaken then, because he cherished his state of soul at that time, and by admitting that it had been due to weakness he would have profaned those moments. He was in painful discord with himself and strained all the forces of his soul to get out of it.[60]

'How's that? Remembers God? Lives for the soul?' Levin almost shouted.

'Everybody knows how—by the truth, by God's way. People are different. Now, take you even, you wouldn't offend anybody either ... '

'Yes, yes, goodbye!' said Levin, breathless with excitement, and, turning, he took his stick and quickly walked off towards home.

A new, joyful feeling came over him. At the muzhik's words about Fokanych living for the soul, by the truth, by God's way, it was as if a host of vague but important thoughts burst from some locked-up place and, all rushing towards the same goal, whirled through his head, blinding him with their light.[61]

That is the real problem of belief. It is the only piece of language, truth, and logic without a number on it. It could go anywhere. 'This piece can have any value and go anywhere.'— That is the real problem of it. The problem of it is not Christianity or some other religion with a name to it or religion per se. Or anything with a doctrine and a content. That just keeps turning the same wheel. The problem is that in any moment some person could believe anything they like. The problem is that *sheer possibility*, when by now it should have been precluded by the *true version of the event*.

When Wittgenstein says—'It is not *how* things are in the world that is mystical, but *that* it exists'[62]—he is not making a rhetorical move on the concept of ontology. Nor is he taking up with something he will later be able to move on from. In a book all about facts, he is simply stating the ultimate, strangest fact of them all; which is that despite all evidence to the contrary, from Heraclitus' 'you can't step into the same river twice' to his own *Remarks on Colour*, there is always something that everyone has to be able to see equally and simultaneously. *The true version of the event*. This is the version as the camera would see it. And the camera fulfils the role of the 'infinity of observers'. The camera becomes the shorthand way of saying: 'If every human who ever walked the earth, past to future, could be consulted in this moment on the event in hand, and if they all saw it unfold in *X* way, then that would also be what this camera now sees.' The camera is, of course, as much an invention as the concept of the infinity of observers (or for that matter, infinity itself), yet without it we are sunk. That is to say: 'Without its concept we would never be able to get out of our own heads.'

> Sufficient evidence passes over into insufficient evidence without a definite borderline. Shall I say that a natural foundation for the way this concept is formed is the complex nature and the variety of human contingencies?
>
> Then given much less variety, a sharply bounded conceptual structure would have to seem natural. And why does it seem so difficult to imagine the simplified case?[63]

But that doesn't mean, of course, that we actually ever *do* get out of our heads. It simply explains what the dream of doing it would look like; and what it would require from us for it to look like that.

All of which is to say that language, as it is used, is really always the language of a place to which none of us have been—Nor can ever go. Even one single letter of its alphabet presents us with an eternal stability of meaning that has immediately to be considered conceptual in relation to the obvious flux and chaos of the *worlds of our own heads*. The only way for us to deal with that really does seem to be that we use language in an endless series of games, in which that same eternal stability of meaning is used to hold in place, momentarily, some other meaning, concocted in private agreement between two minds; then afterwards discarded with the game.

Yes, it really is strange, and anyone who has lived seriously and also seriously worked with words feels it. Language *qua* language exists to script *the true version of an event*. [One can only write one book at a time.] Yet the authentic human experience of truth would have nothing to do with such a scheme. It would have to do instead with the endless dawnings of first contact. The sunrise that is also a sunset. With each step forwards exploding the last.

> There was a special attraction in beginnings, which drove me into everlasting endeavour to free my personality from accretions and project it on a fresh medium, that my curiosity to see its naked shadow might be fed. The invisible self appeared

to be reflected clearest in the still water of another man's yet incurious mind. Considered judgements, which had in them of the past and the future, were worthless compared with the revealing first sight, the instinctive opening or closing of a man as he met the stranger.[64]

That was how T. E. Lawrence put it. Leave it to others and the camera to pick the bones of *afterwards*. You'll be long gone anyway.

THE END

Put a ruler against this body; it does not say that the body is of such-and-such a length. Rather is it in itself—I should like to say—dead, and achieves nothing of what thought achieves.—It is as if we had imagined that the essential thing about a living man was his outward form. Then we made a lump of wood in that form, and were abashed to see the stupid block, which hadn't even any similarity to a living being.

There is a gulf between an order and its execution. It has to be filled by the act of understanding. Only in the act of understanding is it meant that we are to do this. The *order*—WHY, that is nothing but sounds, ink-marks.—

—WITTGENSTEIN, *Philosophical Investigations*, I, 430 & 431

If the carpenter, as he has given the figure, could also give a heart, the carpenter would be worshipped by his own idol!

—AUGUSTINE, *Sermons*, CXLI, 3

The South American balsa raft, which scholars had claimed would sink if it were not regularly dried out ashore, stayed buoyant as a cork.

—THOR HEYERDAHL, *Kon-Tiki*

Appendix

ON LOGIC AND THIS BOOK

Modern logic allows us to speak in abstraction, as though each empirical incident were the proof of the general case. Its schemata are nothing in themselves but rather the ideal representations of the shapes made by real objects in time and space.

* * *

In this book, I have consistently spoken against it, as though it were doing something terribly wrong. As though it *were* wrong. For those of you who have been left interested 'Why?', I have included this, as an appendix, because it was written after the fact of the main book. What follows amounts to a thesis, which I can state very simply for you here, at the outset. Logic, such as it is— where by that I mean, such as it always has been, as a basic function of the human brain—never was in any way related to the question of 'Truth?'. What we can say, is that by choosing always to take the question of truth into our brains, we ensure that it cannot but be handled *logically*. In stating the matter like this, we get to see that we are describing a trait, not a virtue. A disability, not an ability. An interesting side line would be to observe that the historical category difference between 'rational man' and the 'nonrational rest (of the animal kingdom)' probably should not apply. For after all, have we not been living in awe of the other animals' pristine rationality, their pristine logic, their pristine instinct? In them, it never errs, it is never switched off. Or if it is, then they and their errant genetic line are gobbled up by natural selection. Which is itself only the 'greatest logic of them all', for it simply cannot err.

* * *

What should separate us from the rest of the animal kingdom, and for that matter from the rest of physical nature and all its laws, is not logic but the question of 'Truth?'. The rest of the animal kingdom simply does not take this question into their brains, but we do. Or more to the point, if 'brain is brain' across the animal world, if a fish uses its brain to survive as much as we do, then something, or someone, must have once-upon-a-time injected the question into our brains for it to be there now. This process of 'injection', whenever, and however, it was that it happened, must in turn have made use of an inlet—Something in us that was us, but something other than our brains and biology. At this point, one is traditionally obliged to say 'soul'; and the saying of it indicates why Wittgenstein at least thought that all philosophical problems taken to their twentieth-century degree of rigour were really religious problems. Or that they should be approached, in the Western instance, through the great Western religion, which is Christianity. What struck him most about Christianity in this regard, was how it really did define incorporeality, the spiritual, and the soul in terms of the question they admit, rather than ontologically, as some strange 'ether', or categorically, as the difference between time and eternity. For example, many religions contain their own story of the 'fall of man', or, at any rate, of how we have arrived at temporality from out of eternity, given that we can still locate longings for the latter inside us. The Plotinian 'Tolma' would be one prominent such example. These non-Christian treatments operate in the abstract, as though the corporeal and incorporeal were components of the universe at large—As the defining characteristics of classes of things within it. They offer you a story of how things came to this pass and invite you to situate yourself within it, viz., to find the bits of spirit and matter inside you. Only Christianity uses a question—the Serpent's question—to launch you on an infinite logical regress of such questions. Right the way until the only thing you can remain sure of, is the *You* who is framing these questions in the first place. Solipsism's *You*.

I am my world.[1]

For this reason alone, was Wittgenstein bound to take Christianity and its imagery deadly seriously. To try to relate him to it as the believer to a story as so many have done is both unimaginative and misguided. But I have already argued this at length over the course of this book. What I want to do here is to stay on the outside track, in the aftermath of this book, and to show you how things may look now, in the light of it.

* * *

The story of the first three books of Genesis which give us the picture of the human being as a creature which must increasingly live in the universe of its own thoughts was not the only point on which Wittgenstein interacted with Christianity. Christianity for him was—as indeed it was for two of the writers he greatly admired, Augustine and Tolstoy—*Christ*-centred. Here, I really do need to elaborate a little and show you the matter in a way in which you may not have seen it before.

* * *

Nowadays, it is assumed that the ancient religions and Christianity were all of a piece; that collectively they represented a juvenile belief in the supernatural and that Christianity has been that belief's (strangely) enduring hangover. I am afraid the reality may even be worse than that, or better than that, depending on your position in it. You see, we tend to export an unwarranted degree of hindsight to the ancient situation, as though they had the choice of perspectives that we have now. They didn't. Their religious convictions were not optional, in the way that ours are now. They were not items of private choice and behaviour, transacted against the backdrop of a neutral public square. If religion to them was everywhere and obligatory—and it was—then it was because it had simply *always been there*. No one could remember a time before religion. More, that very concept of a 'time before' could not have been constructed. There was no zero hour. There was no social contract. No ancient people carried a tradition of having adopted their religion, and thus, of having legitimized it through that adoption. This explains certain characteristics of ancient, pre-Christian religions that may surprise some, brought up on the fire-in-the-belly tradition of Reformed faith or the exacting logics of the Catholic catechism.

Ancient religion was not personal, it was programmatic. It was not believed, it was learnt. And because of that, approaches to it could be cynical and irreverent in the extreme. By the time of the late empire, for example, the Romans had accrued a veritable phonebook of gods—Each one to be called on for its specifically assigned task. Moreover, the ruling elite could be more than up to manipulating religion as a tool of mass control. There is that fun observation of Alfred North Whitehead's:

> The cult of the Empire was the sort of religion which might be constructed today by the Law School of a University, laudably impressed by the notion that mere penal repression is not the way to avert a crime wave.[2]

Enter, then, Christianity, with its startling claim that Christ had risen from the dead. And with its corresponding insistence that *this*, more than anything else, must be the acme of belief. Forget the supernatural. Forget superstition. Forget irrationalism. This would be the first time in the West that religion had actually been put to the test. Here was an *event in time*. Here was the clean shot of historicity—Something that could be true or something that could be false, in the 'seeing is believing' kind of way. Think about it. Despite all its device and contrivance, ancient religion had never created the opening for the 'doubting Thomas'. It had never presented a person with that particular choice of the mind. Now that category would exist, and nothing in the West would ever be the same again. Where religious belief had once been rote and arbitrary, it would now be associated with a person's sense of self-respect. Where religion had once held in place the common identity of a people, it would now signal the point of arrival of the *individual*—Marked by their right to criticise and discriminate. Let us say that the idea that Christ had actually risen from the dead was simply incredible, and that it very quickly called the bluff on where the ancients *really* stood with regard to religion and belief. It turns out that they were just like us. Religion, understood as something that it was traditional to do, was fine. So, too, was touching wood and crossing your fingers. (Why not, it only takes a second?) But the ancient world was far more familiar with death than we are, and dead men don't return as live men. As ghosts, maybe, but not as fully reconstituted men. Already in the second century, the Greek philosopher Celsus would be dismissing Mary Magdalene's testimony as 'hysterical' and 'hallucinatory'.[3]

The standard way to bring Wittgenstein into this has been to show that religious belief is, in his infamous phrase, a 'form of life'. In other words, that belief in the historicity of an event—in this case, Christ's resurrection from the dead—is only ever really the obverse of the life that then stands in relation to that belief. It is that whole life (of belief) reduced to a single, spoken formula. A pinprick. So that to then go on to regard that pinprick as the truth of the matter, rather than the whole span and reality of the believer's life, would be madness!

I repeat. It has been said that Wittgenstein's move in matters of religious belief was to say that truth only enters to be counted at the point at which it becomes the documented history of the believer's behaviour. Belief becomes real when it becomes the reason that stands behind the actions of that human believer's life; which by that stage must mean that nothing else can matter (from the point of view of analysis). I repeat again. Religious belief *can* explain the actions of a human life; but only at the same time as it forces us to notice that the explanation has occurred after the fact of the belief. This is said to be the sum of the Wittgensteinian response to the Russellian debunking of religious belief. At the end of the domain of known facts, religious belief simply creates a whole new fact of its own. All of which is to say that Christ's resurrection will then exist only insofar as that it has become the point on which the behaviours of countless numbers of historical believers can be seen to have been triangulating. It has become real by virtue of the weight of people who act as though it were real.

As we have seen in this book, this makes for a whole new criterion of truth that flagrantly overpasses the former criteria, which had relied upon proving correspondence with what was *really there*, or in this case, what had *really happened*. To say now that this no longer mattered. To say now that the test of truth in a material world was the outward shapes that human bodies make in time. To say that everything was to be measured in terms of how people acted, rather than how they were internally motivated or moved, was, if nothing else, a brilliant strategical move on Wittgenstein's part. For it gave science the victory it had always craved at the same time it proved that victory could amount to nothing.

* * *

That is to say, a Scientist *acts* like a scientist. So, too, does a Religionist *act*. And most of all does the universe only *act* as though it were lawful and constant. This may sound like madness to you, but whatever it is, you are never going to be able to refute it on its own terms. So perhaps you should think again. It joins Wittgenstein to Augustine on the only thing they really did have in common, which was not an interest in language per se, but the one detail which any exhausted language finally exposes—Which is that *you can never actually know what someone else is thinking*. Which if that is the case, means that most of all can you never know what the universe itself is 'thinking'. Because if the 'not knowing' which hangs over a human life is the fact that its next moment cannot arrive to be counted before it does, then most of all does this 'not knowing' hang over the universe's next moment. Just ask David Hume. But it is a difficult thing to read Wittgenstein and to know how to take this acting of the scientists and the universe seriously. To know *where* to take it. Because if traditional religion and traditional science are as bad as each other, and if the universe is the biggest actor of them all, then it would seem as though we had lost touch with all reality, in the sense in which logic, in the sense in which *acting logically*, had appeared to keep us in touch with it.

* * *

In this book, I have tried to show you that the first step is to realise that Wittgenstein was never using science to make an example of religion, but the other way around. He was saying, 'Religion is one thing. But Science is even worse!'

> Frazer [Namely, James George Frazer of *The Golden Bough*] is much more savage than most of his savages, for they are not as far removed from the understanding of spiritual matter as a twentieth-century Englishman. His explanations of primitive practices are much cruder than the meaning of these practices themselves.[4]
>
> What should we gain by a definition, as it can only lead us to other undefined terms?[5]

If, to him, religion and science are just as bad as each other, if the natural and the supernatural are equally useless examples of each other, then logic is not helping us sift and discriminate our way around an actually existing universe but is *creating* that universe *as we speak*. In the language of this book, we are all of us thinking and acting, writing and speaking, as though there were such a thing as a materially existing universe and us in it. This would be the only explanation of the only fact which really does need explaining, which is that logic cannot actually do the very thing which it was trumpeted to do by Russell and others; which is to *tell the truth*. If an alien race from outside of time and this universe were to abduct a scientist from this century and a shaman from twenty centuries ago, and were to interrogate them about planet earth, they would not be able to tell them apart on the basis of their answers. All that they would be able to conclude is, 'These animals explain things by means of other things. Whatever it is they are after, they have never touched it.' You see, it really doesn't matter whether we say that 'one atom strikes another atom' or that 'fairies push them into each other', for in both cases we have come up with a likely story, and *that*, rather than anything in the stories themselves, is what must distinguish us as a species—No!—as a 'form of life'. We develop likely stories (scientists call them hypotheses), and then we live out our lives in the light of them as though they were the truth. We play with the double-headed penny. Scientists like to respond to such provocations by saying that each new hypothesis anticipates its refinement by trial and error. But to our alien interrogators, that would just be like saying, 'Wait! I'll have an even likelier story for you tomorrow.' No difference. Same difference. By the same token, our alien interrogators might conclude, 'This species always takes the evidence to be "the evidence of *some thing*"; where this *some thing* they then declare to be more real than the evidence itself.' For example, I remember reading in an old treatise on logic the following:

> It was the almost superhuman power with which [Newton] traced out geometrically the consequences of his theory, and submitted them to repeated comparison with experience, which constitutes his pre-eminence over all philosophers.[6]

Yet 'gravity' and all other such denoted things share one glaring quality, which is that no one shall ever be able to put their hand to them—To touch them. All that you can touch is the evidence of them. Nothing is what it is, then—And even this whole world of ours and its 'self-evidence' may not be. This is what I meant when I took things to their immaterial conclusion in Chapter 5. It is an extreme version of the only conclusion which Wittgenstein ever allowed himself to reach on the matter, in words, in his later philosophy. His own kind of *Cogito*, but not one which proves anything at anything else's expense. Least of all your existence. He is saying that if we trawled all the blackness of nothingness for you, we wouldn't find you—Save as your pulsing, *believing* self. While your *believing* self would be—would ensure—the blackness and nothingness of everything else around you. Because as I pointed out at the end of Ch. 5, from the point of view of sense and understanding, belief must always have a 'random value'. It makes for the blackness of nothingness around it because it breaks grammar.

> One can mistrust one's own senses, but not one's own belief.
> If there were a verb meaning 'to believe falsely', it would not have any significant first person, present indicative.[7]

To explain this further, I must run us through this same sequence of thoughts, but in a way which draws in more of the materials of this book.

MODERN LOGIC'S INBUILT ILLOGICALITY

Modern logic's inbuilt illogicality is that it cannot adjudicate between fiction and nonfiction. It can only show you what it would be like to talk and think 'as though each empirical incident were the proof of the general case.' Modern logic can be used to write fairy tales, and this has been done, but what it can never do is to take up a position on the indisputable timeline of events.

Modern logic is not like a knock on the head when an apple falls out of a tree. It is rather what happens when we wish to talk and think as though gravity and all such other laws were there all along. The illogicality is that modern logic cannot verify itself to be true but by turning to these timeline events as to its proper objects. Yet all along it has had no proper objects, because it is just a language. It cannot of itself be the means of telling the difference between fiction and nonfiction. Which would all be fine and well, except for the peculiar insistence in the twentieth century on using the method of logical analysis as though it could so tell the difference. As though the difference between truth and falsehood would be the same as the difference between logic and illogic, a function of mathematics.

We know how this was done. The term logic of old was phased out to be replaced by the propositional logic of the linguistic schools. By this trick, modern logic was meant to have been reconstituted as something belonging within the timeline of events, qualified by its proper objects: apples and heads and what 'actually, verifiably happened'. Thus, it was as though language itself had been brought into the timeline. Before long, it was no longer good enough merely to speak, for if speech was now to be coordinate with the underlying reality of serial events, then one had better learn to speak correctly, to speak truthfully. To speak in step with the left-to-right course of history. To speak incorrectly and untruthfully correspondingly came to be identified with speaking with sincerity and intention about things that did not apparently exist to be observed within the timeline. Things like emotions and gods. The inner and invisible things. Eventually, something had to give. This moment was axiomatic set theory, and Bertrand Russell and Alfred North Whitehead's *Principia Mathematica*. Their project of divinizing the timeline had the effect of giving to modern logic a new, foundational set of proper objects, made out of the hitherto unnamed ratios and relations between numbers. If these ratios and relations and other such infallible operations could be fixed down to named classes, then something truly theurgic might be achieved. Modern logic's 'inbuilt illogicality' might be overcome, because modern logic might at last become a language with its proper domain of objects. A language of language, if you like. The old elusive number-mysticism of the ancient mind would be eradicated like a blood clot. For if the old elusive mysticism of number was that numbers simultaneously occupied themselves and things in the timeline, then the new theurgy of set theory would be to mark the separation between these simultaneous phenomena—The nonfiction of the 'numbers of things (in the universe)' would be separated from the old Platonic fiction of (the world of) perfect-form numbers in the sky, and the effect would be that we should be able to adjudicate, at last, between the very ideas in our heads. A new language that could put names to the invisible wires and rods between *things-as-represented-in-numbers* would do this for us. The old philosophers were right. Numbers were our step into the pure air of ideal objects, always obedient to the rules of the general case. But now the step would be repeated again, from the rules of the general case to the elusive invisible connections between those rules.

However, to try to beat numbers at their own game like this, is to fail. Because numbers are the Devil. And if numbers are the Devil, then failure will look like mathematics become ethics.

The mysticism which Wittgenstein would begin to generate on this insight would be something altogether different to the old number mysticism of Plato and the new ethical mysticism of Russell. It would lack the predetermined objective of both those types, which is the Good Life. It would instead be the mysticism of the *Unknown Next*, a place which can only be stepped into, physically, and which is therefore never the same place twice. Choose to speak a language—any language—and you become the predictable occupant of a single place. Try to speak languages of languages, and beat the numbers a là Russell, and you are just playing games. Wittgenstein's mysticism is the triumph of *his* physical over *this* mental. Two forms of intelligence; only one winner.

THE CHALLENGE OF THAT FOR THIS BOOK

This pinpoint victory is the untold story of Wittgenstein's life that I tried to tell in this book. The difficulty was that it could never make for the traditional subject matter of the traditional biography. You can't beat the numbers, you can't beat the facts. How things really look, in terms of them, on the timeline, is how things really look (in terms of them, on the timeline, in a reductive regression). Biographies which follow their subjects around with a notebook and pencil are not wrong. In fact, they are as right about that form of intelligence as the *Tractatus* was. And if you follow Wittgenstein's life around with a notebook and pencil you get one of the really legendary stories of twentieth-century genius and eccentricity. That story is not wrong, nor can it be replaced by what I have done here. What I have done here is to write a biography that *performs* his untold, private battle against his biographers—Future and imagined. I endeavoured to find ways to make numbers really feel like the Devil. And then against that, to find ways to make the opposite really feel like a kind of salvation—And then again, to frame that salvation in the Christian language on which Wittgenstein so insisted throughout his career.

Does that mean that the 'untold, private battle' of Wittgenstein's life amounts to a kind of paranoia? That is a fair question, I think. Psychology always knows more about you than *you* know about you, and the epsilon of class membership only makes that more complete, right the way up to a kind of predestination. To try to live as Wittgenstein lived—as though *you* always know more about yourself than psychology does—will always, in the end, look like paranoia to those looking on. For this reason, Russell and logical analysis will always be right, and the paranoia of Wittgenstein and all like him will always be wrong or, at any rate, unfounded. For that is the chief and final consequence of ethical mysticism and of allowing modern logic to apparently generate legitimate domain objects of its own. Language was never meant to do this. It was never meant to be the means of adjudicating 'between the very ideas in our heads'. For if there is a legitimate domain of objects, while it is language's job to line up on them, then fiction must become intolerable to nonfiction. The pen in my hand, *qua* pen (*qua* the material atoms of the pen, not *qua* 'penness', as per the Platonic universals of old), must rise to become more concrete and existent than any of the ideas in my head which it just happens to be putting down. And that would be very dangerous, should it ever happen. Because then we would simply be snuffed out and extinguished. In the sense in which the pen, *qua* its material atoms, has already taken care of itself.

It was one of Wittgenstein's very early acts to pronounce on this doom in his *Notebooks*. A doom precisely because—like all real dooms—it cannot be turned around to face itself. That is to say, fiction happens when we make illegitimate use of legitimate signs, when we use a rule to start a revolution. The legitimate signs always have to come first (as language), then the illegitimate use which we may make of them, second. This is the same thing as to say that the purpose of legitimacy is illegitimacy or that the purpose of rulership is arbitrariness. This is in flat defiance of Plato's project in the *Republic* but close to the original elusiveness of his master Socrates, and his notorious antipathy to words written down. Similarly, modern logic does not turn around to face itself and admit this in its great works. Its propositional modus appears to bring actual experience to bear on the question of truth, yet there will always be those like Wittgenstein to point out that this 'actual experience' of the timeline and history is something quite other than what we mean by the 'actual experience' of the first-person human consciousness.

> Logic must take care of herself.
>
> If syntactical rules for functions could at all be fixed up, then the whole theory of things, properties, etc., would become superfluous. It is all too clear that neither the *Grundgesetze* nor the *Principia Mathematica* wish to bring this theory into question. Again: Logic must take care of herself. A *possible* sign must also be capable of designating. Everything that is possible is also legitimate (permitted). Let us remember the explanation why 'Socrates is Plato' is nonsense. That is, because *we* have not made an arbitrary specification, NOT because a sign is, so to speak, illegitimate in itself![8]
>
> The idea that, in order to comprehend the significance of a general term, one must first find the element common to all its applications, has paralysed philosophical research. Not only has it not brought about any clear results, but it has encouraged the philosopher to reject outright (as irrelevant) all those concrete and discrete incidents that would otherwise have been the one true master key to unlocking, for him, the use of the general term. When Socrates put the question, 'What is knowledge?' [*Theaetetus*, 146c], he never imagined that a proper preliminary response should consist in the enumeration of all the possible cases of knowledge. If I wanted to find out what sort of thing is arithmetic, I would find it entirely satisfactory to make an investigation merely of the case of the finite cardinal numbers. In fact:
>
> (a) this would of its own lead me to all the more complicated cases,
>
> (b) an arithmetic of the finite cardinal numbers is not incomplete; it does not have lacunae that are then filled by the rest of arithmetic.[9]

LANGUAGE SHOULD NOT HAVE ITS PROPER DOMAIN OF OBJECTS

Language, like confession before God, does not and should not have its proper domain of objects. Again, as in the act of confession before God, you can only speak about language in theory, or doctrine, up to a point. After that, you can only begin to say (or confess) things that are spontaneous and extempore, come one moment, gone the next. Things that only you can feel, and God can know. The category opposite, in other words, of the eternal things of Russell's ethical mysticism. After a point, you can only speak nonsense, and have nonsense spoken to you by God. When Socrates said—

> I can not help feeling, Phaedrus, that writing is unfortunately like painting; for the creations of the painter have the attitude of life, and yet if you ask them a question they preserve a solemn silence. And the same may be said of speeches. You would imagine that they had intelligence, but if you want to know anything and put a question to one of them, the speaker always gives one unvarying answer. And when they have been once written down they are tossed about anywhere among those who do and among those who do not understand them. And they have no reticences or proprieties towards different classes of persons; and, if they are unjustly assailed or abused, their parent is needed to protect his offspring, for they can not protect or defend themselves.[10]

—He was giving the lie to the nascent dream of the Western mind, and how it was preparing to stake everything on truth and freedom as being like one 'unvarying answer'. And even the things we think and speak, and how we behave and associate, to be such as should stand to reason in this same, unvarying way. Wittgenstein's famous criticism of G. E. Moore's famous proof is arrowed towards this. Yes, you can bring your hand up before your face to prove the whole discourse of existence and everything that hangs on it, but you cannot at the same time escape the possibility that you are only *acting* as though the incident of it were the proof of the general case. In other words, *if you first thought like Moore*, then this is indeed what you would do. As ever, something stands behind the thought and makes it seem the intelligent thing to do. Moore raises his hand, and now the whole universe and everything in it must obey his gesture for ever more. This is absurd. And more absurd, then, that it should be invoked to settle anything so profound as the question of existence. Socrates had an instinct that truth and freedom should be nothing so unvarying as that, but something more like physicality's endless change of place. The river that you can't step into twice.

Moore wasn't wrong. Everything in the Western idea of intelligence really does summit on his proof. Scepticism within the Western ideal of intelligence does have to summit always on scepticism *of the external world*, and therefore his proof works. It is just that there is another kind of scepticism—Wittgenstein's kind of scepticism—that recognizes that each and every one of our acts is a law and a rule and a physics, but only because we first act as though it were. A world of people so acting is the scenario that Wittgenstein's *On Certainty* repeatedly produces for its example. Of course, Moore and all like him must at once counter with the idea that, whilst we may, the world doesn't 'act', and that not acting, its incidents really do represent the proof of the general case! But press this theorem (*Teorema*) in the way that Wittgenstein presses it, and you will find that the 'world' is as much acting as we are—That we can only say that when Moore raises his one hand, and then the other, he is merely acting with the world or aping it. The world might choose to act differently one day, or what is the same thing, God might choose to. And then Moore's proof would no longer work.

A world that is this animate, capricious, and unpredictable becomes the only possible explanation for the otherwise inexplicable statements of credence and certainty that are made to overlay so much of human language; though this is where the mysticism of Wittgenstein's philosophy becomes ultra-demanding. He asks us, over and over, to consider how we are only ever presented—by Moore and others—with the contexts and settings (language-games) in which their proofs would stand to reason. The faith of physics in the laws of nature really does come down to a classroom setting, in which the actions of Professor G. E. Moore in raising his hands are preceded by something that would make them the a-ha moment and the coup de grâce. This something is never in itself contained within the raising of the hands. It is rather something that exists between Moore and his students, and it can only be described by observing that *he* does exactly what *they* would expect him to do as an expert witness.

> Should I rather say, 'I Believe in physics': or 'I know that physics is true'?
>
> They teach me that under *these* circumstances, *this* thing will happen. This has been discovered because the proof of it has been run at least twice. Moreover, we are obliged to take all of this seriously because this experience, and its proof, are not isolated, but constituted in a wider system of such things. Thus, experiments have not only been made on the fall of bodies, but on the resistance of air, and on many other corresponding things, too.
>
> In the end, however, it remains that I simply put my faith in these experiences—or as it may be, in the reports of these experiences—and in accordance with this, and without any scruples, I go on to order the actions of my daily life. But what of this faith itself, then? Can it be said to have given a good proof of itself? As far as I can judge it—yes.
>
> In the setting of a court of law, the pronouncement of a physicist that water boils at 100 degrees centigrade would be unconditionally accepted as the truth. But now say I were to decide not to go along with this, what should I do? Make my own experiments? What could they then prove?
>
> But what if the pronouncements of the physicist were actually superstitions, so that to conform our judgement to them would be as absurd as putting our faith in the 'trial by fire'?
>
> In my opinion, the sheer fact that they were this could not of itself be enough to allow me to assume that my conformation would then be erroneous.—But would it not be a good enough reason to at least imagine that I might be in error? Not at all! It could be no good reason for any uncertainty in my thoughts or actions.
>
> The judge might well say: 'This is the truth insofar as I can know it.' But what effect would this addition of his have? ('beyond all reasonable doubt').
>
> Is it wrong to leave me to judge the propositions of physics from my own bodily actions? Must I ever be allowed to say that I have no good reason to do so?—Because, is it not after all precisely this [seeing is believing], that we call a 'good reason'?
>
> Suppose that we were to encounter people who really did not consider this to be the thing to do. More to the point, how would we set about imagining such a scenario? Perhaps we could do it by imaging that instead of interrogating physicists, they interrogate oracles. (And that for this reason we consider them primitives). Is it wrong that they consult an oracle, and leave all matters of judgement to him?—And does saying as much actually defeat them (within the meaning of this language game)?
>
> And are we right or wrong to put up this fight against them in the first place? Naturally we will go on regardless, supporting our method of proceeding with every manner of watchword and slogan.

For whenever you encounter the meeting of two such mutually exclusive principles, just watch how each will accuse the other of being folly and heresy.

I used the word 'fight'—so would I still produce *reasons* for my stance? Certainly, but where would they come from? At the end of all reasoning stands *persuasion*. (Think of what befell the indigenous peoples when the missionaries came to convert them).

If I now say, 'I know that at the touch of the gas flame the water in the casserole dish will boil rather than freeze', it seems to me that this 'I know' of mine is as justified as *anything* could be. 'If I know some thing, then I know *this*'—or is it that I know with a still *greater* certainty that the man standing next to me is my old friend So-and-So? And how does all of this accord with the proposition that I see with two *eyes*, and that if I look in the mirror I see them?—I do not know quite how I should respond here, but between the two cases there certainly stands a difference. If the water over the flame were to freeze, I would, for sure, be totally stupefied; but without hesitation I would suppose that there was at work some influence of which I was as yet ignorant, and perhaps I would leave it to the physicists to judge.—But what could cause me to doubt that this man might be N. N., who I have known for many years? Here, it would seem, is a doubt that can suck everything into itself and throw everything into chaos.[11]

Wittgenstein is, right, of course. The statements of credence and certainty which are made to overlay so much of human language are a reaction and antidote to this last catastrophic form of doubt. The doubt shouldn't exist. That is to say, if language can be made to line up on its proper domain objects, then there wouldn't be any gap of misalignment for doubt to exploit. Again, we are citing Russell's ethical mysticism. As ever, for Wittgenstein, then, it all comes down to *us*. That Russell and the others don't succeed/can't succeed, comes down to us. And this, after all, was what he really designed his philosophy to do. His infamous style of 'teaching' exemplified it. In his *Lectures on the Foundations of Mathematics* at Cambridge he demonstrated, over and again, that the so-called empiricism by which all language, truth, and logic is said to be guaranteed is much more akin to a plot, in which human beings agree ahead of time to think and act in a certain way. This pre-arranged way of thinking and acting is then imagined to be the empiricism which guaranteed the thought and actions to be 'true' ('in the first place')—Whereas all along they were only 'true' in the sense in which what was agreed upon before, between all, was obeyed and carried out (by all simultaneously). For Wittgenstein, this is what truth, even truth in mathematics, comes to refer to. What is really going on, then, between Moore and his students in the classroom—or between Moore and the readers of his books—is a mutual recognition that the game must go on because the game always has gone on. To try now at this late stage to go against the whole human history of this contract would be awkward, if not impossible.

'If the water over the flame were to freeze, I would, for sure, be totally stupefied; but without hesitation I would suppose that there was at work some influence of which I was as yet ignorant.' Here Wittgenstein wants you to see that what you have been taught to call truth and intelligence can just as easily be written out in this way, in which you see instead that you have been taught only to run from revelation—And how to keep running. When you learn to count, to read, or when later on in life you follow a venerated philosophy professor as he makes out a proof, you obey because of what it would mean to interrupt him and stand up and stop everything. Deduction, induction, reduction, dogma, doctrine, law: to think in these ways is to follow out a fear. What your education calls being reasonable, and seeing the bigger picture, is the ideology of this fear. It might well be that the *real truth* runs against everything ever said by venerated philosophers.

But just try and say that out loud, or write a book on it, and see if the world will let you. They won't! And just think about this. What if the *real truth* really is everything that you could say, but mustn't? And what if the so-called truth of the Western philosophers has been nothing but omertà? These thoughts are shocking, but Wittgenstein makes them also reassuring and viable. Because the standout thing about 'the truth of the Western philosophers' is that it really is a classroom, and a professor, and his way or the highway. This is what the concept of 'meaning' signifies. It signifies that there *shall* be meaning. That there shan't be my version, or your version, but only *meaning*. Each and every something shall mean *something*. If I teach you, I must do it in such a way as that you can write things down. The trick all along has been for Western philosophy to ignore this elephant in the room. This is why I used the word 'omertà'. Language, like mathematics, is, yes, simply the pre-arranged contract between humans that there shall be meaning.[12] This is why Wittgenstein's eye was able to fall to regarding all language events as one-time games—With the significance of the word 'games' meaning that they must play out between people.

WHAT CAN BE DISPUTED

The Western idea of philosophical meaning says that whatever is true is independent of us—Regardless of the human eye, and unswerving. For example, you, as a self-conscious human being, can never be, so to speak, true—or, I should say, perfectly truthful—yet your body can, if we consider it in terms of its unswerving biology. The same unswerving biology that makes an accurate and effective modern medicine possible. Here we have the same construction that I earlier made an example of when I talked about the pen in my hand being more concrete and existent than me (than the ideas in my head). Here we see again that the Western idea of philosophical meaning makes a special and decisive use of physics. The unswerving things in physical nature have been chased and found out over the years, and science's rampant success with this has heaped up a mountain of evidence. But here is what Wittgenstein noticed: in the final analysis, this evidence, however abundant, can tell us nothing about the existence of the Universe of Physics (vis-à-vis the nonexistence of everything that is not it). The fabled ability of physics to predict that something will act in such-and-such a way, on such-and-such a date is as unremarkable and tautological as to say that something that was always going to happen has happened. It is as though physics is like a magician who first tells you the whole exact explanation of the illusion he is about to perform, then performs it. He would be booed off the stage. But this is what physics does; this is the precise nature of its claim to fame. Yet this is to take nothing away from the weirdness of the temporal aspect in this—A weirdness which the *Tractatus* fulsomely explored. By closing the distance between an event that is going to happen and the numbers that predict it, physics seems able to say the same thing twice, but in different moments—The one ahead of the other. This ability of physics to put you in two places at once is, yes, a weird sensation, and a major part of the thrill of the thing. But when Wittgenstein leaves the *Tractatus* behind, it is because he has acknowledged that this thrill is still the aeons-old thrill of superstition and magic, though in its best yet form. The thrill is that the future has not happened yet: but a prediction can put you into it. That is the thrill, and why it is aeons-old. In this strange way, physics claims to be debunking and demolishing the ways of old; yet, it, more than any religion, needs a predestined future in which it can be proved to be right. And physics is not wrong about its predestined future. How could it be? How can you be wrong about what is predestined? So the real story must be something else altogether, which is where Wittgenstein goes next.

Appendix

241

If everything that you do or say has already been done and said, by you, in the future-to-be—and if between all the things you have done and said and connecting them is physics, and also language, truth, and logic (so that none of this can be disputed)—then the real story must lie in what can be disputed. The Universe of Physics tells us all about itself and will continue revealing itself indefinitely. But the special and decisive use that Western philosophy has always made of physics on the question of meaning—on the question of existence—is the thing that can be disputed. If Western philosophy has girded itself over the millennia to teach today that truth and falsehood are exactly coordinate with what does and does not (with what can and cannot be seen to) exist, then Wittgenstein points out in return that this existence itself does not 'exist'. When Moore raises his hands, he does not thereby prove existence while simultaneously vanquishing nonexistence. He simply proves that it is possible to act as though the Universe of Physics exists, and us in it. In turn, this acting out is utterly dependent upon its reception by those in the audience. The full recognition of this was the new deadly seriousness of Wittgenstein's later philosophy. A theory like physics does not need human minds for the sections of it that already coordinate with timeline events, and which therefore cannot strictly speaking be said to amount to a theory at all; what it really needs them for, is the kind of advance-of-time deep space exploration of the *Principia Mathematica* as much as of astrophysics. By allowing its loops to pass through our minds, *we* verify it. That is to say, it is we who tacitly verify that some described point in outer logic, or outer space, really is there, if we are not taking an active step against it. This is not David Hume's 'problem of induction'; though it is not unrelated to it. If Hume was struck by the fact that the future which induction lays claim to can never actually be said to exist, then Wittgenstein is more agitated about the ways in which we are co-opted, or recruited, for this and all the other schemes of mental intelligence.

There is the experience of working in perfect mental concordance with the timeline of events: having the apple hit you on the head, counting with abacus beads, and so on. This is the traditional, empirical basis of positivism, and rightly so. And then there is the experience of what happens next, because none of us can afford to live solely in step with the timeline. The good life has always required forethought and planning, and these things depend in turn upon the mastery of nature and the ability to know what will happen next. Thus it is that these necessities compel us to journey ahead of the timeline, mentally, with the calculating techniques perfected by the scientists and philosophers. And here is where the strangeness happens. When you work in 'perfect mental concordance with the timeline of events', your language lines up on domain objects that are real. But when you voyage ahead of the timeline into the regions of pure theory, your language has to create new domain objects of its own. I have already made a particular example of Russell on this. I have called it 'ethical mysticism' because it comes out, in the end, as a normative theory of human action, in which these created domain objects reach back to verify the infallibility of what has just been spoken over them. It is this necessity of language to create what it simultaneously sees that makes for the final insight into Wittgenstein's philosophy, and explains its mesmeric relationship to empiricism.

THE COLLAPSE INTO UTTER IDENTITY

It is true enough to say, after Russell, that the proven syntax of language offers the advantage of being able to super-compute—A process whereby we take the symbolism of language /re time and space and then re-symbolise it endlessly, each new set of symbols generating the next. What only Wittgenstein seems to notice is that this super-computing must necessarily carry time and space with it, until it becomes something which we must obey: the ideology of numbers. This comes about because computing, or calculating, is an empirical activity which must be run through, whereas the results obtained along the way are simply what it turns up. The corresponding idea that these results were there all along, as objects, is a conclusion that must therefore grow to become totally bewitching after a while. [Think again of how Plato slipped into conceptualizing the Good Life as a set of universal ideas, shimmering in the distance and drawing us on.] Wittgenstein's insight, then, is to see that between the activity and this, its corresponding idea, we have no natural place to occupy—Save to go along with it, to make it into a method of life, and to fashion the City and the Universe of that life. When a philosophy professor like Moore stands before a class of students and orchestrates them in a proof of the external world, *this* is what he is doing. Going along with it. In the life and language of the everyday, this is disguised. We do many things without first saying out loud, 'I am going to do *x*'. Putting a forkful of food into one's mouth, for instance. Yet if we always did this, we would always have Moore's proof of an external world. I repeat: Wittgenstein's insight is to say that it doesn't matter whether you act as though you had just spoken or speak as though you had just acted. Either way shows you that the criterion of truth in all things mental (the classroom of the mind) is something that can only be enacted in the presence of other humans. It does not put us in touch with anything external to us—Anything that could be the final arbiter of truth. I repeat: The disproof of Moore's proof could never be a counter-argument, but only you standing up and saying, 'I don't witness to this!' If everyone in the world did this to Moore, or even just the majority, then he could no longer claim validity for it. It is like Wittgenstein puts it, towards the end of his *Lectures on the Foundations of Mathematics*. (To come, later.)

There is nothing a priori, which being a priori and existing, can guarantee the correctness of the operations of the human mind. (Note that terrifying, totalitarian language.) Mathematics purports to be the test case which proves that there is—That, say, the whole of common sense and the Good Life can be reverse engineered from an atomic fact like, 'Were you to stand in the way of a moving train, you would be killed'. (This is the real, lurking force of Moore's 'here is one hand' proof.) When mathematics gets you to count abacus beads, using your hands and your eyes, it is saying as much. The abacus beads turn up results called numbers; those numbers are simultaneously proved in the movements of the beads. What is simultaneously called mental intelligence and an education is for you to go along with that (on pain of death). This is not to say that two beads can of a sudden, and with no function of addition, become three beads, or that you should step in front of a train. But it is to say that this one way of acting—this one method of life (this one Western education)—happens to be such that it can only exist (that it can only prove itself to be true) by annihilating all the other ways of acting. In non-Western parts of the world, two beads are also two beads, and no one steps in front of trains who wants to remain alive; yet these things are not taken to prove the nonexistence of the supernatural or life after death. Wittgenstein's enduring distress, or paranoia, /re mathematics and logic was this conquest economy and its intolerance. If the only way that you can stand against it is to claim that there is a rhinoceros in the room when there isn't, then that is what you have to do, and so be it. Bertrand Russell may call you a fool, but then what else could he call you? Logic and mathematics must always use an outside agent who can be surprised, mystified, thrilled, enticed, compelled, and convinced by their results. That agent is *you*. The number two can't jump up and down whenever it sees two objects in the world and draw the conclusions for life and knowledge. But you can. As I said, it is like the way Wittgenstein put it towards the end of his *Lectures on the Foundations of Mathematics*, when he was climaxing on the realization that Truth is always that moment when we see ourselves in the mirror of how the numbers would have us be. We have walked their steps, and now we are as they. We have become the experiential to their mathematical. [Which is why the two cannot be separated in climax.]

Suppose we know:

$$\varnothing(1) = \varphi(1)$$

$$\varnothing(n+1) = F(\varnothing n)$$

$$\varphi(n'+1) = F(\varphi n')$$

We can then substitute 1 for n, and so prove that $\varnothing(1+1) = \varphi(1+1)$, and then substitute $1+1$ for n and so prove that $\varnothing(3) = \varphi(3)$, …

On the ground of these equations, we can assert $\varnothing(3000) = \varphi(3000)$. We could prove this by going through all 3000 steps, but this would be very long, so we take a short cut.— Now what's responsible for this? How is it that we can leave all these steps out? Someone might say, 'This is rash.' But of course it isn't. We can even conclude to $\varnothing(n) = \varphi(n)$, which if anything would be more rash.

The interesting thing is this. (1) You haven't the faintest doubt you can do this. (2) You can say you have done the same thing in the two cases. Your mind has gone through all the steps.—But has your mind done this?

What did I do when I tried to persuade you of this? I showed you what would happen with 1, what would happen with 2, and then said 'and so on'. And you were satisfied with this.

You might say:

(1) The real proof would be the whole chain. In some mystical way, I've done all these operations.

(2) In some way, what I've done is the *same as* doing all 3000.—I can only say it's not the same.

Now how is it that we can be so certain that the two steps will lead to the same result as the 3000 steps? Why do we say they must meet?

… If we weigh two crystals separately and each weighs 3 grams, and then weigh them together, must they weigh 6 grams? Obviously not. They might weigh 5 grams. Does this mean that our arithmetic has gone wrong? Of course not.—Our arithmetic doesn't tell us anything about the weights—it is a standard. On the basis of it we judge that something *must* have happened.

So in the case of mathematical induction. How are we going to judge that we made the right steps? If we should go through the 3000 steps and *not* get the predicted result, we're going to say that we've made a mistake. Either we take this as one of the criteria or we don't.

Isn't it all that you can say of a step that it seems to be correct? What is it to say of a step that it is correct, except to say 'It seems to be correct—unless I am crazy'?

... In the mathematical induction case, you might say, 'We *must* get the same result.'

Does this mean that we *do* get the same result? The thing is that we get this result, and *not* by taking the 3000 steps; and in fact we use this result as a criterion of whether our 3000 steps *are* correct.

That our 3000 steps will produce this result is an experiential proposition. But that this result is correct is a *rule*. We don't allow any experiential process either to refute or to establish a rule ... —The difficulty is to make a cut in such a way as to cut the mathematical from the empirical.

It isn't *a priori* clear at all when we should say we've left out numbers. A criterion is that we say we do the same thing.—Our memory agrees with what we write.

We don't know what would happen if things went wrong, or what sort of mistake we should imagine.

There is a case where we all say you left out a number and you don't know you have. What we say is the criterion.

'Don't you see you've left out the number 1000?' You look at the textbook. You say, 'I must have been dreaming.'—Did you ever hear of such a case? Did you ever hear of a man imagining that the number series goes the other way? No. But these are very important facts. If *many* people did such things, this would affect the nature of our calculus. The criterion for our counting correctly is partly our memory, but mostly the constant agreement ...

We are so used to the criteria for certain facts, that we completely forget what the criteria are. We need an enormous number of criteria for knowing that we count the same, etc.[13]

The analogue of this in human life is sex, or, at least, the climax of the sexual act. If self-consciousness is like a narrative that we are all the time writing over our physical movements down below it, so that the traditional strangeness of self consciousness is this strangeness of being in two places at once (subject *and* king is how I put it in my previous book[14]), then it must come inevitably to pass that self-consciousness *as the language of the human condition* must begin to want to line up on its proper domain objects. In no other human act is self-consciousness more implicated than in the human sexual act. In no other human act is it actually required that the language of the human condition collapse into utter identity with physical movements down below for those same movements to actually proceed to their conclusion. As we have seen in this book, this is where Wittgenstein's untold, private battle shows its face in his philosophy. The fact that the human condition is written through with this climactic collapse into utter identity (the Devil), and that it must in fact be gone through religiously for the continuation of the species, is worth pausing over. It links Wittgenstein to the man he so admired—Saint Augustine of Hippo—for whom sex was similarly momentous and similarly suspicious. It can only be simulated up to a point, and then the collapse must occur.

The infamous episode in his *Confessions*, where he recounts his excruciation while having an erection while a teenager in the public baths at Thagaste, is really about this, rather than about a middle-aged man's inability to move on from a normal teenage experience. Augustine's insistence on making an example of the male erection there, and then in numerous other passages in his writings, had nothing to do with Christian prudery or ethics, though that has long been the understanding of it. It was a technical investigation of what, to him, was the only known example in the human experience (apart from counting using the fingers of one's hands; see above) of a state of being that cannot be acted out or rehearsed, but which is itself the criterion of an exact mental state which accompanies it (and vice versa). You cannot pretend to have an erection. You cannot go through the motions of it as you could, say, pretend to be a priest in a film.[15]

When Wittgenstein discussed this same problem in his *Philosophical Investigations*, he did not use the example of the male erection but instead his famous example of the 'beetle in box'.[16] In this example, he showed that because every instantiation of language is a game of rules, it cannot of itself supply the criterion to differentiate between those participants acting it out sincerely or fraudulently. More, it cannot of itself supply the criterion of what it would be 'to act' or 'to pretend'. Language-games are such as that they can only be recognized by their outward movements and sounds. The definition of a language game is exactly that it should be able to be recorded and replayed by a machine. By learning and perfecting the rules of a language-game, you can be a seamless participant in its running, yet be thinking utterly unrelated thoughts. You can look like a priest, act like a priest, and talk like a priest, yet you could have anything but a beetle in your box.

For Wittgenstein as much as for Augustine, this was good news, because to both men, that possibility of having 'anything but a beetle in your box' was a direct reference to your personality—To its total insulation from syntax, and therefore to its requirement of a personal salvation and a personal saviour. Either the whole world is to become one giant language-game played correctly, and that to be called 'Salvation'; or 'Salvation' is to become the private *conversation* (i.e. NOT a *private language*) with a private God that everyone secretly suspects Wittgenstein to have had in imitation of Augustine; but for which his theory of language has eradicated the proof.[17]

'To love one's neighbour' would mean to will![18]

SEX IS THE SYMBOLIC EVENT HORIZON

Sex is the symbolic event horizon between language and fact, art and realism. Sex is therefore the fixation of a Russellian ethical mysticism that would have it that all falsehood is imprecision and all precision would be to only ever act out the proof of the general case. In this way would a new kind of eternity come into being—One made from the annihilation of the temporal sequencing of events. If subjectivity as we know it, is the belief that we are pretending—the belief that there is always a split-second distance between what we would look like through a film camera and the internal craftwork that the camera cannot see, but which secures our personalities—then ethical mysticism imagines the annihilation of that dignity. If self-consciousness is the last bastion between us and how we would look through history's camera anyway (the last bastion of the split-second's free choice, which, if we were to use Christian imagery, we might call 'grace'), then ethical mysticism removes that final impediment so that we can always be acting out the proof of history's general case.

> The feeling of an unbridgeable gulf between consciousness and brain-process: how does it come about that this does not come into the considerations of our ordinary life? This idea of a difference in kind is accompanied by slight giddiness,—which occurs when we are performing a piece of logical sleight of hand. (The same giddiness attacks us when we think of certain theorems in set theory.) When does this feeling occur in the present case? It is when I, for example, turn my attention in a particular way on my own consciousness, and,

astonished, say to myself: THIS is supposed to be produced by a process in the brain!—as it were clutching my forehead.—But what can it mean to speak of 'turning my attention to my own consciousness'? This is surely the queerest thing there could be! It was a particular act of gazing that I called doing this. I stared fixedly in front of me—but *not* at any particular point or object. My eyes were wide open, the brows not contracted (as they mostly are when I am interested in a particular object). No such interest preceded this gazing. My glance was vacant; or again *like* that of someone admiring the illumination of the sky and drinking in the light.

Now bear in mind that the proposition which I uttered as a paradox (THIS is produced by a brain-process!) has nothing paradoxical about it. I could have said it in the course of an experiment whose purpose was to show that an effect of light which I see is produced by stimulation of a particular part of the brain.—But I did not utter the sentence in the surroundings in which it would have had an everyday and unparadoxical sense. And my attention was not such as would have accorded with making an experiment. (If it had been, my look would have been intent, not vacant.)[19]

I don't suggest you get paranoid over sex yourself! In any case, it takes a certain kind of person to get so paranoid. A certain kind of person like Wittgenstein. A certain kind of sensitivity. A certain kind of sensitivity like Wittgenstein's. But next time you are perusing his numerous thoughts on the impossibility of representing intentionality and soul in form and structure, and vice versa, do please give it a thought. If you shared this, his morbid fear of collapsing into history's apparent and apparently insuperable automation, then you would be austere and mysterious with sex, wouldn't you?

The question that Wittgenstein ultimately presents us with is this: Should we take sex and use it to try to learn to speak the language of God, or should God speak to us in a language which (only) we can understand? If you can allow things to come to this final question, then I think it becomes only more natural still to consider him in terms of his deep but deeply unspecified debt to Augustine. For both men, the investigation of language *as language* must eventually bring philosophy out on this question.[20] The last thing to be realized about language is always that it really does eradicate all proof, save of itself. Western philosophy already has a venerable history of probing the disconnect between ideas and things, and then of exploring the startling consequences of that. But language *as language* has never quite been investigated in the same way—Though we have seen in this book how far Wittgenstein got with it. It has simply been the case that we have not been able to afford language to be implicated in anything. It has simply been the case that we have not been able to afford it to be anything other than the neutral currency of human intercourse. The guarantor of this has seemed to be the good sense of sense itself: the discovery that proper speech itself only breaks the surface once it starts to say something about something else. Like when a baby stops babbling and attaches its first word to something real in the world. 'Daddy' or 'Mommy'. What is missed amidst all this innocence is that such speech acquisition launches one on a career of tragic discernment. Like Moore's demonstration or Wittgenstein's beetle in a box or Augustine's experience at the public baths, you can 'divide through' by the empirical component, but never vice versa.

Augustine's horror that his body can automate and drag him with it in thought and words is Wittgenstein's observation that only rules are necessary for a game; in turn, it is Moore's proof that an external world can only be known by those who choose to act with it. If every instance of syntax, however fleeting or fractional, is the proof of something, then it is the proof of this. That is to say, syntax proves itself in results which it cannot but turn up. That is to say again, it is impossible to separate in time and space the imperative (that it makes sense) to classify all 'Daddies' and 'Mommies' under those names from the imperative that all real-life 'Daddies' and 'Mommies' should strive to acquire the qualities of those classifications. The two imperatives work simultaneously, such that real life and virtual life must eventually converge on the same middle. We note again that the sexual act is simply the handiest and most dramatic example of this. But gravity and all the rest of the laws of nature work just as well. In each case, their discovery has been simultaneous with the imperative to act in concert with them. If one tries to press the point of this simultaneity, one can only come up against the disappointment of a dead-end. 'Why should I not leap into the Grand Canyon?' 'Because you will die!' And from this, as we have already noticed, the Good Life and a great deal else of religion and ethics can be reverse engineered. Yet excluded from this scheme is the human freedom to act otherwise and regardless. (To stand up in the classroom, to disagree, to walk out; enough people doing that to become a whole new world.)

The only way to pin this simultaneity down in words is to say that all that can be answered has been answered. That the sum total of those answers is the Good Life. And it is imperative to human beings to formulate then ask the questions of those answers, and then to come into that life. To say it out loud like this is to account at once for the whole long history of Western philosophy—And why Wittgenstein's innocent-enough questioning can put it into such straits and paroxysms.

Wittgenstein's questioning amounts to asking why the 'whole long history of Western philosophy' insists on presenting *The Truth* as though we were building it or discovering it from our end, here, in classrooms and books, when really it must be reaching back for us from its end—That is, if *The Truth* is *The Truth* at all. For of course, whatever is 'true' must simply be whatever has already happened, past or future of the present moment. That Napoleon conquered Moscow is as true as some enormous number that no one has yet counted out. By the same token, Napoleon's conquest of Moscow had already happened when Augustine was writing in the fifth century. Moore, too, knew that raising his two hands had already happened, when he was spelling out his proof of them to his class in the present moment. Wittgenstein's point is that this naturalistic, positivistic conception of truth forces us to declare that what is 'right'—what is 'ethical' and the Good Life—is whatever has already happened. The Good Life is nonfiction, which is why Socrates and classical thinking could not entertain that the Good Life, once seen, would not be acted on.

In this way, Wittgenstein shows that what may now lie in store for us is a new and terrifying kind of *Realism*. One in which language, truth, and logic really can be turned into a virtual world and presented back to us for our imitation. That is to say, it is not that we are going to be replaced by machines, but that we are going to eventually talk and act and look like them. If that is so, then Wittgenstein also supplies the key to the only counterinsurgency which he believes can work. If Leo Tolstoy was right to notice that we have no natural defence against the idea of the laws of nature, so that Knowledge immediately becomes the grammar which gives our intellectual conscience its voice—

> As with astronomy the difficulty in the way of recognizing that the earth moves consisted in having to rid oneself of the immediate sensation that the earth was stationary accompanied by a similar sense of the planets' motion, so in history the obstacle in the way of recognizing

> the subjection of the individual to the laws of space and time and causality lies in the difficulty of renouncing one's personal impression of being independent of those laws. But as in astronomy the new view said: 'True, we are not conscious of the movements of the earth but if we allow that it is stationary we should arrive at an absurdity, whereas if we admit the motion (which we do not feel) we arrive at laws,' likewise in history the new theory says: 'True, we are not conscious of our dependence but if we were to allow that we are free we arrive at an absurdity, whereas by admitting our dependence on the external world, on time and on causality we arrive at laws.'[21]

—And if Augustine was equally right to notice that this intellectual conscience uses rules to reach round and backfill the extempore originality of the human soul—

> So in the speeches of eloquent men, we find rules of eloquence carried out which the speakers did not think of as aids to eloquence at the time that they spoke them.... For it is because they are eloquent that they exemplify these rules; it is not that they were the kinds of characters who were using them in order to be eloquent.[22]

—Then Wittgenstein is the modern-age prophet of this irony. The visionary of the *Tractatus* who preached you are better off saying nothing at all. Or, at least, in keeping your conversation private. The visionary of the *Philosophical Investigations* who foretold that the great public conversation will one day succeed only in connecting all the possible points of view, and all the possible routes of syntax, and destroy us all in some ecstatic vision—Some lightning surge across them all. The God's-eye snapshot of all time. The whole history of freedom through the wrong end of the telescope. Like death, and when you run your whole life through one final scintillating time—And how the seeing of it is a film reel, and how the film reel of it is the reason why all the events form up in a line.

If this is what it takes for there to be meaning, then the only thing that anyone can say is that they acted for meaning's sake. Or we say again: you divide through by the actions of a human life to arrive at Meaning. Western philosophy has no answer to give to Wittgenstein's innocent questions about meaning save than to say that you must act in a certain way to bring it about. Raise your two hands. [The game is up.] *Act like your Biography*. Everything and this world hangs on this commandment.

> Giving grounds, however, justifying the evidence, comes to an end;—but the end is not certain 'propositions' striking us immediately as true, i.e. it is not a kind of *seeing* on our part; it is our *acting*, which lies at the bottom of the language-game.[23]

Act otherwise, and all things and all other worlds are possible. That is the insurgency. Numberless commandments, and numberless worlds. [And the *Voice* that makes them possible.] In the same way that you cannot cut the mathematical from the empirical, you cannot cut the concept of the film reel from the recursion of the examined life. Thus we butt up against the barrier, and why it must be broken.

> It is possible to imagine a case in which I *could* find out that I had two hands. Normally, however, I *cannot* do so. 'But all you need is to hold them up before your eyes!'—If I am *now* in doubt whether I have two hands, I need not believe my eyes either. (I might just as well ask a friend.)

With this is connected the fact that, for instance, the proposition 'The Earth has existed for millions of years' makes clearer sense than 'The Earth has existed in the last five minutes'. For I should ask anyone who asserted the latter: 'What observations does this proposition refer to; and what observations would count against it?'—whereas I know what ideas and observations the former proposition goes with.[24]

Would this situation be conceivable: someone remembers for the first time in his life and says 'Yes, now I know what "remembering" is, what it *feels like* to remember'.—How does he know that this feeling is 'remembering'? Compare: 'Yes, now I know what "tingling" is'. (He has perhaps had an electric shock for the first time.)—Does he know that it is memory because it is caused by something past? And how does he know what the past is? Man learns the concept of the past by remembering.

And how will he know again in the future what remembering feels like?[25]

NOTES

INTRODUCTION

1. Zhao Tingyang is Great Wall Professor of Chinese Philosophy at the Chinese Academy of Social Sciences, Beijing. His books have been national bestsellers in China for years. This quotation is from his paper, 'The Ontology of Co-existence: From *Cogito* to *Facio*', *Diogenes*, vol. 57, no. 4 (2012), 32.
2. Miles Hollingworth, *Inventing Socrates* (New York, London, Bloomsbury, 2015), p. 138.
3. Ludwig Wittgenstein (ed. Cora Diamond), *Lectures on the Foundations of Mathematics, Cambridge, 1939* (Chicago, University of Chicago Press, 1989), XXIX.
4. Ludwig Wittgenstein, *MS* 120, p. 41v-42r (1937).
5. Ludwig Wittgenstein (tr. G. E. M. Anscombe), *Philosophical Investigations* (Oxford, Basil Blackwell, 1976), II, xi, 226.
6. Ludwig Wittgenstein (ed. and tr. G. E. M. Anscombe), *Remarks on Colour* (Oxford, Wiley-Blackwell, 1991), 58e-59e.
7. Brian McGuinness (ed.), *Wittgenstein and the Vienna Circle: Conversations Recorded by F. Waismann* (Oxford, Blackwell, 1979), p. 33.
8. Ludwig Wittgenstein (ed. Rush Rhees; tr. Anthony Kenny), *Philosophical Grammar* (Oxford, Basil Blackwell, 1974), 468.
9. Ludwig Wittgenstein (ed. Rush Rhees), *Philosophical Remarks* (Chicago, University of Chicago Press, 1980), 152.
10. Wittgenstein (ed. & tr. C. G. Luckhardt & M. A. E. Aue), *The Big Typescript TS 213* (Oxford, Basil Blackwell, 2013), 139e.

11. Ludwig Wittgenstein (eds. G. E. M. Anscombe, G. H. von Wright & Denis Paul), *On Certainty* (New York, Harper & Row, 1972), §341.

12. Ibid., §343.

13. Ibid., §30.

14. M. O'C. Drury, 'Conversations with Wittgenstein', in Rush Rhees (ed.), *Ludwig Wittgenstein: Personal Recollections* (Lanham, MD, Rowman & Littlefield, 1981), p. 117.

15. Wittgenstein, *Philosophical Grammar*, 222.

16. Wittgenstein, *Philosophical Remarks*, 73. See also Ludwig Wittgenstein (tr. Peter Winch), *Culture and Value* (Hoboken, NJ, Wiley-Blackwell, 1998), 14e: 'Spengler could be better understood if he said: I am comparing different cultural epochs with the lives of families; within a family there is a family resemblance, though you will also find resemblance between members of different families; family resemblance differs from the other sort of resemblance in such and such ways, etc. What I mean is: we have to be told the object of comparison, the object from which this way of viewing things is derived, otherwise the discussion will constantly be affected by distortions. Because willy-nilly we shall ascribe the properties of the prototype to the object we are viewing in its light; and we claim 'it must always be ...' This is because we want to give the prototype's characteristics a purchase on our way of representing things. But since we confuse prototype and object, we find ourselves dogmatically conferring on the object properties which only the prototype necessarily possesses. On the other hand we think our view will not have the generality we want it to have if it is really true only of the one case. But the prototype ought to be clearly presented for what it is; so that it characterizes the whole discussion and determines its form. This makes it the focal point, so that its general validity will depend on the fact that it determines the form of discussion rather than on the claim that everything which is true only of it holds too for all the things that are being discussed. Similarly the question always to ask when exaggerated, dogmatic assertions are made is: What is actually true in this? Or again: In what case is that actually true?'

17. Wittgenstein, *On Certainty*, 467.

18. Wittgenstein, *Culture and Value*, 77e.

19. Wittgenstein, *On Certainty*, 152.

20. Wittgenstein (ed. G. E. M. Anscombe et al.), *Lectures and Conversations on Aesthetics, Psychology and Religious Belief* (Oxford, Basil Blackwell, 1966), pp. 24–25.

21. Augustine, *Confessions*, VIII, 8, 20.

CHAPTER 1

1. Cf. Wittgenstein, *MS* 183, p. 125 (1931): 'The movement of thought in my philosophy should be reflected in the history of my mind, its moral concepts and its comprehension of the situations in which I found myself.'

2. Ludwig Wittgenstein (tr. Peter Winch), *Culture and Value* (Hoboken, NJ, Wiley-Blackwell, 1998), 31e.

3. Brian McGuinness (ed.), *Wittgenstein and the Vienna Circle: Conversations Recorded by F. Waismann* (Oxford, Blackwell, 1979), pp. 116–117.

4. Cf. Wittgenstein (ed. Rush Rhees; tr. Anthony Kenny), *Philosophical Grammar* (Oxford, Basil Blackwell, 1974), 481: 'One cannot discover any connection between parts of mathematics or logic that was already there without one knowing.'

5. See p. 200, n. 10.
6. Wittgenstein, *Culture and Value*, 28e.
7. Ibid., 86.
8. Ludwig Wittgenstein (ed. & tr. G. E. M. Anscombe), *Zettel* (Oakland, CA, University of California Press, 1970), §173.
9. Here we encounter an assumption that makes possible all of Wittgenstein's writing, and which he never therefore makes explicit in that writing. As an assumption, it also functions to designate him a peculiarly Continental thinker, as I have already suggested. It also describes the great difficulty, from the Anglo-American side, of coming to terms with his handling of ethics and supernaturalism. Because the Anglo-American mind now has a long history of benefitting from the material fruits of science and technology, it can tell itself—and easily believe—that its use of these fruits is creative and original, that it even amounts to, or defines, creativity and originality. Thus, to be told now that it amounts rather to obeying orders, or the diktats of reason, or however you want to describe them, would be shocking and awkward to say the least. It would be disappointing. It would be to have the carpet pulled out from underneath one. Yet Wittgenstein and other Continental thinkers have a long history of doing just this. The fascination and repulsion of Modernism for Pasolini was much as it was for Wittgenstein. For both thinkers—but far more violently and radically for Wittgenstein—the form and function that Modernism reduces to is not merely self-sufficiency. It is that, of course. But whereas the Model T and the production line has trained the Anglo-American mind to regard that self-sufficiency as a self-satisfying full stop, the Continental mind has resources and a history that equip it to see it as a point of ambidexterity. More: As the very point of ambidexterity of the *very point of human experience*. You will later on see what I do with this when I discuss Haus Wittgenstein, across pp. 89–107. Suffice to say here that when the mother Lucia caresses the discarded clothing of Pasolini's Christ, and when Pasolini brings us in to witness it, this ambidextrous point of human experience is what we are witnessing. The Anglo-American mind chooses one way, and goes right. Whereas Pasolini sees that the point of human experience is never such that it can be correctly—or truly—interpreted in accordance with its reduction to fact. A mother caressing the clothes of a man who might be her son only looks sexual because Pasolini has made it that the left-to-right of 'reduction-to-fact' ('the clothes of a man who might be her son') is now going to be independent of, and in opposition to, *her point of experience*. What Lucia is feeling can only be 'wrong' or 'right' in relation to a single world (this world) which has made it that these things shall have the temporal dispensation of natural laws. In another world, Lucia's actions would not look perverse. Her passion for Pasolini's Christ would not look sexual. Yet we have been conditioned away from this insight because we have been educated to bow down to the ethic and the narrative that the left-to-right arrow of time in *this* world suggests. We have been educated to forget the eternity of our *point of experience*. Thus it happens, time and again, that the signal message of Wittgenstein's so-called private language argument is missed. Or, I should say, its true setting remains unannounced. What it was really designed to ridicule was not the idea of a private language *qua* language, but the reasons that make Pasolini's Christ and Lucia's behaviour scandalous and even obscene. What is *really* scandalous and obscene is to hold everything to ransom over the single ethic and narrative that *the facts in this world happen to speak*. Pasolini's great achievement in his *Teorema*—I repeat—was to find a way to put the *points of experience* of all his characters in 'independence and opposition' to this fascist left-to-right. Or I should say again, that the *Teorema* is such as it could be transposed to an infinity of settings; but that its

'true setting would remain always unannounced'. [Which is why it is a *Teorema*.] Thus we come to what only language, truth, and logic can expose, or, at least, what Wittgenstein believed that they only could expose. Which is that temporality is madness; eternity is sanity; and that the infinite (single) universe of language, truth, and logic is what he would ridicule as the 'hocus-pocus' of an arrow pointing on its own: ' "Everything is already there in … " How does it come about that this arrow → *points*? Doesn't it seem to carry in it something besides itself?—No, not the dead line on paper; only the psychical thing, the meaning, can do that.—That is both true and false. The arrow points only in the application that a living being makes of it. The pointing is *not* a hocus-pocus which can be performed only by the soul' (*Philosophical Investigations*, I, 454). And so we arrive at the assumption that makes all of Wittgenstein's writing possible: *if anything is to look like anything, it requires a world in which it can so look; yet that world cannot also, then, become its meaning.* [*The arrow requires a world in which it can so look; yet that world cannot also, then, become its meaning.*] Across pp. 66–68, I discuss this in relation to Kurt Gödel's 'incompleteness theorems'. Those theorems show, truly enough, that meaning can never be a quality of law, or consistency, or temporality, or even a (fake) eternity made out of an infinity of identical temporal moments. Thus, they force us to confront the absurdity that in the infinite (single) universe of language, truth, and logic the capstone of meaning is an event called 'death', which is, albeit, predestinated (by syntax) yet never proved; we should say, 'yet incapable of proof'. Incapable of proof because the method of syntax which generated it is not configured for the doubt that a proof would address. The famous 'All men are mortal' of the ancient syllogism is not an item of term logic that we have since been able to substitute and upgrade with a verifiable proposition. Ancient logic discovered that the death of one man could only be raised from the incident of it to the term 'All men are mortal' by creating a syntax in which that term would cap a world in which mortality *could so look*. And so the modern idea that each death becomes the meaning of mortality and a mortal world, and an empirical event on which a proposition of language can be made, is not a great advance at all but a regression. It is a regression because it only truly succeeds in showing us how our language, truth, and logic would be demolished by 'The Immortal Man'. With this Immortal Man being, of course, the *Suffering Christ*, and in the form in which he is seen to appear all over Wittgenstein's writings—And always at just the moment to confound this cardinal pretension of modern logic. [Don't look for the word 'Christ': Look instead for each moment in which Wittgenstein regrets set theory's divinization of language, and instead prospects for the possibility that God may be willing to speak *our* language (to speak to (each one of) us)).] Like the arrow, we cannot point through sheer occult (soulful) intentionality; we make use of our physical finger to do it. At least, that is what it looks like in a corporeal world. Yet to conclude then that a single finger pointing should exclude all other worlds, and how that point of intentionality (that *point of human experience*) would look in them, is, yes, absurdity. Logic itself disallows it: which is only what Gödel was trying to show. And what Pasolini was trying to show, with his *Suffering Christ*. And *Lucia*.

10. 'Quicksilver' is a deliberate echo of how I approached this subject in my biography of Saint Augustine of Hippo. See Miles Hollingworth, *Saint Augustine of Hippo: An Intellectual Biography* (New York, Oxford University Press, 2013/London, Bloomsbury, 2013), pp. 86, 111, 150–151, 154–155, 163–168, 198, 200. For the 'quicksilver' reference, see p. 184.

11. Pier Paolo Pasolini, *Teorema* (Milano, Garzanti Editore, 2014), I, 12 (translation mine).

12. Ibid., I, 11 (translation mine).

13. This idea: that intentionality in its rawest, purest physical expression can become its own form of intelligence: is one that I take to the nth degree in the next chapter—and indeed through to the end of this book. You can follow it out across these pages under the concept of 'physical intelligence': from p. 59 onwards. At this early point, consider this remark at Wittgenstein, *Philosophical Grammar*, II, ch. 5, §22, p. 365: 'How strange it would be if a geographical expedition were uncertain whether it had a goal, and so whether it had any route whatsoever. We can't imagine such a thing, it's nonsense. But this is precisely what it is like in a mathematical expedition. And so perhaps it is a good idea to drop the comparison altogether.'

14. Pasolini, *Teorema*, I, 1 (translation mine).

15. Ludwig Wittgenstein (tr. D. F. Pears & B. F. McGuinness), *Tractatus Logico-Philosophicus* (London, Routledge & Kegan Paul, 1977), 6.54.

16. Fyodor Dostoyevsky (tr. Ronald Meyer), *The Meek One* (London, Penguin Books, 2015), pp. 54–55.

17. Ludwig Wittgenstein (tr. G. E. M. Anscombe), *Philosophical Investigations* (Oxford, Basil Blackwell, 1976), §109.

18. Wittgenstein, *Tractatus*, 6.43.

19. See how Wittgenstein makes use of just this imagery of points of light on p. 219.

20. Thomas Hobbes (ed. C. B. Macpherson), *Leviathan* (Harmondsworth, Penguin, 1982), IV, 46.

21. Ibid., II, 20.

22. Ibid., II, 21.

23. Ibid.

24. Ludwig Wittgenstein (ed. G. E. M. Anscombe), *Notebooks, 1914-1916* (Chicago, University of Chicago Press, 1984), 84e.

25. Wittgenstein, *Culture and Value*, 67e.

26. Ibid., 50e.

27. See p. 5.

28. Quoted in Rush Rhees, *Ludwig Wittgenstein: Personal Recollections* (New York, Rowman & Littlefield, 1981), p. 96.

29. See, for example, Ludwig Wittgenstein (eds. G. E. M. Anscombe, G. H. von Wright & Denis Paul), *On Certainty* (New York, Harper & Row, 1972), 472, 476: 'When a child learns his language, he learns contemporaneously, what he should look for and also what he should not look for. When he learns that in the room there is a wardrobe, then he learns also not to doubt that that which he will see there a little later will still be a wardrobe ... ' and 'A child does not learn that books exist, or that chairs exist, etc., etc., but he learns to go and take a book, to sit on a chair, etc. Of course, later on, questions on existence do arise: 'Does the unicorn exist?', and so on. But that they do, is only because they are not already settled within the meaning of the learning process. Knowledge and certainty are simply not included within the remit of learning—for whereas the latter is a method that proves itself as it goes along, the former are psychological states which an intellectual criterion cannot ever touch.'

30. Cf. Wittgenstein (eds. G. H. von Wright, R. Rhees & G. E. M. Anscombe), *Remarks on the Foundations of Mathematics* (Cambridge, MA, The MIT Press, 1993)), p. 38: 'The proposition "It is true that this follows from that" means simply: This follows from that.'

31. Wittgenstein, *Philosophical Investigations*, II, 4.

CHAPTER 2

1. Ludwig Wittgenstein (eds. G. E. M. Anscombe, G. H. von Wright & Denis Paul), *On Certainty* (New York, Harper & Row, 1972), 144.
2. Ibid., 205.
3. Ibid., 378.
4. Ian Ground, 'The Relentless Honesty of Ludwig Wittgenstein', *Times Literary Supplement*, 10 October 2017.
5. Ludwig Wittgenstein (ed. Rush Rhees), *Philosophical Remarks* (Chicago, University of Chicago Press, 1980), 151.
6. Cf. Ludwig Wittgenstein (ed. Rush Rhees; tr. Anthony Kenny), *Philosophical Grammar* (Oxford, Basil Blackwell, 1974), II, ch. 5, §22, p. 360: '[W]hen we have supplied a proof, it doesn't prove what was conjectured at all, since I can't conjecture to infinity. I can only conjecture what can be confirmed, but experience can only conjecture a finite number of conjectures, and you can't conjecture the proof until you've got it, and not then either.'
7. Drury in conversation with Wittgenstein in Connemara, Ireland, 1934; quoted in Richard Wall, *Wittgenstein in Ireland* (London, Reaktion Books, 2000), p. 31.
8. Ludwig Wittgenstein, 'A Lecture on Ethics', *Philosophical Review*, vol. 74, no. 1 (1965), 7.
9. Rush Rhees, *Ludwig Wittgenstein: Personal Recollections* (Lanham, MD, Rowman & Littlefield, 1981), p. 184.
10. Ludwig Wittgenstein (tr. G. E. M. Anscombe), *Philosophical Investigations* (Oxford, Basil Blackwell, 1976), II, 11.
11. Ludwig Wittgenstein (tr. D. F. Pears & B. F. McGuinness), *Tractatus Logico-Philosophicus* (London, Routledge & Kegan Paul, 1977), 3.031.
12. Or as we can now have it in Wittgenstein's definition: 'Men have always had a presentiment that there must be a realm in which the answers to questions are symmetrically combined—a priori—to form a self-contained system. A realm subject to the law: Simplex sigillum veri' (Wittgenstein, *Tractatus*, 5.4541).
13. Ludwig Wittgenstein (ed. Rush Rhees), *Preliminary Studies for the 'Philosophical Investigations': Generally Known as the Blue and Brown Books* (Oxford, Basil Blackwell, 1969), p. 19.
14. Cf. Ibid., p. 73: 'Let us now ask: "Can a human *body* have pain?" One is inclined to say: "How can the body have pain? The body in itself is something dead; a body isn't conscious." And here again it is as though we looked into the nature of pain and saw that it lies in its nature that a material object can't have it. And it is as though we saw that what has pain must be an entity of a different nature from that of a material object; that, in fact, it must be of a mental nature. On the other hand we can perfectly well adopt the expression "this body feels pain", and we shall then, just as usual, tell it to go to the doctor, to lie down, and even to remember that when the last time it had pains they went away in a day.'
15. Wittgenstein, *Philosophical Remarks*, §54.
16. Boethius (tr. V. E. Watts), *The Consolations of Philosophy* (Harmondsworth, Penguin, 1978), pp. 54–55.
17. Martin Luther, *A Commentary on St. Paul's Epistle to the Galatians*, II, 16.
18. Ludwig Wittgenstein (ed. & tr. G. E. M. Anscombe), *Zettel* (Oakland, CA, University of California Press, 1970), §60.
19. Alexius Meinong was an Austrian philosopher born in 1853. His famous contribution to philosophy was his systemic rejection of the 'ontological assumption', which is the assumption

that underwrites most all modern empiricist and logical theories; namely, that you can only make true statements about objects that actually, that factually, exist. Against this, Meinong brought the fact that fictitious objects of the human imagination can also, then, evidently, be the bearer of properties: which would leave it that actual factual existence would not need to be a requirement of their being. In fact, Meinong would refer to the being of such fictitious objects as *Sosein* 'so-being', in order to distinguish it from the standard being of actual, factual objects. The infinite totality of fictitious objects which according to Meinong can now be said to be are what is referred to by the term 'Meinong's jungle'. Famous inhabitants of the jungle are 'the golden mountain', 'the square circle' and 'the unicorn'.

20. Wittgenstein, *Zettel*, §55.
21. Ibid., §59.
22. Ibid., §60.
23. Ibid., §61.
24. Ibid., §62.
25. Ibid., §70.
26. Here is something from Augustine's *Confessions* that Wittgenstein really will have read and which says the same thing: 'Memory contains the principles and countless laws of numbers and dimensions, none of which any bodily sense has impressed upon it, since they are not coloured, nor do they give out sound or odour, nor are they tasted or touched. I have heard the sound of the words by which such things are signified when they are discussed, but the sounds are one thing and the things are another. The sounds are of one kind in Greek and of another in Latin, but the things are neither Greek, nor Latin, nor any other kind of language. I have seen lines drawn by builders, even lines so fine as to be like a spider's webs. But those other lines are different: they are not images of things of which the fleshly eye has told me. Anyone who perceives them within himself, without the conception of anybody whatsoever, knows those things. Also, by means of all the bodily senses I have perceived the numbers that we enumerate, but those numbers with which we enumerate are something different. They are not the images of the other ones, and yet they truly exist. Let him who does not perceive them laugh at me for making these statements; I will pity him for laughing at me' (*Confessions*, X, 12, 19).
27. Cf. Wittgenstein, *Philosophical Remarks*, §§47, 48: 'It doesn't strike us at all when we look around us, move about in space, feel our own bodies, etc., etc., because there is nothing that contrasts with the form of our world. The self-evidence of the world expresses itself in the very fact that language can and does only refer to it.'; 'The stream of life, or the stream of the world, flows on and our propositions are so to speak verified only at instants. Then they are commensurable with the present.'
28. Wittgenstein, *Tractatus*, 5.133.
29. Cf. Wittgenstein, *Philosophical Remarks*, §124: 'It isn't just impossible "for us men" to run through the natural numbers one by one; it's *impossible*, it means nothing. The totality is only given as a concept.'
30. Wittgenstein, *Tractatus*, 6.522.
31. He would rather say things like: 'A religious symbol does not rest on any *opinion*. And error belongs only with opinion. One would like to say: This is what took place here; laugh, if you can' (Ludwig Wittgenstein (eds. James Carl Klagge & Alfred Nordmann), *Philosophical Occasions: 1912-1951* (Indianapolis, IN, Hackett Publishing Company, 1993), 123).
32. Cf. Ludwig Wittgenstein (ed. G. E. M. Anscombe), *Notebooks, 1914-1916* (Chicago, University of Chicago Press, 1984), 2.9.14: 'It must in a certain sense be impossible for us to go

wrong in logic. This is already partly expressed by saying: Logic must take care of itself. This is an extremely profound and important insight.'

33. First published in 1936.

34. Oxonian, 'A Visit to Oxford', *New Statesman and Nation*, 6 June 1948, 518–519.

35. A. J. Ayer, *Language, Truth and Logic* (New York, Dover, 2002), p. 35.

36. The deliberateness of this phrasing needs some explanation. I mean to refer to how the nonlinguistic, abstract subject matter of mathematics (numbers and so on) are the acme of what can actually be *seen* and *said* in the world; such that the randomly occurring events of human life have to differ from this paradigm as wisdom has to differ from opinion. We have learnt to overcome this problem in the 'randomly occurring events of human life' by observing that certain laws of process and behaviour can be induced from these events; and in such a way as that one law can imply another. This has allowed formal philosophical logic to achieve its own level of abstraction in its rules of notation. There is thus no naturally occurring truth in philosophical logic. Whatever truth it does exhibit is proxy for the naturally occurring truth of the real, physical world, which means, in turn, that logic is actually nothing to do with truth, but with the human desire to be able to speak a perfectly clean language—To be able, as it were, to 'speak Science'. This desire reveals itself most of all in the high watermark of modern logic: that is, in class, or set, theory. Set theory was famously developed by one man, Georg Cantor, in order to solve the problem of how the visible spectrum of thought grades imperceptibly into the invisible—Viz., the problem of continuity between finite and transfinite numbers. Set theory is therefore the point at which logic moves beyond propositions (that could always in theory be proved true or false by events in the world of fact) and acquires a new notation that coordinates on the transfinite, i.e. the invisible, domain of knowledge. Wittgenstein would himself criticise set theory on this basis. See, for example, his remarks at *Philosophical Remarks*, §129: 'A proposition about all propositions, or all functions, is impossible. *Generality* in arithmetic is indicated by an induction'; and §174: 'Set theory builds on a fictitious symbolism, therefore on nonsense. As if there were something in Logic that could be known, but not by us.'

37. It should be clear now that ever since my invocation of Augustine's *On the Trinity*, I have had in mind this *feeling of freedom* rather than the classic sense-data problem whenever I have talked of the particularity of our private and subjective worlds. As for the classic sense-data problem, I have always liked the summary of it by W. T. Stace: 'I cannot experience anything except *my own* experience. I can see my red but I can never see yours. I can feel a pain in my leg. But I can never feel the pain in your leg. I can feel my emotion but not yours. Even if your anger infects me, so that I feel it in sympathy with you, it is yet, in so far as I feel it, *my* anger, not yours. I can never be you, nor you be me.… All knowledge, all philosophy must be based upon experience. And from whose experience can I begin except from my own? Whatever belief I hold on whatever subject must be either a datum of *my* consciousness or else an inference or mental construction which *I* base upon *my* data. If I accept a scientific belief on your authority, this belief must be an inference which I make from the sounds (words) I hear you utter, and from *my* belief in your repute as a scientific authority. Whatever I believe rests in the end upon the data of my own consciousness.' (W. T. Stace, *The Theory of Knowledge and Existence* (Oxford, Oxford University Press, 1932), p. 67).

38. Wittgenstein, *Philosophical Investigations*, §261.

39. Rhees, *Personal Recollections*, p. 184.

40. Wittgenstein, *Philosophical Investigations*, I, 326.

41. Wittgenstein, *Tractatus*, 6.4311.

42. See, for example, Aristotle, *Politics*, 1253a: 'Language serves to declare what is advantageous and what is the reverse, and it therefore serves to declare what is just and what is unjust. It is the peculiarity of man ... that he alone possesses a conception of good and evil, of the just and the unjust, and of other similar qualities; and it is association [in a common perception of these things] which makes a family and a polis.'

43. Wittgenstein, 'A Lecture on Ethics', 12.

44. Cf. Wittgenstein, *Philosophical Investigations*, I, 240: 'Disputes do not break out (among mathematicians, say) over the question whether a rule has been obeyed or not. People don't come to blows over it, for example. That is part of the framework on which the working of our language is based (for example, in giving descriptions).'

45. Cf. Georg Henrik von Wright's recollection: 'He was of the opinion—justified, I believe—that his ideas were usually misunderstood and distorted even by those who professed to be his disciples. He doubted that he would be better understood in the future. He once said that he felt as though he were writing for people who would think in a quite different way, breathe a different air of life, from that of present-day men' (G. H. von Wright, 'A Biographical Sketch', in Norman Malcolm (ed.) *Ludwig Wittgenstein: A Memoir* (Oxford, Clarendon Press, 2001), p. 3).

46. Wittgenstein, *Philosophical Investigations*, II, 11.

47. Wittgenstein (ed. G. H. von Wright & Heikki Nyman; tr. C. G. Luckhardt & Maximilian E. Aue), *Last Writings on the Philosophy of Psychology*, vol. I (Oxford, Blackwell, 1982), p. 758.

48. Ibid., pp. 664–665.

49. Cf. Wittgenstein, *Philosophical Investigations*, xii: 'For is even our style of painting arbitrary? Can we choose one at pleasure? (The Egyptian, for instance.) Is it a mere question of pleasing and ugly?'

50. Wittgenstein, *Tractatus*, 6.1261.

51. Wittgenstein, *Notebooks*, Appendix I, 3rd MS, pp. 99–100.

52. Karl Wittgenstein (ed. J. C. Nyíri), *Politico-Economic Writings: An Annotated Reprint of Zeitungsartikel und Vorträge* (Amsterdam, John Benjamins, 1984), p. 197. See also p. 203: 'the uneducated peasant, who has himself learned nothing and who allows his son to learn nothing, who stands humbly with his hat in his hand before the *Gutsherr*, the priest or the state official, is the greatest obstacle to the progress of industry, since he is the source and support of all those efforts, both conscious and unconscious, which are braced against it.'

53. Ludwig in a letter to his friend Paul Engelmann in 1920: 'I continually imagined to take my own life—and even now the thought still follows me around and haunts me.' B. F. McGuinness & G. H. von Wright (eds.), *Ludwig Wittgenstein Briefe* (Berlin, Suhrkamp Verlag, 1986), p. 131.

54. Ibid., p. 204.

55. Quoted in Ronald W. Clark, *The Life of Bertrand Russell* (Harmondsworth, Penguin, 1975), pp. 209–210.

56. Hermine Wittgenstein, *Familienerinnerungen* (Vienna, 1944), p. 102.

57. In his article, 'On the Philosophical Relevance of Gödel's Incompleteness Theorems', *Revue Internationale de Philosophie*, vol. 59, no. 234(4) (Oct. 2005), Panu Raatikainen summarizes Gödel's two incompleteness theorems thus: 'Gödel's first incompleteness theorem (as improved by Rosser (1936) [in Barkley Rosser, 'Extensions of Some Theories of Gödel and Church', *Journal of Symbolic Logic* 1, 87–91]) says that for any consistent formalized system F, which contains elementary arithmetic, there exists a sentence G_F of the language of the system which is true

but improvable in that system. Gödel's second incompleteness theorem states that no consistent formal system can prove its own consistency.'

58. George MacDonald, *At the Back of the North Wind* (London, Octopus Books, 1979), p. 289.

59. Wittgenstein, *On Certainty*, 47.

60. Wittgenstein, *MS* 121, 33r-33v (1938). Cf. Wittgenstein, *Philosophical Grammar* (Oxford, Basil Blackwell, 1974), p. 384: '"If we only search long enough" has no meaning (That goes for existence proofs in general.).'

61. Wittgenstein, *Culture and Value*, 73.

62. Cf., *Philosophical Investigations*, I, 425–426: 'In numberless cases we exert ourselves to find a picture and once it is found the application as it were comes about of itself. In this case we already have a picture which forces itself on us at every turn,—but does not help us out of the difficulty, which only begins here. If I ask, for example: "How am I to imagine *this* mechanism going into *this* box?"—perhaps a drawing reduced in scale may serve to answer me. Then I can be told: "You see, it goes in like *this*"; or perhaps even: "Why are you surprised? See how it goes *here*; it is the same there". Of course the latter does not explain anything more: it simply invites me to apply the picture I am given.

A picture is conjured up which seems to fix the sense *unambiguously*. The actual use, compared with that suggested by the picture, seems like something muddled. Here again we get the same thing as in set theory: the form of expression we use seems to have been designed for a god, who knows what we cannot know; he sees the whole of each of these infinite series and he sees into human consciousness. For us, of course, these forms of expression are like pontificals which we may put on, but cannot do much with, since we lack the effective power that would give these vestments meaning and purpose.

In the actual use of expressions we make detours, we go by side-roads. We see the straight highway before us, but of course we cannot use it, because it is permanently closed.'

63. As Ludwig would put it in a letter to the writer and publisher Ludwig von Ficker: 'My work consists of two parts: the one presented here plus all that I have *not* written. And it is precisely the second part that is the important one' (Paul Engelmann (ed. B. F. McGuinness & tr. L. Furtmuller), *Letters from Ludwig Wittgenstein, with a Memoir* (Oxford, Basil Blackwell, 1967), p. 144).

64. Karl Wittgenstein, *Politico-Economic Writings*, p. 201.

65. Wittgenstein, *Philosophical Investigations*, I, 193.

66. Ibid., I, 1.

67. Bertrand Russell, *A Critical Exposition of the Philosophy of Leibniz* (Cambridge, Cambridge University Press, 1900), p. 192.

68. Wittgenstein makes this point in these words: 'It is impossible to speak about the will in so far as it is the subject of ethical attributes' (Wittgenstein, *Tractatus*, 6.423).

69. Augustine, *Confessions*, VIII, 8, 19–20 (tr. John K. Ryan).

70. Apollonius, *Enquiry into Miracles*, 6.2e (tr. Robin Waterfield).

71. Ludwig Wittgenstein (eds. Heikki Nyman & G. H. von Wright), *Last Writings on the Philosophy of Psychology*, vol. II (Oxford, Basil Blackwell, 1992), 47.

72. Ludwig Wittgenstein (tr. Peter Winch), 'Cause and Effect: Intuitive Awareness', in James Carl Klagge & Alfred Nordmann (eds.), *Philosophical Occasions, 1912-1951* (Indianapolis, Hackett, 1993), p. 395.

73. Ludwig Wittgenstein (ed. Cyril Barrett), *Lectures and Conversations on Aesthetics, Psychology and Religious Belief* (Oxford, Basil Blackwell, 1966), p. 71.

74. Hermine Wittgenstein, *Familienerinnerungen*, p. 94 (italics in original).

75. Ibid., pp. 94–95.

76. Wittgenstein, *On Certainty* (New York, Harper & Row, 1972), §4.

77. Mikhail Bulgakov (tr. Carl R. Proffer), 'The Fatal Eggs', in *Diaboliad and Other Stories* (New York, Ardis, 2012), p. 51.

CHAPTER 3

1. Cf. Ludwig Wittgenstein (tr. Peter Winch), *Culture and Value* (Hoboken, NJ, Wiley-Blackwell, 1998), p. 23: 'Nothing we do can be defended definitively. But only by reference to something else that is established. I.e. no reason can be given why you should act (or should have acted) like this, except that by doing so you bring about such and such a situation, which again you have to accept as an aim.'

2. Rush Rhees, *Ludwig Wittgenstein: Personal Recollections* (Lanham, MD, Rowman & Littlefield, 1981), p. 135.

3. Ibid., p. 48.

4. Cf. here Wittgenstein, *Culture and Value*, p. 81: 'The beauty of a star-shaped figure—of a hexagon star perhaps—is spoiled if we see it as symmetrical relative to a given axis.'

5. Ibid., p. 38.

6. Ibid., p. 99.

7. Ibid., p. 53.

8. Ibid.

9. Cf. Ibid., pp. 70–71: 'Nothing seems to me more unlikely than that a scientist or mathematician, who reads me, should be seriously influenced thereby in the way he works. (In that respect my warnings are like the posters on the ticket offices at English railway stations "Is your journey really necessary?" As if anyone reading that would say to himself "On second thoughts, no".) Quite different artillery is needed here from anything I am in a position to muster. Most likely I could still achieve an effect in that, above all, a whole lot of garbage is written in response to my stimulus & that perhaps this provides the stimulus for something good. I ought always to hope only for the most indirect of influences. E.g. nothing more stupid than the chatter about cause & effect in history books; nothing more wrong-headed, more half-baked.—But who could put a stop to it by saying that? (It is as though I wanted to change men's and women's fashions by talking.)'

10. See p. 55.

11. Ludwig Wittgenstein (ed. Rush Rhees), *Philosophical Remarks* (Chicago, University of Chicago Press, 1980), III, 20.

12. Wittgenstein, *Culture and Value*, 8.

13. This is a funny one. It is probably one of the most widely quoted, and certainly one of the most widely applied and caricatured, of all Wittgenstein's remarks. You can buy T-shirts and coffee mugs with it emblazoned. Yet there is no reliable source for it. I am 90% certain that he didn't say it. But I am duty-bound to include it here anyway, because 90% of people have come to *know* Wittgenstein through it. Which goes to show. Something. But I will leave that one up to you to work out!

14. Wittgenstein, *Culture and Value*, p. 98.

15. Ibid., p. 43.

16. Plato (tr. Benjamin Jowett), *Euthyphro* (Oxford, Clarendon Press, 1903), pp. 17–18.

17. Cf. Wittgenstein, *Notebooks*, p. 83.

18. See pp. 75.

19. Ludwig Wittgenstein (ed. G. E. M. Anscombe), *Notebooks, 1914-1916* (Chicago, University of Chicago Press, 1984), 1.10.1917.

20. See p. 89.

21. Rhees, *Personal Recollections*, p. 79.

22. B. F. McGuinness & G. H. von Wright (eds.), *Ludwig Wittgenstein Briefe* (Berlin, Suhrkamp Verlag, 1986), p. 213.

23. Otto Weininger, *Sex and Character* (Charleston, SC, BiblioLife, 2009), p. 7.

24. Cf. Wittgenstein, *Culture and Value*, p. 33: 'If I am thinking just for myself without wanting to write a book, I jump about all round the topic; that is the only way of thinking that is natural to me. Forcing my thoughts into an ordered sequence is a torment for me. Should I even attempt it now??'

25. Cf. these comments about Wittgenstein from Bertrand Russell in a letter to Lady Ottoline Morrell in 1912: 'I love him and feel he will solve the problems I am too old to solve—all kinds of vital problems that are raised by my work, but want a fresh mind and the vigour of youth.... He is *the* young man one hopes for. But as is usual with such men, he is unstable, and may go to pieces. His vigour and life is such a comfort after the washed-out Cambridge type. His attitude justifies all I have hoped about my work ... he has even the same similes I have—a wall, parting him from the truth, which he must pull down somehow' (quoted in Ronald W. Clark, *The Life of Bertrand Russell* (Harmondsworth, Penguin, 1975), pp. 212–213).

26. As Alexander Waugh records in his *The House of Wittgenstein: A Family at War* (New York, Doubleday, 2008), p. 147: 'There were of course (and still are, now) many doubters—those who roll their eyes and mutter about "the Emperor's new clothes!" Ludwig's uncles, aunts and extended family of Austrian cousins were among those who were the least impressed. Many of them were simply embarrassed by what they perceived to be his eccentric behaviour and thought it perverse that he, the dupe of the family—an elementary school teacher—should be honoured as a great philosopher abroad. Shaking their heads, they found it amusing that the world was taken in by the clown of their family, that *that* useless person had suddenly become famous and an intellectual giant in England.'

27. Wittgenstein, *Culture and Value*, p. 4.

28. Ludwig Wittgenstein (eds. G. E. M. Anscombe, G. H. von Wright & Denis Paul), *On Certainty* (New York, Harper & Row, 1972), 248.

29. Wittgenstein, *Culture and Value*, p. 5.

30. Ibid.

31. Ibid.

32. Wittgenstein, *Tractatus*, 6.53–57.

33. Ludwig Wittgenstein (ed. Rush Rhees), *Preliminary Studies for the 'Philosophical Investigations': Generally Known as the Blue and Brown Books* (Oxford, Basil Blackwell, 1969), 48.

34. Hermine Wittgenstein, *Familienerinnerungen* (Vienna, 1944), p. 115.

35. Rhees, *Personal Recollections*, p. 9.

36. Quoted in F. A. Flowers, *Portraits of Wittgenstein*, vol. 2 (Bristol, Thoemmes, 1999), p. 146.

37. Wittgenstein, *The Blue and Brown Books*, p. 65.
38. Wittgenstein, *Culture and Value*, 55e.
39. K. T. Fann, *Ludwig Wittgenstein: The Man and his Philosophy* (New York, Delta, 1967), p. 88.
40. Ibid., p. 86.
41. Rhees, *Personal Recollections*, p. 125.
42. Irving Block, *Perspectives on the Philosophy of Wittgenstein* (Oxford, Basil Blackwell, 1981), p. 12.
43. Quoted in Michael Nedo, *Wittgenstein and Cambridge: Family Resemblances*, catalogue of an exhibition at Clare Hall Cambridge, 31 March to 4 May, 2011, p. 8.
44. G. H. von Wright (ed.), *A Portrait of Wittgenstein as a Young Man from the Diary of David Hume Pinsent, 1912-14* (Oxford, Basil Blackwell, 1990), p. 5.
45. Hermine Wittgenstein, *Familienerinnerungen*, p. 108.
46. von Wright, *A Portrait of Wittgenstein as a Young Man*, p. 6.
47. Ibid., p. 64.
48. McGuinness & von Wright, *Ludwig Wittgenstein Briefe*, p. 27.
49. Ibid., p. 44.
50. Leo Tolstoy (tr. Dustin Condren), *The Gospel in Brief* (New York, HarperCollins, 2011), p. 135.
51. *Fremden-Blatt*, 23.11.1918.
52. Wittgenstein, *Tractatus*, xxii.
53. Clark, *The Life of Bertrand Russell*, p. 545.
54. See p. 51.
55. Clark, *The Life of Bertrand Russell*, 546.
56. Augustine, *Sermons*, LII, 16.
57. See pp. 66–68.
58. Wittgenstein, *Culture and Value*, 11e.
59. See, for example, Alfred North Whitehead and Bertrand Russell, *Principia Mathematica* (Cambridge, Cambridge University Press, 1910), pp. 2-3: '(1) The ideas here employed are more abstract than those familiarly considered in language. Accordingly there are no words which are used mainly in the exact consistent senses which are required here. Any use of words would require unnatural limitations to their ordinary meanings, which would be in fact more difficult to remember consistently than are the definitions of entirely new symbols. (2) The grammatical structure of language is adapted to a wide variety of usages. Thus it possesses no unique simplicity in representing the few simple, though highly abstract, processes and ideas arising in the deductive trains of reasoning employed here. In fact the very abstract simplicity of the ideas of this work defeats language. Language can represent complex ideas more easily. The proposition "a whale is big" represents language at its best, giving terse expression to a complicated fact; while the true analysis of "one is a number" leads, in language, to an intolerable prolixity. Accordingly terseness is gained by using a symbolism especially designed to represent the ideas and processes of deduction which occur in this work. (3) The adaption of the rules of the symbolism to the processes of deduction aids the intuition in regions too abstract for the imagination readily to present to the mind the true relation between the ideas employed. For various collocations of symbols become familiar as representing important collocations of ideas; and in turn the possible relations—according to the rules of the symbolism—between these collocations of symbols become familiar, and these further collocations represent still more complicated relations between the abstract ideas. And

thus the mind is finally led to construct trains of reasoning in regions of thought in which the imagination would be entirely unable to sustain itself without symbolic help. Ordinary language yields no such help. Its grammatical structure does not represent uniquely the relations between the ideas involved. Thus, "a whale is big" and "one is a number" both look alike so that the eye gives no help to the imagination. (4) The terseness of the symbolism enables a whole proposition to be represented to the eyesight as one whole, or at most in two or three parts divided where the natural breaks, represented in the symbolism, occur. This is a humble property, but is in fact very important in connection with the advantages enumerated under the heading (3).'

60. Bertrand Russell, 'A Free Man's Worship', in Paul Edwards (ed.), *Why I Am Not a Christian* (New York, Simon & Schuster, 1957), pp. 115–116.

61. Wittgenstein, *Culture and Value*, p. 13.

62. Ibid., p. 19.

63. Ibid., p. 3.

64. Ibid., p. 46.

65. Ibid., p. 48.

66. Ibid., p. 89.

67. Ibid., p. 30.

68. Rhees, *Personal Recollections*, pp. 121–122.

69. Norman Malcolm (ed.), *Ludwig Wittgenstein: A Memoir* (Oxford, Clarendon Press, 2001), p. 26.

70. Quoted in Hans Sluga & David G. Stern (eds.), *The Cambridge Companion to Wittgenstein* (Cambridge, Cambridge University Press, 2005), p. 454.

71. See p. 113.

72. Wittgenstein, *Culture and Value*, p. 13.

73. Ludwig Wittgenstein (eds. G. H. von Wright, R. Rhees & G. E. M. Anscombe), *Remarks on the Foundations of Mathematics* (Cambridge, MA, The MIT Press, 1993), III, 41.

74. In Wittgenstein's language: 'The philosophical self is not the human being, not the human body or the human soul with the psychological properties, but the metaphysical subject, the boundary (not a part) of the world. The human body, however, my body in particular, is a part of the world among others, among animals, plants, stones, etc., etc.' (Wittgenstein, *Notebooks*, 2.9.1916).

75. Wittgenstein, *The Blue and Brown Books*, p. 4.

76. Ludwig Wittgenstein (ed. Cora Diamond), *Wittgenstein's Lectures on the Foundations of Mathematics, Cambridge, 1939* (Chicago, University of Chicago Press, 1989), IV.

77. Augustine, *Confessions*, XI, 28, 38 & 30, 40.

78. G. H. von Wright, *Wittgenstein* (Minnesota, University of Minnesota Press, 1982), p. 83.

79. Ibid., p. 39.

80. Ibid., pp. 34–35.

81. See p. 112.

82. See p. 123.

83. Wittgenstein, *Philosophical Remarks*, §181 and Wittgenstein, *Philosophical Grammar* (Oxford, Basil Blackwell, 1974), p. 473.

84. See how Kant puts it in his *Critique of Pure Reason*: 'Even if we suppose the whole of nature to be spread out before us, and that of all that is presented to our intuition nothing is concealed from our senses and consciousness, yet still through no experience could the object of our ideas

be known by us *in concreto*. For that purpose, in addition to this exhaustive intuition, we should require what is not possible through any empirical knowledge, namely, a complete synthesis and the consciousness of its absolute totality. Accordingly our question does not require to be raised in the explanation of any given appearance, and is therefore not a question which can be regarded as imposed on us by the object itself. The object can never come before us, since it cannot be given through any possible experience. In all possible perceptions we always remain involved in *conditions*, whether in space or in time, and come upon nothing unconditioned requiring us to determine whether this unconditioned is to be located in an absolute beginning of synthesis, or in an absolute totality of a series that has no beginning.... Appearances demand explanation only so far as the conditions of their explanation are given in perception; but all that may ever be given in this way, when taken together in an *absolute whole*, is not itself a perception. Yet it is just the explanation of this very whole that is demanded in the transcendental problems of reason. Thus the solution of these problems can never be found in experience, and this is precisely the reason why we should not say that it is uncertain what should be ascribed to the object [of our idea]. For as our object is only in our brain, and cannot be given outside of it, we have only to take care to be at one with ourselves' (Immanuel Kant (tr. Martin Kemp Smith), *Immanuel Kant's Critique of Pure Reason* (London, Macmillan, 1964), pp. 434–435).

85. See p. 128.
86. Wittgenstein, *Culture and Value*, p. 16.
87. Ibid.
88. Ibid., p. 42.
89. *City of God*, XXI, 14 (tr. R. W. Dyson).
90. Ludwig Wittgenstein (ed. & tr. G. E. M. Anscombe), *Zettel* (Oakland, CA, University of California Press, 1970), §34.
91. Wittgenstein, *On Certainty*, 59.
92. Brian McGuinness (ed.), *Wittgenstein and the Vienna Circle: Conversations Recorded by F. Waismann* (Oxford, Blackwell, 1979), p. 83. The reference in the quote is to Hermann Weyl, German mathematician, theoretical physicist, and philosopher.
93. Wittgenstein, *Tractatus*, 5.6–5.633.

CHAPTER 4

1. Miles Hollingworth, *Inventing Socrates* (New York: London, Bloomsbury, 2015), p. 147.
2. Ernst Troeltsch, 'Empiricism and Platonism in the Philosophy of Religion: To the Memory of William James', *Harvard Theological Review*, vol. 5, no. 4 (1912), 404.
3. Ludwig Wittgenstein (tr. Peter Winch), *Culture and Value* (Hoboken, NJ, Wiley-Blackwell, 1998), 53*e*.
4. Ibid., 44*e*.
5. Cf. Ludwig Wittgenstein (ed. Rush Rhees), *Philosophical Remarks* (Chicago, University of Chicago Press, 1980), 151: '[T]he difficult mathematical problems are those for whose solution we don't yet possess a *written* system. The mathematician who is looking for a solution then has a system in some sort of psychic symbolism, in images, "in his head", and endeavours to get it down on paper. Once that's done, the rest is easy. But if he has *no kind* of system, either in written or unwritten symbols, then he can't *search* for a solution either, but at best can only grope around.— Now, of course you may find something even by random groping. But in that case, you haven't

searched for it, and, from a logical point of view, the process was synthetic; whereas searching is a process of analysis.'

6. Luke 23:39–43.

7. See p. 128.

8. Ludwig Wittgenstein (tr. G. E. M. Anscombe), *Philosophical Investigations* (Oxford, Basil Blackwell, 1976), I, 65–66.

9. Cf. Ludwig Wittgenstein (ed. Rush Rhees), *Preliminary Studies for the 'Philosophical Investigations': Generally Known as The Blue and Brown Books* (Oxford, Basil-Blackwell, 1969), 18: 'Philosophers constantly see the method of science before their eyes, and are irresistibly tempted to ask and answer questions in the way science does. This tendency ... leads the philosopher into complete darkness.'

10. Wittgenstein (ed. G. E. M. Anscombe & G. H. von Wright; tr. G. E. M. Anscombe), *Remarks on the Philosophy of Psychology*, vol. I (Oxford, Blackwell, 1980), p. 903.

11. Wittgenstein, *Philosophical Investigations*, §217.

12. Matthew 11:27–30.

13. Cf. pp. 78–80.

14. Ludwig Wittgenstein (tr. D. F. Pears & B. F. McGuinness), *Tractatus Logico-Philosophicus* (London, Routledge & Kegan Paul, 1977), 5.1362.

15. See pp. 98–99.

16. See p. 87.

17. Wittgenstein, *Philosophical Investigations*, I, 55.

18. Ibid., I, 283–285.

19. Ibid., I, 275.

20. Wittgenstein, *Tractatus*, 6.423–426.4311. Cf. how I used the last part of this quotation on p. 53.

21. See p. 157.

22. Ernest Hemingway, *For Whom the Bell Tolls* (New York, Scribner Classics, 1996), pp. 184–185.

23. Wittgenstein, *Philosophical Investigations*, I, 1–2.

24. You may remember that I have already referenced it. See pp. 70–71.

25. Wittgenstein, *Philosophical Investigations*, II, 11.

26. Ludwig Wittgenstein (ed. G. E. M. Anscombe), *Remarks on Colour* (Oxford, Wiley-Blackwell, 1991), §1.

27. Wittgenstein, *Tractatus*, 6.5–6.521.

28. See pp. 91–92.

29. Plato, *Republic*, 511*b-c* (tr. Richard W. Sterling & William C. Scott).

30. Aristotle, *Metaphysics*, 1041*a*-1041*b* (tr. Richard Hope).

31. See how I say this same thing at the start of Ch. 3, pp. 82–83.

32. Thomas Hobbes (ed. C. B. Mcpherson), *Leviathan* (Harmondsworth, Penguin, 1982), XLVI.

33. Bertrand Russell, 'On Denoting', *Mind*, vol. 14, no. 56 (Oct. 1905), 483.

34. Ibid., 479–480.

35. Ibid., 480.

36. Ibid., 488.

37. See, for example, the following from his *The New Science*: 'It is noteworthy that in all languages the greater part of the expressions relating to inanimate things are formed by metaphor

from the human body and its parts and from the human senses and passions … The farmers of Latium used to say the fields were thirsty, bore fruit, were swollen with grain; and our rustics speak of plants making love, vines growing mad, resinous trees weeping. Innumerable other examples could be collected from all languages. All of which is a consequence of our axiom that man in his ignorance makes himself the rule of the universe, for in the examples cited he has made of himself an entire world. So that, as rational metaphysics teaches that man becomes all things by understanding them (*homo intelligendo fit omnia*), this imaginative metaphysics shows that man becomes all things by *not* understanding them (*homo non intelligendo fit omnia*); and perhaps the latter proposition is truer than the former, for when man understands he extends his mind and takes in the things, but when he does not understand he makes the things out of himself and becomes them by transforming himself into them' (Giambattista Vico (tr. Thomas Goddard Bergin & Max Harold Fisch), *The New Science of Giambattista Vico* (Ithaca, London, Cornell University Press, 1984), pp. 129–130).

38. Wittgenstein, *Tractatus*, 6.1222.
39. Ibid., 6.1223.
40. Ibid., 6.123.
41. Ibid., 6.1232.
42. Antonio Rosmini (ed. & tr. Terry Watson & Denis Cleary), *The Origin of Thought* (Leominster, Fowler Wright Books, 1987), pp. 65–66.
43. See pp. 65–66.
44. Wittgenstein, *Tractatus*, 6.124
45. Ibid., 6.125.
46. Ibid., 6.1251.
47. Remember what I said about Christ and 'reported speech' on p. 139?
48. Wittgenstein, *Culture and Value*, 50e.
49. See p. 128.
50. Wittgenstein (ed. A. Ambrose), *Wittgenstein's Lectures, Cambridge 1932-1935* (Chicago, University of Chicago Press, 1979), 98.
51. Ludwig Wittgenstein (ed. Cora Diamond), *Wittgenstein's Lectures on the Foundations of Mathematics, Cambridge, 1939* (Chicago, University of Chicago Press, 1989), VIII.
52. See p. 118.
53. See p. 51.
54. I take up with this at the start of chapter 5.
55. Cf. pp. 166–167.
56. See p. 149.
57. Bertrand Russell, *A History of Western Philosophy* (London, George Allen & Unwin, 1946), p. 864.
58. Wittgenstein, *Lectures on the Foundations of Mathematics*, XXV.
59. Ibid., p. 331.
60. Ibid., p. 328.
61. Ludwig Wittgenstein (ed. & tr. G. E. M. Anscombe), *Zettel* (Oakland, CA, University of California Press, 1970), §54.
62. Wittgenstein, *Culture and Value*, 17e.
63. Wittgenstein, *Philosophical Investigations*, II, 223.
64. Wittgenstein, *Culture and Value*, p. 3.
65. See pp. 107–111.

66. See p. 163.

67. Wittgenstein, *Tractatus*, 3.0321.

68. 1 Cor. 2:11.

69. Hermine Wittgenstein et al., *Recollections of Wittgenstein* (Oxford, Oxford University Press, 1981), p. 152.

70. Wittgenstein, *Tractatus*, 5.53.

71. Ibid., 5.5301.

72. Ibid., 5.5302.

73. Ibid., 5.5303.

74. Wittgenstein, *Philosophical Investigations*, II, 229.

75. Ibid.

76. See ibid., II, 228.

77. Plato, *Meno*, 85e–86b (tr. Benjamin Jowett).

78. Wittgenstein, *Philosophical Investigations*, I, 232–234.

CHAPTER 5

1. See pp. 87–88.

2. Ludwig Wittgenstein (eds. G. E. M. Anscombe, G. H. von Wright & Denis Paul), *On Certainty* (New York, Harper & Row, 1972), 108.

3. Ludwig Wittgenstein (ed. G. E. M. Anscombe & G. H. von Wright; tr. G. E. M. Anscombe), *Remarks on the Philosophy of Psychology*, vol. I (Oxford, Blackwell, 1980), p. 220.

4. Ludwig Wittgenstein (tr. Peter Winch), *Culture and Value* (Hoboken, NJ, Wiley-Blackwell, 1998), 7.

5. See how I make the same argument at pp. 64–67.

6. Ludwig Wittgenstein (ed. G. E. M. Anscombe), *Notebooks, 1914–1916* (Chicago, University of Chicago Press, 1984), p. 10.

7. Wittgenstein, *On Certainty*, p. 110.

8. Cf. Wittgenstein (ed. A. Ambrose) *Wittgenstein's Lectures, Cambridge, 1932-1935* (Oxford, Basil Blackwell, 1979), pp. 156–157: 'Suppose we called "2 + 2 = 4" the expression of a convention. This is misleading, though the equation might originally have been the result of one. The situation with respect to it is comparable to the situation supposed in the Social Contract theory, we know that there was no actual contract, but it is as if such a contract had been made. Similarly for 2 + 2 = 4: it is as if a convention had been made.'

9. Wittgenstein, *Culture and Value*, p. 7.

10. This is clear in Heidegger's depiction of the difference between the self-sufficient and indifferent 'being' of scientific knowledge and the 'being' of man as it becomes established against this in the act and event of 'thinking': 'For it is true that what was said so far, and the entire discussion that is to follow, have nothing to do with scientific knowledge, especially not if the discussion itself is to be a thinking. This situation is grounded in the fact that science itself does not think, and cannot think—which is its good fortune, here meaning the assurance of its own appointed course. Science does not think' (Martin Heidegger (tr. Fred D Wieck & J. Glenn Gray), *What is Called Thinking?* (New York, Harper & Row, 1968), pp. 7–8).

11. See especially p. 67.

12. Ludwig Wittgenstein (tr. D. F. Pears & B. F. McGuinness), *Tractatus Logico-Philosophicus* (London, Routledge & Kegan Paul, 1977), 6.4–6.421.

13. Ludwig Wittgenstein (ed. Cora Diamond), *Wittgenstein's Lectures on the Foundations of Mathematics, Cambridge, 1939* (Chicago, University of Chicago Press, 1989), XXVII.

14. Immanuel Kant (tr. Martin Kemp Smith), *Immanuel Kant's Critique of Pure Reason* (London, Macmillan, 1964), p. 7.

15. Fernando Pessoa (tr. Margaret Jull Costa), *The Book of Disquiet* (New York, Serpent's Tail Classics, 2011), p. 118.

16. Kant, *Critique of Pure Reason*, p. 644.

17. See pp. 167–174.

18. Michel de Montaigne (tr. Donald M. Frame), *The Complete Essays of Montaigne* (Stanford, CA, Stanford University Press, 1958), p. 669.

19. Pauline Réage (tr. Sabine d'Estrée), *Story of O* (New York, Ballantine Books, 1965), p. 4.

20. Jean Genet, 'The Maids', in (tr. Bernard Frechtman), *The Maids and Deathwatch: Two Plays by Jean Genet* (New York, Grove Press, 1982), pp. 84–85.

21. Wittgenstein (ed. Alice Ambrose), *Wittgenstein's Lectures, Cambridge, 1932-1935* (Chicago, University of Chicago Press, 1979), 124.

22. Pier Paolo Pasolini, 'Il pianto della scavatrice', in *Carne e cielo: Poesie per giovani* (Milano, Adriano Salani Editore, 2015), p. 62.

23. Ludwig Wittgenstein (ed. Rush Rhees), *Preliminary Studies for the 'Philosophical Investigations': Generally Known as The Blue and Brown Books* (Oxford, Basil Blackwell, 1969), pp. 59–60.

24. See Miles Hollingworth, *Inventing Socrates* (New York: London, Bloomsbury, 2015), p. 125.

25. See the example of Wittgenstein putting this in his own words on p. 128.

26. Ludwig Wittgenstein (eds. James Carl Klagge & Alfred Nordmann), *Philosophical Occasions: 1912–1951* (Indianapolis, IN, Hackett, 1993), 228.

27. Wittgenstein, *Notebooks*, 07/21/16.

28. Ibid., 07/30/16.

29. Wittgenstein, *MS* 103, pp. 14–15.

30. A. E. Housman, 'He looked at me with eyes I thought', in *The Collected Poems of A. E. Housman* (London, Jonathan Cape, 1967), p. 133.

31. Ludwig Wittgenstein (tr. G. E. M. Anscombe), *Philosophical Investigations* (Oxford, Basil Blackwell 1976), I, 620–621.

32. Ludwig Wittgenstein (ed. Rush Rhees), *Philosophical Remarks* (Chicago, University of Chicago Press, 1980), 150.

33. Wittgenstein, *The Blue and Brown Books*, p. 172.

34. Wittgenstein, *Philosophical Investigations*, II, 6.

35. Ludwig Wittgenstein (ed. Rush Rhees; tr. Anthony Kenny), *Philosophical Grammar* (Oxford, Basil Blackwell, 1974), p. 315.

36. Wittgenstein, *Notebooks*, 11/04/16.

37. See Wittgenstein, *MS* 102, p. 40v (1937): 'Certainly we have to admit that Christianity alone pursues the road to happiness, but what happens if I refuse this happiness?'

38. Watch how Wittgenstein expresses love's freedom here: 'Given the two ideas "fat" and "lean", would you be rather inclined to say that Wednesday was fat and Tuesday lean, or *vice versa*? (I incline decisively towards the former.) … Asked "What do you really mean here by 'fat' and 'lean'?"—I could only explain the meanings in the usual way. I could *not* point to the examples of Tuesday and Wednesday … [For example] If I say "For me the vowel *e* is yellow" I do not

mean: "yellow" in a metaphorical sense,—for I could not express what I want to say in any other way than by means of the idea "yellow"' (Wittgenstein, *Philosophical Investigations*, II, 11).

39. Wittgenstein, *Philosophical Investigations*, II, 5.

40. Ibid.

41. Ibid., II, 11.

42. Wittgenstein, *Philosophical Remarks*, §57.

43. Wittgenstein (ed. P. T. Geach), *Wittgenstein's Lectures on Philosophical Psychology* (Chicago, Chicago University Press, 1989), 47.

44. Ludwig Wittgenstein (eds. G. H. von Wright, R. Rhees & G. E. M. Anscombe), *Remarks on the Foundations of Mathematics* (Cambridge, MA, The MIT Press, 1993), p. 34.

45. See p. 145.

46. Wittgenstein, *Philosophical Grammar*, p. 477.

47. Wittgenstein, *Philosophical Occasions*, 357.

48. Wittgenstein *Remarks on the Foundations of Mathematics*, App. III, §8.

49. Ludwig Wittgenstein (ed. G. E. M. Anscombe), *Remarks on Colour* (Oxford, Wiley-Blackwell, 1991), I, 32.

50. Ludwig Wittgenstein, *Philosophical Occasions*, p. 121.

51. Wittgenstein, *Philosophical Grammar*, p. 244.

52. Ludwig Wittgenstein (ed. & tr. G. E. M. Anscombe), *Zettel* (Oakland, CA, University of California Press, 1970), §309.

53. Wittgenstein, *MS* 183, pp. 82–84 (1931).

54. Ibid. 101, p. 21v (1914).

55. Wittgenstein, *Philosophical Occasions*, p. 121.

56. Wittgenstein (ed. G. H. von Wright et al.), *Remarks on the Philosophy of Psychology*, vol. II (Oxford, Blackwell, 1980), 183.

57. Ludwig Wittgenstein (eds. G. E. M. Anscombe, Rush Rhees, Gilbert Ryle & B. F. McGuinness), *Lectures on Ethics, Aesthetics, Psychology and Religious Belief* (Oxford, Basil Blackwell, 1966), 42.

58. William Blake, 'The Human Abstract', in (ed. Peter Butter), *William Blake* (London, J. M. Dent, 1996), p. 38.

59. Bertrand Russell, *The Problems of Philosophy* (London, New York, Oxford University Press, 1970), p. 91.

60. Leo Tolstoy (tr. Richard Pevear & Larissa Volokhonsky), *Anna Karenina* (London, Penguin, 2006), p. 787.

61. Ibid., p. 794.

62. Wittgenstein, *Tractatus*, 6.44.

63. Wittgenstein, *Zettel*, 439.

64. T. E. Lawrence, *Seven Pillars of Wisdom* (London, Penguin, 2000), p. 583.

APPENDIX

1. Ludwig Wittgenstein (ed. G. E. M. Anscombe), *Notebooks, 1914–1916* (Chicago, University of Chicago Press, 1984), 12.10.16.

2. Alfred North Whitehead, *Religion in the Making* (New York, Fordham University Press, 1996), p. 31.

3. See Origen, *Against Celsus*, II, 59.

4. Ludwig Wittgenstein (eds. James Carl Klagge & Alfred Nordmann), *Philosophical Occasions: 1912–1951* (Indianapolis, IN, Hackett Publishing Company, 1993), p. 131.

5. Ludwig Wittgenstein (ed. Rush Rhees), *Preliminary Studies for the 'Philosophical Investigations': Generally Known as The Blue and Brown Books* (Oxford, Basil Blackwell, 1969), p. 26.

6. W. Stanley Jevons, *Elementary Lessons in Logic* (London, Macmillan, 1957), p. 262.

7. Ludwig Wittgenstein (tr. G. E. M. Anscombe), *Philosophical Investigations* (Oxford, Basil Blackwell, 1976), II, p. 126.

8. Wittgenstein, *Notebooks*, 22.8.14.

9. Wittgenstein, *The Blue and Brown Books*, p. 30.

10. Plato, *Phaedrus*, 276b-c (tr. Benjamin Jowett).

11. Ludwig Wittgenstein (eds. G. E. M. Anscombe, G. H. von Wright & Denis Paul), *On Certainty* (New York, Harper & Row, 1972), 602–613.

12. Cf. Wittgenstein (ed. & tr. C. G. Luckhardt & M. A. E. Aue), *The Big Typescript*, (Oxford, Blackwell, 2005), 312: 'The conflict in which we constantly find ourselves when we undertake logical investigations is like the conflict of two people who have concluded a contract with each other, the last formulations of which are expressed in easily misunderstood words, whereas the explanations of these formulations explain everything unmistakeably. Now one of the two people has short memory, constantly forgets the explanations, misinterprets the provisions of the contract, and therefore continually runs into difficulties. The other person has to remind him over and over of the explanations in the contract and remove the difficulty.'

13. Ludwig Wittgenstein (ed. Cora Diamond), *Wittgenstein's Lectures on the Foundations of Mathematics, Cambridge, 1939* (Chicago, University of Chicago Press, 1989), XXXI.

14. Miles Hollingworth, *Inventing Socrates* (New York, London, Bloomsbury, 2015), p. 85.

15. See how he would put it much later on in his life, in the great work of his maturity, the *City of God*: 'This lust triumphs not only over the whole body, and not only outwardly, but inwardly also. When the emotion of the mind is united with the craving of the flesh, it convulses the whole man, so that there follows a pleasure greater than any other: a bodily pleasure so great that, at the moment of time when he achieves his climax, the alertness and, so to speak, vigilance of a man's mind is almost entirely overwhelmed. Any friend of wisdom and holy joys who lives a married life but knows "how to possess his vessel in sanctification and honour", as the apostle admonishes [1 Thess. 4.4]—surely such a one would prefer to beget children without lust of this kind, if such a thing were possible. For the parts created for this purpose would then be the servants of his mind even in the task of procreation, just as his other members serve it in the various tasks distributed to them. They would act at the command of his will, and not because incited by the urging of lust.' (*City of God*, XIV, 16 (tr. R. W. Dyson)).

16. See Wittgenstein, *Philosophical Investigations*, I, 293: 'If I say of myself that it is only from my own case that I know what the word "pain" means—must I not say the same of other people too? And how can I generalize the *one* case so irresponsibly?

Now someone tells me that *he* knows what pain is only from his own case!—Suppose everyone had a box with something in it: we call it a "beetle". No one can look into anyone else's box, and everyone says he knows what a beetle is only by looking at *his* beetle.—Here it would be quite possible for everyone to have something different in his box. One might even imagine such a thing constantly changing.—But suppose the word "beetle" had a use in these people's language?—If so it would not be used as the name of a thing. The thing in the box has no place in the language-game at all; not even as a *something*: for the box might even be empty.—No, one can "divide through" by the thing in the box; it cancels out, whatever it is.

That is to say: if we construe the grammar of the expression of sensation on the model of "object and designation" the object drops out of consideration as irrelevant.

17. The philosopher James Wetzel has bravely gone here. The following words sum up his project thus far; and to me they get better and bigger every time I read them: 'I can confess only to the sin that reminds me that I lack the synoptic view of my condition. Were I to see ahead of all the exits and entries of my shared life with others, I would be making yet another exit and falsely imagining it to be my grand entry. Here Wittgenstein reassures me that a language of timeless definitiveness and a perspective at the limits of my world is not in any case what I want: none of that would meet my "real need". Augustine warns me that I have taken my taste of the foreknowledge that is both disaffecting and full of promise and that now only God can help me. I do not think, despite how it may sound at first, that Wittgenstein and Augustine are speaking to very different forms of deliverance' (James Wetzel, *Parting Knowledge: Essays after Augustine* (Eugene, OR, Wipf & Stock, 2013), p. 246).

18. Wittgenstein, *Notebooks*, 07/29/16.

19. Wittgenstein, *Philosophical Investigations*, I, 412.

20. I was grateful to find Rowan Williams stating this decisively in his new book, *On Augustine*: 'Left to ourselves, we can fantasize about gaining wisdom by effort, but in fact we shall only be locking ourselves up still further in our illusions, admiring not the eternal wisdom but our own spiritual skills.... We have to grow, says Augustine, if we are to feed on truth. And the heart of that growth is humility, facing our essential incompleteness at every level, metaphysical, spiritual, cognitive, moral. Where does God actually meet us? In the free action by which he accepts the limits of mortal life so that he can speak directly to us using our own language. When you see God in Jesus, it is as if you see him at your own feet, the suffering or dead body laid out before you; throw yourself down on that level, "and when He rises, you will rise"' (Rowan Williams, *On Augustine* (London: New York, Bloomsbury, 2016), p. 132).

21. Leo Tolstoy (tr. Rosemary Edmunds), *War and Peace* (Penguin, Harmondsworth, 1974), pp. 1443–1444.

22. Augustine, *On Christian Doctrine*, IV, 3, 4. Cf. now this, from his *Sermons*, CXVII, 5: 'So you think that you can comprehend a body by the eye, but really you cannot at all! For whatever you look at, you do not see the whole of it. If, say, you see a man's face, you do not see his back at the time you see the face; and when you see the back, you do not at that time see the face. You do not then comprehend a body by seeing it all at once; but when you see another part which you had not seen before, memory aids you to remember other parts of the body which you have already seen. With this aid, you could never say that you had comprehended anything—even on the surface. So you find that you tend to handle what you see, turning it about on this side and that. Or you may actually walk yourself round it to see the whole. But all at once in one view you cannot see the whole. And as long as you turn it about to see it, you are seeing the parts; and by putting together those parts, you are fancying that you are seeing the whole. But this must not be understood as the sight of the eyes, but the activity of the memory.'

23. Wittgenstein, *On Certainty*, p. 204.

24. Wittgenstein, *Philosophical Investigations*, II, xi, 221.

25. Ibid., II, xiii, 231.

INDEX OF NAMES

Anscombe, Elizabeth, 32, 37, 46, 121
Aristotle, 53, 54, 72, 147–148, 167–178, 199
Augustine of Hippo, ix–x, xviii–xix, 46–49, 57, 70–71, 75, 80, 107, 113, 116, 124–127, 131–133, 138–139, 147–152, 162, 167, 191, 229, 231–232, 244–248
Aury, Dominique, 208
Ayer, Alfred Jules, 51–52

Bailey, Philip James, 32
Barth, Karl, xv
Beethoven, van Ludwig, 96, 108
Berkeley, George, 38
Bevan, Edward Vaughan, 37
Blake, William, 225
Boethius, 44
Bolstad, Arne, 112
Boltzmann, Ludwig, 108, 131
Bonaparte, Napoleon, 247
Bosanquet, Bernard, 113
Brahms, Johannes, 61, 108
Breuer, Josef, 131
Bruckner, Anton, 102
Bunyan, John, 8

Cantor, Georg, 82, 106, 258
Carnegie, Andrew, 59
Casals, Pablo, 61

Darwin, Charles, 66, 83, 161
Descartes, René, 199
Dix, Otto, 82, 106
Dostoyevsky, Fyodor, 15–18, 223
Drury, Maurice O'Connor, xviii, 32, 36, 84, 96, 108, 120

Eccles, William, 108
Einstein, Albert, 75–76, 86, 94
Engelmann, Paul, 90, 101

Frazer, James George, 233
Frege, Gottlob, 58, 108–109, 125, 131, 173
Freud, Sigmund, 86, 107, 131, 190, 225

Galton, Sir Francis, 50
Genet, Jean, 196
Gödel, Kurt, 66–68, 96, 106, 117, 119, 130, 165–166, 172, 202, 221, 254
Grillparzer, Franz, 102

Groag, Emo, 105
Groag, Jacques, 90, 101, 105
Ground, Ian, 33–34

Haidbauer, Josef, 89
Hayek, Friedrich, 109
Heidegger, Martin, 7, 200–201, 205–208
Hemingway, Ernest, 160–161, 196
Heracleitus, 227
Heron of Alexandria, 108
Hertz, Heinrich Rudolf, 131
Hirschfeld, Magnus, 78
Hobbes, Thomas, 21–24, 28, 170–171
Hoffmann, Josef, 61
Houseman, Alfred Edward, 215
Hume, David, 38, 232, 241

Johnson, William Ernest, 110

Kant, Emmanuel, 123, 129–130, 138, 201–208
Keynes, John Maynard, 51, 116
Klimt, Gustav, 61
Kokoschka, Oskar, 112
Kraus, Karl, 86, 131

Labor, Josef, 102
Lawrence, Thomas Edward, 228
Leibniz, Gottfried Wilhelm, 73–74
Lenau, Nikolaus, 102
Loos, Adolf, 101, 112, 131
Lussac, Boyle-Guy, 97
Luther, Martin, 45

MacDonald, George, 67
Mahler, Gustav, 61, 90
Malcolm, Norman, 120
Mays, Wolfe, 108
Meinong, Alexius, 46, 173, 256–257
Meno, 188, 193–194
Monica (mother of Augustine of Hippo), 80
Montaigne, Michel de, 207–208
Moore, George Edward, 84, 96, 109–110, 112–113, 115, 116, 120, 121, 196, 237–247
Morrell, Lady Ottoline, 60, 109, 262
Mozart, Wolfgang Amadeus, 3

Nietzsche, Friedrich, 135
Nureyev, Rudolf, 139, 147

Pascal, Fanja, 84, 90
Pasolini, Pier Paolo, 10–15, 209, 253–254
Pelagius, 118
Pessoa, Fernando, 204
Pied Piper of Hamelin, 64
Pinsent, David Hume, 110, 111, 115, 216
Plato, 19–20, 66, 72, 166–167, 170, 178, 188, 193, 199, 207, 235–236, 242
Poliakoff, Samuil, 59
Popper, Karl, 121
Pythagoras, 75, 175

Ramsey, Frank, 216–217
Renoir, Pierre-Auguste, 189
Respinger, Marguerite, 29, 215
Reuleaux, Franz, 108
Rhees, Rush, 121
Richards, Ben, 37, 216
Rilke, Rainer Maria, 112
Rosmini, Antonio, 177
Russell, Bertrand, x, xii–xiii, 16, 60–61, 73–74, 82, 88, 89, 108, 109, 110, 111, 112, 115, 116–127, 131, 137, 143, 150, 157, 171–179, 181–189, 192, 216, 221–222, 225, 232–245

Salzer, Max, 78
Schoenberg, Arnold, 61
Schopenhauer, Arthur, 108, 131
Singer, Isaac Bashevis, 137
Skinner, Francis, 216
Smythies, Yorick, 37
Socrates, 14, 68, 72, 91–92, 123, 166, 170, 171, 178, 192, 193–194, 199, 209, 236, 237, 247
Spengler, Oswald, 86, 131, 252
Spinoza, Baruch, 115
Sraffa, Piero, 131
Stonborough, Jerome, 78
Strauss, Richard, 61
Swift, Jonathan, 135

Thales, 16, 66
Thomas Aquinas, 39
Tolstoy, Leo, 37, 114, 224, 226, 231, 247
Trakl, Georg, 112
Tsar Alexander II, 59
Turing, Alan, 117–118, 125–126, 162–163, 193

Vico, Giambattista, 175
Voltaire, 36

Index of Names

Wagner, Richard, 108
Weininger, Otto, 96–98, 108, 131
Weyl, Hermann, 133
Whitehead, Alfred North, xii, 118–119, 171–172, 231, 234, 263–264
Wittgenstein, Dora, 77
Wittgenstein, Helene, 77
Wittgenstein, Hermine, 62, 76, 77, 78, 104–105, 110–111
Wittgenstein, Johannes, 77, 78
Wittgenstein, Karl, 58–69, 72, 76, 77–79, 88, 90, 94–95, 112, 129, 259

Wittgenstein, Konrad, 77
Wittgenstein, Leopoldine, 58, 76–79, 88, 90, 94–95, 129
Wittgenstein, Margaret, 77, 78, 90, 101, 105, 115
Wittgenstein, Paul, 77–78, 114–115
Wittgenstein, Rudolf, 77, 78
Wright von, Georg Henrik, 46, 259

Zhao, Tingyang, x–xi

www.ingramcontent.com/pod-product-compliance
Ingram Content Group UK Ltd.
Pitfield, Milton Keynes, MK11 3LW, UK
UKHW022152230426
12049UKWH00003BA/64